THE UNIVERSITY OF WINCHESTER

Martial Rose Library
Tel: 01962 827306

To be returned on or before the day marked above, subject to recall.

MUSIC THEATRE IN BRITAIN
1960–1975

MUSIC THEATRE IN BRITAIN
1960–1975

Michael Hall

THE BOYDELL PRESS

First published 2015
The Boydell Press, Woodbridge

ISBN 978 1 78327 012 5

The Boydell Press is an imprint of Boydell & Brewer Ltd
PO Box 9, Woodbridge, Suffolk IP12 3DF, UK
and of Boydell & Brewer Inc.
668 Mount Hope Ave, Rochester, NY 14620–2731, USA
website: www.boydellandbrewer.com

A catalogue record for this book is available
from the British Library

The publisher has no responsibility for the continued existence or accuracy of URLs for
external or third-party internet websites referred to in this book, and does not guarantee that
any content on such websites is, or will remain, accurate or appropriate.

This publication is printed on acid-free paper

Printed and bound in Great Britain by
TJ International Ltd. Padstow, Cornwall

Contents

Illustrations

The author and publishers are grateful to all the institutions and individuals
listed for permission to reproduce the materials in which they hold copyright.
Every effort has been made to trace the copyright holders; apologies are offered
for any omission, and the publishers will be pleased to add any necessary
acknowledgement in subsequent editions.

Music Examples

7.3: Peter Maxwell Davies, *Missa super L'homme armé* © Copyright 1978 by Boosey & Hawkes Music Publishers Ltd. Reproduced by permission of Boosey & Hawkes Music Publishers Ltd   152

7.4: Peter Maxwell Davies, *Eight Songs for a Mad King* © Copyright 1971 by Boosey & Hawkes Music Publishers Ltd. Reproduced by permission of Boosey & Hawkes Music Publishers Ltd   157

7.5: Peter Maxwell Davies, *Vesalii Icones* © Copyright 1978 by Boosey & Hawkes Music Publishers Ltd. Reproduced by permission of Boosey & Hawkes Music Publishers Ltd   163

8.1: Cornelius Cardew, *Schooltime Compositions* (1967–8). London: Experimental Music Catalogue, 2006. Used by permission of Horace Cardew   171

8.2: *Anti-World*, music by Nicola LeFanu © Copyright 1972 Novello & Company Limited. All Rights Reserved. International Copyright Secured. Used by permission of Novello & Co. Ltd   179

8.3: Jeremy Dale Roberts, *Reconciliation* (1969). Used by permission of the composer   182

8.4: George Newson, *Arena* (Alfred Lengnick & Co. Ltd, 1971). Used by permission of the composer   190

8.5: Anthony Gilbert, *The Scene-Machine*, text by George MacBeth (Kassel, Schott & Co., 1970). Used by permission of Schott Music Ltd   196

9.1: Chamber Concerto No. 2, music by Thea Musgrave © Copyright 1966 Chester Music Limited. All Rights Reserved. International Copyright Secured. Used by permission of Chester Music Ltd   201

9.2: Concerto for Clarinet and Orchestra, music by Thea Musgrave © Copyright 1968 Chester Music Limited. All Rights Reserved. International Copyright Secured. Used by permission of Chester Music Ltd   204

9.3: Concerto for Horn and Orchestra, music by Thea Musgrave © Copyright 1971 Chester Music Limited. All Rights Reserved. International Copyright Secured. Used by permission of Chester Music Ltd   206

9.4: Harrison Birtwistle, *Verses for Ensembles* (1968–9). Used by permission of Universal Edition (London) Ltd   216

9.5: Erika Fox, *Lamentations for Four* (1973). Used by permission of the composer   220

10.1: *Celtic Requiem*, words by Henry Vaughan, John Henry Newman and Blathnac, music by John Tavener © Copyright 1969 Chester Music Limited. All Rights Reserved. International Copyright Secured. Used by Permission of Chester Music Ltd   229

Foreword by Alexander Goehr

Music Theatre, as so known, was and is the descendant of operetta and flourished on Broadway in the earliest part of the twentieth century. Its influence spread throughout the world. But this is not how the nomenclature is understood in the late Michael Hall's book. 'Our' much more modest Music Theatre has in common with the senior American version only a general belief that opera/Music Theatre must relate in some way to the preoccupations, scope and style of contemporary spoken theatre. 'Opera' as practised in the opera houses reflects its eighteenth- and nineteenth-century origins and repertoire and its excursions into new forms have only rarely succeeded.

Britten himself, the most successful twentieth-century composer for the opera house, was, at best, ambivalent about it and much of his best work moves away into what were, in his time, new forms of presentation, reduction of scale and scope, and, most radically, the building of his own theatre replacing the churches and church halls where much of his work was first shown.

When, in the early 1970s, John Cox and I were given the opportunity by the impresario Ian Hunter to come up with new forms of presenting new music, we devised a new version of the music-theatre concept. The scale was to be significantly reduced, approximating to the size of the Royal Court Theatre. We might perform in theatres, but also, following Britten's example, in any available space (acoustics permitting). Gone would be the large orchestras; singers chosen for their carrying voices were less in demand than singers who could speak, act and even mime. Our long-term ambition, following the work of Kagel and Ligeti (*Sur scène* and *Aventures*) was to replace the idea of sung play with instrumental accompaniment, with a form where vocal performance, instrumental expression and circus-derived virtuosity for its own sake existed in contrapuntal balance. In my time this ideal was rarely, if at all, achieved.

I believed that new forms of Music Theatre, created by ourselves and like-minded friends, would only succeed if I could find a pedigree of existing related repertoire to perform along with new pieces. The already mentioned Kagel and Ligeti pieces existed, and chronologically previous to them were the Stravinsky pieces (*Renard*, *The Soldier's Tale*), the Hindemith and Brecht–Weill collaborations at the Baden-Baden Festivals of the late 1920s, the play with music by Satie, or Milhaud's miniature operas. Looking further back, Monteverdi's *Il combattimento di Tancredi e Clorinda*, some of Handel's smaller pieces (*Acis and Galatea*) and the possible re-examination of the Jacobean masque might yield new ways of working.

In the short life of my Music Theatre Ensemble, some of what I have mentioned was attempted. But it did not go far enough. What, it appears, did survive was the ideal. This ideal has spawned a whole variety of new ensembles committed to the creating of new work and even the building of a new theatre at the Royal Opera House (the Linbury) where new work is presented. Further, the ideal and even the name appears not only in Britain (e.g. Music Theatre Wales) but in many countries. Naturally the styles and preferences of these organisations will differ, as indeed they should. The significance of the ideal appears now to be firmly established.

Editorial Preface

This book was a long time in the making and it is a great sadness for me that my husband did not live to see it published. In the early years of the new millennium we had many discussions with friends who came to visit us at our home in south-west France about what Michael's next project would be. Despite being weakened by heart disease, he had recently completed two books that were to be published in 2003 and was impatient to find the next topic to write about. During one such discussion, Michael talked spiritedly about his interest in the music of the sixties, reminding us that he knew many of the composers of the period from his time as a music producer at the BBC as well as from his earlier conducting years, when new music had been a special enthusiasm. The germ of an idea had been sown, and between 2003 and 2005 Michael was busy working his way around the UK interviewing as many composers, musicians and other key people as possible.

He amassed a vast amount of material and sometimes despaired of finding a coherent means of dealing with it. Eventually he decided that two books would be needed: one on Music Theatre and a second on other genres. By now, however, his health was deteriorating further and the writing process was slow. In 2006 life in rural France was no longer practicable and we returned to the UK. The upheaval caused yet more delays in the writing. Furthermore, repeated spells in hospital, followed by the need to recuperate, made him almost give up. However, with characteristic tenacity, he decided to make a supreme effort to complete the first of the planned books by his eightieth birthday. He did so and the manuscript was submitted to the publisher two months later in May 2012, after his friend, the composer Anthony Gilbert, had helped him edit his final draft. But Michael was gravely ill by now and he died not knowing if the book had been accepted for publication or not.

When an author dies before being able to discuss the editing of his manuscript, those with the responsibility of bringing the project to fruition face a dilemma. The publisher's criteria have to be met but the author's intentions must also be respected. Robert Adlington, a reputed scholar in the same field, who also knew Michael personally, made helpful proposals for editing the book. These involved structural reorganisation, mainly of the first chapters, to provide a less repetitive and more coherent line to the material, the inclusion of music examples, and the underpinning of the first part of the book with a light referential framework.

These amendments all seemed to me to reinforce and clarify my late husband's intentions.

However, once the structural changes had been agreed, it was clear that the book fell into two distinct parts: the background information and the discussion of the selected works. Robert's editorial suggestions for the first part of the book have been largely incorporated without interfering with the main arguments Michael expounded. This provides a context for the works of the British composers discussed in the main part of the book.

The second and main part, on the other hand, apart from some biographical material for readers' information and some additional references, I felt needed to be left as far as possible as Michael had written it. The reason for this decision was that Michael had never intended to write an academic treatise. As a music producer with the BBC during the sixties, he had personal experience of what he considered to be a uniquely exciting and innovative time for British composers, who were interacting with experimental music in the USA and Europe. The voices of those with direct involvement in this period are inevitably being silenced with the passage of time. But it is this involvement that makes Michael's book especially valuable. His style is unpretentious, direct and enthusiastic, as those who have been fortunate to attend his lectures or hear his broadcasts will recognise. I have no doubt that a later generation of scholars would approach the topic differently, but they were not there and they did not experience the events first hand.

The book concludes with a chapter looking beyond the period selected. Michael wanted to indicate the direction that British Music Theatre took after its heyday. He looks at how the major composers continued to compose music-theatre pieces and he wished further to show how contemporary composers have embraced the genre. I have added some brief references to the music-theatre scene as it continues today.

Research on British composers from the core era is of great current interest and the major figures are already the subject of much analysis, with several important studies having been published since Michael completed his manuscript. Michael's book, however, places the better-known works of Birtwistle, Maxwell Davies and Goehr in a much fuller context. He shows how lesser known composers were enthused by the genre and were given opportunities to have their experimental work performed through a burgeoning array of festivals and ensembles. The close relationship between composers, performers and conductors is also of great interest, revealing as it does the influence that certain performance styles had on how composers went about their work. The economic, social and political frenzy of those times is seen to provide a significant backdrop to the ideas being expressed in music, and it is clear that many of the composers felt their works should be of direct relevance to these events.

The book will be of interest to researchers and students in the field of British music of the late twentieth century in that it discusses topics and composers that have been hitherto largely neglected. It will be relevant also to students of composition, who will learn much about the experimental nature of composition at that time. A broader readership with a general interest in the cultural legacy of the era will find the material informative and, given Michael's clear writing style, very accessible. Those currently working in Music Theatre as composers, performers or producers will also be able to learn much from the procedures and processes of their predecessors.

I have had to make difficult decisions about the extent of editorial intervention for this book but I hope that my main objectives, of respecting Michael's aims and preserving his style, will permit as wide a readership as possible to obtain maximum benefit from his last work.

Brenda Hall
Exeter, September 2014

Acknowledgements

This book could not have been written without the participation of the composers, performers and others involved in the music scene of the 1960s and 1970s whom the author interviewed between 2003 and 2005, several of whom have, sadly, since died. This appraisal of the genre, therefore, owes a great deal to, among others, David Bedford, Harrison Birtwistle, David Blake, Susan Bradshaw, Bruce Cole, Edward Cowie, Gordon Crosse, Jeremy Dale Roberts, Peter Maxwell Davies, Peter Dickinson, Archer Endrich, Erika Fox, Alexander Goehr, Alan Hacker, Robin Holloway, Nicola LeFanu, David Lumsdaine, Catherine Macintosh, Jane Manning, Peter Manning, Nicholas Maw, Wilfrid Mellers, Dominic Muldowney, George Newson, Anthony Payne, Edwin Roxburgh, John Tilbury, Hugh Wood and John Woolf.

Special thanks go to Anthony Gilbert for his encouragement, support, editorial help and superb memory of events, and to Roger Marsh for his unstinting help with the music-theatre pieces written and performed at York. Valuable editorial advice was given by Robert Adlington and technical assistance was provided by James Whittle and Paul Sild.

The following quotations from texts have been made possible with the kind permission of the publishers or composers:

Luciano Berio, *Recital 1 for Cathy*, Universal Edition (London) Ltd, 1972. Used by permission of Universal Edition (London) Ltd.

Harrison Birtwistle, *Punch and Judy*, text by Stephen Pruslin, Universal Edition (London) Ltd, 1966–7. Used by permission of Universal Edition (London) Ltd.

Harrison Birtwistle, *Down by the Greenwood Side*, libretto by Michael Nyman, Universal Edition (London) Ltd, 1968–9. Used by permission of Universal Edition (London) Ltd.

Harrison Birtwistle, *Nenia: The Death of Orpheus*, text by Peter Zinovieff, Universal Edition (London) Ltd, 1970. Used by permission of Universal Edition (London) Ltd.

Harrison Birtwistle, *Bow Down*, text by Tony Harrison, Universal Edition (London) Ltd, 1977. Used by permission of Universal Edition (London) Ltd.

Harrison Birtwistle, *The Io Passion*, libretto by Stephen Plaice © Copyright 2004 by Boosey & Hawkes Music Publishers Ltd. Reproduced by permission of Boosey & Hawkes Music Publishers Ltd.

Bruce Cole, *The House on Secker Street*, text by Michael Johnson © Copyright by Boosey & Hawkes Music Publishers Ltd. Reproduced by permission of Boosey & Hawkes Music Publishers Ltd.

Peter Maxwell Davies, *Revelation and Fall*, text by Georg Trakl, translated by Stephen Pruslin © Copyright 1971 by Boosey & Hawkes Music Publishers Ltd. Reproduced by permission of Boosey & Hawkes Music Publishers Ltd.

Peter Maxwell Davies, *Eight Songs for a Mad King*, text by Randolph Stow © Copyright 1971 by Boosey & Hawkes Music Publishers Ltd. Reproduced by permission of Boosey & Hawkes Music Publishers Ltd.

Peter Maxwell Davies, *Miss Donnithorne's Maggot*, text by Randolph Stow © Copyright 1977 by Boosey & Hawkes Music Publishers Ltd. Reproduced by permission of Boosey & Hawkes Music Publishers Ltd.

Peter Maxwell Davies, *Blind Man's Buff*, words and music by Peter Maxwell Davies © Copyright 1972 Chester Music Limited. All Rights Reserved. International Copyright Secured. Used by permission of Chester Music Ltd.

Peter Maxwell Davies, *Mr Emmet Takes a Walk*, text by David Pountney © Copyright 2000, 2006 by Boosey & Hawkes Music Publishers Ltd. Reproduced by permission of Boosey & Hawkes Music Publishers Ltd.

Anthony Gilbert, *The Scene-Machine*, text by George MacBeth, Schott Music Ltd, 1970.

Alexander Goehr, *Shadowplay*, text adapted from Kenneth Cavander's translation of Book VII of Plato's *Republic*, Schott Music Ltd, 1970.

Alexander Goehr, *Sonata about Jerusalem*, texts adapted by Recha Freier and the composer, Schott Music Ltd, 1970.

Eve Harrison, *Hera's List* and *The Rose Collector*, by permission of the composer.

George Newson, *Arena* (Alfred Lengnick & Co. Ltd, 1971). Used by permission of the composer.

John Tavener, *Celtic Requiem*, words by Henry Vaughan, John Henry Newman and Blathnac, music by John Tavener © Copyright 1969 Chester Music Limited. All Rights Reserved. International Copyright Secured. Used by Permission of Chester Music Ltd.

Thanks also to Wiltshire and Swindon Archives for permission to quote from *Odyssey*, Summer 1961 (Cranborne Chase School Magazine).

PART ONE

An Emerging Genre

CHAPTER ONE

Definitions and Overview

THIS book discusses the Music Theatre composed mainly by British composers during the 1960s and 1970s. By Music Theatre I mean in essence, to quote
the 2009 *Concise English Oxford Dictionary*, 'a combination of music and drama
in a modern form distinct from traditional opera, typically for a small number of
performers'. However, this is only one of the meanings the term has had and its
gradual emergence as a distinct genre is worth exploring.

It was certainly used in the nineteenth century in America as an abbreviation of musical theatre, a generic term for popular forms of musical entertainment such as the minstrel show, vaudeville and, after 1895, the music comedy or
musical. In the early 1950s, a theatrical licensing agency specialising in Broadway
and West End musicals began calling itself 'Music Theatre International'.[1] More
recently, however, the term has veered away from popular music towards opera.
Philip Glass's book, *Opera on the Beach*, about his operas *Einstein on the Beach*,
Satyagraha and *Akhnaten*, has as its subtitle, *Philip Glass on his New World of
Music Theatre*.[2]

In Europe, it was used by Walter Felsenstein in the 1950s 'to designate a theatrical work (or performance) in which dramatic and musical elements are used so as
to melt into one another and to create the total impression of "seamless unity"',[3]
but it only came into general use in the 1960s. There is, for example, no entry for
Music Theatre in the 1954 edition of *The Grove Dictionary of Music and Musicians*,
but there is in the following edition, *The New Grove* of 1980. By then the heyday
of Music Theatre had been over for several years, but the contributor, Andrew
Porter, a London music critic with a special interest in opera, still could not really
see it as being 'distinct from traditional opera'. For him the term is 'a catch-phrase
that became common in the 1960s, particularly among composers, producers
and critics who had artistic or social objections to the cost of traditional grand
opera and the conservatism of grand opera companies and their audiences'. He
maintained that the term is loosely used in three senses:

---

[1] http://www.mtishows.com/content.asp?id=1_2_0 (accessed 17 February 2014).
[2] Philip Glass, *Opera on the Beach: Philip Glass on his New World of Music Theatre*, ed.
Robert T. Jones (London, Faber, 1988).
[3] Peter Paul Fuchs, Foreword to *The Music Theatre of Walter Felsenstein*, ed. Peter Paul
Fuchs (London, Quartet Books, 1991), preliminary pages not numbered.

1) to designate musical works for small or moderate forces that involve a dramatic element in their presentation; 2) to describe an opera in which the theatrical element is deemed powerful enough to compensate for an indifferent or insubstantial score; 3) to describe a manner of opera performance in which the acting and staging are thought to be so vivid as to compensate for mediocre, or complement admirable singing and playing.[4]

Porter's first definition includes 'small-scale operas' such as Alexander Goehr's *Naboth's Vineyard*, 'song cycles with instrumental accompaniment that are "staged" and enacted on a concert platform', such as Maxwell Davies's *Eight Songs for a Mad King*, as well as György Ligeti's *Aventures et Nouvelles aventures*, Cornelius Cardew's *School Operas* and 'numerous but unspecified works by Mauricio Kagel, some with no recognisable musical component, and which resist any precise definition'. Among earlier examples he cites 'Stravinsky's *The Soldier's Tale* and *Renard*, Weill's *Mahagonny Songspiel* and Paul Hindemith's *Wir bauen eine Stadt* for children and, for that matter, Monteverdi's *Il combattimento di Tancredi e Clorinda*.

As an example of his second definition, Porter cites Penderecki's *The Devils of Loudun*, which, he says, 'may not be very good music, but is excellent music theatre'. His third definition refers to 'Walter Felsenstein's carefully acted productions of the traditional operatic repertory'. However, he believes that in these second and third senses 'music theatre is little more than a handy term of approved use, in the age-old struggle for supremacy that underlies the history of opera and has prompted so many reformers to champion the claims of drama against those of music'.

There is no entry for Music Theatre in the second edition of *The Harvard Dictionary of Music* of 1969, and in *The New Harvard Dictionary of Music* of 1986, the contributor Robert P. Morgan makes no mention of the various American meanings; these are given a separate entry in the dictionary under the heading Musical (comedy), nor does he allude to Porter's second and third senses of the term. He confines himself solely to Porter's first sense. But whereas Porter seemed unsure about some of the contents in it, Morgan confidently asserts that the genre is 'the combination of elements from music and drama in new forms distinct from traditional opera, although some action is usually specified, music theatre

---

[4] See Porter's article on Music Theatre in *The New Grove Dictionary of Music and Musicians*, ed. Stanley Sadie (London, Macmillan, 1980), vol. 12, 863. In the 2001 edition of the *NGDMM*, Andrew Clements defines Music Theatre as: 'A term used to characterize a kind of opera and opera production in which spectacle and dramatic impact are emphasized over purely musical factors. It was first used specifically in the 1960s to describe the small-scale musico-dramatic works of the postwar generations that proliferated in western Europe and North America during that decade,' vol. 17, 534.

is normally non-realistic and often non-representational'.[5] He cites Schoenberg's *Pierrot lunaire* (1912) as an early example, but claims that 'the most active early 20th century composer in developing alternative musico-theatrical approaches' was Stravinsky. With *Renard* (1916), *L'histoire du soldat* (1918) and *Les noces* (1922), Stravinsky 'anticipated the separation of musical and dramatic elements later advocated by the German playwright Bertolt Brecht, who became an important force in creating new forms of music theatre in the 1920s and 30s, working in collaboration with such composers as Paul Hindemith and Kurt Weill'. Morgan concludes by saying that the genre:

> has flourished especially in the second half of the century, during which a number of composers have come to view much of their work, including instrumental music, in essentially dramatic terms. Singers or instrumentalists may be required to wear masks (e.g George Crumb's *Vox balaenae* (1971)) or full costume (Peter Maxwell Davies's *Eight Songs for a Mad King* (1969)); or the musical performance itself may be treated as a 'staged' dramatic event (Luciano Berio's *Recital 1* (1972), and numerous works by John Cage and Mauricio Kagel).[6]

My own definition of Music Theatre is that it is a flexible genre distinct from opera or ballet. The works I discuss in this book never rely exclusively on singing, dancing or speaking, but combine these elements, or draw on folk or popular types of theatre, to create a unique composite style for each of them. They are intended for the concert hall or a theatre with an open stage, and are generally short enough to be included as an item in a concert containing other types of music. Sometimes the instrumentalists are asked to take part in the action. The works often require neither scenery nor elaborate lighting, but costumes and masks are sometimes worn, and props and screens may be employed. As at a concert, all the performers are typically required to be on the platform throughout the duration of the work. Apart from at the beginning and end, the works exclude entrances and exits. Unlike fully staged opera and ballet or theatre, Music Theatre allows composers to take control of all aspects of the performance. Only occasionally do they need the assistance of a producer, director or conductor.[7] Without exception they set out to

---

[5] *The New Harvard Dictionary of Music*, ed. Don Michael Randel (Cambridge, Mass., Belknap Press of Harvard University Press, 1986), 522.

[6] Ibid.

[7] According to W. Anthony Sheppard, *Revealing Masks: Exotic Influences and Ritualized Performance in Modernist Music Theater* (Berkeley and London, University of California Press, 2001), 6, the small-scale of Music Theatre 'had its roots in economic and social concerns'.

be surprising, to include moments of humour even when the topic is serious, and to convey a spirit of adventure.[8]

Yet, despite the gradual development of a distinct term, the genre is not really a new phenomenon. I want to use for my initial example the first specimen of what may be called Music Theatre: Monteverdi's *Il combattimento di Tancredi e Clorinda*. This can be found in Monteverdi's eighth book of madrigals: the 'Madrigals of War and Love' (1638). First performed in a concert of madrigals given in the palace of a Venetian nobleman in 1624, it was the first work in an experimental style, which Monteverdi termed the *stile concitato*, designed to express anger and warfare. I discuss it in depth in Chapter Two, but briefly it concerns the combat between Tancredi, a Norman knight, and Clorinda, a Saracen amazon dressed in armour as a man, as described by Tasso in his *Gerusalemme liberata*. Scored for soprano, tenor (narrator), baritone and six instruments (five strings and keyboard), all the action is mimed by the soprano and baritone wearing masks. They sing only during an interlude in the fighting when they need to rest, and at the end, when Clorinda is wounded. No scenery is required, and apart from swords and a '*Cavallo Mariano*' (a kind of hobbyhorse) there is no need for any other props. Monteverdi's explanatory preface to the work suggests that the tenor should stand apart from the instrumentalists. He should avoid using ornaments other than in the third stanza, when he contemplates what the event will mean for future generations. During this the combatants must presumably 'freeze' before resuming the action.

In 1968 Alexander Goehr used *Il combattimento* as the model for *Naboth's Vineyard*, 'a dramatic madrigal with a text in Latin and English adapted from 1 Kings xxi'. This I discuss in detail in Chapter Six, but, briefly, the narrative tells how Jezebel arranges to have Naboth stoned to death so that her husband, King Achab, can take possession of the vineyard, which Naboth has refused to relinquish. Goehr scores the work for two mimes, three voices and six instruments. When the voices sing as a chorus they narrate the story in English; when they sing separately they sing the lines for Jezebel, Achab, Naboth, Elijah and the Elders in Latin. As in *Il combattimento,* all the action is performed in mime, not by the singers but by two mimes dressed identically alike in shifts, but wearing masks to differentiate the characters they represent. Whereas the mimes occupy the acting area centre stage, the singers and instrumentalists dressed in casual modern clothes should stand or sit at the back or sides of the stage.

---

[8] Further discussions of Music Theatre as a genre can be found in 'Music Theatre since the 1960s', by Robert Adlington, in *The Cambridge Companion to Twentieth-Century Opera*, ed. Mervyn Cooke (Cambridge, Cambridge University Press, 2005), 225–43; and Nicholas Till, 'Post-Operatic Music Theatre in Europe', in Joe Kelleher and Nicholas Ridout (eds), *Contemporary Theatres in Europe* (London, Routledge, 2006).

The key differences between Monteverdi and Goehr lie in Goehr's use of the modernisms of his time. His instrumentalists playing flute, clarinet, bass trombone, violin, double bass and piano (four hands) cover not only the extremes of the tonal spectrum but also the extremes of twentieth-century instrumental techniques. His language is atonal not modal. His separation of music and action is also extreme. Whereas Monteverdi wanted the mimes to conform exactly to the music of the *stile concitato* provided by the instruments, Goehr asks his mimes to be independent of the music, to be comic even when the situation is serious.[9] He also makes extensive use of montage. Whereas Monteverdi extended real time by stopping the action for the lyrical realisation of Tasso's third stanza, Goehr contracts time by abruptly juxtaposing different passages or by superimposing one on another. In so doing, he applies cinematic techniques to his piece: he compresses actions that may take several days, weeks or even months into twenty minutes.

But Goehr had another mentor in mind when composing *Naboth's Vineyard*, and that was Bertolt Brecht. He asks the chorus to sing in English and the individual characters in Latin, so that he can conform to Brecht's concept of Epic Theatre, the type of theatre intended to keep the audience estranged from the action so that they can make a rational judgement of its outcome.[10] It means that the audience will understand that they are getting a report of past events, and will be more likely to assess these with critical detachment. Although Goehr did not publicly refer to *Naboth's Vineyard* as Music Theatre, he had nevertheless been using the term privately among friends and fellow composers since visiting East Berlin in 1963 to report on the use of music in the Brecht plays being given by the Berliner Ensemble at the Theater am Schiffbauerdamm. He had been sent by Bernard Miles, who wanted to perform some Brecht plays at the Mermaid Theatre, Puddle Dock. When there, he also went to performances at the Komische Oper in East Berlin, where Walter Felsenstein, its Director, had been using the term *Musiktheater* to describe the operatic productions he had been mounting since 1947.[11]

---

[9] By asking the mimes to be amusing, Goehr is calling on an ancient popular type of mime theatre, broad comic shows with a strong emphasis on action and gesture. I believe it is a tradition that Monteverdi was also calling on, for although *Il combattimento* ends tragically, the sight of mimes acting and gesturing in strict accordance with the music must have also been amusing.

[10] See *Brecht on Theatre: The Development of an Aesthetic*, ed. and tr. John Willett (London, Eyre Methuen, 1978).

[11] Unless otherwise indicated, information and quotations from the British composers, musicians and performers discussed in his book are taken from the interviews conducted with the author in 2003 and 2004.

Felsenstein's reason for adopting this term was because the opera productions of the time laid too much emphasis on singing and were neglecting the theatrical aspect of the genre. Felsenstein made a composite noun out of 'Musik' and 'Theater' to indicate that, when producing an opera, the director should place the aural and the visual on a more or less equal footing. Although music, because it unfolds in time, can create a sense of action, nevertheless action per se, the process of doing, can only take place in a physical dimension, the dimension that can be seen. He insisted that producers should never allow singers to assume that operas were concerts in costume. They should be persuaded to think of themselves as 'singing actors'. The character, feelings and thoughts of those they represent should be indicated through their gestures, their facial expression, body language, physical responses and movements as well as through their singing.[12]

In England, the first mention in print of Music Theatre in Felsenstein's meaning of the term appears to be in an article by the composer David Blake about the music of Hanns Eisler in *The Listener* in September 1966.[13] It appears in the sentence 'The dramatic style of music theatre, strangely, could not hold him long, even if it left traces on his musical physiognomy.' On the recommendation of Alexander Goehr, who had befriended Eisler in the mid-fifties, Blake studied composition under Eisler in East Berlin during the academic year 1960-1, and he too had been able to attend Felsenstein's productions at the Komische Oper on several occasions. Blake recalls that when he wrote that sentence he had in mind Eisler's collaboration with Bertolt Brecht on *Die Massnahme* (1930) and *Die Mutter* (1932). Initially he thought he could categorise them using the American term 'musical theatre', but because both are serious in character, he realised he could never relate them to *Oklahoma!* or *Annie Get Your Gun* and therefore he had to borrow Felsenstein's term.

Although the separation of music and action, a defining characteristic of Brecht's Epic Theatre, is a feature of many later specimens of Music Theatre, there has been an equally strong tendency to integrate the two. One early example, Schoenberg's *Pierrot lunaire* (1912), stands in both camps. Scored for an actress and five instrumentalists, it is a setting of twenty-one poems expressing the bizarre fantasies of a clown who has been cut off from reality. Schoenberg intended the instrumentalists to be hidden behind screens so that the actress had the stage to herself. But she does not speak the lines; she performs them using a form of articulation, which is neither speech nor song but a simultaneous combination of the two, *Sprechstimme* or *Sprechgesang*. By this means she conveys not only the split personality of the clown, she also participates in the music. Physically she

[12] Fuchs, *Music Theatre*, 15–25.
[13] 'Hanns Eisler', *The Listener* (15 September 1966), 398.

may be separated from the instrumentalists, but in her own way she contributes to their music.

Most of the other works that set out to integrate rather than separate belong to the seventies. Harrison Birtwistle's *Bow Down* dates from 1977, when the composer was Music Director of the National Theatre and was regularly working with actors as well as musicians. To explore the common territory between actors and musicians, *Bow Down* employs five actors, three of whom must dance, and four musicians, who between them play bamboo flute, bamboo pipes, oboes, penny whistles and percussion; all the performers contribute to both the acting and the music. The three people needed to perform Richard Orton's *Mug Grunt* (1972) similarly have to be both actors and musicians, each gesturing and vocalising to produce elaborate patterns in which the visual and the aural appear to be totally integrated. Total integration was also Stockhausen's aim when he composed *Inori* (1974) for one or two mimes and a large symphony orchestra, and *Harlekin* (1975) for a clarinettist who can dance (discussed further in Chapter Four). In *Inori*, Stockhausen assigned a pitch, duration, tempo and timbre for each of the mime's gestures, so that every visual gesture has its musical equivalent. In *Harlekin*, he devised a choreography of mime, gesture and movement so that her dancing would be totally at one with his music.

As a piece for a dancer who can accompany herself on the clarinet, *Harlekin* is Music Theatre. But as a piece for a clarinettist who can dance, it is, more accurately, Instrumental Theatre. There are no separate entries for Instrumental Theatre in the standard late twentieth-century music dictionaries, the 2001 edition of *The New Grove* included. Dictionaries place instrumental-theatre works among the music-theatre works they are listing or discussing. Paul Griffiths does separate Instrumental Theatre from Music Theatre in his book *Modern Music and After*:[14] while Music Theatre, for him, grew out of 'the dotage of opera', with 'new possibilities in smaller, more flexible combinations of music and drama',[15] Instrumental Theatre was characterised by 'musicians in movement'. However, no real discussion making a distinction between these two forms ensues. In the second edition of *The New Grove Dictionary of Music and Musicians* (2001), Andrew Clements classifies Mauricio Kagel's *Match* for two cellos and percussion (1964) as Music Theatre, even though it is one of the best-known specimens of Instrumental Theatre.

Essentially, an instrumental work becomes Instrumental Theatre when it includes a meaningful visual dimension and involves actions that go beyond those normally needed to produce music. In *The New Harvard Dictionary*, Morgan

---

[14] *Modern Music and After*, 3rd edn (Oxford, Oxford University Press, 2011), 90–202.
[15] Ibid., 196.

includes George Crumb's *Vox balaenae* (The Voice of the Whale) in the category of Music Theatre: 'a number of composers have come to view much of their work, including purely instrumental work in dramatic terms ... the musical performance itself may be treated as a "staged" event'.[16] In *Vox balaenae*, the instrumentalists (amplified flute, amplified cello and amplified piano) have to wear black masks throughout the performance, and the platform should be bathed in deep-blue stage lighting to represent the sea. But although Crumb produces some very whale-like sounds from his instrumentalists, the work is equally effective without the visual elements. Instrumental Theatre demands that at least some of the instrumentalists taking part should behave like actors.[17]

This is clear for the three works I instinctively select to represent the continental contribution to Instrumental Theatre in this introductory chapter: Kagel's *Match*, Stockhausen's *Trans* and Berio's *Sequenza V*. Perhaps it is no coincidence that all three are comedies, because when you act with an instrument in your hands, it is easier to be a clown than a tragedian. In Kagel's *Match* (discussed further in Chapter Four), two cellists battle with each other to discover which has the more virtuoso technique; the clown is the percussionist, who acts as the referee. The cellists appear to 'act' because the music Kagel gives them is so difficult that only exaggerated movements can cope with what is demanded.

'Trans' is an abbreviation of 'transpersonal', and Stockhausen says that the work 'has something to do with the beyond, with what's on the other side'.[18] In this instance, what lies on the other side is suggested by four groups of wind and percussion instruments playing softly and slowly behind a gauze curtain bathed in a violet light, in front of which is a bank of strings behaving like automata. In an attempt to penetrate this barrier, the principal viola, cello and violin take it in turns to put on an act, each triggered by a stage hand or the amplified sounds of a weaving loom shuttle.

Instrumental Theatre need not always be non-representational, however. Berio's solo trombone piece *Sequenza V* represents Karl Adrian 'Grock' Wettach (1880-1959), the Swiss-born, self-styled 'king of clowns'.[19] Although Grock preferred to play the violin, he was said to be skilled on twenty-four instruments,

---

[16] *The New Harvard Dictionary of Music*, 522.
[17] For further discussion of Instrumental Theatre in relation to Music Theatre, see F. Huebner, 'Entering the Stage: Musicians as Performance in Contemporary Music Theatre', *New Sounds*, 36:2 (Dept. of Musicology, Faculty of Music, University of Belgrade, November 2010), 63–74.
[18] Jonathan Cott, *Stockhausen: Conversations with the Composer* (London, Robson Books, 1974), 56.
[19] His autobiography was entitled *Grock: King of Clowns*, 2nd edn, tr. Basil Creighton, ed. Ernst Konstantin (London, Methuen, 1957).

among them the trombone. His act consisted of a series of mishaps, and after each of them he would plaintively ask, 'Warum?' Modern trombonists have developed techniques that have made their instrument so versatile that, with the aid of different types of embouchures and mutes, players can use it as a vehicle for singing, talking and even producing chords. *Sequenza V* creates a comic drama out of the struggle to convert sound into speech and then speech into sound. After each failure, the trombonist attempts to say 'why' through his instrument. But the technique of playing and speaking at the same time is so difficult that, in Berio's words, the execution becomes 'simultaneously grotesque and desperate', hence, in Grock's case, comic.[20]

British Instrumental Theatre generally avoids the overt comedy of these European works. Instead it falls into two types: one expands the concerto principle, the other relates to rituals. Four concertos composed by Thea Musgrave between 1967 and 1973 dramatise, often humorously, the conflict between soloist, orchestral musicians and conductor. The visual component involves musicians walking from position to position either within the orchestra or around the auditorium, or the simple expedient of having players stand when they would normally be sitting. Jeremy Dale Roberts's Cello Concerto, on the other hand, manages to create a strong sense of movement even though none actually takes place. The work requires that one of the orchestral cellists, hidden behind a screen at the back of the platform, should function as the first soloist's distorted mirror image, his ghostly double or Doppelgänger. His playing is amplified, with his loudspeakers positioned so that his sounds suggest a wandering location. Stockhausen had done something similar in *Kontakte* for piano, percussion and tape (1958–60), which should be considered the harbinger of Instrumental Theatre. In this the instrumentalists are trying to make contact with the electronic sounds that seem to be coming from outer space. But the players are only really successful after they have walked from their positions at the sides of the platform to the centre, where they summons the mysterious 'beyond' by beating a tam-tam and a gong.

It is notable that works representative of Instrumental Theatre as ritual frequently make extensive use of percussion instruments. The advantage in composing for percussionists is that they are always on the move, and therefore provide a visual spectacle. Anthony Gilbert's *Brighton Piece* for two percussionists and small ensemble (1968) takes as its model the Roman Catholic Mass, with its four movements labelled Introit, Gradual, Choral I and Choral II. But he uses the terms in their literal meanings in addition to their religious associations: Introit 'entry' (the two percussionists commence their activities facing each other

[20] Rossana Dalmonte and Bálint András Varga, *Luciano Berio: Two Interviews*, tr. and ed. David Osmond-Smith (New York: Marion Boyars Publishers, 1981), 93.

downstage); Gradual 'taking steps' (the rapid movement between one percussion instrument and another); and Choral 'coming together', such as at the end, when all the instrumentalists play percussion instruments. The two percussionists in Fox's *Lamentations for Four* for percussion and two cellos (1972) are clearly going through a ritual performed by undertakers at a funeral. They move slowly with measured steps between three percussion 'positions' placed behind the two cellists, and are instructed to play 'with calm, formal and deliberate movements'.

Birtwistle's *Verses for Ensembles*, for five woodwind, five brass and two percussion players (1969), has no obvious religious ceremony lying behind it, even though it uses the two kinds of chant found in the Christian liturgy: antiphonal chant (the alternation of two or more choirs) and responsorial chant (the alternation of a soloist and a single choir). It is Instrumental Theatre because, apart from the trombones, the players have to walk from position to position to play different instruments or perform different roles; it is a ritual simply because all Birtwistle's works are highly formal, involving repetitions that are constantly being transformed.

During the twentieth century, Music Theatre was cultivated in three periods: between 1912 and 1921, when Schoenberg's *Pierrot lunaire*, Satie's *Le piège de Méduse* and Stravinsky's *Les noces, Renard* and *L'histoire du soldat* were composed; between 1927 and 1933 when Weill's *Mahagonny Songspiel* and *Die Sieben Todsünden*, Hindemith and Weill's *Der Flug der Lindberghs*, Hindemith's *Das Badener Lehrstück* and Eisler's *Die Massnahme* saw the light of day; and between 1958 and 1974 when the composers who are my main concern in this book were active in the field.

Like Monteverdi's *Il combattimento di Tancredi e Clorinda,* their distant seventeenth-century precursor, all of these works were experimental. Monteverdi's adaptation of ancient Greek metric theories to create a rhythmic style suitable for warlike emotions was as new as the experiments in opera: chordal harmony, tonality, the more expressive use of the dissonance, and the polarisation of melody and bass. Three hundred years later, between 1912 and 1921, when several composers felt that these techniques had run their course, experimentation was again in the air. *Pierrot lunaire* was composed after Schoenberg had abandoned tonality, emancipated dissonance, and was experimenting with how deeply disturbed states of mind could be dramatised. *Le piège de Méduse* was the outcome of Satie's interest in musical non-sequiturs and mosaic-like structures; while Stravinsky's three pieces were written in the wake of the radical innovations of *The Rite of Spring,* and were experiments in how other examples from the Russian folk-theatre tradition could be adapted for the modern theatre.

In Germany between 1927 and 1933, experimentation was driven mainly by political and social circumstances. Although only Eisler was a member of the

Communist Party, Hindemith, Weill and Bertolt Brecht, the playwright who initiated the experiments, also followed a left-wing agenda. Brecht sought to replace the contemporary theatre of illusion with a type of theatre in which the audience, instead of identifying with the hero, could make rational judgements about the events portrayed. Likewise, the music of Eisler, Hindemith and Weill sought to be as objective as possible so that it too could serve a rational and useful purpose.

The dates of the third period, 1958–74, are those the historian Arthur Marwick believes mark the beginning and end of the sixties, a period he claims witnessed a cultural revolution in Britain, France, Italy and the United States (the countries he chose to investigate). The year 1958 was when the austerities and restrictions occasioned by the Second World War had come, or were coming, to an end; 1974 the year after the Organization of Petrol-Exporting Countries (OPEC) quadrupled oil prices, as a result of which an economic crisis ensued and confidence evaporated.[21]

Music Theatre's ethos reflected the revolutionary atmosphere and the spirit of adventure that characterised that era. However, the revolution in music took place even earlier. After 1958, avant-garde composers were merely coming to terms with what Pierre Boulez in Europe and John Cage in America had instigated in the period between 1945 and 1952. For different reasons both men had wanted to make a completely new start in music, and consequently both were revolutionaries. The height of their radicalism occurred in 1952 when Boulez produced his first book of *Structures* for two pianos in which everything, other than the selection of registers, was produced by automatic processes. Then, in the same year, Cage produced his 'silent' piano piece *4'33"* conceived under the influence of Zen philosophy. In *4'33"* all the pianist does is lift or lower the lid of the piano after specific periods of time. There are no sounds other than those going on in the concert hall during its performance: the rustling of programmes, coughs, yawns, stifled laughter, etc.[22] Neither the first book of *Structures* nor *4'33"* lasts more than a few minutes, but the influence of both pieces was profound in the years that followed. Boulez's piece, which had been initiated by combining the innovations of Messiaen, Stravinsky and Webern, established the principle of integral serialism, soon to be an almost unshakeable orthodoxy for those composers who met

[21] Arthur Marwick, *The Sixties: Cultural Revolution in Britain, France, Italy and the United States, c.1958–c.1974* (Oxford, Oxford University Press, 1998).
[22] 'But *4'33"* also stands at the end of a road … it is silent. Though it has been claimed, reasonably enough, that 4'33" consists not of silence but of the environmental sounds which an audience might otherwise ignore, and though the piece may be described as a prototype of music-theatre, in that the performer or performers … are asked to make it clear that a musical performance is in progress, these are incidental features.' Paul Griffiths, *Modern Music: The Avant Garde since 1945* (London, J.M. Dent, 1981), 70.

annually at the summer festival held at Darmstadt; while Cage's piece established indeterminacy and ultimately led to minimalism.[23]

Cage's philosophy that the composer must 'give up the desire to control sound, clear his mind of music, and set about discovering means to let sounds be themselves rather than vehicles for man-made theories or expressions of human sentiments'[24] was further exemplified in his first 'happening' which took place in the grounds of Black Mountain College in North Carolina also in 1952. The event required that the poets, painters, dancers and musicians he recruited should each 'do their own thing' independently of a medley of films, slides and gramophone records being shown or played at the same time. Cage imposed a degree of order on the proceedings by telling each person when to start and how much time they had for their activities, and he had the audience sit in the centre of the activities to demonstrate that 'the theatre is all around us'.[25]

For Boulez, however, the theatre meant opera, and for someone who wanted to rid music of its extra-musical associations,[26] who wanted to let music be itself, opera was taboo, as indeed it was for most of the composers who followed in his footsteps during the rest of the fifties. Nevertheless, the work he composed after his first book of *Structures, Le marteau sans maître* (1955), included a singer, and singers, because they have to use words, which are the principal carriers of extra-musical associations in music. However, in Boulez's hands the meaning of the words, and their associations, took second place to their sound and syntax.[27] It was only when other avant-garde composers adopted this procedure, and then realised that for expressive reasons words and other extra-musical associations could not be avoided, that the situation became ripe for the emergence of Music Theatre.

In his book Marwick divides the sixties into three distinctive sub-periods, 1958–63, 'the first stirrings of a cultural revolution'; 1964–9, 'the high sixties', and 1969–74 'everything goes and catching up'. As far as Music Theatre was concerned, the 'first stirrings' involved a wide range of experiments, a number of which are recounted in Chapter Three. In 1959, Berio, for example, produced *Allez Hop* for mimes and symphony orchestra, about a travelling showman with a flea circus who shouted 'Allez Hop' when he wanted his fleas to jump. He followed

---

[23] See Michael Nyman, *Experimental Music: Cage and Beyond*, 2nd edn (Cambridge, Cambridge University Press, 1999).

[24] Quoted in ibid., 50

[25] Ibid.,72.

[26] See Michael Hall, *Leaving Home* (London, Faber and Faber, 1988), 16–18.

[27] 'the poem disappears as such but continues to control purely musical features by the continuations of its structures in the music. Structure and form are the things that I wish finally to emphasize.' Pierre Boulez, *Orientations: Collected Writings* (London, Faber, 1986), 198.

this in 1960 with *Circles* for mezzo-soprano, harp and two percussionists, which incorporates closely circumscribed movements for the musicians. *Passaggio* (1962), on the other hand, requires an opera house, an opera singer, an eight-part chorus situated in the orchestral pit alongside twenty-five instrumentalists, and five speaking choruses seated among the audience in the auditorium. Despite the work's dependency upon the resources of opera, it anticipates later Music Theatre in significant respects, notably in its Brechtian anti-realism and upsetting of the conventional relationship between audience and performers.

Stockhausen also embraced extremes in those years. Earlier, I called *Kontakte*, his piece for piano, percussion and tape (1959), 'the harbinger of Instrumental Theatre'. It was certainly the harbinger of a more fully blown music-theatre work called *Originale* (1961), which Stockhausen based on the music of *Kontakte*, and modelled on Cage's Black Mountain Happening. Like Cage, he recruited as many 'originals' as were available, including a film crew, a street vendor, an attendant from Cologne Zoo's monkey house, and a child playing with toy bricks. The participants were left free to improvise their own actions more or less obliviously of each other. The result put Stockhausen in line with what was happening in the contemporary Theatre of the Absurd [28] except that in his case the absurdities were writ large. The same influence was at work in Kagel's *Sur scène* (1960), which satirises contemporary musical practice, and Ligeti's *Aventures* (1962), which makes nonsense out of operatic conventions.

In Britain the 'first stirrings' did not really begin until 1964. The leading figures were Alexander Goehr, Peter Maxwell Davies and Harrison Birtwistle, who had been fellow students at the Royal Manchester College of Music in the mid-fifties. They differed from their continental colleagues in that they had no wish to sever themselves from the past. Like John Dunstable six centuries earlier, they sought to reconcile the great innovations taking place on the continent with tradition, not necessarily the English harmonic tradition that Dunstable had wanted to preserve, but the tradition they had inherited in their different ways as music students. For Goehr this meant reconciling serialism with modality and the German tradition that Bach had established; for Maxwell Davies it meant reconciling serialism with late medieval and Renaissance procedures; for Birtwistle it meant reconciling early medieval organum with the chance operations that Cage had been recommending.[29]

---

[28] The term was coined by Martin Esslin, *The Theatre of the Absurd*, rev. and enlarged edn (London, Pelican, 1967) and defined as: 'The Theatre of the Absurd strives to express its sense of the senselessness of the human condition and the inadequacy of the rational approach by the open abandonment of rational devices and discursive thought' (24).

[29] For discussion of Birtwistle's use of chance and random numbers, see Michael Hall, *Harrison Birtwistle* (London, Robson Books, 1984), 87–91.

The establishment of two permanent opera houses in London after the war, and the success of the operas by Britten and Tippett, encouraged young British composers to follow in their footsteps. Maxwell Davies began to sketch plans for his opera *Taverner* when he was still a student, even though he knew that such an avant-garde work would not be commissioned until he had established his name. To be commissioned to write an opera in the late fifties and early sixties, composers had to prove they could write in a style acceptable to the opera-going public. Sadler's Wells commissioned Malcolm Williamson's *Our Man in Havana* (1963) because the performance of his Organ Concerto at the 1961 Proms had shown that his music could be highly exuberant and extrovert. The same company commissioned Richard Rodney Bennett's *The Mines of Sulphur* (1963) not only because he was a well-known film composer but also because he had written *The Ledge,* a one-act opera that had been well received in 1961. And it was Nicholas Maw's highly romantic *Scenes and Arias* at the 1962 Proms that persuaded the London County Council to ask him to write *One Man Show* for the 1974 opening of the Jeanetta Cochrane Theatre.

The importance of opera for British composers was reflected in the first of two Summer Schools of Music at Wardour Castle that Birtwistle organised in 1964 and 1965. For these Goehr and Maxwell Davies took the composition seminars, the Melos Ensemble gave recitals and taught the instrumentalists, and Michael Tippett was asked to be President. The Schools lasted a week from Saturday to Saturday, and the first opened with a lecture by Goehr on 'Music in Our Time', the gist of which was that, although a great deal of new music was going to be played and discussed, there would be relatively little that was really new; most of it had been done before. In other words, the new music was rooted in tradition.

Opera took centre stage at an open forum called 'Opera Today' on the Wednesday evening of the first Summer School. As well as including a discussion about Britten's church parable, *Curlew River,* which had received its first performance a few months earlier, Goehr, Maxwell Davies and Birtwistle gave summaries of *Arden Must Die, Taverner* and *Punch and Judy,* the operas they were either composing or planning to compose. But the topic that received most interest came from the floor, when Anthony Gilbert took the bull by the horns by attacking the whole concept of traditional opera in the mid-twentieth century. In his opinion opera had had its day, and he asked why Tippett persisted in writing such works as *Midsummer Marriage,* which seemed more like Mozart than anything that could belong to the twentieth century. He felt that composers should develop a much more concentrated form of opera, that it should be relevant to contemporary situations, and cited as an example Hindemith's *Das Badener Lehrstück,* a work that dates from 1929, lasts fifty minutes and has a text by Brecht about four airmen who attempt to cross the Atlantic as Charles Lindbergh had done two years earlier. According to Gilbert, the general discussion that ensued eventually led to a consensus among the composers present. They decided that 'Music Theatre', as all agreed to call it, should be 'concise, contain no stage fripperies, no large orchestra, no divas, no gigantic arias. It could include the spoken word, ideally be done in the round, and music and theatre should be integrated for the clear purpose of putting across a socio-political message. In its purest form, the idea of plot could be dispensed with, in which case the content could be abstract.'

Of the many composers present, only Birtwistle, Maxwell Davies, Goehr and Gilbert were to compose Music Theatre, Gilbert's being *The Scene-Machine*, a *Lehrstück* commissioned by a German opera house, and first performed in 1972. However, apart from Gilbert, who stuck to his principle that Music Theatre should be relevant to contemporary situations, the other three persistently drew on ideas from the past. Like Goehr in his opening lecture, they opted for a traditional approach. It was not until 1972 that some composers turned from the past to the present, as Gilbert was to do in *The Scene-Machine*, Nicola LeFanu in *Anti-World* and George Newson in *Arena* (discussed in Chapter Eight). Nor was the idea of putting across a socio-political message of importance to more than a handful of composers, notably Goehr, Gilbert, Newson and, much later, Eve Harrison, a contemporary composer. Furthermore it was only Richard Orton in *Mug Grunt* (1972) who came near to producing a music-theatre work that could be described as 'abstract'.

The first work to comply with most of the points in the consensus was Goehr's *Naboth's Vineyard*, and that was not until 1968. Between 1965 and 1968 Music Theatre was in the hands of Birtwistle and Maxwell Davies. The most striking feature of the examples they produced (Maxwell Davies's *Revelation and Fall* (1965), Birtwistle's *Monodrama* (1967) and Maxwell Davies's *Missa super L'homme armé*) was that the music conveyed the drama. Gilbert's model for Music Theatre may have been Hindemith's *Das Badener Lehrstück*, but it was not theirs. Their model was Schoenberg's *Pierrot lunaire,* which had been given an extremely theatrical performance by Bethany Beardslee and the Melos Ensemble on the Monday evening of the second Wardour Castle Summer School (see the discussion in Chapter Seven). This was a demonstration of the consensus reached in the discussion on 'Opera Today' the previous year; so too was Birtwistle's *Tragoedia*, an instrumental work that the Melos Ensemble had commissioned for performance on the Friday evening.

Even though they may disagree about how it should be performed, most musicians consider *Pierrot lunaire* a masterpiece, and its impact upon British composers during this period is indisputable. Contemporaneous with its performance at Wardour Castle in August 1965, Jane Manning and the Vesuvius Ensemble under Susan Bradshaw gave a quite different rendition at the Dartington Summer

School, one that emphasised the work's musical qualities. On the grounds that the reciter's theatricality tends to distract the audience from Schoenberg's music, Susan Bradshaw had Jane Manning wear a modern evening dress and stand among the instrumentalists to deliver her part unhindered by extraneous movement. The performance had been initiated by William Glock, the director of the Summer School and the BBC's Controller of Music. Four years earlier at one of his Invitation Concerts at the BBC he had placed side by side a concert performance of *Pierrot lunaire* with a performance of Bach's Goldberg Variations specifically to draw attention to the variety, the elaborate counterpoint and remarkable contrapuntal sections of both works. The value of *Pierrot lunaire* as music *per se* had persuaded Maxwell Davies and Goehr, who ran the two composition seminars taking place each morning at Wardour Castle, to devote several of their sessions to the work. Maxwell Davies relates that he still has the analytical notes he prepared for his seminars, and those who were at Goehr's seminars still remember the session devoted entirely to 'Der kranke Mond' (the seventh setting) in which rhythm was the prime concern.

As a result of this musical interest, British composers, particularly Maxwell Davies and Birtwistle, looked at *Pierrot lunaire* from two perspectives. They acknowledged that when performed by a reciter with acting skills, *Pierrot* is a box-office draw, hence the reason why, when Birtwistle initiated a group to perform Music Theatre, he called it The Pierrot Players, and made *Pierrot* the mainstay of the group's activities. But they also acknowledged that what is unique about the work is its sound, the strange world created by its combination of atonal harmony, *Sprechgesang*, erudite procedures and parodies of popular music such as the Viennese waltz. For them it seemed clear that the predominant entity in Music Theatre is music, and this is why their early examples followed suit. In works such as Maxwell Davies's *Revelation and Fall* (1965–6) and *Missa super L'Homme armé* (1968), and Birtwistle's *Monodrama* (1967), the opportunities for the solo singer to act are either limited or curtailed altogether, to allow the instrumental music's intricate structures and knowing parodies to have their full effect.

Five months after the concert in which *Revelation and Fall* and *Missa super L'homme armé* had their premières on 26 February 1968, Goehr's *Naboth's Vineyard* received its first performance. I have already drawn attention to it in order to comment on its relationship to Monteverdi's *Il combattimento*. I refer to it here because it was the first specimen of Music Theatre in Britain to achieve a balance between music and theatre. Unlike the other examples, it is not a monodrama; it involves several characters (three singers and two mimes). It also takes pains to separate the music from the action, following Brechtian principles, thus giving different perspectives, musical and dramatic, on the same event. These features, I believe, were responsible for initiating the developments that were to take place in British Music Theatre during the following few years. They influenced all of the works produced in 1969, the *annus mirabilis* of the genre: Birtwistle's *Verses for Ensembles*, Maxwell Davies's *Eight Songs for a Mad King*, Birtwistle's *Down by the Greenwood Side*, John Tavener's *Celtic Requiem* and Maxwell Davies's *Vesalii Icones*. All five works, each of which is discussed in detail in later chapters, involve several characters or instrumentalists who can interact with each other. And each manifests a concern with multiple perspectives upon a dramatic theme or musical object, presented either in succession or simultaneously.

Later, when Birtwistle and Maxwell Davies ran a music-theatre course at the 1970 Dartington Summer School, they chose to devote it entirely to the presentation of the same event from different perspectives. The task given to the students was to think of an idea that could be realised in both mime and music, and to assist the students a professional mime-actor was engaged. Among the students were Nicola LeFanu, Erika Fox and Bruce Cole, each of whose subsequent contributions to Music Theatre are described in later chapters. Their works make clear that during the early seventies the relationship between music and action was constantly subject to experiment. The continuing interest in separating music and action was further counterpointed by the move, discussed earlier, to integrate the two, exemplified in works such as Birtwistle's *Bow Down* and Orton's *Mug Grunt*. Another important change that took place after 1969 was the shift in orientation from the past to the present, although not everybody wanted to be as up to date politically and socially as George Newson in *Arena*, Anthony Gilbert in *The Scene-Machine* or LeFanu in *Anti-World*.

Between 1970 and 1977, British composers who cultivated Music Theatre were divided into two groups: those who worked in and around London, and those who taught or studied at York University. The Music Theatre composed by the London group included six written with children in mind. Some were written for professional actors, others were intended to be performed by children themselves. Because children demand a strong visual dimension, plenty of action, a sense of the surreal, and an imaginative world that they can identify with, these works brought a new vitality to Music Theatre, as discussed in Chapter Ten.

Two of these children's works are by Bruce Cole, who since 1986 has been Fellow in Community Music at York University, an institution that made its own distinctive contribution to Music Theatre in the early seventies. Unlike their colleagues in London, the York composers had no professional actors or musicians at hand to perform their works, so they had to write for each other. The first performance of Orton's *Mug Grunt*, for example, was given by Bernard Rands, a member of the music faculty, and two postgraduate students. Secondly, most of them compensated for the lack of singers in their midst by calling on Berio's use of vocal gestures and phonemes in works such as *Visage* (1960–1). And thirdly, all of them were indebted to the concept of *musica poetica*, the close relationship between music and poetry that had been the basis of the Music Theatre produced by Wilfrid Mellers, who was the Professor of Music at York.

These and other developments in British Music Theatre are the main focus of this book. First, however, the key antecedents to the late twentieth-century tradition of Music Theatre, and contemporary developments in Europe and America, are examined. Both earlier and contemporary repertoires were prominent in the programmes of the performance institutions that pioneered British music-theatre works during the 1960s and early 1970s. No account of Music Theatre in Britain can be considered complete without a fuller understanding of the historical and contemporary context for the genre.

CHAPTER TWO

Antecedents

ITALIAN music in the first half of the seventeenth century acknowledged two styles: the *prima prattica*, a continuation of the polyphonic style of the sixteenth century, which composers used mainly for church music, and the *seconda prattica*, which embraced all the innovations that had emerged in secular music during the sixteenth century. Monteverdi made significant contributions to both, but above all he is remembered for his contribution to the *seconda prattica*. *Il combattimento di Tancredi e Clorinda*, which he composed for a concert of madrigals in the *palazzo* of the Venetian nobleman Girolamo Mocenigo in 1624, represents his indebtedness to what he and others had already achieved in the 'second practice': declamatory solo singing (the *stile rappresentativo*), the basso continuo, the use of instruments, the expressive use of dissonance and the increasing gravitation towards tonality. As mentioned in Chapter One, it also introduced into music a technique that was entirely new, the *stile concitato*, or 'agitated style'.

Monteverdi published *Il combattimento* in his eighth book of madrigals, *Madrigali guerrieri et amorosi* (Madrigals of War and Love) of 1638. In the preface he tells us that, in his opinion, the three fundamental passions are anger, moderation and humility. Although previous composers had expressed moderation and humility by writing 'in a gentle and tempered style', none had been able to express anger or warlike emotions. For these, an agitated style was needed. Basing his invention on ancient Greek metric theories, he maintained that, to achieve agitation, the spondaic beat (the semibreve) had to be divided into sixteen semiquavers, these being the sixteen 'hammer strokes' of the pyrrhic measure used for lively and warlike dances. 'If performed on a single note or chord, and combined with words expressing anger or disdain, this will produce an effect expressive of the excitement of battle.' He then adds an important provision: 'But since music depends on the juxtaposition of contrary passions anger must be contrasted with humility.'

To illustrate his innovation, Monteverdi chose to tell the story of the combat between Tancredi and Clorinda contained in the twelfth canto of Torquato Tasso's epic poem, *Gerusalemme liberata*, where it occupies sixteen stanzas of *ottava rima*. He scores the work for soprano (Clorinda), tenor (Testo, the narrator), high baritone (Tancredi), four viole da braccio (soprano, alto, tenor and bass) and a continuo of great bass viol and harpsichord. To be faithful to Tasso's text, which is mainly a narrative interspersed with occasional lines of direct speech, Monteverdi had to give the bulk of the singing to the tenor. When not singing their few lines of direct speech, the soprano and the baritone mime the events Testo describes. Since the work was experimental, Monteverdi provided instructions on how to perform it. If the performers want to present it in a theatrical manner it should be preceded by madrigals that require only to be sung, thus ensuring that the entrance of Clorinda, from the side of the stage where the instrumentalists are playing, is unexpected. Clorinda, armed and on foot, should enter first, followed by Tancredi, armed and riding a *cavallo mariano* (presumably some kind of hobbyhorse). The characters must move and act as the text dictates, their steps and gestures strictly observing the tempo and beat.

The instrumentalists also have to strictly observe the difference between loud and soft. (To specify this may seem unnecessary given the professional musicians he employed, but when Clorinda acknowledges defeat in the fourteenth stanza, and says that her baptism will wash away her sins, the strings illustrate her transformation from warrior to supplicant through the highly unusual procedure of chords played *forte* for half of their length and *piano* for the other half). Furthermore, the narrator should regulate the timing of his words in such a way that a sense of unity is conferred upon the whole: he should not individualise his delivery with rubato. The instruments must play in a manner consistent with the emotions of the words. The narrator, in a position somewhat removed from the instrumentalists so that he can be heard the better, must sing his part in a clear, firm voice and have good pronunciation so that the text is comprehensible. This suggests that the narrator and the instrumentalists should stand or sit on opposite sides of the stage or platform, and that, apart from when they enter, Tancredi and Clorinda should occupy centre stage.

The narrator should not insert any vocal ornaments and trills except in the passage where he calls on night to 'illuminate' his words for the benefit of future generations. This exception occurs in the third stanza, when the combatants rest; the action is suspended and the narrator becomes reflective and employs an expressive version of the *stile rappresentativo*. On other occasions ornaments and trills would draw too much attention to the art of singing and would detract the audience from focusing on the mime. But although Monteverdi's instructions make certain things clear, he leaves it to the soprano and baritone to decide what they should do or not do during this third stanza. They have already displayed their warlike intentions before the stanza begins, but Testo's singing in the *stile rappresentativo* demands that all attention must be focused on him. The two combatants cannot just lower their swords and stand aside during the three or four minutes his singing takes, so the most appropriate solution is for them to 'freeze', holding their positions without moving until the music and text indicate they can fight again.

If this is what Monteverdi required, then he was extending 'the juxtaposition of contrary passions' to include 'the juxtaposition of contrary actions'. Another example can be found in the work's opening section. When Clorinda enters, the music indicates that she is walking steadily and purposively. Testo tells us that she is skirting a steep hill and making for the gate that takes her into Jerusalem. As she walks, Tancredi enters on his hobbyhorse, first trotting then galloping. Clorinda stops walking as the clash of his armour makes her turn. The contrast between these two types of movement serves to highlight the absence of movement in the third stanza. After Clorinda accepts Tancredi's challenge they approach each other 'with slow and bellicose steps'. The music, consisting of four identical minim phrases separated by rests, suggests that their movements should be identical, and that during the rests they should pause. But when they confront each other 'like two rival bulls inflamed with rage', they quiver with intense agitation (see Ex. 2.1). To convey this we are introduced to Monteverdi's new technique. But it is only a dramatic 'taster'.

When the battle proper begins, the *stile concitato* is only one of about twenty different musical gestures Monteverdi provides to counterpoint Testo's words. One is the first use of pizzicato in music, a gesture intended to illustrate the clashing of the hilts of their swords and casques. The increase in excitement, which Testo enhances by singing in the *stile concitato*, eventually leads to the moment when Tancredi and Clorinda are forced to rest. Since Tancredi wants to know whom he is fighting, he asks Clorinda to reveal her name and title. But when she refuses, he resumes his onslaught more fiercely. This time the fighting ends when Tancredi plunges his sword into her breast. We hear falling semitones, indicating the imminence of death. Clorinda acknowledges defeat, her anger being transformed into humility. This is when the strings play their series of *forte-piano* chords.

But these are purely musical symbols requiring nothing visual to mirror them. So too is the playing of the strings when Clorinda utters her last words. Monteverdi instructs them to play *arcate soave,* to bow smoothly, which means that their long strokes stand in marked contrast to the short rapid strokes needed for the *stile concitato*. Like Clorinda, they go in peace.

The period not represented in this chapter is the one when the High Baroque style was replaced by the Classical during the second half of the eighteenth century. The dramatic melodramas of Georg Benda (1722–95), in which music and the spoken word are set against each other, might be considered a prototype for Music Theatre. Mozart certainly admired Benda's *Ariadne auf Naxos* (1776), and made use of melodrama in his Singspiel, *Zaide* (1779–80). But melodrama failed to rival the attractions of opera, and apart from rare incidences, such as the dungeon scene in Beethoven's *Fidelio*, it fell out of use in the theatre. It was not until speech became closer to song in the speech-notation scheme which

Ex. 2.1 Claudio Monteverdi, *Il combattimento di Tancredi e Clorinda* (1624). Arranged by Luciano Berio. Reproduced by permission of Universal Edition A.G. Wien.

Humperdinck invented for his melodrama *Königskinder* (1867), a scheme he subsequently abandoned but which Schoenberg adapted for the twenty-one melodramas that constitute *Pierrot lunaire*, that melodrama became a resource that composers could call upon again.

Schoenberg intended *Pierrot lunaire*, his 'seven times three melodramas' to poems by the Belgian poet Albert Giraud (1860–1929), to be 'light, ironical and satirical in tone'.[1] He selected the poems from the cycle of fifty that Giraud had published under the same title in 1884. Schoenberg received the commission for the work in 1912. It came from Albertine Zehme, a former actress who had been touring Germany giving readings of Otto Erich Hartleben's translations of Giraud's poems with piano accompaniment. On those occasions her accompaniment had been music by Otto Vrieslander. However, Vrieslander's music was in the Brahmsian style and she considered it too tame for the outlandish behaviour of the clown. What she required from Schoenberg was something bizarre.[2] This suggests that she must have heard Etta Werndorff perform Schoenberg's Six Little Piano Pieces Op. 19 in Vienna the previous year. To anyone not *au fait* with what Schoenberg had been composing over the previous three years, these pieces would certainly have sounded bizarre, for they are cast in a style in which the tradition that Monteverdi had helped to establish three hundred years earlier had been virtually abolished. Harmony was no longer rooted in tonality; instead, it emerged from melodic figurations, which, in the Little Piano Pieces, were often little more than elusive fragments. Only in the second and sixth pieces, where Schoenberg has a recurring chord to bind the fragmentary texture together, is there a reminder of the stability that music had apparently lost.

Zehme had expected that Schoenberg's work would also be a series of piano pieces, but as soon as the contract was sealed and Schoenberg began to compose the music, he sought her permission to include other instruments as well. Eventually he scored the work for flute doubling piccolo, clarinet doubling bass clarinet, violin doubling viola, cello and piano. This was about the size of the ensemble Schoenberg had conducted when he was music director of a literary cabaret in Berlin during the early years of the century, an intimate theatre where Hartleben (1864–1905) might have recited his *Pierrot* translations as he had been doing at literary gatherings in Germany and Austria since 1891.

Like his rival Harlequin, Pierrot had been one of the mischievous valets contending for the hand of the servant girl, Columbine, in the old *commedia dell'arte*.

---

[1] See Jonathan Dunsby, *Schoenberg, Pierrot Lunaire*, (Cambridge, Cambridge University Press, 1992), 2, and Willi Reich, *Schoenberg: A Critical Biography* (London, Longman 1971), 74.
[2] Dunsby, *Pierrot*, 22.

But he was made famous in the first half of the nineteenth century by the mime Jean-Gaspard Deburau (1796–1846), who established French pantomime at the Théâtre des Funambules in Paris. Like the Pierrots of the *commedia dell'arte*, Deburau dressed himself totally in white, using chalk or powder to whiten his face; but instead of casting Pierrot as a mere mischief-maker, he transformed him into a moonstruck lover who exaggerates his suffering and who lives in an inner world totally given over to fantasy.

Albert Giraud was able to convey the dichotomy between outer and inner by encasing Pierrot's bizarre imagery in the extremely formal mould of the French rondel. This consists of a thirteen-line stanza in which the first and second lines return to make the seventh and eighth, and the first comes back again to round the poem off. All Schoenberg's twenty-one melodramas are through-composed, meaning that the repetitions in the poetry function as a counterpoint to his music. To represent Pierrot's split personality in musical terms, he did what Humperdinck had done in his melodrama *Königskinder* (1897). This was to use a type of speech-melody, which was neither speech nor song but a combination of them. He called it *Sprechstimme* (speaking voice), although later it has more frequently been called *Sprechgesang* (speech song). In his preface to his score, Schoenberg gave instructions on how it should be performed. He begins by saying that notes with crosses halfway up their stems 'are not intended for singing (except for specially marked isolated exceptions)'. The task of the performer is to transform them into speech-melody. To do this she must maintain the rhythm as accurately as if she were singing. She must also become acutely aware of the difference between singing tone and speaking tone. As Schoenberg writes, 'Singing tone unalterably stays on the pitch, whereas speaking tone gives the pitch but immediately leaves it again by falling or rising. However, the performer must be very careful not to adopt a singsong speech pattern. That is not intended at all. Nor should she strive for realistic, natural speech.'

On the surface, these instructions seem clear enough, but in practice they are extremely difficult to realise. The vocal line covers a range from E flat below middle C to the A flat/G sharp two octaves and a fourth above, and this is the range of a highly trained mezzo-soprano. If an actress had this range she would also need absolute pitch to cope with the leaps Schoenberg writes for her. Since Albertine Zehme first performed the work, most if not all Pierrots have been singers. But even they have found it difficult to hit the pitch and then leave it immediately by falling or rising, especially when the notes follow each other in rapid succession. At best only approximations are possible. Nevertheless these approximations make a strong contrast to the accuracy of the instruments, and it is this dichotomy that defines the essence of the piece: the difference between the normal and the abnormal.

That Giraud intended his fifty poems to be theatrical is made clear in the first of them:

Je rêve d'un théâtre de chambre,
Dont Breughel peindrait les volets,
Shakspeare [sic] les féeriques palais,
Et Watteau, les fonds couleur d'ambre.[3]

Breughel, Shakespeare and Watteau appear again in Giraud's cycle, but Hartleben's translation restricts their names to the first poem, and Schoenberg eliminates them altogether. His intention was clearly to cut out all references to real people, and to devote all his attention to Pierrot's highly unstable inner world. The work is therefore in line with the other dramatic pieces he wrote between 1909 and 1913 after he abandoned tonality, except that *Erwartung* and *Die glückliche Hand* totally lack the 'light, ironical and satirical tone' of *Pierrot*. The events in *Erwartung* – a woman's search for her lover, her discovery of his dead body, her subsequent dementia and jealous outpourings about the other 'she' – could all be taking place inside her head. Those in *Die glückliche Hand*, which begin and end with a man lying face down with the teeth of a cat-like creature fastened to his neck, seem to be the fantasy of someone who cannot relate to the world at all.

Pierrot, however, ultimately does make contact with reality, for *Pierrot lunaire* ends with him putting his fantasies aside and returning to his home in Bergamo (where the *commedia dell'arte* originated). Although the sequence of events appears to be as bizarre as the imagery, Schoenberg chose poems from Giraud's cycle to provide an overall structure that seems to have been common to all who have undergone a spiritual transformation: a movement in and out of 'a long, dark night of the soul'. The work is in three parts. In the second, the moon, which has dominated the imagery in the first part, has waned. But Pierrot's 'long, dark night of the soul' is not the kind that mystics talk about, for Pierrot's soul is not empty but full of the images betraying his horror of the night. He steals from coffins full of rubies, he celebrates a red mass, he sees himself on the gallows being kissed by a harlot, and when the new moon appears, it seems to be a scimitar about to fall on his neck. In the last part the moon gradually waxes. In its light Pierrot forgets his tragic manner. His laughter and outrageous pranks return, and when he reaches Bergamo his 'sorrow is dispelled'. From his 'sun-encircled window' he sees 'the lovely world again'.

At the first performance in Berlin's small Choralion Hall, Albertine Zehme, dressed as Columbine, was surrounded back and sides by dark screens with the instrumentalists, conducted by Schoenberg, placed out of view behind them. It

---

[3] *Pierrot lunaire*, (Paris, Alphonse Lemerre, 1884), 2.

is almost unbelievable that Schoenberg, who was so meticulous over musical matters, should allow the actress to wear the costume of Columbine rather than Pierrot. Perhaps he felt that, having paid for the work and having sponsored the concert, she had the right to do what she wanted. Presumably she dressed as Columbine because most of the poems are in the third person singular, as in No. 3 *Der Dandy*: 'Pierrot with waxen countenance / Stands musing and thinks how he will paint tonight'. Only three poems use the first person singular: *Colombine* (No. 2), *Gebet an Pierrot* (No. 9) and *O alter Duft* (No. 21). But the work is not a description of Pierrot's behaviour; it is an enactment of it. Pierrot is a clown putting on a show. He refers to himself in the third person singular because his actions are those of 'the other', his other self. He reserves the first person singular for when he no longer needs to put on a show – such as when he addresses Columbine as a lover with a heavy heart; when in *Gebet an Pierrot* he pleads with his other self to restore his laughter; and when in *O alter Duft* he addresses 'the ancient scent from far-off days'.

The only instructions Schoenberg provided for the performer are given in the final paragraph of his preface to the score:

> It is never the task of performers to recreate the mood and character of the individual pieces on the basis of the meaning of the words, but solely on the basis of the music. Those events and emotions that were important to the composer are in the music. If the performer finds them lacking he should abstain from presenting something that was not included by the composer. He would not be adding but detracting.

It seems Schoenberg feared that, if the performer followed the meaning of the words, she would be tempted to overact. This is apparently what Hartleben did when he recited the poems at literary cabarets in a flamboyant manner. If Schoenberg had Hartleben in mind when he wrote his preface, this may explain why he addressed the performer as if she were a man, i.e. 'He would not be adding but detracting.'

It is possible that Schoenberg's decision to place the instrumentalists behind screens was because he wanted the audience's attention to be focused on the actress. However, the decision meant that it would have been impossible for Albertine Zehme to see his baton, and equally impossible for the two of them to make eye contact. It can only be assumed that the attainment of a good ensemble took second place to the symbolism of the separation and the practicalities of obtaining a good balance. On the grounds that the central feature of the work is the split personality of the clown, then this dichotomy could be mirrored not only by the platform's layout, but also by Schoenberg's music. Lying behind its atonal, modernist style were the remnants of tonality and tradition.

When he abandoned tonality in 1908, Schoenberg replaced a harmonic way of thinking with a melodic way of thinking. Instead of basing his music on how its harmony related to a tonal centre, he based it almost exclusively on counterpoint, the interplay of melodic lines generated and developed by motifs. At the local level, within each of the twenty-one melodramas, the motifs are melodic, but at the global level *Pierrot lunaire* depends on a rhythmical motif, basically seven equally spaced notes that can be varied in ways that preserve its identity (see Ex. 2.2a–c). Furthermore, although the work lacks an established tonal centre, it sometimes seems to be veering toward E major, particularly in the first and last items. Indeed in *O alter Duft* (No. 21) E major is hinted at so

Ex. 2.2a Schoenberg, *Pierrot lunaire*, opening passages of 1, 10 and 15.

Ex. 2.2b

Ex. 2.2c

strongly that, like Pierrot, we have a sense of having arrived home. Its stream of parallel thirds and implicit appoggiaturas have all the hallmarks of late romantic harmony. They suggest, in retrospect, that apart from those moments when Pierrot is totally disorientated, late romantic harmony has been lying behind the work from the start.

The remnants of other aspects of tradition are even more apparent, not only in the parodies of popular styles such as the barcarole and the ubiquitous waltz, but also the satirical use of traditional contrapuntal styles, notably the passacaglia in *Nacht* (No. 8) and the canons in *Parodie* (No. 17) and *Der Mondfleck* (No. 18). *Parodie* involves three types of strict canon to illustrate the way the knitting needles stuck in the hair of the old Duenna are mimicked by flickering moonbeams. *Der Mondfleck* consists of a double canon which turns round on itself halfway through to illustrate how the moon has created what appears to be flecks of snow on Pierrot's best frockcoat, which Pierrot attempts to brush away. Schoenberg conducted three performances of *Pierrot lunaire* in Berlin in 1912. At one of them Igor Stravinsky was in the audience. In his later years he called the work, 'the solar plexus as well as the mind of early twentieth-century music'.[4]

Satie's contribution to Music Theatre is confined to one slender work composed in 1913, *Le piège de Méduse* (Medusa's Snare). Satie is often seen as being little more than a humorist, a precursor of Dada and Surrealism. But in at least one respect he was as radical as Schoenberg and Stravinsky. Jean Cocteau touched on his importance, viewing him as the supreme anti-Romantic.[5] Yet Satie was not just opposed to romanticism; his opposition extended to the whole of the post-Renaissance tradition. It is clear even from his earliest works that his main objection to this tradition was its obsession with linear, goal-orientated time, with a sense of 'becoming'. In works such as the *Trois gymnopédies* of 1888, Satie makes clear that he was more concerned with 'being' than with 'becoming'. Gymnopaedia were dances performed by young naked males to show off their manly beauty at festivals dedicated to Apollo. Satie's three dances are therefore Apollonian in nature, cool, refined, unhurried, totally without rhetoric. All three are in the same tempo, and are similar both melodically and harmonically. The result is like looking at the same object from different perspectives. Time has become a circular, long-range form, without direction.

Le piège de Méduse is about a man who is so confused that he can carry nothing through to its logical conclusion. As a theatrical piece it can be considered a forerunner of the Theatre of the Absurd, which flourished in the fifties and early sixties. The work consists of nine short scenes with seven equally short pieces of music inserted between scenes one to three and four to nine. Baron Medusa is a 'very rich *rentier*'[6] who has Frisette for a daughter, Astolfo for a prospective son-in-law, and

---

[4]   Igor Stravinsky and Robert Craft, *Dialogues* (London, Faber Music in association with Faber, 1982), 105.

[5]   See *The Rough Guide to Classical Music*, ed. Joe Staines (London, Rough Guides, 2010), 468.

[6]   A person of private means. The description comes from Satie's score.

Polycarp for a servant who perpetually uses the familiar *tu* in addressing him. The action takes place in Paris, 'the day before yesterday', and the setting is the baron's study, which has furniture 'a la mode' and 'an elegant and enormous monkey stuffed by a master-hand' at the rear. 'The monkey', the stage directions tell us, 'is a superb mechanical toy which the baron has made for his personal diversion'. Between the scenes, the monkey dances to music containing wrong notes, illogical progressions, sudden and inexplicable changes of key and unresolved cadences (see Ex. 2.3). In other words, it is as confused and illogical as the baron.

Ex. 2.3 Satie, *Le piège de Méduse*, 'Valse'

The baron's main problem is that he cannot put his accounts in order. He either forgets what he's doing, becomes muddled or is interrupted by his servant. Polycarp, however, has no such problems; he knows precisely what is what. In this instance he insists on going to a billiards match that evening. Frisette and Astolfo, on the other hand, are confused by the baron's behaviour. Even though he consents to their marriage, he decides to set Astolfo a trap. This is not to prove that the young man is worthy of his daughter, it is simply because he wants a son-in-law 'who will be all mine'. Putting a finger to his right eye he asks Astolfo if he can dance on his left eye. When Astolfo tells him he cannot, the baron is delighted: 'You are a straightforward man, no evasions, no wiles.' He then, like everyone else, turns to the monkey and embraces him.

At the first performance in a private salon, Satie played the musical numbers on the piano, placing sheets of paper between the strings to make the sound more mechanical. Eight years later, in 1921, when *Le piège de Méduse* was performed at the Théâtre des Bouffes, he scored the music for clarinet, trumpet, trombone, violin, cello, double bass and percussion. But it was the first version that put the work on the music-theatre map, when John Cage had it performed at Black Mountain College, North Carolina in 1948. On that occasion Cage played the piano, Buckminster Fuller the baron, Elaine de Kooning Frisette, and Merce Cunningham the monkey.

During the First World War Stravinsky was isolated in Switzerland and unable to compose another full-length ballet for Diaghilev, to follow the three great successes he had scored with *The Firebird*, *Petrushka* and *Le sacre du printemps*. The theatrical works he did compose between 1914 and 1918, *Les noces*, *Renard* and *L'histoire du soldat*, although scored for smaller forces than *Le sacre du printemps*, were still indebted to it because they also draw on the Russian folk tradition and are examples of ritual theatre.

He conceived *Les noces* (The Wedding), which he ultimately subtitled 'Russian choreographic scenes with song and music', while composing *Le sacre du printemps*, but he did not begin to compose the music for it until 1914. Three years later, when he completed the short score, he felt that since it celebrated a domestic ritual, it did not call for the large symphony orchestra he had planned for the accompaniment.[7] It took him another four years before he realised that the scoring should be based on the sound of wedding bells. To represent them he chose four pianos and an array of percussion instruments for six players.

Princess Edmond de Polignac commissioned *Renard* in 1915. She wanted Stravinsky to write something that did not require the huge orchestral forces that

---

[7] Igor Stravinsky and Robert Craft, *Expositions and Developments* (London, Faber and Faber, 1962), 118

were popular before the war. Stravinsky chose to compose for her a burlesque based on Russian folk stories which he called a 'Burlesque story about the fox, the cock, the cat and the goat [or ram], to be sung and played on the stage'.[8] Clowns, actors or acrobats mimed the animals, two tenors and two basses sang the songs, and an ensemble of fifteen, including a cimbalom, supplied the accompaniment.

L'histoire du soldat was even more modest in its scoring. Early in 1918 Stravinsky and the novelist C.F. Ramuz, both of whom had had their assets frozen because of the war, decided to write something that could be performed with ease throughout Switzerland, and might therefore supply them with a living.[9] The work is the story of a soldier who ultimately has to yield his soul to the devil. It requires three actors, a female dancer and an ensemble strongly resembling a New Orleans jazz band: clarinet, bassoon, cornet, trombone, violin, double bass and percussion.

According to Simon Karlinsky, *Les noces*, *Renard* and *L'histoire du soldat* along with *Petrushka* and *Le sacre du printemps* 'add up to a compendium of the native theatrical genres of old Russia'.[10] *Le sacre du printemps*, *Les noces* and *Renard* have their roots in Russian history before Peter the Great (1672–1725). *Le sacre du printemps* relates to 'enactments of surviving pagan rituals that date back to pre-Christian times'. Initially these had agrarian significance, and were timed to take place when the seasons changed. 'Usually (though not always)', Karlinsky notes, 'they were disguised as Christian holidays or ceremonies'. *Les noces* has its roots in 'highly dramatised village customs of betrothal, wedding and post-wedding celebration, which also combined pre-Christian and post-baptismal elements'. *Renard* celebrates 'performances by itinerant folk entertainers, the *skomorokhi*, Russian minstrels who also doubled as buffoons, musicians and animal impersonators'.

Petrushka and *L'histoire du soldat*, on the other hand, have their roots in more recent types of folk theatre. *Petrushka* relates to 'the pre-Lenten carnival, with its bearded carnival barkers, puppet shows, masked mummers and trained bears', while *L'histoire du soldat* relates to 'the performance of orally transmitted plays about peasants, devils, and foreign royalty that were put on by illiterate soldiers and convicts in Siberian penal settlements'.[11]

Although Stravinsky makes little mention of these types of folk theatre in his dialogues with Robert Craft, nevertheless in *Expositions and Developments* he says

---

[8] Eric Walter White, *Stravinsky: The Composer and His Works*, 2nd edn (London, Faber and Faber, 1979), 239.

[9] Ibid., 264–5.

[10] Simon Karlinsky, 'Russian Preliterate Theatre', in *Confronting Stravinsky: Man, Musician, and Modernist*, ed. Jann Pasler (Berkeley, University of California Press, 1986), 4.

[11] Ibid., 4–5.

a lot about the three works under discussion. He says that his texts for *Les noces* and *Renard*, and C.F. Ramuz's text for *L'histoire du soldat*, were based on the 'two great treasures of the Russian language and spirit', Afanasiev's anthology of Russia folk tales and Kireevsky's collection of Russian folk poetry, with *Les noces* deriving 'almost entirely from Kireevsky'.[12] He divided the latter into two parts, the first consisting of scenes in the bride's house, where she has her hair bound, in the groom's house, where he is dressed, and then back to the bride's house for her departure. The second part is devoted to what would now be called the wedding reception, during which the bridal bed is warmed by another pair before the married couple occupy it, and concludes with the newly-weds entering the bedroom, and having the door closed behind them.

Stravinsky described *Les noces* as:

a suite of typical wedding episodes told through quotations of typical talk. The latter, whether the bride's, the groom's, the parents' or the guests', is always ritualistic. As a collection of clichés and quotations of typical wedding sayings it might be compared to one of those scenes in *Ulysses* in which the reader seems to be overhearing scraps of conversation without the connecting thread of discourse. But *Les noces* might also be compared to *Ulysses* in the larger sense that both works are trying to *present* rather than to *describe*. Individual roles do not exist in *Les noces*, the solo voices impersonate now one type of character and now another. Thus the soprano in the first scene is not the bride, but merely the bride's voice; the same voice is associated with the goose in the last scene. Similarly, the fiancé's words are sung by a tenor in the grooming scene, but by a bass at the end; and the two unaccompanied bass voices in the second scene, however much their voices may suggest the actual reading of the marriage service, are not to be identified with two priests. Even the proper names such as Palagai and Saveliushka belong to no one in particular. They were chosen for their sound, their syllables, and their Russian typicality.[13]

Although Stravinsky originally thought of *Les noces* as being a cantata, and the singing is continuous, it is fairly clear from the score that everyone should dance as well as sing, including the vocal soloists. The instruments are to be spread across the stage and the dancers should perform their parts in the gaps between them. He also said he wanted the dancers to wear early nineteenth-century peasant costumes and the instrumentalists modern evening dress. 'This', he said, 'not only did

[12] Stravinsky and Craft, *Expositions and Developments*, 115.
[13] Ibid., 115.

not embarrass me, but, on the contrary, was perfectly in keeping with my idea of a *divertissement* of the masquerade type.'[14] However, when the Ballets Russes first performed the work in 1923, Diaghilev insisted that the work should be presented as a ballet. The singers were not required to double as dancers. They and the percussion instrumentalists were hidden out of view in the orchestra pit. Only the dancers and the four pianos were visible but the pianos were placed at the sides of the stage. Although Stravinsky later expressed considerable dissatisfaction with Diaghilev's staging, it was generally compatible with his conception of the work as being ritualistic and non-personal. 'The curtain was not used', he said, 'and the dancers did not leave the stage even during the lamentation of the two mothers, a wailing ritual which presupposes an empty stage ... But though the bride and groom are always present, the guests are able to talk about them as if they were not there – a stylization not unlike Kabuki theatre.'[15]

According to Simon Karlinsky, *Renard*, at its basic level:

> depicts four *skomorokhi* in a pre-Petrine village who put on animal masks to perform a satirical, anticlerical skit about the victimisation of a wealthy peasant (the cock) by a con woman disguised as an itinerant nun (the fox is a vixen in the Russian text). The cock's two fellow peasants, the tomcat and the ram, rescue him twice. Then the peasants kill the predator and blame the murder on the hounds of the local nobleman, whereupon the performers remove their masks and demand a payment of a crock of butter for their performance.[16]

Because the story was too short for his purposes, Stravinsky lengthened it by telling the fox's deceit of the cock twice. After pretending to be a nun, the vixen returns with the promise that the cock can have a barn full of corn if he comes down from his perch. Both episodes end with a dance for the cock, cat and ram, and at the end of the performance the *skomorokhi* pass round a collection box instead of asking for butter.

In *Expositions and Developments* Stravinsky tells us that when he planned the staging, it was:

> always with the consideration that *Renard* should not be confounded with opera. The players are to be dancing acrobats, and the singers are not to be identified with them; the relationship between the vocal parts and the stage

---

[14] Stravinsky, cited in White, *Stravinsky*, 259.
[15] Stravinsky and Craft, *Expositions and Developments*, 117.
[16] Karlinsky, 'Russian Preliterate Theatre', 10.

characters is the same as it is in *Les noces* and, again, as in *Les noces* the performers, musical and mimetic, should all be together on the stage, with the
singers in the centre of the instrumental ensemble. Moreover *Renard* does
not need symbolic overtones. It is a banal moral tale, no more. The religious
satire (the fox disguised as a nun; nuns were untouchables in Russia) is not
so much satire as gentle mockery, and good fun.[17]

Stravinsky wanted the work to be played on a trestle stage with the instrumental ensemble and singers placed behind it. If performed in a theatre, he noted
in a preface to the score, he wanted it to be played in front of the curtain with
the players entering together, to the accompaniment of the little introductory
march, and their exeunt managed in the same way. As soon as the action begins,
Stravinsky introduces us to the sound of the cimbalom, which throughout the
work he associates with the fox. The instrument is a substitution for the *gusli*, a
Russian psaltery (a plucked zither with a flat wooden sound box and a variable
number of strings), an instrument that had been traditionally associated with the
skomorokhi but was no longer available even in Russia. Musically, the humour of
the work has its origins in the sound of the cimbalom and its four-octave flourish
whenever the fox enters. To match it, the two tenors and two basses sitting in the
orchestra also leap over wide intervals, much wider than any found in *Les noces*.
Indeed, on one occasion Stravinsky demands a leap of a double octave, as well as
asking for falsetto to cover some of the really high notes. Although the rhythmic
procedures are similar to those in *Les noces,* the melodic character of *Renard* is
totally individual.

This could also be said about *L'histoire du soldat*, but as this involves only actors
and a dancer, the music is entirely instrumental. It consists of eleven numbers,
eight of which Stravinsky later arranged into a concert suite. These are distributed
within a two-part structure, each part containing three scenes. The structure of the
first part resembles a play with incidental music, but during the second part, from
the fifth number onwards, the music becomes continuous so that the action can
be taken to a convincing climax. In this part, music accompanies dancing as well
as speech and action. Central to the work is the narrator, who sits at the side of the
stage telling the Faust-like story ostensibly from a manuscript.

His story concerns a soldier on a fortnight's leave. On his march home the
soldier encounters the devil disguised as an old man with a butterfly net who
offers him a magic book in exchange for his violin. Later, disguised as a cattle
merchant, the devil shows the soldier how to make a fortune with the help of the
book. Eventually the soldier becomes disillusioned by wealth and is then accosted

---

[17] Stravinsky and Craft, *Expositions and Developments*, 22.

by the devil dressed as an old woman selling clothes. In the basket containing her wares, he finds his lost violin. But when he discovers that he can get no sound out of it he throws it away. His next encounter with the devil occurs when he travels to a town where the king has promised that whoever can cure his invalid daughter can marry her. On this occasion the devil is disguised as a virtuoso violinist. Now the tables are turned. The soldier manages to deceive the devil. They play cards and the soldier regains his violin after getting the devil drunk and pretending to lose. He can then play his violin for the princess. She is immediately cured and in gratitude she dances a tango, waltz and ragtime to his fiddle playing. They marry, but when they decide to visit the soldier's home they enter what has become the devil's territory. The devil now appears dressed gorgeously in scarlet with the violin in his possession again. Unable to resist him, the soldier follows him down to hell.

Stravinsky maintained that every piece of good music is marked by its own characteristic sound.[18] In *Les noces* it is the sound of four pianos, in *Renard* that of the cimbalom, while in *L'histoire du soldat* the characteristic sounds are 'the scrape of the violin and the punctuation of the drums. The violin is the soldier's soul and the drums are the *diablerie*.'[19] Yet in Stravinsky's hands the sound of the violin is nothing like how it sounds traditionally. He writes nothing for it that demands vibrato, for instance. He gives it double or triple stops, and asks for staccato rather than legato bowing. Its most memorable feature is a figure consisting of two-crotchet double stops played with down bows on the violin's lowest strings. It is a figure that represents more succinctly than any other the characteristic rhythm of the soldier's march. Variants of this appear throughout the work, but the two down-bow crotchets become particularly significant in the last number, 'The Triumphal March of the Devil'. Here the figure is distorted. The double-stopped thirds become highly discordant triple stops, and the crotchets become heavily accented quavers followed by quaver rests. During the course of the march the figure becomes increasingly more isolated until it is eventually superseded by its opposite, a highly irregular rhythm played by instruments with very unclear pitch and virtually no tone quality: a tambourine, two side drums and a bass drum (Ex. 2.4).

L'histoire du soldat requires an outer stage with the narrator sitting at one side of it and the instrumentalists at the other side. Between the two there should be a small inner stage mounted on a platform with a curtain that can be raised and lowered whenever the soldier, devil or princess have to act or dance. The narrator should sit on a stool or barrel at a small table on which there are a carafe of white

---

[18] Ibid., 92.
[19] Ibid.

Ex. 2.4 Stravinsky, *L'histoire du soldat*

wine and a glass. Stravinsky maintained that the piece was his only staged work with a contemporary reference. In the first production the soldier was dressed in the uniform of a Swiss army private of 1918. But although Switzerland was neutral in the First World War, the soldier was 'very definitely understood to be the victim of the then world conflict'.[20]

L'histoire du soldat is a forerunner to the Music Theatre that Brecht and his associates, Eisler, Hindemith and Weill, produced in Germany in the late twenties and early thirties, for in several respects Stravinsky anticipated some of the dramatic and musical features of Brecht and his associates. Brecht's Epic Theatre, for example, a type of theatre intended to appeal to the spectator's reason rather than his feelings, was anticipated by Stravinky's use of the narrator in *L'histoire du soldat*. Whereas in *Il combattimento* the narrator conveys empathy through his expressive singing, Stravinsky's narrator distances the spectator from the action by speaking his part, and, as a consequence, the spectator is more likely to think about the soldier's plight than to empathise with it. Thinking rather than feeling was also the purpose behind the 'objective' musical styles that Eisler, Hindemith and Weill were to adopt. These too are anticipated in *L'histoire du soldat*. The fact that Stravinsky's instrumentation is similar to that of the Original Dixieland

---

[20] Ibid., 90–1.

Jazz Band, and that he makes the violin sound like a percussion instrument, bears witness to the fact that Stravinsky too had embraced an objective style.

Although only Eisler was a communist, Brecht, Hindemith and Weill also shared his views. The purpose of their Music Theatre was to make people politically aware, hence the need for a theatre that made people think. The first of the five works they produced between 1927 and 1933, Weill's *Mahagonny Songspiel*, was commissioned by Hindemith for the closing concert of the 1927 week-long Baden-Baden Festival of Modern Music, whose administration he was partly responsible for. The other works in the programme were to be three short chamber operas: Milhaud's *L'enlèvement d'Europe*, Ernst Toch's *Die Prinzessin auf der Erbse* and Hindemith's *Hin und Zurück*. Knowing this, Weill decided to set Brecht's five Mahagonny songs, first published in 1926, as a *Songspiel*, a hybrid term to indicate that the songs were to be like 'the better type of American popular song'.[21] He and Brecht had already embarked on expanding the poems into a three-act opera to be called *The Rise and Fall of the City of Mahagonny*, and Weill realised that if the poems were turned into a small-scale dramatic work they could be a useful 'style study' for the opera. Brecht changed the order of the poems to provide better continuity, and added a sixth to bring the sequence to a close. He arranged them in three parts: Part I (Prologue) consists of *Off to Mahagonny* and *Alabama Song*; Part II (Life in Mahagonny) contains *If you had five bucks a day, Benares Song* and *God in Mahagonny*; while Part III (Revolution in Mahagonny) is devoted to *People only dream of Mahagonny*. For the music to be more or less continuous, Weill provided short instrumental links or introductions between or before the songs.

The programme note for the first performance declared that:

In his more recent works, Weill has been moving in the same direction as other artists from all spheres who foretell the extinction of the bourgeois forms of art. The modest epic piece *Mahagonny* merely draws conclusions from the irreversible breakdown of the existing social order. Already he is appealing to a naive audience which simply wants a bit of fun in the theatre.

The 'fun' consists of a series of mismatches and incongruities intended to defy conventions. For example, for no apparent reason four of the songs are in German and two (the Alabama and Benares songs) are in English. They are sung by two sopranos, two tenors and two basses who in the first production were opera singers, except that at the final stage of casting one of the sopranos was replaced by Weill's wife, Lotte Lenya, who was a singing actress not a trained singer. This particular mismatch reflected the kind of vocal lines the singers were required to

[21]   Interview with Kurt Weill, *New York World Telegram*, 21 December 1935.

sing, for like the ten-piece ensemble which accompanied them they belong to the world of the cabaret rather than opera. Nevertheless the singers were required to stand in a line as if giving a concert performance of an opera. All six of them had to be dressed identically in male evening dress, except that the men had to wear black bowler hats, the women white boaters. They were contained within a boxing ring with a bucket of water in one corner and an American bar in another. Behind them was a large screen on which were projected illustrations, texts and slogans designed by Caspar Neher to make visually explicit the events referred to in the songs.

Essentially these events reflect the conditions that prevailed in Germany during the 1920s, particularly the feeling of helplessness provoked by the financial crisis, except that they are presented as if they were taking place in a mythical city in America. Although Weill names the singers Bessie, Jessie, Charlie, Billy, Johnny and Bobbie, they have no individual characterisation other than suggesting that the men are roughnecks and the women prostitutes. All are off to Mahagonny for the easy life. The men want booze, poker tables, good whores and good horseflesh, the women want whisky ('Oh, don't ask why'). But when they get to their Utopia they discover that the only law is money, and since they have little or none of it, they are soon destitute. Their only solution is to leave Mahagonny for Benares, 'where the sun is shining'. But they discover that Benares has been destroyed in an earthquake so they are forced to remain where they are. One morning, quite incongruously, God decides to visit the city, and since He finds it a den of iniquity He condemns the inhabitants to Hell. For them this will make no difference for they are already in Hell. Finally they confess that in a world where everything is rotten, Mahagonny is a dream: 'There is no peace in us / And no compassion / And there is nothing / A man could depend on.' As they sing this the singers march round and round the boxing ring with placards proclaiming 'Up with the morality of the soul', 'Down with syphilis', 'Up with Weill'. Unsurprisingly, it brought the first Baden-Baden Festival to a highly controversial conclusion.

At the second Baden-Baden Music Week in 1928, the festival ended with two works that were even more controversial. They were works Brecht labelled 'didactic': *Der Flug der Lindberghs* (The Flight of Lindbergh) was followed the next evening by *Das Badener Lehrstück vom Einverständnis* (The Didactic Play of Baden on Consent). Didactic drama (or *Lehrstück*) was intended to be educational. Instead of arousing emotions by depicting the fate of individuals, it would focus entirely on abstract social and moral concepts in the hope that these would be of benefit to both the audience and those who performed the work. *Der Flug der Lindberghs* was described as 'a didactic radio play for boys and girls'. This, however, was rather misleading, for although the piece includes a radio and might indeed be instructive for children, no radio production at that time could recapture Brecht's stereophonic production of it at the festival.

The work, based on Charles Lindbergh's solo flight across the Atlantic in May 1927, is essentially a celebration of the science and technology that made it possible. To eliminate any sense of individuality, Brecht had the role of Lindbergh performed by a chorus rather than a soloist (hence the title *The Flight of the Lindberghs*), and he confined his text to bald facts: 'My name is Charles Lindbergh – I am twenty-four years old – My grandfather was Swedish – I am American – I have picked my aircraft myself – Its name is *Spirit of St. Louis* – The Ryan Aircraft works in San Diego – Have built it in sixty days – etc'. At one side of the stage under a board inscribed 'The Radio' (which in 1928 was an innovation exemplifying the achievements of technology) were placed a tenor, baritone and bass with a small ensemble. These relayed what the American newspapers were saying about the weather conditions and Lindbergh's chances of success. A gramophone provided the sound effects: the noise of the engine, the sound of the waves, the cheers of the crowds. Those events taking place within the aircraft were placed at the other side of the stage under a board inscribed 'The Listener'. This is where the chorus representing Lindbergh stood. But since Lindbergh needed to keep his payload as light as possible, his aircraft did not have a radio. The listener is not listening to the radio; he is listening to himself listing the facts about his journey. They include facts about himself and the equipment he is carrying, and facts about his battle with the force of nature, a battle that will result in sweeping away the idea of God from the heavens. This was perhaps Brecht's main point, and he enhanced it by having the cheers that greeted Lindbergh on his arrival represent the triumph of enlightenment. Throughout these proceedings a screen at the back of the stage had visual representations of the journey projected on it, the last pointing to the moral, 'Doing is better than Telling'.

The music for the thirteen sung numbers in *The Flight of Lindbergh* was to have been composed by Weill, but after completing the first seven and a half, he realized he could not meet the deadline, so Hindemith helped him out by completing the eighth and quickly supplying the remaining five. The result was stylistically somewhat incongruous. Both men had wanted to create a popular style based on the principles of *Neue Sachlichkeit* (new objectivity), but whereas Weill's fusion of jazz and German cabaret music laced with the astringency he had cultivated in his earlier music was designed for professionals, Hindemith had embarked on *Gebrauchsmusik* (useful music), a style designed specifically for amateurs to perform. This was why when he elected to write a piece for this second Baden-Baden Music Week he asked Brecht to supply a text in which the audience could sing.

Brecht responded by writing *Das Badener Lehrstück vom Einverständnis*, a play involving a debate between two choruses: a 'skilled' professional chorus, and a 'mass' chorus performed by the audience with simple hymn-like material to sing. To accompany them are an off-stage brass band and an orchestra composed of those members of the audience who play instruments. In this piece there are four airmen, a pilot and three mechanics, who are trying to cross the Atlantic. But unlike Lindbergh's flight, their attempt is a failure for they are forced to crash-land. Since they have no wish to die they ask mankind for help. Mankind duly debates the issue, and during the course of it Carl Kock's film *The Dance of Death* is shown on a screen. At one stage a scene between three clowns is inserted to ask the question 'does man help man?' Herr Schmitt, a huge clown on stilts, complains of being in pain, so the other two clowns systematically saw off the limbs that hurt him including his arms, legs and head. The conclusion is that man does not help man; the airmen must die. After this insert, the pilot refuses to accept the necessity of his death. He wants to preserve his individual desire for life and glory. This being so, mankind decides he must perish. The mechanics, on the other hand, accept the instructions delivered by mankind that death can only be overcome by accepting the necessity of history. They are therefore redeemed, the moral being that death and violence cannot be overcome by palliatives. Man's inhumanity to man will be overcome only after a just world order has been established.

Brecht had clear ideas about the use of music in his plays. Its main purpose was to interrupt the action and allow the audience to reflect on it.[22] But in these music-theatre type works, music has a greater relevance than in his full-length plays. In fact the *Badener Lehrstück* is frequently called an oratorio, and Brecht termed his next didactic piece, *Die Massnahme* (The Measures Taken), a cantata, even though it also contains spoken dialogue. The latter work is generally considered to be one of his masterpieces, as is the music Hanns Eisler composed for it. Eisler had been a pupil of Schoenberg, but had modified his style when he became a member of the Communist Party in 1926. The series of choral works and marching songs he composed between 1926 and 1933 were so compelling for left-wing groups throughout Europe that they made them their own. This is why he had no difficulty in persuading the Greater Berlin Workers' Choir to take part in the first performance of *Die Massnahme* in December 1930, after Hindemith had been reluctant to have it performed at the Berlin New Music Festival, the successor to the Baden-Baden Music Week, because of its overtly political nature.

Die Massnahme is true Music Theatre. Scored for tenor, three actors, mixed chorus, two horns, three trumpets, two trombones, two timpanists, percussion

---

22 See Martin Esslin, *Brecht: A Choice of Evils* (London, Heinemann Educational Books, 1970), 113–14.

and piano, it lasts for just under an hour. It needs no scenery, costumes or props other than masks. The chorus represents the conscience of the Communist Party, which has to decide whether the action that three young communist agitators had to take when on a mission to China was justified. Since it involved the elimination of a fourth agitator who had put the mission in jeopardy, the three have to act out the circumstances to the Party in speech and song, taking it in turns to play the part of the young agitator. Before they get to China the three comrades are joined by a young agitator on the border, and all four put on masks so that they can look Chinese. But when they get to China the young agitator is so appalled by the condition of the coolies that he takes it into his own hands to help them. First he attempts to organise a revolution, then he tears off his mask to reveal that he is a Russian who lives in freedom. But his actions have put the purpose of the mission in jeopardy. His three comrades tell him that the revolution he tries to incite is premature and will result in failure, so they decide he must be eliminated. When he is told about the measure they must take, he himself leads them to the lime pit where they will shoot him. Eventually the Party decides that what they did was in the interests of communism, and that the disciplinary measure was justified.

This description gives no account of Eisler's music, but a performance of *Die Massnahme* from the Bergen International Festival, 2007, is available on the Internet.[23] From this, the quality and extent of the music, as well as the role of the tenor as an intermediary between the chorus and the comrades, is vividly clear.

Brecht's next and last piece of Music Theatre was written in 1933 in Paris, where he and Weill had gone to escape the Nazis. Essentially *Die Sieben Todsünden* (The Seven Deadly Sins) returns to what concerned them in *Mahagonny Songspiel*: life under capitalism. This time, however, having condemned individualism in his didactic works, Brecht based the whole piece on the personality of an American girl called Anna, and gave, even more surprisingly, priority to instinct over reason.

Anna has a split personality. Her instinctive side is expressed through dance, her rational side through song. This means that the character must be played by two women, a singer (Anna I) and a dancer (Anna II). The work is therefore half ballet, half Songspiel. Anna II, the dancer, travels around America trying to make money to pay for a house her family wants to build in Louisiana. If she is to achieve her ambition she must avoid the seven deadly sins, the seven indulgences she feels instinctively drawn to. Throughout the journey, Anna I, the singer, who represents the bourgeoisie, keeps her on the straight and narrow by constantly urging her to be reasonable and to never let her emotions get the better of her. In the end, after a seven-year pilgrimage through seven American cities, Anna II, having repressed her instincts and made enough money to build the house,

[23] http://www.youtube.com/watch?v=1faRq5oBTno (accessed 9 February 2014).

returns home. To be successful in a commercial society emotions and instincts must give way to calculation. Nevertheless, the house could never have been built had not Anna II, the instinctive one, taken the initiative.

In this chapter, a number of significant precursors for Music Theatre have been outlined. In exploring new ways of combining words, music and action, and in offering alternatives to the traditions and grand scale of opera, they directly anticipate the later genre. As will be seen in the next two chapters, this is no coincidence: works such as *Il combattimento di Tancredi e Clorinda*, *Pierrot lunaire*, *Le piège de Méduse* and *Die Massnahme* received significant new productions in the post-war decades, productions which in turn inspired young composers to turn to Music Theatre. Of equal importance to British composers of Music Theatre, however, were the experiments of leading figures of the post-war avant-garde in Europe and the United States discussed in the next chapter.

CHAPTER THREE

European and American Contemporaries

TRADITIONALLY, theatre, including opera, has been primarily concerned with character: how characters are responsible for situations they have created, or how they respond to situations created by circumstances or by the actions of others. Eight of the specimens of Music Theatre discussed in the previous chapter fall into this category. Not all are as sharply focused as *Pierrot lunaire,* but even when actions take precedence over character, as initially in Monteverdi's *Il combattimento*, it is the transformation of Tancredi and Clorinda's belligerency into compassion and tranquillity that determines the outcome of the plot.

In two of the examples discussed in Chapter Two, *Les noces* and *Der Flug der Lindberghs*, the interest lies not in character but in the situations being celebrated: the ritual of a peasant wedding and the first flight across the Atlantic. To ensure that the audience will not empathise with the feelings of those on stage, all references to personal emotions are eliminated, Stravinsky has the exchanges between the bride and the groom in the wedding feast sung by the chorus, and when the groom speaks, his words are sung first by a tenor then by a bass. Likewise, Weill and Hindemith have Lindbergh's words sung by a chorus, not by an individual. Here the emphasis is on the triumph of modern technology in the overcoming of adversity. Satie's *Le piège de Méduse* lies somewhere between the theatre of character and that of situation. As I mentioned in the previous chapter, it anticipates what became known as the Theatre of the Absurd. Although the character of the Baron determines the action, the non sequiturs in the instrumental interludes exemplify the absurdity of the piece as a whole.

In my consideration of the work of the main figures in Music and Instrumental Theatre in Europe and America during the sixties and early seventies, I group them according to the types of theatre they cultivated, types that can be traced back to earlier twentieth-century antecedents. For me the Music Theatre of Luigi Nono, John Cage and Pierre Boulez represents the Theatre of Situation; that of Harry Partch, Luciano Berio and Hans Werner Henze, the Theatre of Character; and that of Karlheinz Stockhausen, Mauricio Kagel and György Ligeti, the Theatre of the Absurd.

In the sixties, when Music Theatre came into its own as a separate and timely genre, the distinction between theatre as character and theatre as situation first emerged in Luigi Nono's *Intolleranza 1960*, which the composer called an *azione scenica* (stage activity or stage action) to differentiate it from opera. A Venetian

by birth, Nono had joined the Communist Party in 1952, and although he was a leading avant-garde figure, and therefore an unequivocal advocate of the new, he nevertheless did not exclude from his works elements that had become taboo among his colleagues in their attempt to make music as unsullied as possible. These elements included extra-musical associations, in particular the setting of words, the principal carriers of external meanings in music. Without words he would have been unable to propagate his political views, as can be clearly seen by his use of words in *Epitaffio per Federico García Lorca* (1952–3) and *Il canto sospeso* (1956), his two anti-fascist choral works. Similarly, he had no qualms about composing an opera about an unemployed worker from the south of Italy, who in 1960 could find only intolerance as he travelled north to find employment.

Nono believed that to deliver his message about the plight of refugees and itin- erant workers in a modern capitalist society he needed to convert the 'theatre of character' into a 'theatre of situation', and that this meant the creation of a 'total' theatre in which the audience would be bombarded both aurally and visually with material coming from several sources simultaneously.[1]

The first performance of *Intolleranza 1960* took place in Venice's La Fenice, and in addition to having a large orchestra in the pit and an equally large chorus on stage, it required films and slides with electronic music and sounds coming from loudspeakers situated throughout the auditorium. With the acoustics of St Mark's Basilica in mind, Nono said that his purpose was 'to see how sound arranges itself with other sounds in space'.[2] Structurally the work replaces narra- tive with a series of episodes that take the worker and his female companion from one example of intolerance to the next, most of the action being performed by the chorus representing those responsible for the abuse. At no time are the characters of the worker and his companion open to scrutiny, since all attention is focused on the situations in which they find themselves.

In the event, the audience was so hostile at the first performance of *Intolleranza 1960* that Nono was forced to conclude that at least in the immediate future he would have to direct his activities to workers in their factories rather than to members of the public who attend opera houses. This meant that he had to reduce his forces to a minimum. Consequently he scored *La fabbrica illuminata* (The Enlightened Factory) for soprano and tape (1964), the tape consisting of sounds recorded in a factory, workers' voices, a choir and the soloist herself. The theme is social injustice, and how it can be overcome in an 'enlightened factory'. But the work involves no *azione scenica*, so essentially it is a concert piece.

---

[1] See Raymond Fearn, *Italian Opera since 1945* (London, Routledge, 1998), 68.
[2] Ibid.

Nono did not produce his first music-theatre work until 1966. This was after he had seen the American experimental theatre company, Living Theatre,[3] perform its version of *Frankenstein* at the 1965 Venice Biennale. This was 'total' theatre without the need for a symphony orchestra and large chorus. It was based on the ideas of Antonin Artaud (1896–1948), the French director, playwright and theorist who advocated a 'theatre of cruelty' on the grounds that drama's job was to expose the deepest conflicts in the human mind, to express things that could not be put into words.[4] He held that the function of words in drama should be purely ritualistic and incantatory. As a consequence, the action in *Frankenstein* relied mainly on its visual presentation. The set Living Theatre constructed consisted of scaffolding with three platforms and two vertical partitions on which a number of events could take place simultaneously. The head of Frankenstein's monster was outlined on the scaffold by lights. What must have particularly interested Nono was that, within the collage of Grand Guignol, shadow-play, yoga, meditation, gymnastics, howls, grunts and groans, were slogans denouncing the escalation of the war in Vietnam; fundamentally the piece was political.

With this as his model, and with the participation of three actors from Living Theatre, Nono composed and had performed in Venice *A floresta è jovem e cheja de vida* (The Forest is Young and Full of Life) for soprano, three actors, clarinet, five suspended copper plates and eight-track tape (1966). He dedicated the work to the National Front for the Liberation of Vietnam. As well as making use of words by a Vietnamese partisan (in the original language) and the slogans shouted out by American students in their anti-war demonstrations, he quoted passages from speeches by Fidel Castro, Frantz Fanon and Patrice Lumumba. Like Living Theatre, his purpose was to create total theatre, but being a composer he gave more emphasis to the aural than the visual. As Charles Ives had done in *The Unanswered Question* (1908), he relied on spatial positioning to create a sense of the visual. The loudspeakers needed for the 8-track tape were placed throughout the auditorium; on stage the actors and musicians were situated on or around podiums rather than on scaffolding, while the soprano's role was to sing what was intended to sound like a Vietnamese lament. For this she needed to make use of micro-intervals. The clarinettist had to supply flutter-tonguing and multiphonics to blend with both the soprano and the multiphonic electronic sounds on the tape. Combined with warlike rumblings of the copper plates, these various sounds, like those in *Intolleranza 1960*, virtually flooded the auditorium.

---

[3] Founded in 1947 as an imaginative alternative to the commercial theatre by Judith Malina, the German-born student of Erwin Piscator, and Julian Beck, an abstract expressionist painter of the New York School.
[4] Fearn, *Italian Opera since 1945*, 110.

This meant that with his subtle use of lighting, Nono felt he had no need for *azione scenica*. Nevertheless he did not rule out the inclusion of such scenic action in future performances.

The Theatre of Situation was an almost inevitable consequence of the radical changes in style that emerged after the Second World War. After the 1914–18 War the younger generation of European composers chose to abandon romanticism and cultivate more 'objective', neo-classical styles. After the Second World War, neo-classicism was abandoned for not being objective enough. When Stravinsky's neo-classical *Danses concertantes* (1942) was given its first European performance at one of the concerts devoted to Stravinsky in Paris during the winter of 1944–5, Pierre Boulez, then a student at the Paris Conservatoire, led the booing.

During the next few years Boulez combined the pitch innovations of Webern with the rhythmic innovations of Messiaen and early Stravinsky to create a style that eliminated all subjective feeling and extra-musical associations. As mentioned in Chapter One, the style was fully revealed in his first book of *Structures* for two pianos (1952), based on the highest of the three scales in Messiaen's equally revolutionary piano piece, *Mode de valeurs et d'intensités*. Boulez said that his intention was to discover:

> how far automatism in musical matters would go, with individual invention appearing only in some really very simple forms of disposition: in the matter of densities, for example … It was an experiment in what one might call Cartesian doubt, to bring everything into question again, make a clean sweep of one's heritage and start all over again from scratch, to see how it might be possible to reconstitute a way of writing that begins with something that eliminates personal invention.[5]

In later works, Boulez was never as radical. He allowed not only himself, but in some cases the performers of his music, a degree of personal invention. His *Domaines* for solo clarinet and twenty-one instruments (1961–8) not only permits the latter, it also employs a visual dimension to help clarify the structure of the work. In so doing he produces instrumental theatre that highlights the 'situation' of performance. The accompanying instruments are divided into six groups placed within six domains, each with a different number of players and each with a distinctive sonority: A, a trombone quartet; B, a string sextet; C, a marimba/double bass duo; D, a mixed quintet (flute, trumpet, saxophone, bassoon and harp); E, a mixed trio (oboe, horn and harp); and F, a bass clarinet. Ideally the

---

[5] Pierre Boulez and Célestin Deliège, *Conversations with Célestin Deliège* (London, Eulenburg Books, 1976), 56.

domains should form a circle with the conductor standing in the middle of them. The clarinet soloist has at his disposal six sheets of material (*cahiers*) labelled ABCDEF, each containing six variants arranged in two different symmetrical patterns. He is at liberty to play the *cahiers* in whatever order he chooses. If he chooses the order CDBEAF, for instance, then this is the order of the domains he must visit. In front of domain C he must play the *cahier* C. Once he has presented it, the marimba and double bass within this domain respond to him by proliferating his material.

When all six domains have been visited, the soloist must make a return journey, but this time the conductor must choose the order of his visitations. On this return journey the instrumentalists take the lead by playing variants of what they originally played, while the soloist responds by playing a mirror version of the *cahier* associated with their domain. To explain why the soloist has to walk from domain to domain, Boulez says:

> There is no way in which one can make the structure itself more clear than by rendering it visibly through the instrumentalist's movements: but this is no more than a geographical representation of what happens in the score. It could be played without moving about, but this would give a false perspective of a piece that actually has a clear tendency to individualise its various component parts.[6]

In 1952 John Cage produced his silent piece, *4'33"*, and his first 'Happening', works that in their own way were as radical as Boulez's first book of *Structures*. But whereas *Structures* sprang from the extensions of the European tradition that Webern, Messiaen and Stravinsky had introduced, *4'33"* was conceived under the influence of Zen philosophy and was therefore totally at odds with the European tradition. It was first performed at a piano recital given by David Tudor at Woodstock, New York on 29 August 1952. Among the other items in the programme was Boulez's First Piano Sonata (1946) and works by Morton Feldman and Earle Brown. As well as bringing onto the platform what was assumed to be a score of *4'33"*, Tudor also had with him a stopwatch. With this he timed the beginning and end of each of the work's three silent movements. They lasted 0'30", 2'23" and 1'40" respectively. Before each movement Tudor raised the piano's lid, and when the time limit was completed he lowered it. 'What they thought was silence, because they didn't know how to listen, was full of accidental sounds. You could hear the wind stirring outside during the first movement. During the second, raindrops began pattering the roof and during the third people made all

---

[6] Ibid., 87.

kinds of interesting sounds as they talked or walked out.'[7] Although Cage did not control these events, he had nevertheless enabled the audience to hear the music of the environment, and this is what the European tradition had never bothered about.

If *4'33"* was a prime example of the theatre of situation, so too was the Happening that had occurred a few weeks earlier at Black Mountain College, North Carolina, which is briefly described in Chapter Two. Black Mountain was where many of the leading figures of the American avant-garde had studied or were teachers. Among those Cage recruited for the event were the poets M.C. Richards and Charles Olson, the painter Robert Rauschenberg, the dancer Merce Cunningham, and pianist David Tudor.

The Happening required that each of them should 'do their own thing' while various films, slides and gramophone records were being shown or played at the same time. Cage had the audience sit in the centre of these various activities to demonstrate that the theatre is all around us. He too took part, but although he wanted each event to be itself, he nevertheless imposed a degree of order on the proceedings. Each person was told when to start and how long their activities should last, whether these be reciting, dancing, lecturing, playing the gramophone or making music. This ensured that their activities would overlap. In that the number of participants involved amounted to dozens rather than one, that it took place in the open air rather than the concert hall, and that it was noisy rather than silent, the Happening represented the extreme opposite of *4'33"*, but in both works each 'event' was given a specific duration and they therefore shared the same structural principle.

Shortly afterwards, Cage called the Happening *Theatre Piece No. 1*, but he dropped this title when, six years later, he composed his *Theatre Piece*. This too consisted of a series of timed, independent events occurring simultaneously. But since the work was limited to at most eight participants, and since these could be singers, instrumentalists, dancers, actors or mimes, it was possible that if only dancers, actors or mimes were involved, it too could be a silent piece. Once again Cage wanted to reduce his control over the event to a minimum. Those who took part were given a set of instructions, two packs of twenty numbered blank cards on which they had to write either a noun or a verb, a set of transparent rulers to measure the time they could take over each action their words suggested, and a diagrammatic score consisting of a vertical string of numbers in both large and small print, and signs indicating multiplication, addition and subtraction, and horizontal brackets. By following Cage's instructions about when the cards

---

[7] See Kyle Gann, *No Such Thing as Silence: John Cage's 4'33"* (New Haven, Yale University Press, 2010), 3–4.

should be shuffled, how the rulers should be used, and how the diagram could be interpreted, the participants could produce a thirty-minute programme of actions which, like the events in the Black Mountain Happening, were entirely their own.

American composers can be divided into two main categories, those born and bred in the Eastern States, who tend to be orientated to European culture, and those born and bred in the Western States, who tend to turn their faces to the East. Milton Babbitt and Elliott Carter represent the first category, John Cage and Harry Partch the second. Partch spent much of his childhood in the Arizona desert, and was largely self-taught as a musician. Before he was twenty he had already become dissatisfied with 'both the intonational system of modern Europe and its concert system'.[8] The music that interested him, he later claimed, was that of 'Yaqui Indians, Chinese lullabies, Hebrew chants for the dead, Christian hymns, Congo puberty rites …'.[9] By 1928 he had written the first version of his book *Genesis of a Music*, in which he put forward what he called 'his new philosophy of music'.[10] He rejected Western harmony and polyphony, insisting that music should go back to its roots: the single melodic line, conceived in relation to the human voice. He rejected the twelve-note tempered scale of Western music and replaced it with a forty-three-note scale derived from the pure intervals of just intonation. He also rejected the abstraction of Western music, holding that music was corporeal as well as aural. His contention was that in musical performances the visual should be as important as the aural. This is why the instruments he invented and built to play his music, with names such as 'blue rainbow', 'Castor and Pollux', 'cloud chamber bowls', 'diamond marimba' are as beautiful to look at as they are to listen to.

Partch's first dramatic work, *U.S. Highball* (1943), subtitled 'A Musical Account of a Transcontinental Hobo Trip', focuses upon an individual figure thus implying a much greater interest in character. It can also be regarded as prototype Music Theatre. The stage is occupied by a single figure, a hobo called Mac, who is riding the trains to get to Chicago. Also on stage are some of Partch's early instruments to accompany Mac. They play snatches of popular tunes, represent railway noises and also the presence of other hobos. The work is cast in three acts, each devoted to a stage on the journey, with Mac chanting or intoning about what he sees and thinks on the way. His last word, when he draws into its station, is simply: 'Chicago'. The instrumental music following this bald statement is meant

---

[8] Harry Partch, *Genesis of a Music: An Account of a Creative Work, its Roots, and its Fulfillments*, 2nd edn (New York, Da Capo Press, 1979), 6.

[9] Ibid., viii.

[10] Ibid., 4.

to suggest that, now the excitement of getting there is over, 'all that's left is a tremendous letdown', a sense of 'bewilderment'.[11]

If *U.S. Highball* can be considered prototype Music Theatre then Partch's last dramatic work, *Delusion of the Fury* (1965–6), represents its full flowering. Apart from demanding more participants and being much longer than other examples, it is a paradigm of the genre. Its first act is based on a Japanese Noh play, its second on an Ethiopian folk tale, one being serious, the other comic. It needs two men and a woman to be the principals, a chorus of between eighteen and twenty, and twenty-five instrumentalists, some of whom must double as actors or attendants when not required to play. The central theme of the work is reconciliation. In the Noh play the man, who has slain a princely warrior, goes back to where the murder took place, taking with him the warrior's son, who was born after his father's death. The boy hopes to see a vision of his father, and, in effect, when he encounters his father's ghost, he does. The ghost is furious that he had to die before seeing his son, and he re-enacts the ordeal of his death. This and the presence of his son enables him to be reconciled to what had been denied him.

In the Ethiopian folk tale, a young vagabond is cooking a meal on a fire among some rocks, when an old female goatherd approaches looking for a kid she has lost. Later she finds the kid, but because of a misunderstanding with the vagabond who happens to be deaf, she has a furious row with him. Villagers gather to witness it, and during a violent dance they force the quarrelling couple to appear before a justice of the peace, who is not only deaf himself but near-sighted too. Nevertheless he manages to reconcile the two, and afterwards the villagers sing in unison, 'Oh, how did we ever get by without justice?'

Delusion of the Fury contains very few words, only a dozen in Act I and about three dozen in Act II. Some are spoken, others sung. Those given to the principals must be sung in an oriental, 'somewhat disembodied voice', while those given to the chorus must be chanted or intoned. All the performers have to wear costumes, and in addition the instrumentalists wear 'fantastic headpieces'. Their instruments should be prominent but not crowded together. They should be positioned so that the acting can take place between them. Partch insists that all the acting should be intense. In the first act the performers should move slowly, in the second vigorously: their movements should be as stylised as those in oriental theatre.

Luciano Berio's position on the avoidance of extra-musical associations in the early fifties was ambiguous. Although he composed nothing for voice between completing *Chamber Music* in 1953 and composing *Circles* in 1960, he nevertheless produced two pieces for a 'theatre of the imagination'. He called both

[11] Ibid., 321.

Mimusique. The first, written in 1953, was an electronic piece based on the sound of a gunshot; the second, from 1955, a work for a symphony orchestra without its string section. Both were rich in musical gestures, and by giving them a title that combined 'mime' and 'musique', Berio hoped that listeners would supply for themselves a theatrical scenario. In other words he wanted listeners to invent their own extra-musical associations. Later in 1955 and 1959 he used *Mimusique No. 2* for two theatre works for mimes in which the scenarios were supplied by first Roberto Leydi then Italo Calvino. Leydi's *Tre modi per sopportare la vita* has a left-wing slant, while Calvino's *Allez Hop* has a travelling showman with a flea-circus putting his fleas through their paces, and is more subtly left-wing.

Circles, for mezzo-soprano, harp and two percussionists, is closer to being true Music Theatre than *Allez Hop*, even though its visual content is limited. For his texts Berio chose three poems by e.e. cummings, whose experimental typography, eccentric punctuation, fragmentation and broken syntax lent themselves admirably to the task of restoring to words their function as bearers of meaning, as well as allowing him to make extensive use of their sounds for their own sake. The circles are not just confined to the way the texts move from semantic continuity to fragmentation and back, or the way the singer moves from melismatic singing to speech and back; they also involve physical movements. The singer has to walk round her instrumental colleagues in a half circle during the course of the work; the percussionists must perform gyrations around their instruments during the third of the work's five sections; and in the last of them, one has to use a cymbal to describe circles in space. The prominence of the solo singer in the piece tips the work towards the theatre of character despite the nature of the texts.

But if *Circles*, unlike *Allez Hop*, is on the fringes of being a theatre of character, Berio's next theatrical work, *Passaggio* (1962), with its focus on the persona of the solo singer, demonstrates his total commitment to it. Since it requires large forces it must be performed in an opera house, indeed as far as the composer was concerned 'its subject is the opera house itself'.[12] As well as a virtuoso soprano, it requires an eight-part chorus situated in the orchestral pit alongside twenty-five instrumentalists, and five speaking choruses seated among the audience in the auditorium. The work exists on two levels: one relates to events on stage, the other to what goes on in the mind of the soprano as well as in the minds of the five choruses representing the audience.

On stage, the soprano, whom Berio calls 'She', slowly traces a passage from one side of the stage to the other, stopping from time to time to enact roles which together make a skeletal story. They describe a woman being hunted down,

---

[12] *Luciano Berio: Two Interviews with Rossana Dalmonte and Balint Andras Varga*, tr. and ed. David Osmond-Smith (London, Boyars, 1981), 93.

arrested, subjected to brutal interrogation and torture, and finally obliged to live in the squalor of an urban bedsit. Most of this has to be inferred from visual clues and from the reactions of the choruses. While the chorus in the pit acts as a commentator, those sitting in the audience represent the bourgeoisie speaking in a variety of languages and exposing their thoughts about what is happening or what is not happening on stage. They range from the abusive to the lustful. But the soprano is so absorbed in her own inner thoughts that she appears to be indifferent to their raillery. Eventually she leaves the stage, but after a reflective choral epilogue delivered by those in the pit she returns to put on her raincoat. She then revisits the stopping places, acknowledges what was represented in them, then curtly tells the audience to leave.

Although *Passaggio* needs to be performed in an opera house and requires an opera singer and a large number of people to accompany her, it is nevertheless a rare type of Music Theatre, even though Berio and his librettist Eduardo Sanguinetti called it a *messa in scena* (a staged mass). So too is *Sequenza III*, which Berio completed in 1966. Being a solo piece scored for one soprano, this goes to the opposite end of the numerical pendulum. However, it too exposes a singer's private world to public scrutiny. Another example is *Monodrama* (1970), in which an ageing tenor works himself up into a frenzy worrying about whether he can reach the top G in a Heine setting he has been asked to sing.[13]

But dramatically the most vivid of these psychological studies is *Recital I (for Cathy)* for mezzo-soprano and seventeen instruments, which Berio composed in 1972, three years after completing his *Sinfonia* for eight amplified voices and orchestra. *Sinfonia* has a third movement in which a stream of quotations from orchestral music ranging from Bach to Stockhausen is held together by the scherzo in Mahler's Second Symphony weaving in and out of them, a procedure Berio likens to a skeleton that often re-emerges fully fleshed out, then disappears, then comes back again.[14] A stream of quotations also runs through *Recital I* except that here they represent a history of solo vocal music. Both works also contain spoken material. In *Sinfonia* this consists of remarks made by Harvard undergraduates, slogans written by students on the walls of the Sorbonne during the 1968 Paris insurrection, and a collage of other literary and popular quotations. What binds them together is the refrain: 'Keep going, keep going,' a quotation from Samuel Beckett's novel *The Unnamable*. The spoken commentary in *Recital I*, on the other hand, is a private affair. It represents the singer's inner speech:

[13]   Ibid., 97.

[14]   A detailed study of *Sinfonia* is given by David Osmond-Smith, in *Playing on Words: Guide to Luciano Berio's 'Sinfonia'* (Royal Musical Association Monographs, London, Ashgate, 1985).

when you come down to it I've seen everything ... I've heard everything, in fact as I stand here with my hand on the piano looking into all those faces I couldn't care less about seeing and feeling all those things I couldn't care less about singing

Her musical quotations include references to such operas as *Dido and Aeneas*, *Carmen*, *Manon*, *Lakmé*, *Rigoletto*, *The Fairy Queen* and *La Cenerentola*, and to cantatas and songs both ancient and modern.[15] Here, in contrast to *Sinfonia*, there is no musical 'skeleton' running through the work; the quotations are triggered not by music but by whatever enters the singer's mind. As a result she gives the impression that there is nothing to hold her together, either as a singer or as a person.

Although continuous, the work falls into two parts, each beginning with the performance of a complete number. The first has 'Se i languidi miei sguardi' from Monteverdi's *La lettera amorosa* at its head, the second Berio's 1948 setting of 'Avendo gran desio', a poem by the twelfth-century poet Jacopo da Lentini. Both concern absent love, which we can only assume is also the singer's preoccupation. In the Monteverdi she had been accompanied by a harpsichordist, but at the end of it, before she embarks on another Monteverdi number, 'Amor dov'é la fé', she notices that her pianist has not turned up. Her first thoughts indicate her concern for him as she notes that he hadn't been aware of being alone and had always been so. As her monologue unfolds, it becomes evident that it is she, not the pianist, who is experiencing loneliness: loneliness and the feeling that, as a professional singer who must perform a number of roles in her career, she lacks a firm identity. In the second part, five members of the seventeen-piece ensemble supplying the accompaniment don masks, and stand in a circle around her. They too appear to lack a firm identity, for as well as exchanging masks they also exchange instruments. Meanwhile a wardrobe mistress has started to drape the singer in more and more costumes, the last two being a net with a rope, which she places around the singer's neck, and a transparent veil covered with huge drops of blood that she places over her head. So robed, all the singer can do is to ask the audience to laugh or applaud, her last vocal contribution being: 'libera nos', sung *sotto voce*.

Hans Werner Henze was not an overtly political figure, but in 1967, when Che Guevara was executed in Bolivia for attempting to rouse the tin-miners to rebellion, the event was one of a number that drew him to sympathise with the

---

[15] A comprehensive list of the quoted musical fragments is offered in David Metzer, *Quotation and Musical Meaning in Twentieth-Century Music* (Cambridge, Cambridge University Press, 2003), 219–20.

revolutionary movements then prevalent.[16] He dedicated his 'oratorio volgare e militare', *The Raft of the Medusa* (1968), to the memory of Guevara, and during the course of the next seven years he laid aside his interest in opera to compose a number of works that either celebrated revolution or cast doubts on whether he himself could have been an active revolutionary. Three of them are Music Theatre: *El Cimarrón* (1969-70), *Das langwierige Weg in der Wohnung der Natascha Ungeheuer* (1971) and his Second Violin Concerto (1971), which contains both physical action and a part for a singer.

El Cimarrón, a seventy-six-minute 'recital' for an actor-singer, flute, guitar and percussion, was composed shortly after Henze arrived in Cuba on the first of two extended visits made to support the revolution Fidel Castro had successfully concluded. The singer, a baritone, is cast in the role of Esteban Montejo, a Cuban slave, who tells how he became a revolutionary fighter after escaping his Spanish masters, and how he ended up a member of Castro's victorious army. Henze gives the singer and the three musicians accompanying him the freedom to improvise, thus ensuring that, because of their creative contribution to the work, he was able to establish an egalitarian relationship between himself and his performers.

Das langwierige Weg in der Wohnung der Natascha Ungeheuer (The Tedious Way to the Apartment of Natascha Ungeheuer), on the other hand, is where Henze and his librettist, the Chilian poet Gaston Salvatore, question their abilities to be active revolutionaries themselves, even though Salvatore had taken part in the 1967-8 student uprising in Berlin, and afterwards Henze had given protection to its leader, Rudi Dutschke. Henze's doubts were founded on the knowledge that in the early fifties, when he had been a supporter of the musical revolution that Boulez and others had instigated, he had turned away from the avant-garde to devote himself to opera, then considered to be the epitome of old-fashioned, middle-class, anti-revolutionary values. *Natascha Ungeheuer* lasts just under one hour, and is in eleven named sections. Henze scores the work for a baritone and seventeen instrumentalists. The baritone, representing the would-be revolutionary, is dressed in the obligatory gear of jeans, fatigues and dark glasses. The instrumentalists are also dressed in the manner of prototypes. Fifteen of them are split up into three groups of five: the instruments Schoenberg chose for *Pierrot lunaire* are dressed in bloodstained hospital overalls to represent the sick bourgeoisie; a brass quintet wearing police helmets represent agents of the oppressive state machine; and a five-piece jazz/rock band, dressed like hippies, represent the voice of the underground.

---

[16] 'I decided ... to turn the work into a sort of allegorical requiem for Che Guevara.' Hans Werner Henze, *Bohemian Fifths*, tr. Stewart Spencer (London, Faber and Faber, 1998), 229.

There are also two soloists: a Hammond organist dressed in lounge suit to represent a plutocrat; and a percussionist dressed as a garage mechanic in blue overalls to represent the kind of man the baritone cannot be: a man used to doing things, a man of action. In addition there is a tape montage containing the voices of Henze and Salvatore, Berlin street sounds, crowd noises, snatches from the triumphal march in *Aida*, the funeral march in Mahler's Fifth Symphony and the voice of a woman called Natascha, who represents, says Salvatore, 'the siren of a false Utopia'.

The would-be revolutionary is clearly, like Henze and Salvatore, a left-wing intellectual. The work opens with him standing in his study with a map, reading instructions on a piece of paper. But the journey he plans to take takes place in his mind, not on the streets of Berlin. Both text and music indicate that we are listening to an internal monologue of a man trapped by his bourgeois proclivities, and suffering extreme *angst*. Although given actions to perform, these are limited to the area immediately surrounding him. In the seventh section, for example, he has to take off his shoes and shirt, roll up his trousers, stand on a podium and fold his hands behind his back so that physically he looks like a condemned man awaiting execution. His words, however, speak of other things, and include references to Guevara, Castro and Baron Münchhausen struggling to get out of the swamp into which he has fallen. This seventh section contains four stanzas. In the first and third we hear the distorted voices of Henze and Salvatore on tape, in the second the spoken voice of the baritone, in the fourth his hysterical singing, hysterical because it represents the culmination of his mental torment. Accompanying him are conflicting strands of music played by the three instrumental groups including an obsessive repetition of scales belonging to some unrecognisable romantic piano piece. Henze calls this seventh section 'Attempted Return No. 2', and at the end of the work in 'Attempted Return No. 3' he makes it clear that, although Natascha is unable to lure the would-be revolutionary into her apartment, the man has come full circle. He will have to find another, less tedious, route to where he wants to go.

Baron Münchhausen crops up again in Henze's Second Violin Concerto, which also includes Hans Magnus Enzensberger's poem 'Hommage an Gödel'. At the heart of the poem is 'Gödel's proof', that contends: 'In every sufficiently complex system propositions can be formulated that are neither verifiable nor refutable within that system, unless the system itself is inconsistent.'[17] Münchhausen is introduced because he was an inveterate liar and the antithesis of the rigidly logical. Henze's concerto has the soloist accompanied by a baritone singing a setting of Enzensberger's poem, as well as a thirty-three-piece orchestra and a

[17] Ibid., 304.

tape. It becomes Music Theatre on the grounds that the composer states in the score that the violinist enters dressed in 'a flowing black tailcoat lined in red and a plumed tricorn' to represent Münchhausen, and Enzensberger's words must be sung by a 'young buffo, a comic baritone'. The violinist establishes the comic nature of the piece by hurrying on to the platform after the orchestra has begun to play, then being prevented from playing himself until the baritone has fully revealed Gödel's Proof.

The work has six movements, the third and fifth being fantasias. In these the violinist moves into the background, switches on a contact microphone attached to his instrument, and, with a spotlight shining on him, plays a duet with the comically surreal sounds on the tape. Among them can be heard quotations from Elizabethan lute songs. In the other movements the singer presents us with a commentary on Gödel's Proof, one of his points being that 'for its own justification any conceivable system must transcend itself, which means destroy itself'. But Münchhausen is outside the system. He has the capacity to fantasise, and this means, says the composer, that the last movement can be brought to an end 'with seemingly unremitting optimism'.

Nono and Berio were the heirs to the Italian vocal tradition; Karlheinz Stockhausen, however, had the German instrumental tradition standing behind him. It was therefore inevitable that his first contribution to the theatre in the concert hall should be an Instrumental Theatre piece.

There are two versions of *Kontakte*. One is a tape piece for electronic sounds alone, the other a tape piece with additional parts for a percussionist and a pianist who also has a number of percussion instruments to play. Apart from short studies, the tape piece was the first work composed entirely from electronically generated material without recourse to *musique concrète* (music derived from recorded sound). In this respect it was absolutely new. Furthermore, although it sounds 'other-worldly', it contains no extra-musical associations. It becomes dramatically significant only when the familiar sounds of piano and percussion are juxtaposed to it. This means that although it is not a fully fledged specimen of Instrumental Theatre, it nevertheless contains the basic ingredient of the genre.

Stockhausen had been working in the electronic studio run by West German Radio in Cologne since 1953. He began to compose *Kontakte* (1958–60) a year after the Russians had put their first Sputnik satellite into space. Space exploration was thus an exciting new development, opening up for the first time the real possibility that man might establish contact with other worlds.

Stockhausen had already composed *Gesang der Jünglinge* (1955–6), a tape piece combining electronically generated sounds and a recording of a boy's voice singing the *Benedicite*, but although this brought the familiar and the unfamiliar into contact with each other, the situation was not dramatised. The two components were integrated rather than set against each other as they are in *Kontakte*. Here the electronic sounds are relayed through four loudspeakers encircling the listeners, while two performers, sitting as far apart from each other as possible, play the live sounds. However, on several occasions they move from their positions at the sides of the platform to play a gong and a large tam-tam situated in the centre.

The work begins with the pianist walking to the centre of the platform, and taking a long knitting needle out of his pocket. He then touches the rim of the tam-tam with the needle and slowly moves the needle around it to produce what Stockhausen calls a 'ssschhhoouuu' sound. This is immediately picked up by the tape so that the first contact between the live and the electronic has been made. During the course of the work there are many more contacts. Most of them demonstrate how easily the live instruments can respond to the tape, but how tardily the tape responds to them. Its second response occurs as the result of a dramatic and amusing incident engineered by the instrumentalists. The pianist and percussionist play from their positions on either side of the platform a succession of overlapping crescendos, the pianist on cow-bells, the percussionist on hi-hat. But when they get no response from the tape, they move into the centre, where the pianist playing the tam-tam, and the percussionist the gong, produce even louder crescendos. When these reach their peak the tape replies with equally loud sounds strongly resembling those of the tam-tam. Equally amusing is the occasion when the tape produces a sound that zigzags through space so that it sounds like a wasp or bee about to land. When it does, the impulses that have been the only source of the noises it makes throughout the work slow down until they reach the pace of a heart beat. By this means the unfamiliar is transformed into the unmistakably familiar.

Temperamentally, Stockhausen enjoyed going to extremes. A year after completing *Kontakte* he turned it into Music Theatre by superimposing upon it a host of multimedia 'events' in the fashion of Cage's Black Mountain Happening. He called it *Originale*, and to make a work lasting an hour and a half, he lengthened *Kontakte* by repeating some of its sections and adding seven minutes of music from a recording of his choral work, *Carré* (1959–60). Like Cage, he recruited as many participants as were available, and asked them to 'do their own thing' more or less oblivious of each other. The activities included a child playing with some building blocks, a cameraman, a sound engineer, a lighting technician and a film producer making a film and a recording of *Kontakte*; as well as a female attendant from Cologne Zoo's Monkey House and a newspaper vendor known throughout Cologne for her witty comments on the headlines each wandering on and off the stage. In addition, five actors under Stockhausen's direction created a 'formant'[18]

---

[18] 'the actors even speak in what Stockhausen calls "formant rhythms": in a span of four minutes one actor speaks three equally spaced words, a second actor has five equally

from rhythms based on the Fibonacci series;[19] the composer, Nam June Paik, covered himself with shaving cream and threw peas at the audience, and the pianist and percussionist needed for *Kontakte* dressed themselves in an array of exotic costumes and even made tea for each other. But although all these activities appeared to be spontaneous, Stockhausen, like Cage in his Black Mountain Happening, timed when and for how long they should occur meticulously.

Originale created such a scandal when it was performed at Cologne's Theater am Dom that apart from a rather childish improvised theatre piece called *Oben und Unten* (1968), based on the breakdown of Stockhausen's relationship with his companion, the painter Mary Bauermeister, Stockhausen produced no more theatre pieces until *Trans* appeared in 1971. 'Trans' is an abbreviation of 'transpersonal': 'it has something to do with the beyond, with what's on the other side'.[20] Here, what lies on the other side is suggested not by electronics or short waves, but by four groups of wind and percussion instruments playing behind a gauze curtain bathed in a violet light. In front of them, and obscuring them, is a wall of stringed instruments two tiers deep. Aurally this wall consists of dense chords that change only when an electronic device sounding like a shuttle passes from left to right. Stockhausen requires no movement from the string section other than the movement of their bows. When one group are at the point of their bows, others are at the heel: they behave like automata. The wind and percussion instruments behind them, on the other hand, play composed music consisting mainly of parallel lines above a low melody.

To create a sense of action, Stockhausen includes four short events to mark a transition from the purely mechanical to something more spontaneous. Like those in *Originale*, they are absurd. A crazy virtuoso solo for the principal viola, that sounds as if the player had been wound up like a toy, is triggered by a percussion player entering from behind the curtain and marching like a toy soldier. A lugubrious solo for the principal cello, played with sweeping bow strokes, is instigated by a stage hand coming on the platform with a music stand with a theatre light attached to it. A solo for the principal violin, on the other hand, simply needs the flight of the shuttle to get it started. This involves only canary-like noises

spaced words, a third has eight, and yet another has thirteen, while a fifth provides a "noise band" of completely irregular rhythms.' Jonathan Harvey, *The Music of Stockhausen: An Introduction* (Berkeley and Los Angeles: University of California Press, 1975), 90.

[19]   Sequence of numbers in which 1 appears twice as the first two numbers, and every subsequent number is the sum of two preceding numbers: 1, 1, 2, 3, 5, 8, 13 etc. In the West, the Fibonacci sequence first appears in the book, *Liber Abaci* (1202) by Leonardo of Pisa, aka Fibonacci.

[20]   Cott, ed., *Stockhausen*, 59.

at which the other violinists turn and stare at the player in amazement. This response proves to be a harbinger of the denouement, an event set in motion by the appearance of the principal trumpet whose head and shoulders rise up from behind the strings. We now get a glimpse of what lies hidden behind the wall, and with this revelation, the strings and wind section join forces. The seen and the hidden, the here and the beyond, are at one.

Stockhausen thought of *Trans* as representing a stepping-stone to death, a piece that would give the terminally ill a glimpse of the beyond. He originally intended to call it 'Music for the next to die'. Two years later when he composed *Inori*, another piece devoted to making contact with the beyond, the hidden is never exposed. We are constantly made conscious of the beyond but it never makes contact with us. The work is an hour-long piece for one or two dancers or mimes and a large orchestra in which the high instruments sit on the opposite side of the platform to the low instruments. In it Stockhausen relates music to gesture more closely than anyone else had done before. The gestures are those that people from various regions of the world make with their fingers, hands or arms when they pray.

For each prayerful position Stockhausen assigns a pitch, a dynamic, a duration, a tempo and a timbre relating to a particular vowel sound. These enable him to write out the dancer's part as if it were a thirteen-note melody covering the thirteen chromatic notes from middle C to C♯, an augmented octave above. He gives the greatest importance to G, the note lying at the centre of this scale. When G sounds, the dancer's hands must be closed and placed near to the heart. G's dynamic is pianissimo, its duration a minim, its tempo that of the heartbeat, and its timbre the syllable 'Hu'. (According to the Sufi musician Hazrat Inayat Khan, Hu is 'the origin and end of all sounds, the divine name'[21]). These are the parameters that dictate what the orchestra plays to co-ordinate with the dancer. But Stockhausen allows a degree of variety, for the orchestra's textures also mirror how the dancer moves her arms and hands: whether they move away from or towards her body, whether they sink or rise, or whether they drift apart.

From time to time the dancer cups her hand to her ear as if listening for a response. But the response she receives comes only from the orchestra, which although very much 'in tune' with what she is doing, can only rustle up allusions to music of the past when she requires an answer. From time to time she has also to stamp her foot, her purpose being to silence the bass tuba, who is clearly intent on disrupting the proceedings. Stockhausen had a boyish sense of humour, and even when he is at his most serious or devout, he could not resist introducing a joker

[21] Michael Kurz, *Stockhausen: A Biography*, tr. Richard Troop (London, Faber and Faber 1994), 197.

into his pack. This is undoubtedly the impetus behind the antics of the pianist and percussionist in *Kontakte*, the even greater number of antics in *Originale* and the bizarre events in *Trans*. They may seem childish, but without them Stockhausen's music theatre would not be as accessible as it is. By provoking laughter they bring his spatial explorations and search for the spiritual back down to earth.

Laughter also lies behind *Harlekin*, which I discussed at the end of Chapter One, for Harlequin is the mischievous valet who dances around the word seeing off rivals for the hand of his sweetheart, Columbine. By scoring it for a clarinettist who can also dance or a dancer who can also play the clarinet, and by having music and movement co-ordinate so closely, Stockhausen ultimately achieved the epitome of what he was trying to perfect in *Inori*: the ideal balance between the aural and visual.

Mauricio Kagel began composing his first contribution to Music Theatre, *Sur scène*, in 1958, a year after leaving his native Argentina to settle in Cologne. Essentially it is a mocking critique of the contemporary music scene, how new music is presented at concerts devoted to the avant-garde. His target is the introductory lectures given at concerts, when talk about contemporary music takes up more time than the music itself. He almost certainly had in mind the concerts he had been attending at Darmstadt since 1957 and where he taught after 1960. He called the piece a 'Theatrical Chamber Music Work in One Act', and scored it for speaker, mime, singer and three instrumentalists. Throughout the piece the speaker delivers a long-winded, seemingly erudite but basically nonsensical discourse about contemporary music. Kagel gives him precise instructions on where to pitch his voice, how loud he should be, how fast he should go, when he should pause and where he should look at every juncture of his ramblings. Essentially he provides him with what could be a piece of avant-garde music in itself. Meanwhile the singer, mime and instrumentalists practise pre-performance warming-up exercises. They even rehearse the bows and gestures they will take and make before, during and after the performance. They too are given precise instructions: how to react to the speaker and each other, what to do, where to look. But after about an hour it becomes clear that no music is going to be performed. The audience has had all that is on offer.

Fifteen years later when Kagel composed *Kantrimiusik* [sic], i.e. 'Country Music', the Theatre of the Absurd was on the wane. Its innovations were being absorbed into other types of theatre. But Kagel still held to its principles. Scored for clarinet, trumpet, tuba, violin, piano, two guitars, tape and at least three singers, the work has eight movements with seven interludes all devoted to 'folksy' music of various types. In the third movement the tape reproduces the sound of woodland on a winter's day followed by that of a forest on a summer's day, while in the fifth a band playing a waltz seemingly *in perpetuo* has to contend with the tape's rendition of a storm. The interludes on the other hand are mainly given over to the singers providing in different languages every conceivable cliché used to describe the countryside. As in *Sur scène*, everything is notated meticulously, including the visual components of the piece. These comprise life-size inflatable plastic dolls, and an elaborate piece of stage machinery that can be manipulated to provide 'synthetic' images of what can be seen in the countryside: not fields or forests but clouds, a gable of a house, a redbrick chimney, distant mountains: in other words objects that can also be seen in towns. Thus everything in *Kantrimiusik* is a sham.

So too is Kagel's *Staatstheater* (1957–60), a work the Hamburg State Opera commissioned, and which has to be classified as 'anti-opera' because it asks the personnel of an opera company to take on roles they were not employed to perform. He described it as being not just a negation of opera, but of the whole tradition of 'musical theatre'. For example, those who are normally employed to sing the solo roles have to sing as a chorus, those who are members of the chorus are given solo lines to perform alone or in duets or trios with others. There is a ballet for those who cannot dance, a piece for stage hands with squeaky shoes, and at the first performance in Hamburg on 25 April 1971, twenty minutes of deafening sound representing 'anti-music'.

Even before the work was first performed, Kagel had extracted and prepared for publication nine sections that could be performed separately as Music or Instrumental Theatre, or in some cases just as concert pieces. The first in order of publication was *Repertoire*, which Kagel calls a scenic concert piece, but which is actually a piece of Instrumental Theatre taken to an extreme, not just because of the number of instrumentalists taking part but because none of them is on stage for more than a few seconds. The participants are the hundred members of the State Theatre's orchestra who instead of playing their own instruments have to choose to play one of 125 different objects, including household utensils and a chamber pot. Each player has his own scene, and in each scene there is a quasi-musical gesture and a physical gesture to go with it. As in all Kagel's works they have to be performed according to his detailed instructions. The first and simplest is scored for a metal ball between 5 and 50 cm in diameter that Kagel calls a 'styroporkugel'. All the instrumentalist has to do is to drop it and pick it up a number of times. As well as having a sketch of the object in one corner of the score and another sketch of the player dropping it in the opposite corner, there are instructions for the performance in writing, and the notation of a single demi-semi-quaver marked staccato and *fff* within double bars containing vertical pairs of dots indicating that it has to be repeated (Ex. 3.1).

These instructions ensure that the instrumentalist will perform the piece as conscientiously and seriously as he would when playing his instrument in the orchestra. But even though Kagel manages to devise ninety-nine more 'scenic

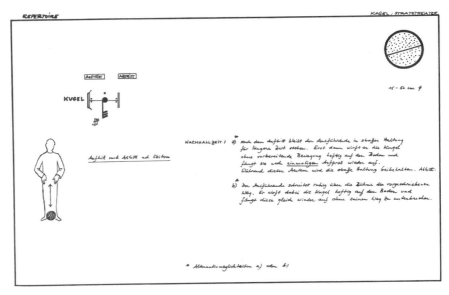

Ex. 3.1 Kagel, *Repertoire, Action 1*

gestures', each with a different object, there comes a time when, however ingenious and amusing they may be, *Repertoire* becomes tedious. This is because, as in *Sur scène*, Kagel wants to use the absurdities to mock not only the musicians but the audience as well. When it comes to the last member of the orchestra to perform, instead of having an object to play, he has only his mouth. He walks to the front of the stage and laughs. At first naturally, but then after breathing in through his teeth, he shapes his lips as if he is about to say 'ee' and proceeds to smile, then pause, then smile, then pause, then smile.

György Ligeti's *Aventures* and its sequel *Nouvelles aventures* (1962–5) is also about opera, but whereas Kagel's *Staatstheater* makes the personnel of an opera house do things they are not employed to do, Ligeti asks a soprano, contralto and baritone to be opera singers but in such a concentrated manner, and at such a hectic pace, that their efforts resemble the speeded-up antics in a comic strip. Since the form of *Aventures* relates to Baroque or Classical 'number' opera, and the two movements of *Nouvelles aventures* to continuous music drama, the two together could be said to constitute a comic history of opera. Ligeti has said that the work 'involves the adventures of imaginary characters on an imaginary stage singing in an imaginary language, a language which is semantically meaningless and has only emotional content'.[22] He goes on to tell us that the three singers play five roles simultaneously, and that in its form the work has five parallel streams

---

[22] György Ligeti, *Ligeti in Conversation* (London, Eulenburg Books, 1983), 45.

of events: five 'stories' that diverge from one another. Each stream consists of a number of separate episodes (seven to eleven per stream), and each episode has its own very distinctive expressive character (e.g. mystical, idyllic, nostalgic, funereal, redeemed, excited, ironic, erotic). To provide an illustration of the vocal complexity of the work, Paul Griffiths, one of Ligeti's biographers, has drawn attention to a passage for the baritone in *Aventures* cast in two overlapping phrases.[23] The first is an impassioned outburst addressed to the audience, and consists of six heavily accented notes marked 'senza tempo', 'zum publicum', 'eroico' and 'triple forte'; while the second, uttered mainly under the breath (à la Monteverdi), consists of rapid repetitions of single notes preceded by accents and marked 'prestissimo capriccioso, staccatissimo', and 'triple pianissimo'. Finally, when a brief variation of the first phrase appears in a slightly altered form to terminate the passage, the marking becomes, 'aggressivo', 'fortissimo'.

Originally Ligeti intended the work to be a concert piece, but after its first performance in 1966, he turned it into Music Theatre by devising a stage scenario with an additional part for a male dancer or mime. In the scene containing that passage for the baritone, there must be at one side of the stage or platform a Golem, in Jewish folklore an animated being created entirely from inanimate material, usually clay. From the other side of the stage the dancer or mime as an Olympic runner enters carrying a scroll and with a torch in his hands. When the baritone sees him they both hide behind an invisible three-person-wide screen, the baritone appearing and disappearing from one side of it, the dancer doing likewise from the other side. With his gestures the dancer also mimics the baritone's singing, making it appear that he is about to announce an extremely important message. The effort, however, exhausts him, and when he catches sight of the Golem he falls lifeless to the ground. The torch goes out and the scroll rolls away.

Although *Aventures et Nouvelles aventures* is a single, bipartite example of Music Theatre, its two components can still be performed separately as concert pieces. The superimposed stage scenario detracts attention from the scenario implicit in the music. It takes absurdity to a ludicrous extreme.

This brief outline of the European and American interest and experiments in Music Theatre provides the context for what was happening in Britain. In the second half of the book, it will be seen that Music Theatre in Britain was an area of creative experimentation, not just for the major figures of the period, but for many lesser known composers, whose works from that time may have been largely forgotten, but which contributed significantly to the richness and innovative nature of the genre.

[23] Paul Griffiths, *György Ligeti* (London, Robson Books, 1983), 40–4.

PART TWO

A Genre for the Times

CHAPTER FOUR

Performers and Performances

THREE composers dominated British Music Theatre during the 1960s and 1970s: Harrison Birtwistle, Peter Maxwell Davies and Alexander Goehr. As well as producing more music-theatre pieces than anyone else, they also ran two of the six organisations devoted to mounting them. Birtwistle and Maxwell Davies ran the Pierrot Players (later The Fires of London), and Goehr the Brighton Festival Ensemble (later the MusicTheatre Ensemble).

Another group, Focus Opera, entered the music-theatre arena in March 1968, when it gave a programme of works by Kagel, Ligeti and Cornelius Cardew, which it billed as '*Three? Avant-Garde? Operas?*' Focus Opera was founded in 1963 to perform little-known one-act operas by classical or twentieth-century composers writing in a traditional style. But from 1968 until 1975 it presented at least twice a year, sometimes in association with the Morley College Music Theatre Group, programmes that usually included music-theatre works by young composers.

Even more consistently devoted to Music Theatre by young composers was the Music Department at York University. Here the composers had to create works to perform themselves, as no trained singers or professional instrumentalists were available to them. Before 1973 most of their work was performed at the university in the Jack Lyons Concert Hall, but in 1973 a Music Theatre group called 'Clap' was formed. Roger Marsh told me that its founder members were Bernard Rands, Vic Hoyland, Melody Lovelace, Tom (Archer) Endrich, Dominic Muldowney, Jonty Harrison and himself. 'Clap', he told me, toured arts centres and colleges in the UK with programmes that combined classic works such as Berio's *Sequenza for Voice*, Berberian's *Stripsody* and Rands's *Ballad II*, with new pieces by members of the group. The ensemble enjoyed success for about two years, before a disastrous appearance at the Shaw Theatre in London in 1974, playing to an audience of about thirty on a stage dominated by a London bus left there for an impending production.

The largest organisations involved with Music Theatre were the London Sinfonietta and the BBC Symphony Orchestra, when it performed at the Roundhouse, which it first used for a Prom in 1971, when George Newson's *Arena*, discussed below and in Chapter Eight, was performed.

The Pierrot Players

Although Birtwistle was always the keenest to form a music-theatre ensemble, Goehr beat him to the post when the Brighton Festival Ensemble gave its first concert on 16 April 1967, while Birtwistle's Pierrot Players had to wait until 30 May before it could give theirs. This was because Birtwistle wanted to make use of the newly opened Queen Elizabeth Hall, and had to wait for a booking. Birtwistle was the first to realise that if what he then called 'limited theatre' was to be successful it would have to be undertaken by people who were wholly committed to the genre. This excluded the Melos Ensemble, which had been his mainstay at Wardour Castle, because their main interest lay in the performance of the standard chamber music repertoire involving strings and wind. It also excluded the New Music Ensemble, whose conductor, John Carewe, had been the conductor of the student orchestra at Wardour Castle, but to everyone's surprise had shown little interest in the contemporary music being performed at the Summer School. It also excluded the newly formed Vesuvius Ensemble, whose performance of *Pierrot lunaire* at the 1965 Dartington Summer School had shown that its director, Susan Bradshaw, preferred to focus on the piece as music rather than as theatre. She had the reciter, Jane Manning, stand in modern evening dress among the instrumentalists. However, as it was Bethany Beardslee's highly theatrical performance of *Pierrot* at Wardour Castle that had generated Birtwistle's interest in 'limited theatre', it was inevitable that a new ensemble had to be created that would place theatrical performances of *Pierrot* at the centre of its activities.

The formation of the Pierrot Players was Birtwistle's idea, but the Harkness Fellowship he won in early 1966 to study in America meant that he depended on Alan Hacker and Stephen Pruslin to organise the first concert. Pruslin had delivered a lecture at Wardour Castle, and with Alan Hacker, had given the first performance of Birtwistle's *Verses* for clarinet and piano in October 1965. Having been in close contact with him they were familiar with his ideas for a music-theatre ensemble.

Pruslin, the librettist of *Punch and Judy*, came up with the name, 'The Pierrot Players', and recruited the mezzo-soprano Mary Thomas to be the singer. Hacker chose the instrumentalists, the five players needed for *Pierrot* plus, on Birtwistle's instructions, a percussionist. The flutes were to be played by Judith Pearce, the clarinets by himself, the violin and viola by Duncan Druce, the cello by Jennifer Ward Clarke, the keyboard instruments by Stephen Pruslin and the percussion by Tristan Fry. Birtwistle selected the programme, obtained a commission from the Anglo-Austrian Music Society for the work he wanted to write for the first concert, and asked Maxwell Davies to join him as joint artistic director, and to supply a curtain raiser.

The concert took place on 30 May 1967 in the newly opened Queen Elizabeth Hall, the programme consisting of: Maxwell Davies's *Antechrist*, Birtwistle's *Monodrama* and Schoenberg's *Pierrot lunaire*. In addition to Mary Thomas and the basic ensemble, an actor and an extra percussionist were needed for *Monodrama*, and two extra percussionists for *Antechrist*. Thomas's performance of Pierrot was as spectacular as Bethany Beardslee's had been at Wardour Castle and, as a result, the concert was a resounding success. It resulted in an invitation from Anne Macnaghten to repeat the Schoenberg in a Macnaghten[1] concert at the Cheltenham Festival for which new works by Birtwistle and Maxwell Davies were commissioned.

For Birtwistle, however, the first concert was a disappointment, at least as far as *Monodrama* was concerned. Although Maxwell Davies holds it in high esteem, Birtwistle never allowed it to be performed again, and has never really explained why. My own view is that the reason lay in Stephen Pruslin's libretto, which like his libretto for *Punch and Judy* was heavily reliant on puns and alliteration. These devices were admirable for the child-like atmosphere of the opera, but entirely unsuitable for a work that deals with the psychological dilemmas of an adult. They obscured rather than clarified. The music critic William Mann, in his vacillating review for *The Times* (31 May 1967), wrote: 'But even so, there remains the obfuscated mandarin style of Mr Pruslin's text, which hinders the communicability of Birtwistle's music and makes it seem more pretentious and vacuous than, on one attentive hearing, it promises to be.'

Neither of the works Birtwistle and Davies composed for the Macnaghten concert in the Town Hall, Cheltenham on 17 July 1967 was theatrical, except that Maxwell Davies's *Hymnos* for clarinet and piano was certainly highly dramatic in its virtuosity. This was a piece in which Alan Hacker could shine, while Birtwistle's *Three Lessons in a Frame* allowed Pruslin's piano playing to stand out. In it Birtwistle attempted to find a way of writing for the Pierrot Players that would satisfy his need to pit a soloist against an ensemble, then reconcile the two elements. The first lesson is for piano alone, the second for the other five instrumentalists as an ensemble. Essentially, the second lesson complements the first in that what is implicit in the first can be found in the second fully realised. The function of the third lesson is to interlock the material in the first and second so that that they make a perfect fit. Even so, Birtwistle was unhappy with the piece, and as with *Monodrama*, he withdrew it from his catalogue.

---

[1] Anne Macnaghten (1908–2008), violinist and teacher, founded the Macnaghten concerts in 1931 with the composer Elisabeth Lutyens and the conductor Iris Lemare, to champion the works of young, unknown contemporary composers.

Although he continued to write pieces for the Pierrot Players, apart from *Cantata* (1969), he did not write a work of any substance for the group that satisfied him. To pursue his interest in music and Instrumental Theatre he had to make use of other ensembles: Goehr's Music Theatre Ensemble, the London Sinfonietta and Matrix, an ensemble for soprano, three clarinets, piano and percussion, which Alan Hacker was to form in 1970. This meant that, for Music Theatre, the activities of the Pierrot Players were left in the hands of Maxwell Davies. Significantly, when Macnaghten Concerts asked the ensemble to play at London's Conway Hall on 26 February 1968, the first part of the programme was devoted exclusively to two pieces by Maxwell Davies: *Revelation and Fall* for soprano and fifteen instruments, and *Missa super L'homme armé*, which included the recorded voice of a boy reciting passages of St Luke's Gospel. *Revelation and Fall* had been completed two years earlier in 1966, and was Maxwell Davies's response to hearing Bethany Beardslee perform *Pierrot lunaire* at Wardour Castle. However, *Revelation and Fall* is not a sequence of melodramas but a scena lasting half an hour, which takes expressionism and the virtuosity of the soloist to extremes.

Missa super L'homme armé deals with betrayal, a topic that had been preoccupying Maxwell Davies ever since he had embarked on his opera *Taverner* in 1956. The passages the boy recites concern Judas's acceptance of bribes, Peter's denial and the reference to betrayal at the Last Supper. But Maxwell Davies's main means of dealing with betrayal is through music rather than words. The basis of his technique since the mid-fifties had been the use of parody: parody in the musical sense of the Parody Mass[2] in that he borrowed material from sources other than his own, often a short piece of plainsong. From this he would build a whole edifice, his purpose being to gradually transform it into something else. But when the transformation mocks the original, Parody Mass becomes general parody, a travesty of the original. *Antechrist* took a thirteenth-century motet and transformed into a state where the mocking *diabolus in musica*[3] was the inevitable outcome. *Missa super L'homme armé* is the gradual transformation of the Agnus Dei from an unfinished fifteenth-century *L' homme armé* Mass into a foxtrot.

Three years later he revised the work, replacing the recorded boy's voice with an actor – if a man, dressed as a nun, or if a woman, as a monk – who makes a dramatic entrance through the audience, delivers the text and then, pointing to the audience, repeats the word 'tradetur' while foxtrotting off. Clearly

---

[2] Popular in the sixteenth century, this was a mass with the text added to music borrowed from an existing composition.

[3] The Tritone is an interval consisting of three whole tones. Since the Middle Ages, when it was prohibited and given its nickname the 'Devil's chord', it has been associated with dissonance.

by then Maxwell Davies had realised the importance of visual gestures in Music
Theatre.

The opportunity to compose a work that would be not only visually and aurally
startling but also much more theatrical came two months later when Randolph
Stow introduced him to Sir Steven Runciman, who showed him the small mechanical hand-organ King George III, the so-called 'mad king', had used to teach his
pet bullfinches to sing. With a text provided by Stow and the extraordinary voice
of the South African baritone Roy Hart, Maxwell Davies produced a piece that
created a sensation when it was performed on 22 April 1969 and proved to be
the work usually referred to by musicologists as being the most representative of
British Music Theatre.[4]

But *Eight Songs for a Mad King* was not the only music-theatre work Maxwell
Davies composed in 1969. On 9 December *Vesalii Icones* was performed in the
Queen Elizabeth Hall. This was a set of fourteen dances based on the sixteenth-
century drawings showing the structure of the human body by Andreas Vesalius[5]
on to which Maxwell Davies had superimposed the fourteen Stations of the Cross.
In the event it was as sensational as the *Eight Songs*, for to be true to Vesalius
the dancer had to be well-nigh naked. In the last dance, the Resurrection, the
Christ-story is modified so that it is the Antichrist who emerges from the tomb, a
situation the audience might have predicted from the amount of mocking parody
contained in the score. However, as far as Music Theatre is concerned, the most
significant feature of the work is the relationship between physical and musical
gesture. Unlike *Revelation and Fall*, where the singer has to invent gestures
suggested by the words and music alone, the gestures in *Vesalii Icones* can be
invented within a framework that contains, as well as music, clear visual images
(the Vesalius drawings) and a familiar dramatic progression (the Stations of the
Cross). At the first performance it was a framework that the black American
dancer William Louther exploited to the full.

When Birtwistle and Maxwell Davies were asked to teach a two-week advanced
composers' course on Music Theatre at the 1970 Dartington Summer School of
Music, they both elected to make the relationship between aural and physical
gesture their main concern. Their model was a performance of *Vesalii Icones* that
William Louther and the Pierrot Players had given at the School on 10 August

---

[4] William Mann, writing in *The Times* (23 April 1969), concluded his review of the piece:
'The piece is meant to have a nerve-wracking effect, and does so. It also discloses many
disturbing, moving facets of musical expression. And Mr Hart's performance is truly
extraordinary.'

[5] Andreas Vesalius (1514–64) was a Flemish-born anatomist whose dissections of the
human body helped to correct the ideas about the human form that dated from ancient
times.

along with Maxwell Davies's arrangement of a piece that made an ironic prelude to it: Buxtehude's cantata, *Also hat Gott die Welt geliebt.*[6] To assist their teaching they had the services of two mimes: Mark Furneaux and, for a shorter period, Photes Constantinedes. Among their students were Bruce Cole, George Brown, Erika Fox, Bradley Giles, James Ingram and Nicola LeFanu. Their most memorable exercise was provided by Birtwistle, who asked them to compose pieces based on two parallel lines he had drawn on a blackboard. They were told that the relationship between aural and physical gesture was stronger if it was based on contrast rather than similarity.

The following year Birtwistle taught this music-theatre course by himself. On this occasion, Oliver Knussen and Dominic Muldowney were among his students. The reason Maxwell Davies had dropped out was because a serious rift had developed between the two composers. In 1968 when the Players were in dire need for someone to look after their affairs, Maxwell Davies recruited James Murdoch,[7] an Australian entrepreneur and impresario, to fulfil the task. They had met when Maxwell Davies had been teaching at Adelaide University, and Murdoch had been putting on concerts of Maxwell Davies's music in Melbourne.

Murdoch, who had a flair for publicity and who arranged for the Players to give concerts abroad, was undoubtedly successful in his job. But for the Players to succeed, they needed works that created a sensation and could draw in the crowds. This is what Maxwell Davies could produce for Murdoch, as *Eight Songs for a Mad King* and *Vesalii Icones* show. Murdoch therefore put all his money on Maxwell Davies and engineered circumstances that undermined Birtwistle's position. According to Alan Hacker, the crunch came when the Players were in Italy during the early winter of 1970. Murdoch deliberately did not tell Birtwistle about a reception being held in their honour. When Birtwistle heard about it he was so affronted that he packed his bags and took the first plane home. Ever since they were students together in Manchester he and Maxwell Davies had been friends, and Birtwistle claimed he had learned more from Maxwell Davies than anyone else. Now his friend, who was so obsessed with betrayal, seemed to have become a betrayer himself. 'Why could Max let it happen?' was what he repeatedly asked Hacker.

But of course there are always two sides to a conflict. Murdoch's view was that Birtwistle was not providing enough material for the Pierrot Players to perform.

---

[6] Dieterich Buxtehude (1637–1707), Solo Cantata no. 5 for soprano, two violins, viola da gamba/violoncello, basso continuo.

[7] James Murdoch (1930–2010), musician, arts administrator, author and consultant. James Murdoch was born in Sydney. He was a pianist and musical director before moving to London in 1968 as director of James Murdoch Management Pty Ltd, managing musicians, composers, singers, dancers and choreographers.

'As manager of the Pierrot Players, I had a product to sell,' he told biographer, Mike Seabrook. 'Max supplied that product. Harry dried up. I had nothing of Harry to sell … We were a Music Theatre group – the best – and needed Music Theatre works. Harry didn't write any … Simple!'[8]

The Pierrot Players were taken over by Maxwell Davies, who on the recommendation of Stephen Pruslin, changed the ensemble's name to The Fires of London. Critic William Mann, commenting on the new ensemble after its first performance in December 1970, wrote in *The Times*: 'The whole concert brought us a larger complement of performers than the compact septet of the Pierrot Players. It remains to be discovered whether The Fires of London will consist basically of their old complement or, even for touring purposes, expand their membership.'[9]

Thereafter Maxwell Davies composed two Music Theatre works: *Blind Man's Buff* for the BBC in 1972, and two years later, *Miss Donnithorne's Maggot* for Mary Thomas and The Fires of London, which they performed at a concert in Adelaide on 9 March 1974. Significantly, perhaps, the topic of betrayal was dropped in favour of another piece about madness. Here it was the madness of a woman who had been jilted on her wedding day and who, like Miss Havisham in *Great Expectations*, had remained in her house for the rest of her life without disturbing her wedding reception preparations. As in his previous music-theatre pieces, Davies makes extensive use of parody, except that now Victorian salon music became the object of his satire. By 1974 most of the original members of the Pierrot Players had left. The ensemble continued for more than a decade but failed to generate the excitement it had done in its early days. The group was disbanded by Maxwell Davies after its twentieth anniversary concert in 1987. Maxwell Davies's works are discussed in Chapters Seven and Twelve.

The Music Theatre Ensemble

The Music Theatre Ensemble had its roots in the Brighton Festival Ensemble, which Alexander Goehr, with the help of Alan Hacker, established for three concerts featuring music-theatre works at the first Brighton Festival between 14 and 30 April 1967. Goehr played a prominent role in the first festival. In addition to organising the three concerts by the Festival Ensemble and advising Ian Hunter, the festival's founder and Artistic Director, on programme building for some of the other concerts, he was also the vice-chairman of a music conference that met

---

[8] Mike Seabrook, *Max: The Life and Music of Peter Maxwell Davies* (London, Victor Gollancz, 1994), 121.

[9] *The Times*, 14 December 1970.

three times to discuss 'Developments in the Arts during the next Twenty-Five Years'.

When the festival was being planned, Goehr knew that Birtwistle was going to name his ensemble the Pierrot Players, therefore the one music-theatre work he admired above all, Schoenberg's *Pierrot lunaire*, was not included in the programmes he devised; this he left to Birtwistle. Instead he persuaded Ian Hunter to have it performed by the Vesuvius Ensemble along with a Suite from Stravinsky's *The Soldier's Tale* at a concert in the Royal Pavilion on 25 April. The Vesuvius Ensemble had first given *Pierrot* at the request of William Glock at the 1965 Dartington Summer School when Bethany Beardslee and the Melos Ensemble were performing it at the Wardour Castle Summer School. Susan Bradshaw, the pianist and director of the Vesuvius Ensemble, had insisted that Schoenberg's music should not be overshadowed by histrionics, so that, as mentioned above, Jane Manning, the reciter, did not don a costume or act as Bethany Beardslee was doing, or Mary Thomas was to do later; she stood among the instrumentalists as if she were one of them. Susan Bradshaw's decision won the full approval of Schoenberg aficionados such as Goehr and Hans Keller,[10] who later, for a European Broadcasting Union concert on the BBC, had the Vesuvius Ensemble perform the work twice, first without the reciter and then with her.

The Brighton Festival Ensemble, even though it varied in size from concert to concert, was a larger unit than either the Vesuvius Ensemble or the Pierrot Players. This meant that, as well as *The Soldier's Tale* and *Pierrot lunaire*, Goehr could include other works by the predecessors of Music Theatre such as Satie's *Le piège de Méduse* and Weill's *Mahagonny Songspiel* in the festival. These provided a background for the other dramatic music he wanted to present, which were a cross-section of what was being produced in America, Russia and Britain. America was represented in an early piece by Cage and a new work by the percussionist Michael Colgrass; Russia in a recent symphony by Boris Tischenko, a one-time pupil of Shostakovich, and a work by Edison Denisov, *The Son of the Incas*, which had recently caused a storm in Russia; Britain in pieces by Birtwistle and Maxwell Davies dating from 1964–5, and a specially commissioned work, *Brighton Piece*, by Anthony Gilbert.

The first concert took place on Sunday 16 April, and included Webern's Concerto for Nine Instruments, Tischenko's Third Symphony and Colgrass's dramatic work, *Virgil's Dream*. Goehr had hoped that between the Tischenko and Colgrass would be a work that he himself would have composed for the festival, but because he had been busy attending rehearsals for his opera *Arden muss Sterben*, which received its first performance in Hamburg on 5 March, he

---

[10] Hans Keller (1919–85) was an Austrian-born British musician and writer.

had not had the time to realise his plan. The inclusion of Tischenko's Symphony was strange given that Goehr was not a supporter of Shostakovich or his school. But the work was a meditation on Anna Akhmatova's *Requiem*, a cycle of poems about the Stalinist terror in the thirties, and Goehr was deeply sympathetic to texts 'which speak of a human condition within hostile or destructive environments'. Colgrass's *Virgil's Dream* provided a complete contrast to this, for, in the score, Colgrass described it as being 'a satiric fantasy for confused mezzo, naive tenor, hysterical tenor, and conservative bass-baritone'. But this was not the end of what Goehr and Ian Hunter had to offer lovers of contemporary music that Sunday afternoon. Immediately after this concert came the second of two lectures by Goehr's one-time teacher, Olivier Messiaen, on 'The Use of Birdsong in Music'.

The second concert took place on the following Saturday evening, when the programme was Satie's *Le piège de Méduse*, Maxwell Davies's *Shakespeare Music*, Anthony Gilbert's *Brighton Piece* and Weill's *Mahagonny Songspiel*. Both the Satie and the Weill were staged. The Satie was produced by Walter Eysselinck, the Weill by David Drew, and both were first performances in Britain. Gilbert says that he knew what the programme would be before he began composing *Brighton Piece*, and that he was led to believe he could make use of the services of Michael Colgrass, 'who could play anything' and who wanted a show case for his virtuosity as a percussionist. But because he was an American, and had not been billed as a soloist, the Musicians' Union forbade Colgrass to take part in the work, so Gilbert had to rewrite the part for two English players. In the event a third had to be employed to help cope with the difficulties.

The last concert the Brighton Festival Ensemble performed at this Brighton Festival took place on Saturday 29 April. In consisted of Birtwistle's *Ring a Dumb Carillon*, Cage's Sonata for clarinet solo (1933), a second performance of Weill's *Mahagonny Songspiel* and the first performance in Britain of Edison Denisov's cantata, *The Son of the Incas*. This was a setting for soprano and ten instrumentalists of poems by the French Provençal poet Frédéric Mistral, which Denisov had dedicated to Boulez, and which had given rise to a storm of abuse from the Russian authorities when first performed in Leningrad three years earlier. Goehr included it because it was one of the first Russian works to embrace Western avant-garde techniques, and had therefore created great interest in British music circles.

In 1968 the Brighton Festival Ensemble became the Music Theatre Ensemble because Ian Hunter had also become the Artistic Director of the newly initiated City of London Festival, and it was felt that the ensemble he and Goehr had founded should not be tied to one particular place. For the Brighton Festival Goehr composed a Romanza for cello and orchestra for Jacqueline du Pré, while for the London Festival he completed *Naboth's Vineyard*, the music-theatre piece he had intended to compose the previous year. Had it been ready for the 1967 Brighton Festival he would have been able to complete the festival's references to five of the seven predecessors of Music Theatre: Monteverdi, Schoenberg, Stravinsky, Satie and Weill. *Naboth's Vineyard* would also have had relevance to Tischenko's Symphony, because the story of Naboth's unjust trial and summary execution mirrors the events in Stalinist Russia that Anna Akhmatova describes. It would have made visible what Tischenko was meditating on, and it would also have shown, through God's condemnation of Jezebel, that justice will ultimately prevail.

For the 1969 Brighton Festival Goehr composed a *Konzertstück* for Daniel Barenboim and the English Chamber Orchestra. He gave Birtwistle the task of composing a piece for the Music Theatre Ensemble. It was just the opportunity Birtwistle had been waiting for because he now had larger forces than the Pierrot Players at his disposal. For his librettist he chose Michael Nyman, and between them they devised *Down by the Greenwood Side*, a work, which, as I mentioned earlier, combined the traditional Mummers' Play with versions of the ballad of 'The Cruel Mother'.

Following *Shadowplay*, the music-theatre piece he composed for the 1970 City of London Festival, Goehr completed his triptych of music-theatre works with *Sonata about Jerusalem*, which was first performed in Tel Aviv in January 1971. When Goehr conducted the triptych at the 1971 Brighton Festival, the Music Theatre Ensemble was coming to the end of its existence. After teaching in America between 1968 and 1970, he became a visiting lecturer at Southampton University; then in 1971 he was appointed Professor of Music at Leeds University. Goehr and I also had plans to have the Music Theatre Ensemble perform Eisler's *Die Massnahme* on the radio, but the executors of Brecht's estate refused to give their permission. We presumed that they thought the work would still be considered too outspoken.

Focus Opera

The Focus Opera Group was founded in 1963 by Michael Sargent, a young school-teacher, who wanted to present new, unusual or little-known small-scale operas using singers who had just completed their training, and instrumentalist who were either young professionals or highly skilled amateurs. His first productions were given as a fringe event at the 1963 Edinburgh Festival, and consisted of two works that would have been relatively familiar at the time: Menotti's *The Telephone* and Holst's *Savitri*, as well as the first British performance of the American composer, Jack Beeson's *Hallo Out There*.

Between then and November 1967, the Group presented nine different programmes mounted either in the University of London Senate House or in the theatre of the London Academy of Music and Dramatic Art. They were mainly double or triple bills of works which, with the exception of Monteverdi's *Il combattimento* and Stravinsky's *Soldier's Tale*, were in styles associated with traditional opera. But when, in 1967, Michael Graubart took over the conducting duties for a performance of Mozart's *La finta giardiniera*, his enthusiasm for experimental forms of opera and, indeed, for experimental music in general persuaded Michael Sargent to change tack. In the International Students' House on 11 and 12 March 1968, Focus Opera presented a programme that brought into question the nature of opera itself. The first two works – Ligeti's *Aventures et Nouvelles aventures* for soprano, contralto, baritone and seven instrumentalists (1962–5), and Kagel's *Sur scène* for speaker, singer, mime and three instrumentalists (1960) – were receiving their first performances in Britain; the third, Cornelius Cardew's *Schooltime Compositions*, had been specially commissioned for the occasion.

As the term Music Theatre was not then in general use, Focus Opera advertised the programme as 'Three? Avant-Garde? Operas?' Although for Ligeti *Aventures et Nouvelles aventures* were a kind of opera, the two pieces that make up the work are actually a parody of opera. Ligeti took as his starting point the difficulty an audience has in hearing the words in opera. Therefore his texts consist of sounds that amount to semantic nonsense. 'I put together a kind of "scenario"', he said, 'by joining five areas of emotions: humour, ghostly-horror, sentimental, mystical-funereal and erotic. All five areas are present throughout, and switch from one to the other so abruptly and quickly that there is a virtual simultaneity.'[11] There is no story other than the hint that the three singers may be involved in a love triangle. In 1966 Ligeti devised a stage scenario for the work, but in the version Focus Opera mounted, the three singers (Gillian Walker, Meriel Dickinson and Alan Reddish) stood in a line as if giving a concert version of an opera.

Kagel's *Sur scène* is a parody of what tends to happen at concerts of contemporary music. It is called 'Theatrical Chamber Music Work in One Act', and throughout the piece the speaker delivers a long-winded, seemingly erudite but basically nonsensical discourse about contemporary music as a whole rather than just an introduction to a work that is about to be performed. Meanwhile the singer, mime and instrumentalists practise pre-performance warming-up exercises. They even rehearse the bows and gestures they will take and make before, during and after the performance.

Cornelius Cardew also set out to be deliberately absurd when he composed *Schooltime Compositions*. For him opera meant 'many people working'.[12] As a

[11] Griffiths, *Gyorgy Ligeti*, 44.
[12] Desmond Shawe-Taylor, 'How Many Ping-Pong Balls Make an Opera?', *Sunday Times*, 17 March 1968.

disciple of John Cage, whose music he encountered when helping Stockhausen compose *Carré* in 1959 and 1960, his model was the Black Mountain College 'Happening' of 1952, when Cage asked friends and colleagues at the college to present 'their own thing' while various films, slides and gramophone records were being shown or played at the same time. To ensure that their activities would overlap, each person was told when to start and how long their activities should last. In *Schooltime Compositions*, the performers also 'do their own thing' in the way they perform the exercises contained in a school exercise book they are given. One exercise tests their ability to make use of the words 'loyal, honest, lovely, good, nice, pretty, friendly, graceful, kind' written on the white notes of a keyboard. Another contains nine rising phrases with the instruction: 'play each phrase to make the preceding phrase seem as though it had been played by a child' written in a corner.

Those taking part included Lou Gare and Keith Rowe (who were colleagues of Cardew in the improvisation group known as AMM), John Tilbury, his friend and piano-duet partner for many years, Christian Wolff, an American 'experimental' composer, while others, such as Eric Brown, Robin Page and John Pitchford, were either friends or his students at the Royal Academy of Music, where Cardew taught composition.

None of the music critics who attended the first evening returned for the second performance the following day. Most confessed to being bored (the performance of *Sur scène* in which Michael Sargent was the spoof musicologist lasted fifty minutes), but nevertheless all were prepared to devote a great many column inches to discussing the event. Their main criticism was that what they had seen were not operas, or if they were they were Neo-Dada specimens. John Warrack's headline in *The Sunday Telegraph* was 'Da-da goes Ga-ga'.[13] Stanley Sadie (*The Times*, 12 March 1968) concluded, 'In a mild way it was faintly amusing; but I should hate to think that anything so poverty-stricken is artistic progress.' Their comments made it clear that not only were the London critics unfamiliar with what was happening in musical circles in America and in Europe, they were also unable to see the parallels with the absurdist drama being performed in theatres on their doorstep. The piece is further discussed in Chapter Eight.

The programmes that Focus Opera mounted in January and April 1969 were much more conservative. The main ingredients were Satie's *Socrate*, David Rowland's *Postil* and Cimarosa's *Il matrimonio segreto*. In 1969 Michael Graubart became the Director of Music at Morley College, the principal further education institution in London. He asked Cardew to tutor a composition class there, and in 1970 he initiated a music-theatre group with Michael Sargent as tutor. During 1970–1, Focus Opera shifted its attention to what young composers outside Britain

[13] *The Sunday Telegraph*, 17 March 1968.

were doing. On three successive evenings in June 1970, Sargent and Graubart presented Bent Lorentzen's *Music-Theatre for Three*, Toshiro Mayuzumi's *Campanology* and Franco Evangelisti's *Die Schachtel*. Then the following March, as well as Monteverdi's *Il combattimento* and Robin Orr's *Full Circle*, a one-act opera from the thirties, they introduced London to Mogens Winkel Holm's *Sonata for Four Opera Singers*, a macabre dream sequence in which three anonymous travellers arrive at a lonely inn, where a waitress in a desperate attempt to amuse them starts a series of animal games and is murdered. The sonata form is completed by the travellers returning to their everyday lives and continuing their journey as if nothing had happened. The piece was highly praised by the critics, one of whom, Hugo Cole, writing in *The Guardian*, compared it favourably 'to the prolonged improvisatory charades by Ligeti, Kagel and Cardew put on by the group three years ago'.[14]

Focus Opera, however, had not finished with Kagel's *Sur scène*, for in their next show on 29 and 30 June and 1 July 1972 they performed it again, but this time in the second half of the programme, the first half being devoted to Birtwistle's *Down by the Greenwood Side* and *Anti-World*, a new work by Nicola LeFanu (discussed in more detail in Chapter Eight), who had been on the Music Theatre course given by Birtwistle and Maxwell Davies at Dartington in 1970. She tells me that the piece she composed on that course was a dry-run for *Anti-World*. Within a year of joining the Morley College Music Theatre Group in 1970, she began to take an active role in organising the improvisation exercises considered necessary for the integration of the group.

The purpose of these exercises was to develop what Birtwistle and Maxwell Davies had been concerned with at Dartington, namely the relationship between the aural and the visual, musical gestures and physical gestures. The catalyst for *Anti-World*, however, was purely visual. It was a scene in Jacques Tati's film *Trafic*, where a large showroom is being prepared for an exhibition of cars. Instead of marking out the areas designated for each car with white lines, the compartments were divided off from each other by wires placed about a foot above the ground. This meant that everybody working in the showroom had to step over the wires, but as the wires were invisible to the onlooker it looked as if the workers were constantly confronting barriers that only they were aware of. *Anti-World* is therefore about invisible barriers, a situation LeFanu explores with a dancer, two singers, three instrumentalists and poems by Russian dissident writers attempting to surmount invisible political barriers.

The programme was the third Focus Opera gave in the Cockpit Theatre, a small theatre-in-the-round owned by the Inner London Education Authority. But this

---

[14] *The Guardian*, 27 June 1970.

location had to be abandoned when Focus Opera became more closely associated with Morley College in the autumn of 1972. The performers in their next production in December 1972 were all members of Morley groups: the Morley College Music Theatre Group, Graubart's Musica Viva ensemble and dancers from the Creative Dance Group. Nicola LeFanu became tutor of the Music Theatre Group, and just as she had directed and conducted the performance of *Anti-World* in the production in June and July, she also directed and conducted a work in this. The programme consisted of Stravinsky's *Renard*, Jeremy Dale Roberts's *Reconciliation*, involving two poems by the American poet Philip Oxman, and Melanie Daiken's *Mayakovsky and the Sun*, based on seven poems by the Russian Futurist poet who committed suicide in 1930.

Mayakovsky and the Sun had first been performed at a concert in the Edinburgh Festival's Fringe the previous August. It was scored for spoken voice, singers, chorus, mime and an instrumental ensemble, which was replaced by two pianos at the first London performance. Mayakovsky, one of the leading poets of the Russian Revolution in 1917, was the principal advocate of Russian Futurism, a movement that lasted until Lenin condemned it in 1923. The purpose of Daiken's work was to have translations of seven of Mayakovsky's poems presented in a context representing the tenets of Futurism, the poems being linked by Mayakovsky's references to the sun in each of them. To this end she had sets constructed in the experimental, non-realistic style of Meyerhold, and music which represented the Italian Futurist Luigi Rossolo's belief that music should 'seek those combinations of sounds that fall most dissonantly, strangely and harshly on the ear'. However, the range of Mayakovsky's poetry was so large and frequently so dramatic that Daiken's music had to take second place to the self-assurance and rhetoric of the spoken word. Nevertheless her choice of Mayakovsky's verse enabled her to convey his perpetual concern with impossible fate and impossible love, and the tensions that led to his untimely death.

Focus Opera, in association with the Morley College Music Theatre Group, continued to exist until 1975, when Michael Sargent took a theatrical post outside London. Among the music-theatre works performed in its final years were Goehr's *Naboth's Vineyard* and *Shadowplay*, Cage's *Theatre Piece* and Francis Shaw's *The Metamorphosis of Narcissus*.

The London Sinfonietta

The Sinfonietta, founded by Nicholas Snowman and David Atherton, gave its first concert on 24 January 1968. Atherton and Snowman had recently been at Cambridge together, and wanted respectively to conduct and administer an ensemble that would present contemporary music imaginatively and to the highest standards. Its aim to concentrate on twentieth-century music was welcomed by Stephen Walsh, writing in *The Observer*:[15] 'its object, thank goodness, is not to churn out still more of those interminable eighteenth-century concerts that plague our smaller halls. Instead it will concentrate on twentieth-century music, its composition being fluid enough to cope with all but the most wayward of modern scores.'

The programme consisted of Henze's cantata *Apollo et Hyazinthus* (1949) for mezzo-soprano and a small ensemble of eight players including harpsichord; the first performance of John Tavener's dramatic cantata *The Whale* (1965–6) for mezzo-soprano, baritone, narrator, six male actors with loudhailers, chorus, childrens' chorus, orchestra, organ and electric organ, and, in the second half, Richard Strauss's Symphony for Wind (1944–5). The number of performers involved indicates that in its early days it was not the basic fourteen-piece ensemble it was later to become in the mid-seventies but an ensemble that varied its size according to the works Atherton and Snowman wanted to perform.

The Whale created a sensation. It had been composed before Music Theatre had become established, and performed before Maxwell Davies's *Revelation and Fall* and *Missa super L'homme armé* had been performed by the Pierrot Players and before Focus Opera had given those music-theatre works by Ligeti, Kagel and Cardew, and Goehr had presented *Naboth's Vineyard* at the City of London Festival. The audience was therefore unprepared and taken aback by its theatricality. Stanley Sadie, writing in *The Times*, described it as 'one of the most exciting works by a young composer I can remember hearing'.[16] It contained no visual dimension, but its progression from a matter-of-fact description of the whale to the highly dramatic storm scene, Jonah's descent into the whale's belly and the equally surreal vomiting of him on to the sand, proved to be so arresting that Atherton and Snowman had no difficulty in persuading the Calouste Gulbenkian Foundation to assist them in commissioning from Tavener what turned out to be genuine Music Theatre on an equally large scale for July 1969: *Celtic Requiem*.

The Sinfonietta had already demonstrated its interest in Music Theatre in the concert they devised for 18 February 1969. This contained Penderecki's *Strophes* (1959) and Gordon Crosse's *Concerto da camera* (1962) in the first half, and Schoenberg's *Pierrot lunaire* in the second. Their inclusion of *Pierrot* was not intended to spite the Pierrot Players, it was because *Strophes* had been highly acclaimed on the continent nine years earlier, and contained a part for a speaker using *Sprechstimme*. The work is a little cantata consisting of eight miniatures with texts drawn from Menander, Sophocles, Isaiah, Jeremiah and Omar Khayyám,

---

[15] *The Observer*, 28 January 1968.
[16] *The Times*, 25 January 1968.

which must be performed in their original languages: Greek, Hebrew and Persian. The *Sprechstimme* is rhythmically fixed, but unlike *Pierrot* only some of the pitch intervals are stipulated. To balance *Pierrot* in length, the Sinfonietta performed *Strophes* twice.

In the five years between January 1968 and November 1973, when the Sinfonietta performed all the instrumental and chamber music of Schoenberg and Roberto Gerhard over a four-week period, it presented nearly all the music-theatre pieces produced by the predecessors of the genre, most of them staged. As well as at least two performances of *Pierrot*, it performed *Il combattimento di Tancredi e Clorinda*, Stravinsky's *Renard* and *The Soldier's Tale*, Satie's *Le piège de Méduse*, Ives's instrumental theatre piece *The Unanswered Question* and two works by the Brecht/Weill partnership, the *Mahagonny Songspiel* and *Der Jasager*, a didactic 'school opera' composed shortly after *Das Badener Lehrstück*.

The Sinfonietta's performances of *Il combattimento* were all directed by Luciano Berio and given in his own arrangement of the work for modern instruments. In an Invitation Concert at the BBC it was presented with Berio's *Laborintus II*, a prime example of Berio's 'theatre of the imagination'. It was also performed by the Sinfonietta in Italy in 1970. On this occasion the programme included the first European performance of Berio's *Melodrama*, one of the autonomous episodes in his opera, *Opera*, which on the concert platform becomes Music Theatre. It concerns a tenor who is past his best and having trouble with his top G. As he nervously prepares to perform a Heine setting, he remonstrates against himself with a barrage of Anglo-American clichés only to discover that in the event he can actually reach top A. His struggle is reminiscent of the trombone player in *Sequenza V*. But Berio's preoccupation with performance neuroses reaches its zenith in *Recital I (for Cathy)*, which Cathy Berberian accompanied by the London Sinfonietta, performed for the first time in Lisbon in 1972.

The Sinfonietta gave five concerts in 1968, four in the Queen Elizabeth Hall, the main venue for its concerts, and one in the Purcell Room for the first performance of David Bedford's *Pentomino*, a work it had commissioned using its own financial resources. Thereafter, having established itself on the London scene, it was able to draw on finance supplied by the London Orchestral Concert Board representing the Arts Council. Its first concert, on 12 February 1969, included the first performance of another work it had commissioned, Birtwistle's *Verses for Ensembles*.

Tavener's *Celtic Requiem* followed five months later on 16 July 1969. For this the London Sinfonietta had to hire the Royal Festival Hall. A year later, however, when they performed it a second time, they managed to squeeze the performers into the much smaller Queen Elizabeth Hall. This concert took place on 19 September 1970, and they devoted the first half to two representatives of

Crossover: Don Banks's *Meeting Place*, in which an electronic synthesiser acts as a mediator between a 'classical' ensemble and a jazz group, and David Bedford's *The Garden of Love*, in which the two groups are a classical ensemble and a pop group. Bedford's score also includes 'six beautiful girls for dancing and turning pages'. With these he created a semblance of Music Theatre, for to be in line with other pop concerts at the time he needed a visual dimension. At the climax of the work, when the groups unite, and the pop group sings a setting of William Blake's poem 'The Garden of Love', the audience is invited to join the girls as they dance on the platform and in the auditorium. In this context, the *Celtic Requiem* could also be considered a crossover piece, high art being represented by the Requiem Mass, Cardinal Newman's hymn, and the Henry Vaughan and Irish settings, and popular art by the children's songs, with the two being united by the ever-present chord of E♭ major.

The Sinfonietta performed nine works by Tavener in its early years, including seven first performances, the last being *Canciones españolas*, which it commissioned for a concert in 1972. Its association with Birtwistle, on the other hand, has been more or less continuous since *Verses for Ensembles*. In the twenty-five years between 1971 and 1996 it gave the first performances of fifteen of his works, including *Secret Theatre*, the work the Sinfonietta commissioned from him for his fiftieth birthday in 1984. In this the relationship between soloists and ensemble is given a new twist. He calls the music the soloists play the cantus, and the music given to the accompanying instruments the continuum. The theatrical aspect of the piece is not just the movement of the players to and from the continuum and cantus positions, it also involves a drama which has its origins in the role-playing taking place in the background. At first this is mainly confined to the flute, whose lyricism 'leads the dance' and has a calming influence over the buffoon-like trombone and the plaintive bassoon, but during the course of the piece these characteristics are gradually transferred from single instruments to groups of instruments, and it is the dramatic interplay between these groups that takes the music to its climax.

The BBC Symphony Orchestra

Between 1959 and 1973, when William Glock[17] was Controller of Music, the BBC's music programmes were the most adventurous in its history. Glock's criterion was that programmes had to be 'vital', they had to include items that could throw new light on each other even though they seemed to be totally incongruous. He first established his reputation as a programme builder when he initiated the Thursday

---

[17] William Glock (1908–2000), Controller of Music for the BBC from 1959 to 1972. From 1960 to 1973, he was also Controller of the Proms.

Invitation Concerts on the Third Programme in January 1960. In the first two, string quintets by Mozart framed Boulez's *Le marteau sans maître*; the second juxtaposed Janáček's *The Diary of a Man who Disappeared* and Berg's Chamber Concerto. One concert had Machaut's *Messe de Nostre Dame* at its centre, Boulez's two *Improvisations sur Mallarmé* on either side of it, and motets by Byrd to begin and end the programme. And for the fourteenth, on 19 April, he placed a concert performance of *Pierrot lunaire* next to Bach's Goldberg Variations.

Although Music Theatre was not ideally suited for radio, most of the works by the predecessors of the genre were broadcast when Music Theatre became fashionable between 1967 and 1974. Glock even arranged to have Kurt Weill's *The Flight of Lindbergh* performed by members of the BBC Symphony Orchestra and Chorus under Colin Davis at one of the 1970 Proms. After establishing the Invitation Concerts, Glock gave most of his attention to the BBC Symphony Orchestra and the Proms. He allowed the regional orchestras to go their own way. Once the standard of the orchestra's playing had improved under Antal Doráti, the Chief Conductor between 1962 and 1966, he engaged first Colin Davis (1967–71) and then Pierre Boulez (1971–4), and with these conductors the programmes became as enterprising as the Invitation Concerts. The one Boulez helped Glock construct for his first appearance as a guest conductor in 1964, for example, consisted in the first half of Boulez's *Le soleil des eaux*, Stravinsky's Symphonies of wind instruments, Webern's arrangement of Bach's six-part *Ricercare*, and Mozart's C minor Adagio and Fugue, and in the second half Debussy's *Images*.

When Boulez became Chief Conductor in 1971, he devised most of the programmes himself. Interviewed by Peter Heyworth for *The Observer*,[18] he said that he had planned a series of 'retrospective' concerts consisting of music by Haydn and Stravinsky, which half the orchestra would perform in St John's, Smith Square, and a series of 'prospective' concerts designed for the Roundhouse, which would be given by the other half of the orchestra. Here the accent would be on discovery of new works, new media, new composers, new ways of expression. The Roundhouse, a former railway-engine turntable shed in Chalk Farm, was converted into an arts centre by the London County Council in 1966. At first mostly pop groups hired it, but it soon became the venue for other types of experimental events. Peter Brook presented his experimental workshop production of *The Tempest* there in 1968, and the following year Living Theatre from New York hired it for *Frankenstein*. When the BBC's Roundhouse concerts got under way, Boulez insisted that his players should abandon their white ties and tails.

At first the Roundhouse concerts were grouped in pairs, the last item in the second being a specimen of Music Theatre. But when Boulez's choice of items

---

[18] *The Observer*, 3 October 1971.

became increasingly more unsuitable for radio, the BBC had to ensure that the chosen works would be comprehensible to listeners, even though they had not heard the introductory announcements explaining the piece.

The BBC first made use of it on 6 September 1971, when it transferred to the Roundhouse a Prom originally intended for the Royal Albert Hall. The highlight was a music-theatre piece that Glock commissioned from George Newson. Not only was it a new work by a relatively new composer, it was also a new type of Music Theatre expressing things that were entirely up to the minute. Newson called it *Arena* because the Royal Albert Hall was an arena for a cross-section of public events. His model was the old-fashioned music hall with a master of ceremonies to comment on current events, and to introduce the orchestra, the conductor and the singers each of whom would have their 'turn'. The King's Singers presented a 'Black Magnificat' about people in the public arena constantly vying with each other for attention; Jane Manning sang a lament inspired by the death of Stravinsky in 1970; and Cleo Laine told the story of Adam and Eve from Eve's point of view. After this, the master of ceremonies became silent, the whole piece was taken over by the political events that took place in 1970, notably the general election, what Enoch Powell had to say about immigration, and most specifically the anti-Vietnam War student demonstrations in America, which culminated in the shooting to death by members of the Ohio national guard of four students at Kent State University. Throughout the whole of this section, a film devoted to other disturbing events taking place in society and the world of politics during 1970 and the first half of 1971 was shown to the audience on a large screen.

The inclusion of a film bore evidence of a weakness in the programme planning, for Glock and Boulez, who conducted *Arena*, had directed their attention to listeners in the hall rather than to listeners on the radio. This became even more evident when the 'progressive' concerts got under way at the Roundhouse. Two were given in January and two in May 1972. Boulez insisted that he should introduce each item, and at the end of the concert the audience should be allowed to discuss the works. All the pieces were either world premières or first performances in Britain, and each pair of concerts was to end with a specially commissioned music-theatre work. On the evidence of *The Garden of Love*, David Bedford was asked to compose the first, and Maxwell Davies, whose opera *Taverner* was scheduled for production in July 1972, the second.

Unfortunately Bedford thought his commission was for a piece in which, as in *The Garden of Love*, the audience could participate. To the great disapproval of Glock and Boulez, he produced *With 100 Kazoos*, a piece containing a section in which a hundred members of the audience would improvise their responses to images projected on a screen with the kazoos they had been given. They therefore withdrew the work and substituted *Foxes and Hedgehogs* by the American Eric

Salzman, a work inspired by the distinction between those who relate to many ideas and those who relate to one big idea.[19] As well as involving movement, visual effects and costumes, sections of the piece had to be recorded and played back during the performance. I was unable to attend the concert or listen to it on the air, but according to William Mann, writing in *The Times* (2 February 1972), the piece 'is a multi-medium, come-all-ye, with unsynchronized moving pictures on two screens, orchestral groups upstairs and downstairs, vocal soloists constantly on the move, a jazz saxophonist, periphonic taped sounds, lights, rock music and much else'. Salzman subsequently noted:

> When *Foxes and Hedgehogs* was performed by Pierre Boulez and the BBC Orchestra in London in the 1970s, it was savaged by the British critics, who obviously understood it quite well and also found its message and technique to be inadmissible (abruptly ending my career in the U.K. although, fortunately, not in Europe).[20]

The music-theatre work Maxwell Davies produced was *Blind Man's Buff*, 'a masque for boy treble, mezzo soprano, dancer, mime and chamber ensemble', based on the last scene in Georg Büchner's comedy *Leonce und Lena*[21] about the foibles and foolishness of men. Ironically, given that apart from *Vesalii Icones* his early music-theatre pieces were visually slim, and that he was writing for radio, this turned out to be the most visual of all Maxwell Davies's works in the genre.

After this second 'prospective' concert, Boulez's initial idea for them had to be amended. His introductions had been long-winded, and the critics thought he tended to be off-hand during the discussions. It was also thought that the programmes ought not to deal exclusively with the new. They ought to include one première, one revival of a recent work and one twentieth-century masterpiece. The programme for the concert on 19 February 1973 contained Stockhausen's *Kreuzspiel*, Schoenberg's *Song of the Wood Dove* and the first performance of Roger Smalley's Sonata for Strings, but instead of having Boulez introduce each item himself, I was roped in to interview him. And in the following concert when Boulez conducted Berio's *Recital I* and Cathy Berberian was the singer, Berio and not Boulez was interviewed before it.

---

[19] 'The fox knows many things, but the hedgehog knows one big thing,' Greek poet, Archilochus (c. 680–c. 645 BC).
[20] 'Speaking in Tongues, or Why Should *Eclectic* Be a Bad Word?', *Theater Magazine*, 39:3 (Durham, NC, Duke University Press, 2009), 8.
[21] German dramatist and poet, b. 1813, d. 1837.

Ill. 4.1 Maxwell Davies, *Blind Man's Buff*, first performance, 1972

Recital I contains a visual component, but it is not as vital to the understanding of the work as the visual components in *Blind Man's Buff* (Ill. 4.1). Indeed, under Robert Ponsonby, who succeeded Glock as Controller of Music in 1973, all the music-theatre pieces presented at the Roundhouse after the Berio concert on 26 March 1973 had visual components that did not demand to be seen but could be easily imagined. In addition, the speech content was limited to scripted talks about the twentieth-century masterpiece given by English composers who were not otherwise engaged in the concert, so that listeners heard Hugh Wood introduce *Pierrot lunaire*, and Bernard Rands, Berio's *Circles*.

The last music-theatre work presented by the BBC at the Roundhouse was the first complete performance of John Buller's *The Mime of Mick, Nick and the Maggies*, which took place on 6 February 1978. It called for three soloists, a narrator, a chorus and an ensemble, and was one of the longest music-theatre pieces produced by a British composer. It was also one of the most complex, less in its music but certainly in its text, for it is a setting of the whole of the 'Children's Night Games' section in James Joyce's *Finnegans Wake*. The work is discussed briefly in Chapter Ten.

Two years earlier, in August 1976, the BBC had broadcast the first forty-five minutes of the work preceded by a reading of the text by Patrick Magee. But, when the whole work was given at the Roundhouse, the BBC decided that, because the text was too long to be read before the performance, the audience should be given the printed text when they entered the auditorium. The concert began with Berio's two-track tape piece *Thema (Omaggio a Joyce)* based on Cathy Berberian's reading of the 'overture' from the Sirens' chapter of Joyce's *Ulysses*. But before the main work of the evening began, the BBC producer inexplicably lowered the house lights so that the text of Buller's work became illegible. Writing in *The Guardian*, Edward Greenfield was scathing: 'The BBC had kindly provided us in the programme notes with the complete text … Then what does the producer do but switch all the lights out for the actual performance, leaving those of us who don't make a habit of memorising *Finnegans Wake* in the dark in every sense.'[22] A sad end to what had promised to be one of the main arenas for Music Theatre.

[22] *The Guardian*, 7 February 1978.

CHAPTER FIVE

Birtwistle's Rituals

As a pioneer of Music Theatre in Britain,[1] Birtwistle has been more closely involved with the genre, and indeed with the theatre in general, than any other composer since the death of Britten. Even so, he has called only *Bow Down* Music Theatre, this being the work he composed in 1977 for performance at the Cottesloe Theatre when he was the Music Director of the National Theatre. Earlier, Birtwistle's term for Music Theatre had been 'limited theatre'. He called *Bow Down* Music Theatre because in it he wanted to get closer to the integration of music and theatre than he had been able to do previously. He was able to do this because his work at the National Theatre had brought him into greater contact with actors and, crucially, with the poet Tony Harrison. These two had already planned to write ...*agm*..., a choral work based on the *Fayum* fragments of Sappho, but their purpose in devising *Bow Down* was to explore the common territory between actors and musicians, to ensure that as much time was allocated to recitation as to music.

They composed the piece for five actors (two female, three male), three of whom had to dance, and four musicians playing between them bamboo flute, bamboo pipes, oboes, penny whistles and percussion. The nine sit in a circle on the floor, and in this arrangement they constitute the chorus. The actors occupy positions 2, 3, 5, 7 and 8, the musicians 1, 4, 6 and 9 (Ill. 5.1).

The work is based on the 'Ballad of the Two Sisters', of which there are over a hundred versions from Scandinavia, North America and throughout the British Isles. Tony Harrison draws on about twenty versions. Although the details vary, all tell the same basic story: how the dark sister's jealousy of the fair sister (after she has been rejected by a suitor, who has had to make a choice between them) leads her to drown her sister in a river. As the body of the fair sister floats down the river, it is seen by a miller and his servant. They haul it on to the bank, lust after it, strip it of all its jewels and mutilate it. The scene then changes to the court, where the king, the father of the two sisters, is overseeing the wedding of the dark sister. During the wedding the ghost of the fair sister appears and speaks. On hearing how she died, the king extorts a confession from the dark sister by having her tortured on a rack. He then has her buried alive in a pit on the seashore.

---

[1] For a recent study of Birtwistle's Music Theatre, see David Beard, *Harrison Birtwistle's Operas and Music Theatre* (Cambridge, Cambridge University Press, 2012).

Ill. 5.1. Birtwistle, *Bow Down* with Morag Hood and Judith Paris. Workshop rehearsal at the National Theatre, London, 1977

While the story may be gruesome, it is alleviated by the way it unfolds. Birtwistle's model was Japanese theatre in which the actors, dancers and musicians are interchangeable, and the action proceeds slowly. Although the story can be told in a few sentences, the inclusion of different versions of the ballad means that *Bow Down* lasts fifty minutes.

Birtwistle restricts himself to one basic pulse and three basic intervals so that musically the piece is very simple. 'The very economy of the music,' reported William Mann in *The Times* after the first performance on 5 July 1977,[2] 'drumbeats, gently hummed chords, sparse plaints for two oboes, served to heighten the presentation's hieratic slowness to an almost Kabuki-like intensity.'

The nature of the work can be best illustrated by referring to the events occurring in its first few minutes. Here we see how closely actors and musicians have to work together, and also how Tony Harrison and Birtwistle move the story backwards and forwards in time to provide a preview of the action that will follow. The work opens with the chorus sitting silently in their positions. At the sound of two drumbeats, a choral pulse based on breathing is initiated. As it proceeds, Chorus No. 7 does a forward roll into the circle to become the fair sister drowning, in this version, in the sea. Her calls for help are taken up by Chorus No. 2, who becomes a blind harper composing a ballad in Danish as he walks round the

---

[2] *The Times*, 6 July 1977.

outside of the choral circle. From the way he walks we realise he is on the seashore very close to the water. His wavering 'dance' follows the ebb and flow of the tides, and it suggests he has been doing this for centuries. As he mutters his ballad, each member of the chorus takes up in turn a different pitch from his recitation so that a hummed chord is built up. In the course of it Chorus No. 3 becomes the dark sister. She goes into the circle behind the drowned fair sister so that we get the impression she is emerging from her. As the dark sister's arms slowly open behind her sister, we see that they are the rigid arms of someone being racked and tortured. After the blind harper momentarily obscures our vision of them, the two sisters re-emerge as young girls sitting in a bower. First they sing a duet to the words, 'I'll be true to my true love if my love will be true to me,' after which they dance together. As they dance, three members of the chorus recite passages from different versions of the ballad to reveal that a knight is coming to be their suitor. His role is given to Chorus No. 5, who must mime a journey on horseback around the circle. When he returns to his chorus position, he joins the sisters in a new dance, this time to music provided by the other members of the chorus, actors as well as musicians.

I have based this account mainly on Tony Harrison's stage directions because they show how, when writing a text for Birtwistle, the poet has to bear in mind that, as well as requiring a sense of ritual, Birtwistle nearly always bases his theatrical works on the relationship between chorus and protagonist. This can be detected even in his first published piece, *Refrains and Choruses* for wind quintet (1957), whose structure is on three levels. On the first lies something absolutely regular and predictable, the formal repetition of a refrain followed by a chorus, each of which is repetitive in itself. Superimposed on this cyclic process is a linear process involving the development of the material as it is passed from one to the other. And further superimposed on these is the drama created by treating the wind quintet as a chorus, and the horn, the only brass instrument in the group, as a protagonist bent on asserting its individuality. Gradually its tonal power and defiance of the others take the music to a climax, after which the others have to coax it back to its origins. Birtwistle regards this progression as being the essence of early Greek theatre.

Yet he did not exploit this relationship again until he composed *Tragoedia* in 1965. In the intervening years he explored other structural possibilities. And it was during this period that he became involved in Music Theatre. In 1960 he was engaged to teach the clarinet in four private schools in Dorset and Wiltshire. Three of them were preparatory schools where his duties were exactly as the job specified, but the fourth was Cranborne Chase, a girls' independent boarding school which had just moved from Crichel House in Moor Crichel in Dorset to its new home in Wardour Castle in Wiltshire. In this post he had scope for composition. In his first year at Wardour Castle, as well as arranging instrumental canzonas by the Franco-Flemish Renaissance composer Heinrich Isaac for his pupils, and composing a Trio for flute, harp and bass clarinet for a concert to be given at the school, Birtwistle wrote music for *The Green Man*, a mime play which, according to a report in *Odyssey*, the school magazine, was the event which gave the school its 'identity' in its new home.

I had already written two books about Birtwistle[3] without *The Green Man* ever being mentioned in any of our numerous conversations. I first heard about it at a luncheon party given by the composer at which his wife, Sheila, and a friend, who had also attended a performance of *The Green Man* at Wardour Castle, were present. Yet although these last two spoke about it with enthusiasm, neither was able to supply me with details. I had hoped that Birtwistle might be more informative, but he said nothing, only smiled. I have therefore had to rely on *Odyssey*, the school magazine, for a description of the work. From this it would seem that the setting is a Punch and Judy booth, and that the action is based on a medieval Romance. One paragraph in a rather gushing report reads:

> The stage is for make-believe. Instantly we were translated into a paradoxi-cal world. The puppet man drew his little curtain across his Punch and Judy box and it covered the whole stage. His puppets were all obedient to the strings, and yet as large as life. We quickly learnt their special language of gesture and glance, so that every move in the story had the unhurried inevi-tability of the truest fairy tales. Of course, our Good Knight succumbed to our Bad Knight (he always does), and only by some miraculous intervention did he win the fair Princess (as we all hope to do).[4]

Underneath this schoolgirl's account is a paragraph about the musical score 'by a visitor to Friday night's performance':

> Mr. Harrison Birtwistle's music to this mime was quite fascinating in the way it accompanied and interpreted the emotional and dramatic devel-opment of the action, and in its clever use of instrumental resources. In the hands of the eleven players were only two melodic instruments, both woodwind, the rest being percussion. At first one thought of Boulez and *Le marteau sans maître,* but the impression that Mr. Birtwistle's music might be derivative soon passed as the purposeful counterpoint of

---

[3]   Michael Hall, *Harrison Birtwistle* (London, Robson Books, 1984) and *Harrison Birtwistle in Recent Years* (London, Robson Books, 1988).

[4]   *Odyssey* (Summer Term, 1961, 13, Wiltshire and Swindon Archives).

rhythms began to have its effect. There was none of Boulez's sensational scattiness, but a steady and serious building up of tension by genuinely musical means. The climaxes were tremendous, not only in volume but in the quite extraordinary brilliance of the tone colours produced by the ingenious orchestration.[5]

The only explanation I can offer for Birtwistle's silence concerning *The Green Man* is that it was the source of several works he was to compose later, and that he did not want to reveal that his ideas originated from a school mime group. His first opera is a combination of Punch and Judy and medieval Romance, which features a scene where the characters dance around a maypole and one of them is dressed as the Green Man; his second is based on the medieval poem *Sir Gawain and the Green Knight*, so too is his choral work, *Narration: A Description of the Passing of a Year*; and the Green Man appears at the end of *Down by the Greenwood Side* in the guise of Jack Finney, the personification of Spring.

However, the real importance of *The Green Man* is that it was Birtwistle's first excursion into Music Theatre. Not only that, it is the first and only example of Music Theatre in which the stage action takes place entirely through mime. This shows that he was involved in the relationship between physical gesture and musical gesture from the very beginning. Judging from his practice when composing music for plays at the National Theatre later in his career, he would have attended most of the stage rehearsals for *The Green Man* before finding a way to match his music to the 'special language of gesture and glance' that characterised the production. He would not, of course, have wanted to 'mickey-mouse' each movement, but he would surely have found musical gestures appropriate for the general character of each episode, as for example in the scene where the Good Knight and the Bad Knight fight. A photograph in the school magazine shows that they were both dressed in fencing gear so that the whole scene must have been cast as a fencing match. What was needed here was music to convey the tension of the situation through its gestures without the fencers having their movements dictated by the music as they lunged and parried.

Although *The Green Man* met nearly all the characteristics of Music Theatre I listed in Chapter One, Birtwistle did not produce another specimen until he composed *Monodrama* six years later, when, surprisingly, he focused on vocal rather than physical gestures. The route to that work also had its beginnings at Wardour Castle. In the autumn of 1962 he was asked to teach the music GCE O-level class as well as the clarinet at Cranborne Chase School. According to the violinist Catherine Macintosh, who was one of his pupils, Birtwistle began by making a

---

[5] Ibid., 14.

list of all the works they should study over the year. It stretched from Machaut to Tippett. At the beginning of the following summer term, however, when the exam was only a matter of weeks away he had only got as far as Bach.

Fortunately his pupils quickly made up the missing ground for themselves. But because 'there was never any time to do what we wanted musically', he asked them if they would like to get together again in the summer holidays when they would have all the time and space they needed. In the event it took him a year to get the first summer school organised. Although the governors of Cranborne Chase School said it could take place between Sunday 16 and Saturday 22 of August 1964, they insisted that a committee of local dignitaries should oversee it. But Birtwistle rejected their advice that it should be as popular as possible, and went his own way. He asked Michael Tippett to be the president, recruited Goehr and Maxwell Davies to teach composition, and through Goehr, he engaged the Melos Ensemble, the most prestigious chamber ensemble of the time, to give concerts and take master-classes. In addition he asked John Alldis to conduct the Summer School Choir, and John Carewe the Summer School Orchestra. Over eighty people attended the School, and he was therefore able to pay the Melos Ensemble their fees, cover all his running costs and even provide subsidies for certain impoverished composers he wanted to attend.

Among the composers were David Bedford, Edward Cowie, David Ellis, Brian Ferneyhough, Anthony Gilbert, Robin Holloway, Bill Hopkins, David Lumsdaine, Michael Nyman, Roger Smalley and Hugh Wood. They could choose to attend one of two seminars taking place every morning, one taken by Goehr, the other by Maxwell Davies. There were also composition workshops supervised by the members of the Melos Ensemble in the afternoons. Although contemporary music was the main topic of the conversations in the seminars, over meals and in the spacious gardens, Maxwell Davies asked those who wanted to join his seminars to be armed with scores of Bach's Two-Part Inventions, Beethoven's Piano Sonata in E minor Op. 90 and Mahler's Third Symphony, while those who chose Goehr's were required to bring along volumes of Scarlatti's Sonatas and Chopin's Waltzes. Mostly these were for reference purposes, but Maxwell Davies analysed the first movement of Mahler's symphony in detail.

Concerts or lectures took place at 5 o'clock each afternoon and 8.30 each evening, and were open to the general public. At 5 o'clock on the Sunday, Goehr opened proceedings with a lecture on 'Music in our Time'. As I was unable to attend the Summer School I have had to rely on those with good memories to recall what was discussed forty years earlier. All that Goehr can remember is that he based the lecture on Boulez's book *Penser la musique aujourd'hui* (1963), but Edward Cowie tells me that this was not so. Goehr's main point was that what the avant-garde composers were doing was an illusion. 'He told us that what we were going to experience was apparently something new, but in percentage terms it will probably be relatively familiar: it has all happened before.'

For the development of Music Theatre, the most significant event took place on the Wednesday evening. The afternoon concert had been devoted to flute and harpsichord music by Bach and Couperin, but the evening session was a discussion on 'Opera Today' by Tippett, Maxwell Davies and Goehr, with Birtwistle in the chair. The reason for this was that all the composers on the rostrum were either writing, or thinking of writing, an opera. Maxwell Davies had just completed the first act of *Taverner* in America; Goehr had been commissioned to write *Arden muss sterben* (*Arden Must Die*) for the Hamburg State Opera and was beginning to compose his music for it; Tippett was making plans for his third opera, *The Knot Garden*, while Birtwistle had plans to write an opera about Punch and Judy.

However, before he could write an opera Birtwistle had to change his approach to rhythm and pacing. Until the winter of 1964/5 when he composed *Ring a Dumb Carillon* for soprano, clarinet and percussion, his practice was to base a whole work on one rhythmic cell, usually the short-long / strong-weak rhythm of the heartbeat. He would subject this cell to all manner of variations and extensions, including extending it into groupings that alternate between rational and irrational numerical formations. The result was often so fluid that, even though there may be an underlying pulse behind the changing rhythms, its regularity would be difficult to detect. On the other hand, in *Ring a Dumb Carillon* he based his rhythms on a series of regularly pulsating ostinatos moving at different rates. By superimposing one regular pulse on another, or by having one get faster or another slower, the result can become quite complex. But even when the various pulses are amalgamated into a single voice, Birtwistle found it easier to convey a sense of changing pace than was possible with his earlier practice. He had the capacity not only to meet the rhythmical needs of opera but also most of his other works as well, including *Tragoedia*, the work that was given its first performance at the Second Wardour Castle Summer School in August 1965.

I mentioned in Chapter One that it was in the discussion following Anthony Gilbert's questioning of the contemporary relevance of opera's various forms of presentation in the 'Opera Today' forum that the ideas for Music Theatre emerged. Although it took several years before they could be put in practice, the two theatrical works given in the 1965 Summer School, Schoenberg's *Pierrot lunaire* and Birtwistle's *Tragoedia*, set the trajectory of English Music and Instrumental Theatre.

Tragoedia originally meant 'goat dance' and in this meaning it refers to the Dionysian festival from which Greek tragedy arose. Birtwistle's work is scored for two instrumental choruses (a wind quintet and a string quartet) plus a harp to both link and act as mediator between the two choruses. The members of the wind quintet are also required to play claves (wooden clappers producing dry percussive sounds, ideal for background ostinatos). For his protagonists, Birtwistle chose the horn and the cello from the wind quintet and string quartet. The work is divided into eight sections corresponding to the formal units in Greek tragedy, but Birtwistle superimposes on their bilateral symmetry a unilateral symmetry that alternates between violent and peaceful: Parodos (violent), Episodion 1 (peaceful), Antistrophe 1 (violent), Stasimon (peaceful), Episodion 2 (violent), Antistrophe 2 (peaceful), Exodos (violent).

That the work is based on a goat dance is established in a Prologue that stands outside these two types of ritual structures. To convey its violent, bucking nature, the horn and cello use rhythmic ostinatos to aggressively vie with each other until they eventually explode into plunging contrapuntal lines (Ex. 5.1a).

* notes marked staccato must be played as near the table as possible

Ex. 5.1a Birtwistle, *Trageodia*, Prologue, bb. 8–17

The following seven sections then exploit this juxtaposition of ostinatos and contrapuntal lines. They form a broken symmetry around Stasimon, the central section, which is the pivot for the whole work. In stark contrast to the Dionysian character of the Prologue it offers a moment of Apollonian serenity. The tempo is

Ex. 5.1b Birtwistle, *Trageodia*, 'Stasimon', bb. 9–20

slow, the dynamics soft; the plunging lines have become gentle undulations, while the conflicting ostinatos have become four different kinds of pulses lying softly in the background. These are a steady, regular pulse, a pulse that gets faster, a pulse that gets slower and a pulse that is 'bent' or drawn out in the additive manner of Birtwistle's earlier music. The combination produces the musical equivalent of a mobile floating waywardly in space. As a result this movement makes a perfect foil for the violent, tightly controlled sections that proceed and follow it (Ex. 5.1b).

Its predecessor, Antistrophe 1, pits the cello against the wind quintet, while its successor, Episodion 2, recasts the peaceful duet contained in Episodion 1 into a violent exchange between the two choruses. The duet in Episodion 1, on the other hand, anticipates the character of the central Stasimon. It opens with a melody introduced by the horn and then passed from horn to cello as if the two were in complete agreement. Six years later Birtwistle made use of this duet in *Meridian* for mezzo-soprano, horn, cello, two choirs of sopranos and two choirs of instruments. Here it functions as an instrumental love duet, which terminates with the mezzo speaking the line: 'The song is lie or nonsense.' I believe Birtwistle felt that

Ex. 5.1b (*continued*)

this had also been true of *Tragoedia*, for thereafter there is no sense of agreement between the horn and cello. Their relationship has to be deduced from hints. It only resurfaces clearly in the violent Exodos, when the two protagonists are as competitive as they were in the Prologue. Ultimately the other instruments silence them with a barrage of repeated notes played by high pizzicatos and claves. All that remains is a final cadence from the harp, a cadence consisting of two lines of three crotchets, each descending softly and slowly, one crotchet apart, to the instrument's lowest depths. In the context of the work it is the simplest version of the plunging lines that first appeared in the Prologue, just as the barrage of repeated notes in rhythmic unison is the simplest version of the ostinatos that preceded the lines.

In a later programme note for *Tragoedia*, Birtwistle says that its music appears practically note for note in his opera *Punch and Judy*, for which it was a preliminary study. If this is so, it is difficult to detect. What I find of greater interest is the remark he made in 2004 when I interviewed him for this book, when he claimed that *Punch and Judy* was more Music Theatre than opera. This was because, unlike opera, Music Theatre can embrace different types of theatre. Not only does the work combine the Punch and Judy show with a medieval Romance, as *The Green Man* had done, it also draws on facets of the medieval morality play and Greek tragedy.

When performed at fêtes and fairs the basic events of the traditional Punch and Judy show consist of Punch throwing Baby out of the window, beating and killing Judy and various other characters, cheating the hangman into hanging himself and then disposing of the Devil. Birtwistle decided to arrange these into four melodramas, and to slot into them three quests for Punch's idealised lady, who could be Pretty Polly, a doll on a stick originally contained in the puppet show until it was reshaped at the beginning of the nineteenth century. He also included a part for the puppeteer whom he decided to call Choregos, after the person who paid the actors in the ancient Greek theatre. His role would be that of a one-man chorus who commentates on Punch's behaviour. He could therefore be one of Punch's victims. But in killing him, Punch would be killing his *raison d'être*. This would be the work's *peripetia*, its turning point. In a nightmare, Punch's former victims would turn against him, Pretty Polly's pedestal would be deserted, and Punch would go to prison to wait for Jack Ketch, the hangman. Jack Ketch, the public executioner between 1663 and 1686, was nicknamed Satan for his botched executions, and therefore his presence would justify Punch's conviction that, when he persuades the hangman to hang himself, he has defeated the Devil.

Given the episodic nature of the plot, Birtwistle realised that the piece could not be through composed, it would have to be a number opera. For his librettist, he chose the American pianist Stephen Pruslin, who had given a perceptive and highly amusing lecture on Mozart's operas at the first Wardour Castle Summer School. In the event he produced a text, which through his use of alliteration, childish puns and riddle games was equally amusing.

The work requires six singers (high soprano, mezzo soprano, high tenor, higher baritone, lower baritone and basso profondo, taking respectively the parts of Pretty Polly (later Witch), Judy (later Fortune Teller), Lawyer, Punch, Choregos (later Jack Ketch and Doctor); five mime dancers; a wind quintet on stage, and a ten-piece ensemble in the pit. The mime dancers are required to represent the Bacchanal that leads to Choregos's murder, to take part in the Black Wedding Procession during the nightmare, and to complete the Maying celebrations, when one of them is dressed as the Green Man. When not dancing they should stand above the action on the Altar of Murder. The members of the wind quintet are to be dressed in Victorian bandsmen's uniforms, and duet with the characters in the drama: the flute with Pretty Polly, the oboe with Judy, the clarinet with Punch, the bassoon with Doctor, the horn with Lawyer.

The suggested stage plan consists of Choregos's booth and the stage band on the extreme left and right of the apron in front of the drop curtain. Behind it on a platform at the back of the stage is the Altar of Murder doubling as Punch's Travel Frame, and in front of this on stage right are four gibbets where Judy, Lawyer and Doctor form a chorus after they have been murdered. Opposite this on stage left is Pretty Polly's pedestal.

In a prologue Choregos welcomes the audience to the 'littel play', and the curtain rises on Punch serenading Baby, who, in this version, he throws into the fire. After Punch sings a homage to Judy, he stabs her to death on the Altar of Murder. His first quest for Pretty Polly takes place 'on a shining summer afternoon'. He offers her a flower, but she dismisses it imperiously: 'The flaw in this flower is a flicker of flame.' In the next melodrama Punch encounters Doctor and Lawyer, killing one with a hypodermic needle, the other with a quill. Then 'in the ashen autumn twilight' he embarks on another quest for Pretty Polly, offering her this time an oversized prism-like gem. This too is rejected: 'This prism of peace is a prison of pain.' He then confronts Choregos, who perishes in a bass viol case amid an orgy of *Gebrauchsmusik*.[6] The quest then takes Punch northward 'to the land of infinite night'. But on the journey he experiences a nightmare. All his victims turn against him: Judy is a fortune-teller with a wicked pack of tarot cards, Pretty Polly a witch taking part in a Black Wedding. When he awakens in terror to continue his journey, Pretty Polly's pedestal is deserted. In the last melodrama Punch is in prison awaiting Jack Ketch. After Punch has tricked the hangman into hanging himself, Pretty Polly comes to life. She hails the Spring, joins Punch and together they sing a love duet. The gallows are turned into a maypole around which everyone dances. When the curtain comes down, Choregos from his booth tells the audience that the tale is told, the damage done, the hurlyburly's lost and won.

The structure of the melodramas varies according to which person is to be murdered, but there are always two parts containing the following events: Punch's encounter with the victim, who establishes the principle he or she represents; a question-and-answer game (the kind children play when they want to eliminate someone); then, in the second part, a murder ensemble consisting of a proclamation from Choregos about the arrogance of Punch 'that high priest of pain'; couplets on the bitter sweetness of death; the murder; and Punch's resolve to search for Pretty Polly. Except when Punch finds the pedestal empty, the quests are all basically the same: travel music followed by a weather report from the chorus, a prayer from Choregos and the chorus, Punch's serenade and Polly's dismissal. Then Choregos, sounding like the Evangelist when reporting Peter's denial in the *St Matthew Passion*, says 'Weep, my Punch. Weep out your unfathomable, inexpressive sorrow.'

---

[6]   Utility music usually associated with Hindemith.

This is not the only reference to the *St Matthew Passion* in *Punch and Judy*: it contains three Passion Chorales and two Passion Arias. The Chorales are sung by Choregos and the chorus after the deaths of Judy and Baby, the Doctor and Lawyer, and Punch's discovery of Pretty Polly's absence; the Arias come before the deaths of Judy and Choregos, the second being an extended da capo aria with oboe d'amore obbligato for Judy: 'Be silent, strings of my heart, / The rainbow on this bridge reveals suspensions of eternal harmony.' But these are only five of the over one hundred separate items in the work: it is a number opera *par excellence*. Some, like the Toccatas which frame the Passion Chorales, last only a few seconds, but all conform to the baroque doctrine of *Affektenlehre*[7] in that each encapsulates a specific attitude or response that can be morally assessed. The Toccatas, for instance, are meant to sound 'like some mechanical process switched on and off' so that the Passion Chorales seem to be an automatic rather than a spontaneous response.

The work was eventually commissioned by the English Opera Group, and performed in Aldeburgh's Jubilee Hall as part of the 1968 Aldeburgh Festival. But although children seem to enjoy the ritual murders in the traditional Punch and Judy show, adults can find them offensive. Perhaps this was why Britten and Peter Pears might have walked out during the première.[8] Nevertheless, the work is still performed, and those who approve of modernism consider it to be one of the most characteristic works of the sixties. If nothing else it demonstrates that it is possible to achieve a close relationship between musical and physical gestures. This point is crucial because, on the evidence of *The Visions of Francesco Petrarca* and *Melodrama*, the two music-theatre works Birtwistle composed in 1966 and 1967, during and just after composing *Punch and Judy*, he had difficulty in establishing a satisfactory relationship between music and gesture.

The Visions of Francesco Petrarca, an allegory for baritone, mime ensemble, chamber ensemble and school orchestra, was composed for the 1966 York Festival, but was later withdrawn for revision. The commission was for a music-theatre work in which local children could take part. The text is Edmund Spenser's translations of seven sonnets by Petrarch, the first six describing how beautiful things (a hind, a tall ship, a laurel bush, a waterfall, a phoenix and a fair lady) are savagely destroyed 'by troublesome fate', the seventh delivering the spiritual homily, 'And

---

[7] This is the theory that music can arouse specific emotions in the listener so that, by using the appropriate musical procedure or device, the composer could evoke a particular emotional response in his audience.

[8] The evidence is anecdotal and was disputed by Birtwistle himself when interviewed for BBC Radio 4's *Desert Island Discs* by Sue Lawley in 1994. William Mann writing in *The Times* (10 June 1968) states obliquely: 'Some people could not bear to stay until the end and clumped out noisily.'

though ye be the fairest of God's creatures, Yet think, that death shall spoil your godly features'. The baritone, accompanied by the professional chamber ensemble, sings the settings of the first six sonnets and, after each of them, the children accompanied by a school orchestra retell them in mime. It is only for the setting of the seventh sonnet that the professionals and amateurs join forces. Varied repetition is, as we have seen, of paramount importance to Birtwistle, but on this occasion the separation of song and dance in order to achieve varied repetition meant that for most of the piece he had to abandon the opposition between protagonist and chorus as well as the close relationship between music and gesture he had so carefully established in *The Green Man* and *Punch and Judy*.

He faced a similar dilemma when composing *Monodrama*. This was written for the Pierrot Players' first concert in May 1967. Although he had himself decided that the ensemble should consist of the same instrumentalists needed for *Pierrot lunaire* plus a percussionist and a soprano, he nevertheless found himself saddled with the prospect of having to compose for an ensemble that was not to his taste. The basis of all his theatrical works is the relationship between a soloist and a chorus. But the combination of flute, clarinet, violin, cello, piano and percussion is too heterogeneous to be a chorus. All he could do in *Monodrama* was to replace the pianist with a second percussionist, and to have the soprano in dramatic relationship with the amplified voice of a male speaker standing off stage. He calls this speaker Choregos, thus implying that he functions as a chorus. The soprano, on the other hand, functions as protagonist, herald and prophetess, which she differentiates visually by wearing different masks.

As in *Tragoedia*, Birtwistle had gone back to a form of Greek tragedy for his topic. In essence, I believe, *Monodrama* is another elaboration of the quotation from Sophocles that stands at the head of the score of *Punch and Judy*: 'Who is the slayer, who the victim? Speak'.[9] Birtwistle and Pruslin, who wrote the libretto, take as their starting point the ancient Greek tradition of having a violent incident such as murder take place off stage. Birtwistle's piece begins with Choregos silencing those instrumentalists who are still tuning up then asking the Protagonist the question, 'Who screamed in pain behind the portal?' This question stands behind the whole piece for it is entirely devoted to the protagonist's attempts to find an answer to it. She asks first a prophetess then a herald to help her. When neither of these can give her a satisfactory answer she turns to the prophetess again. This marks the turning point in the drama for it is here that we get the first hint that the solution will involve a reversal. Initially it was Choregos who silenced the musicians who were tuning up, now it is the prophetess who silences Choregos. She then turns to the instrumentalists, who

---

[9]   Spoken by the Chorus in *Antigone*.

start tuning up again in order to fulfil her request for a 'savage euphony'. This is the trigger that leads to the work's catastrophe. During it the instrumentalists become silent of their own accord. Choregos screams 'Ah! They have struck from within,' and the protagonist, now speaking instead of singing, asks the question 'Who screamed in pain behind the portal?', to which Choregos replies 'Speak, A scream is the portal of pain.' This reversal of their positions at the beginning of the work is now the trigger for what the Greeks called *anagnorisis*, the moment of recognition or discovery, in this instance the discovery is that Choregos and the protagonist are both killers and victims, that they are one and the same, that in psychological terms they are facets of the same psyche. This is reinforced when in the section Pruslin calls 'Triumph', the protagonist calls Choregos 'my beloved' and says: 'Slaying we are slain, Slain, we will slay.' At the end, when Choregos says 'Only an ultra-violet light will infer one red and imply one white,' he is echoed by the protagonist who, as her voice fades away, slowly turns her back on the audience.

I have done my best to understand the plot and to summarise it accurately, but Pruslin's text is very obscure and convoluted so the task has been far from easy. His alliterations worked well in *Punch and Judy*, but in this context they make the process of comprehension almost impossible. Added to which Birtwistle's vocal lines, especially those he gives to the prophetess and also, for most of the time, to the protagonist as well, are so highly melismatic that the words get swallowed up in the proliferation of pitches. I believe this is why the work was withdrawn after its first performance. Nevertheless, the music is of great interest, and in my opinion more than worthy of further performances.

As in *Tragoedia*, the work begins and ends with a Parodos and Exodos. In between them are three cycles divided into a number of shorter sections all of which are labelled. Most of them return varied so that the whole structure, apart from when the climax occurs, is deliberately very formal. Among them, for example, are two Oracles for the prophetess, two Soliloquies for the protagonist, three Cryptograms for Choregos and the protagonist during which one of them gradually reduces their contribution to a single word, and four solo Interstices for the four melody instruments. Because the formal, ritualistic characteristics of the work contain a narrative plot, the order in which these sections occur within the three cycles varies in accordance with the different circumstances. I believe Birtwistle included the Interstices because all are slow, very quiet and so are indicative of a state of contemplation (Ex. 5.2). They are the only sections Birtwistle made use of later, for they became the music for his *Four Interludes for a Tragedy* for basset clarinet and electronic sounds.

These Interstices, however, caused problems when the work was performed, because while they lasted the soprano had to remain more or less motionless.

Ex. 5.2 Birtwistle, *Monodrama*, Interstice III for violin

Indeed there is very little opportunity for her to move at all in the work. She acts the parts of the protagonist, prophetess and herald mainly through her voice.

Having the soprano act different parts vocally while remaining more or less motionless is also a feature of *Nenia: The Death of Orpheus* (1970). But before that Birtwistle had composed two works in which movement is vital. I shall deal with his instrumental theatre piece *Verses for Ensembles* in Chapter Nine, but first I want to discuss *Down by the Greenwood Side*, which he composed for Goehr's Music Theatre Ensemble to perform at the 1969 Brighton Festival. It is scored for soprano, five actors, mime and nine instruments. The actors and mime as a chorus of highly differentiated individuals base their activities on the traditional Mummers' Play, a pantomime that was acted in rural communities every Christmas to celebrate the prospect of spring. For his librettist he chose Michael Nyman, who selected versions of the ballad of the Cruel Mother for the songs, and versions of the Mummers' Play that involve speech as well as mime. Just as Punch and Judy is the oldest surviving specimen of urban entertainment,[10] this type of folk drama is probably the oldest surviving form of secular rural entertainment in Britain, although nothing concrete can be traced back before the eighteenth century.[11] It is cast in the form sometimes referred to as 'Hero-Combat',[12] but

[10] Fully discussed in Robert Leach, *The Punch and Judy Show: History, Tradition and Meaning* (London, Batsford Academic and Educational, 1985).

[11] The genre is comprehensively analysed by Peter Millington in an unpublished doctoral thesis: 'The Origins and Development of English Folk Plays', University of Sheffield, 2002.

[12] Term used by Alex Helm, 'In Comes I, St George', *Folklore*, 76:2 (1965), 118–36.

unlike the story of the Cruel Mother, which focuses only on death, it tells of death and resurrection: death in winter and spiritual regeneration in spring. Although no longer a pantomime in the old-fashioned sense, i.e. a dumb show, Nyman's version is certainly a pantomime in the modern sense, for it abounds in child-like jokes. Father Christmas is the master of ceremonies who gets things going by defining the acting area with a circular flourish of his broom. The action takes place inside this circumscribed area, the actors entering it only when called to do so by Father Christmas, their first words being 'In Comes I'. Mrs Green, on the other hand, enters the area near the end of the show on her own volition. Until then, when not singing, she walks slowly round the perimeter of the circle.

The ballad of the Cruel Mother, of which there are many versions deriving from Scandinavia, Scotland, Northern England and America, tells the story of a woman who gives birth to two illegitimate boys down by the greenwood side, and then kills them to escape the shame they would bring her. Some time later, when walking in the same forest, she sees two naked boys at play. She tells them that if they were hers she would care for them and dress them in fineries. 'When we were thine', they tell her, 'you dressed us in our own hearts' blood.' Nyman calls the mother Mrs Green after the most modern version of the ballad, which Nyman places near the end of the work, when Father Christmas tells how she murdered the boys with a penknife. Before that the soprano playing the part of Mrs Green sings texts from three other versions. These give a more detailed account of the murders as well as her seduction and her meeting with the boys in the forest.

For his orchestra Birtwistle chose the instruments mentioned in the Cornish Floral Dance: 'We danced to the band with the curious tone of cornet, clarinet and big trombone; fiddle, cello, big bass drum, flute, bassoon and euphonium.' This means that, despite his reservations about the instrumentation of the Pierrot Players, he still has a heterogeneous mixture. But on this occasion the chorus is not defined by its instrumentation, instead the Mummers are the chorus. Nevertheless Birtwistle differentiates soloist and Mummers instrumentally. For her first two songs Mrs Green is accompanied by an ensemble consisting of flute, clarinet, bassoon, violin, cello and percussion, i.e. the instrumentation of the Pierrot Players without the piano; and for the Mummers he removes the strings and adds cornet, trombone and euphonium. They all come together for the last song and episode.

The first person Father Christmas ushers in after Mrs Green has sung the first version of the ballad and he has introduced himself is St George, the personification of England, the land and its people. After Father Christmas has told us how brave he is, St George issues a challenge: 'Where is the man who dares to bid me stand? I'll knock him down with my creatious hand. I'll cut him and stew him into as small as flies. And send him to the cookshop to be made into mince pies.' His evil opponent, Bold Slasher, the Saracen infidel, representative of the hardness of the frost-bound winter, answers him in similar fashion. They fight and St George dies.

Following Mrs Green's second song, Father Christmas calls on Dr Blood to cure him. This he does, after which St George and Bold Slasher fight again, and again St George dies. Mrs Green then sings her third song, but before she does, her solemn walking changes into a dance. This time the cure is effected in mime by Jack Finney, who acts the part of the Green Man. As soon as he appears, Bold Slasher leaves. But before Mrs Green completes her song, Father Christmas interpolates a mocking verse which echoes what the boys had said to Mrs Green in the forest. In other words he enters into her world.

Yet no sooner has he embarked on another version of her song than she crosses over the perimeter and enters his world, the acting area. As well as dancing and stabbing a doll she has with her – when Father Christmas tells how, in this version, she killed her child with a knife – she sings lightly and gaily a short diatonic refrain, 'Fair-a-lair-a-li-do'. This is the refrain she eventually sings without any gaiety as she leaves the stage after Father Christmas tells us that on the day after she committed the crime the bobbies came to take her off to prison. 'And that was the end of Mrs Green,' he says, to which the others reply slowly and softly, 'Fair-a-lair-a-li-do.'

About a year after the first performance of *Down by the Greenwood Side* in 1969, Birtwistle received a commission to write an opera for Covent Garden. The topic he chose was the story of Orpheus and Euridice, and during the following sixteen years, before it was produced by the English National Opera, it was always at the back of his mind. As a result his composition of smaller theatrical works was limited to *Nenia: The Death of Orpheus* and *Bow Down*.

I have already mentioned that, before composing *Bow Down*, Birtwistle called Music Theatre 'limited theatre'. This was on the grounds that he could make theatre from any ensemble he had at his disposal, even though the ensemble had only limited means. He composed *Tragoedia* for the Melos Ensemble, for instance, because they commissioned it for the 1965 Wardour Castle Summer School. But it meant that he had to write a theatrical work for instruments. Likewise in 1970, when the soprano Jane Manning commissioned him to write a work for the newly formed Matrix ensemble in which she was the soloist, he composed a theatrical piece for soprano, three clarinets, piano and percussion: *Nenia: The Death of Orpheus*. The words were by Peter Zinovieff, who would also be the librettist of his opera for Covent Garden. It received its first performance at a BBC Invitation Concert on 29 November 1970. Birtwistle knew it was initially intended for the radio, so that the visual had to be conveyed through the singing and the music.

Nenia is a Roman funeral lament, and the story of Orpheus's death is told in Book XI of Ovid's *Metamorphoses*. Having lost Euridice for the second time when he turned to look back at her as they were ascending from Hades, Orpheus rejects women and sits on a mountain top singing only to trees and stones. This rouses the fury of the Maenads, the female followers of Dionysus, who come up the mountain and tear him into pieces. They throw his lyre and still singing head into the river Hebrus, and later, after crossing the sea, his head is washed up on the shore of Lesbos, where it is stung by a snake.

Birtwistle's work operates on two levels. On the first, the soprano using *Sprechgesang* relates the dry facts of the story accompanied by a chorus of three bass clarinets, crotales and piano doubling prepared piano. These suggest in succession the ominous tread of the Maenads coming up the mountain, the tearing apart of Orpheus, and the floating of his head and lyre downstream. On the other level, in the interstices of the narrator's *Sprechgesang*, he has the voices of Orpheus and Euridice calling to each other across time and space. As Orpheus, the soprano sings in the melismatic, *fioriture* style associated with Monteverdi; as Euridice, in the *bel canto* style associated with Gluck. Both have lyrical passages at the centre of the work. Orpheus's text is entirely devoted to repeating Euridice's name, but Euridice responds to this by asking: 'What blame? What sin? That of having too much loved me? Orpheus, my love, love me still too much. Love me. Love me.' And as she too reiterates her beloved's name, the first bass clarinet changes to a soprano instrument for the tearing apart. Its music indicates the violence of the murder. But immediately after it reaches a climax to indicate Orpheus's death, we hear free-floating 'mobiles' that create a floating quality for the head and lyre drifting downstream. This is when the chorus of clarinets, piano and crotales are at one with the voice, in this case the voice of Euridice repeating Orpheus's name seemingly *ad infinitum*. And this, I believe, is ritual in the making.

CHAPTER SIX

Goehr's Triptych

As I explained in Chapter Four, Alexander Goehr's own ensemble grew out of the Brighton Festival Ensemble. The concert brochure for the first Brighton Festival in 1967 noted that Goehr had been commissioned to write a new work to be performed at the first concert on Sunday 16 April. The assumption was that this would be a theatrical piece like nearly all the other works the Brighton Festival Ensemble were performing in their three concerts. However, the work did not materialise. The commission was transferred to his *Romanza* for cello and orchestra played by Jacqueline du Pré and the New Philharmonia Orchestra under Daniel Barenboim the following year in the 1968 Festival. The expected music-theatre piece did not appear until nearly two months later than the *Romanza*, on 16 July, by which time the Brighton Festival Ensemble had changed its name to the Music Theatre Ensemble and was to perform at the City of London Festival in the Cripplegate Theatre.

The work was *Naboth's Vineyard*, a dramatic madrigal with a text in Latin and English, adapted from I Kings 21, and written for two mimes, three singers and seven instruments. The description 'dramatic madrigal' refers to Monteverdi's *Il combattimento di Tancredi e Clorinda*, which the following year Goehr was to paraphrase for solo clarinet. *Il combattimento*, as we have seen, may be said to be the first piece of Music Theatre, as well as the first to be written in the *stile concitato*, the agitated style Monteverdi introduced to express warlike emotions. As detailed in Chapter Two, the action takes place outside the walls of Jerusalem, and the warlike emotions are aroused in the conflict between Tancred, the Norman hero of the First Crusade, and Clorinda, a female Saracen warrior. Both must wear armour and be masked. Most of the singing is undertaken by the narrator. Clorinda, for example, sings only when she is mortally wounded and asks to become a Christian before she dies. The main function of the combatants is to mime the actions described by the narrator, who sits at the side of the stage near the instrumentalists. Similarly, the action in *Naboth's Vineyard* is performed by masked mimes, the singers representing Achab, Jezebel, Elijah and Naboth also positioned near the instrumentalists. Moreover, when Naboth is being stoned to death Goehr makes use of instrumental features associated with the *stile concitato*.

The second piece in the Triptych, *Shadowplay*, 'Music Theatre to a text from book VII of Plato's *Republic* for actor, tenor and five instruments', was first performed at the 1970 City of London Festival at the City Temple Theatre. Throughout this the tenor as the narrator also stands at the side of the stage, while the actor playing the part of the prisoner mimes the episodes in the cave but speaks when he ascends into the outside world. The tenor remains silent until the prisoner sees first the moon and then the sun and he is then required to sing in a highly lyrical style to express the prisoner's emotions. *Sonata about Jerusalem*, the last piece in the Triptych, is described as a cantata, and employs the largest number of people of the three works: two mimes, two solo singers (soprano and bass), a small female chorus (SSA), a boy's speaking voice and nine instruments. The title 'Sonata' and the description 'cantata' come from an unchanging refrain sung five times by the chorus. The word 'Sonata' refers to Monteverdi's *Sonata sopra Sancta Maria* in the *Vespers* where a refrain is sung eleven times by a soprano as an insistent petition to the Virgin. The word 'cantata' is a reference to Stravinsky's *Cantata* of 1952 which has a refrain setting the eight verses of the *Lyke-Wake Dirge*[1] also for female chorus, each verse ending with the plea: 'And Christ receive thy soul'. In *Sonata about Jerusalem*, however, the refrain is not a plea, but a constant reminder that the day of the Lord's coming will be 'magnificent and terrible'.

The work was commissioned by Testimonium of Jerusalem,[2] and first performed in Tel Aviv and Jerusalem in January 1971 as part of a collection of new pieces using texts from the Jewish, Christian and Arab history of Jerusalem. The words are drawn from the autobiography of Obadiah the Proselyte, a twelfth-century Italian monk who became a convert to Judaism and fled to the East where he observed and wrote about Jewish communities, and the twelfth-century chronicle of Samuel be Yahya ben al Maghribi. From these sources Recha Freier[3] together with the composer compiled an account of the persecuted Jews of twelfth-century Baghdad, who are told by a crazed boy that the time has come when the Lord will gather up his people Israel from all the world and bring them to Jerusalem. The Jews then dress in green, the colour of paradise, and climb to the roofs of their houses to await the miracle that will enable them to fly without wings to Jerusalem. But in the morning when nothing has happened they descend from their roofs and are mocked.

When the Triptych was given its complete performance as a composite work in the 1971 Brighton Festival, it was clear that the individual items made a

---

[1] This is an anonymous fourteenth-century funeral chant originating in Cleveland, North Yorkshire.

[2] Each year, the City of Jerusalem sponsors a festival called Testimonium, in which four composers from around the world are commissioned to write music based on Jewish texts.

[3] Recha Freier (1892–1984) founded the Youth Aliyah organisation in 1933, an organisation that saved the lives of 22,000 Jewish children by helping them to leave Germany and travel to Palestine. She also founded the Testimonium Festival.

well-balanced and coherent three-part structure. Nevertheless, the features that welded them into a unit cannot fully be appreciated unless they are seen in the context of Goehr's previous dramatic works. These consist of two cantatas: *The Deluge* for soprano, contralto and eight instruments (1957–8), *Sutter's Gold* for bass, mixed chorus and orchestra (1959–60), and the two-act opera *Arden Must Die* (1963–6).

Goehr has said that all the texts he uses 'speak of the human condition within hostile or destructive environments'. *The Deluge* and *Sutter's Gold* are based on scenarios that Sergei Eisenstein had planned to make into films. For *The Deluge* Eisenstein had used a text by Leonardo da Vinci about men and animals battling for survival in the Great Flood.

Goehr composed the work shortly after returning to London after studying in Paris with Olivier Messiaen. He had become totally disillusioned with the young continental avant-garde composers who had severed all relations with the music of the past, and were pursuing a style based on single notes rather than lines. As a gesture of defiance to this view, he and his father, the conductor Walter Goehr, wrote an essay called 'Arnold Schoenberg's Development towards the Twelve-Tone System', which begins:

> Although the conditions and problems facing a creative artist vary at dif-
> ferent times, an ethnic culture imposes a certain common tradition and
> leads to a fundamental similarity of outlook. An understanding of the roots
> and historic development of a culture is essential for an assessment of any
> individual artist.[4]

This elucidates how tradition was fundamental to Goehr's way of thinking. In *The Deluge* he uses short, highly diversified lines that clearly show the influence of Schoenberg, and are ideal for conveying the impression that the environment is being overwhelmed by wind and water. However, he underpinned this sense of flux by encasing his music in a series of blocks that he likens to the blocks found in Bach's Brandenburg Concertos, where the texture alternates between ritornellos and episodes, between tutti sections and solo sections. In other words he was indicating that not only did he belong to a tradition, but that he also had a predilection for using models, even though they may be difficult to discern in his music.

Bach-inspired blocks also underpin *Sutter's Gold*. This takes place in the California gold rush of 1848. John Sutter had acquired large tracts of land from

---

[4] The essay can be found in *European Music in the Twentieth Century*, ed. Howard Hartog (first published by Routledge and Kegan Paul in 1957 and then in a revised edition published by Pelican Books 1961), 88–106.

the Mexican authorities, and had set up a colony near Sacramento. When gold was discovered on his lands they were devastated by the influx of hordes of gold diggers. He could do nothing to prevent it, and in the end he had to take refuge 'in the darkness of the forest'. Like *The Deluge*, *Sutter's Gold* is serial, but after its first performance at the 1961 Leeds Triennial Festival, Goehr removed it from his catalogue because he had completely miscalculated what a large amateur choir was capable of singing. The members found his rhythms and, above all, his harmony too difficult for them. He therefore felt the need to create a harmonic vocabulary that could relate to common chords while still adhering to the twelve-note system. He did it by adapting and extending Schoenberg's technique of controlling the relationship between two different forms of the row used simultaneously. This was flexible enough to enable him to produce chords and short passages with strong leanings towards tonality, even though they were contained in his chromatic, basically serial technique. It was a way of proceeding he first developed in his *Two Choruses*, and it was to serve him for the next ten years or more.

The *Two Choruses* date from 1962 and are dedicated to the memory of Hanns Eisler, who died in September 1962. Goehr had met him as a student in Paris, and he renewed his acquaintance with him when Eisler came to London earlier in the year to attend a performance of his Deutscher Sinfonie. Like Goehr's father, Eisler had been a pupil of Schoenberg, but in the thirties and forties he became closely associated with Bertolt Brecht, supplying music in the epic style for six of his plays.

According to Goehr, Eisler was one of the first to appreciate the importance of Janáček, and it was to him that he owes his love for the Czech composer. Speaking of the great innovators of the twentieth century, Eisler had suggested they were Schoenberg, Stravinsky and Janáček. While everybody will agree with the first two, Janáček is not so obvious. Eisler held that Schoenberg and Stravinsky achieved new musical forms and languages but that, although Janáček did not, he was a genuine innovator in expression. He was a great Realist. It was with this in mind that, when Goehr was toying with the idea of writing an opera during the latter part of 1962, he decided Janáček should be his model. But as it happened he found the model for his plot not in Janáček but in Shostakovich, whose opera *Lady Macbeth of the Mtsensk District* (*Katerina Ismailova*) was given its first British performance at the Coliseum in December 1962. Shostakovich intended it to be the first of three operas about the plight of women in pre-Revolutionary Russia looked at from a Soviet point of view.

After attending a performance of Shostakovich's opera, Goehr heard a production of the anonymous late sixteenth-century play *Arden of Faversham* on the radio. This too is realistic for it is based on a true incident; it also concerns a woman who murders her husband. But, whereas Shostakovich said that as far as the musical language of *Katerina Ismailova* was concerned everything he wrote for Katerina was designed to attract our sympathy ('all her music has as its purpose the justification of her crimes'), there is nothing about Alice Arden that calls out for sympathy. She does not live in a hostile environment. Her husband may be a ruthless businessman, but he loves his wife. She kills him simply to have her lover, Mosby, replace him.

Goehr's work was commissioned by the Hamburg State Opera and therefore his opera had to be in German. For his librettist he chose Erich Fried, a poet with a wide reputation in Germany, known as much for his controversial left-wing views as for his poetry. Like Goehr's father, who escaped to Britain with his family as soon as Hitler came to power in 1933, Fried came to Britain in 1938 after the Nazis invaded his native Austria. Since then he had been working in the German section of the BBC's World Service. But although Goehr also worked at the BBC, they had little or no contact with each other when the libretto was being written. To Goehr's disappointment, Fried produced a text that bore no resemblance to what he had wanted. 'It stopped being Janáček', he told me, 'it became Brecht, except that it was written in rhyming couplets like Peter Weiss's *Marat/Sade*. I then had the problem of composing it in a new way. I remember Tippett saying you couldn't collaborate with anyone of distinction because they would pull a fast one on you. As poets, they would always have a clear idea of how it should be done, but it wouldn't necessarily be your idea. Fried loathed music, and he loathed opera so he had no sympathy for Janáček and had to make it political.'

However, given the plot of *Arden of Faversham*, he could not have turned it into a tragic opera in the Janáček or Shostakovich manner. What Goehr might have objected to is that Fried saw in the play an opportunity to levy an attack on the behaviour of the Germans towards the Jews during and after the war. This is why at the first performance in Hamburg in March 1967, there was a storm of protests when Fried took his curtain call. For example, in the play the murder of Arden is initiated by Alice alone. Others who feel they have been wronged by her husband become conspirators after she has failed to poison him. In the libretto, on the other hand, the decision to murder Arden is taken jointly. It becomes a communal decision rather than a personal one. Fried also calculated that most Germans would recognise the lute song that the servant Susan sings before the murder, 'Am Weg so rot die Rose glüht', a song that Alice and Mosby take up after the murder as they are passing the bloody knife from one to the other. They would recognise it as being closely related to the Nazi wartime song 'Am Weg die Rose blüht, wenn die SA nach Moskau zieht'.

Fried's most effective way of making his point was achieved through the character he invented for the opera: Mrs Bradshaw, a neighbour of the Ardens. She is present throughout the plotting of the murder, and although she disapproves she also witnesses it. Yet she does nothing to prevent it happening. She merely looks on. At the first performance in Hamburg, Fried added a spoken epilogue in which he points his accusation at the audience, saying it was not guilty of murder or of any other crime, and, unlike Alice, was further off and much better organised.

As a result of Fried's changes, Goehr says he was forced to adopt a musical style closer to Eisler than Janáček. The influence of Janáček can be heard in the declamatory style of the vocal lines, but in other respects the score is indebted to what Brecht called the epic style. 'I had been working at the Mermaid Theatre', Goehr told me, 'and because I spoke German, Bernard Miles sent me to Berlin to find out how the Berliner Ensemble used music for the Brecht plays he wanted to put on at the Mermaid. Some of the ideas I incorporated into the opera.'

Although Goehr put one or two of the ideas into practice in his opera, it was not until he composed the Triptych that he incorporated them fully. All three works are structured in accordance with the autonomous musical forms of the classical tradition; two of them have their action performed by masked mimes; and all three make use of a narrator. He also took over Fried's denunciation of the German attitude to the Jews, openly in *Sonata about Jerusalem*, more covertly in *Naboth's Vineyard* and *Shadowplay*. In *Shadowplay* and *Sonata about Jerusalem* the narrator is a single singer, but in *Naboth's Vineyard* two or three of the soloists singing as a chorus in rhythmic unison take on the role. When they function as a narrator they sing in English, otherwise they sing in Latin. The use of a dead language for direct speech serves two purposes: it affirms that the action is taking place in the past and it helps to distance the audience from the sometimes violent events on stage.

Naboth's Vineyard has two features in common with *Arden Must Die*: it involves a scheming woman who instigates murder, and the use of a figure like Mrs Bradshaw, in this case, Achab, who repents of the crime to save his skin even though he did not commit it. Achab, King of Israel, wants to acquire Naboth's vineyard in order to make a garden for himself. He offers Naboth money or another vineyard in exchange, but Naboth refuses on the grounds that it is his inheritance and that God has forbidden him to part with it. Achab then returns to his palace in a state of great dejection. He retires to his bed, turns his face to the wall, covers his head and refuses all food. His wife, Jezebel, tries to console him, but when she fails to do so, she says she will obtain the vineyard on his behalf. Using Achab's seal, she writes letters to the Elders instructing them to declare a feast, to invite Naboth to it, to have two sons of Belial (Baal) sit opposite him to accuse him of blasphemy against God and the King, then to have him stoned to death. They duly obey her instructions, and when Naboth's death is accomplished, Achab takes possession of the vineyard. At this point Elijah arrives to deliver

Ill. 6.1 Production of Goehr, *Naboth's Vineyard*, 1968

God's judgement. Achab is told that God will bring disaster upon his house, and that Jezebel will be devoured by dogs. At this point, Achab rends his clothes, puts on sackcloth and behaves like an outcast. His contrition is so abject that God sends Elijah to him a second time. He is now told that because he has humbled himself God will not bring disaster upon his house in his own lifetime, but in his son's.

It must be remembered that the singers do not take part in the action. This has to be performed by the mimes. In the introduction to the score the director, John Cox, gives suggestions on how it could be done (Ill. 6.1):

> In the original production of *Naboth's Vineyard* the action was represented by two mimes wearing identical costumes. They put on masks to represent the characters in the drama, exchanging them as the exigencies of the action required. Every attempt was made to keep the mimes indistinguishable from one another, so that the masks were the only 'characters'. The only property was a vine.

Although Goehr asks for the mimes to be indistinguishable from each other, the music he writes for the characters they represent is highly differentiated. This allows him, in characteristic Brechtian manner, to create a dichotomy between what is seen and what is heard. For example, there is nothing in the music to suggest Achab's tantrums or that Naboth is a bully. Achab's vocal line is obsessive and imperious. Goehr characterises this with narrow intervals, frequent repetitions, tight rhythms, strong accents and loud dynamics. In the five bars Naboth has to sing, on the other hand, single notes are articulated evenly and calmly. In contrast, Jezebel's music is extravagantly excessive. Her intervals are wide, and in her vocal range, rhythms and dynamics she goes rapidly from one extreme to the other. These are the features that also characterise Elijah's music, the main difference being that, whereas hers is hysterical, his has to be sung with nobility and without being measured. It could be said to be outside time.

He also characterises the instruments. These make an unusual ensemble: flute, clarinet, bass trombone, piano (four hands), violin and double bass. The flautist must also play alto flute and piccolo, the clarinettist bass clarinet, with both players using the extended techniques exploited in the late sixties. Achab has the clarinet and bass trombone to accompany him, and when he marches to and from the vineyard the piano. Naboth is mainly represented by the flute and clarinet playing evenly and calmly, Jezebel by the Bb clarinet, which like her must also go to the extremes of its range and technique. And when the bass clarinet is joined by the alto flute to accompany Elijah, even more extended techniques are employed: fluttertonguing, key tapping, glissandos and accelerating tremolos.

In Chapter One I focused on *Naboth's Vineyard*'s relationship to *Il combattimento*. Here I want to focus on its structure. Goehr divides the work into six unequal parts, the longer ones also being subdivided. The structure of the work as a whole relates both to classical instrumental sonata form (exposition, development, recapitulation) and to classical three-act opera form (exposition of a conflict, development leading to a climax, denouement). The work begins and ends with the same material altered to suit the circumstances, thus serving as both prelude and postlude. The prelude is given to the narrator in the form of a three-part chorus telling us that we are being taken to Naboth's vineyard. When this is turned into a postlude at the end of the work it is expanded to become the voice of God giving his final judgement. For this the text is given in both Latin and English simultaneously.

The structure's exposition is a contrast between the different singing styles of Achab and Jezebel rather than a difference in interests. The conflict of interests is confined to the first 'subject', when Achab and Naboth confront each other. Here the structure reflects the work as a whole: exposition, development to a climax and denouement. It begins with Achab's march to the vineyard. Like Achab's music when he is singing, it is narrow in its pitch range and tight in its rhythm.

The confrontation between Achab and Naboth has Achab speaking in an assertive tone and Naboth remaining silent, his contribution being represented by the evenly pulsating music which characterises him played by instruments (Ex. 6.1a).

When he does speak he is still relatively calm. Anger overtakes him suddenly, and this marks the beginning of the first subject's development. Now the tables are turned. In a passage in which neither of them speaks, the aggression comes from Naboth, the confusion from Achab. The climax is reached when Naboth throws Achab out of the vineyard. Achab's return to his palace uses the opening march with its pitches played backwards and, inserted within it, we hear the narrator's report on the state of his dejection.

The second subject deals with the outcome of this situation. Here the dialogue is between Achab and Jezebel, but here it is Achab who is silent. She is decisive; he passive. In her first virtuoso passage she demands an explanation from him, and when he indicates that he has been humiliated by Naboth she embarks on a second virtuoso passage in which she says that she herself will acquire the vineyard. This passage is also in the form of a dialogue, her interlocutor being the clarinet (Ex. 6.1b).

Goehr casts the development of this exposition in four sections. Through them the tension gathers pace to reach a climax in a mighty tam-tam stroke played by a mime when Naboth is dead. In the first section Jezebel writes letters in Achab's name to the Elders, and the narrator makes his comments against an antiphonal exchange between a piercingly high piccolo and the violin representing the sound of her nib on the parchment. She then reads out the letter to the Elders and they repeat the instructions back to her. During this section the mimes acting the part of the Elders have double masks, one side representing the Elders, the other the Sons of Belial. When Naboth comes to the feast, the masks are alternated so rapidly that he becomes confused and appeals to the Elders for an explanation. Yet when he looks at them they are no longer the Elders but the Sons of Belial. A note in the score says: 'He realises it is a frame-up. He is trapped.' Suddenly all activity ceases. Jezebel reads out the instruction to have Naboth executed and he is dragged out and stoned.

The stoning is conveyed purely instrumentally: the singers play tambourines with bells to represent the showers of stones falling to the ground, and on one occasion the bass trombone plays a plaintive unaccompanied solo. That this represents Naboth who has been given a few seconds' respite is made clear when it shifts from its bottom register to its top and reiterates a note culminating in extremely loud fluttertonguing to mark the victim's last agonised gasp. Appropriately, the fifth part takes place in silence. It is devoted entirely to the mimes indicating that Jezebel is telling Achab about Naboth's death, and that he can now go to the vineyard to take possession of it.

Ex. 6.1a Goehr, *Naboth's Vineyard*, opening bars of Achab's aria, bb. 18–26

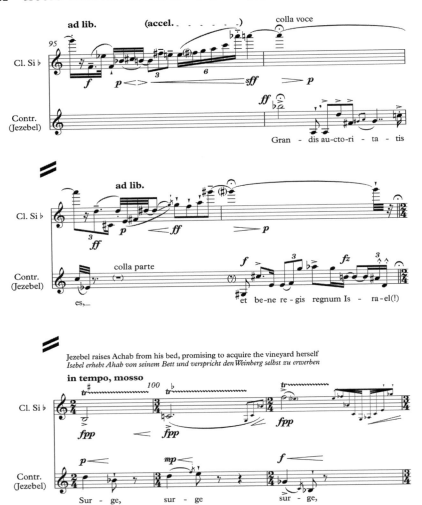

Ex.6.1b Goehr, *Naboth's Vineyard*, second verse of Jezebel's aria, bb. 95–101

The last part combines denouement and recapitulation. It begins with the slowest and simplest music in the work: music that conveys both an *in memoriam* for Naboth and, when the music becomes louder, an indication that God is about to intervene. What follows is an integration of the tight music associated with Achab and the extremely free music associated with Jezebel, which we met in the work's exposition, except that now it is not Jezebel who speaks but Elijah. The two may be polar opposites in terms of their characters, but they are closely related in their music. The relationship means that Goehr is able to conform to the classical tradition in which the contrasting subjects of the exposition are drawn closer together in the recapitulation. In a classical score this would be done by having them both in the home key. Here, however, Goehr manages to integrate Elijah's music with Achab's by shifting the focus from one character to the other as in a dialogue, a technique he has been using throughout the work. This creates the impression that Achab is responding closely to what Elijah is telling him. The last of these responses marks the moment when he humbles himself. At this point the music can return to its beginning to round off the process of recapitulation and integration.

While *Naboth's Vineyard* is the equivalent of an opening sonata-allegro in a three-movement classical design, *Shadowplay* functions as a slow movement. There are two reasons for calling it a slow movement. One is that, although it contains a great many rapid gestures, the basic tempo throughout the piece is Andante. The other is that, like most slow movements, it is contemplative. The passage from Plato's *Republic* (Book VII) Goehr chose is the allegory of the cave because it deals with a philosophical issue that has to be pondered. It illustrates Plato's belief that behind the mutable, material world lies an ideal world. The allegory marks the philosophical ascent from illusion and error to enlightenment, enlightenment being knowledge of the intelligible world that is universal yet invisible. Plato's metaphor for the first is the shadows and for the second the sun. At the end of the story, when the prisoner returns to the cave, he draws the moral that for those who have not experienced knowledge of the intelligible world it is easier to accept illusions and lies even when told the truth.

Plato's text is a dialogue between Socrates and his pupil Glaucon. Goehr uses a translation by Kenneth Cavander, who provides the words for when the prisoner releases himself from his fetters and ascends into the outside world. Goehr cuts out Socrates's questions and Glaucon's answers and comments so that we hear only the basic story. This is told by the narrator (tenor) except that in the central section, when in Goehr's version the prisoner speaks, the tenor moves into the ensemble to deliver in conjunction with the alto saxophone an intensely lyrical passage in praise of the sun. The prisoner's sight of the sun is the climax of the story. However, Plato fails to convey the prisoner's inner feelings at this moment, but Goehr, abandoning Brecht's principle of alienation, instead of distancing the audience from the emotional content of the situation, draws them into it.. Although Plato's parable does not itself call for them, Goehr inserts instrumental intermezzos into the work to create what are in effect four scenes. The first covers the 'shadowplay' on and behind the wall of the cave; the second the prisoners' mistaken belief that what they see is reality as well as the confusion of the prisoner who is released; the third covers the events taking place from twilight to sunrise outside the cave; the fourth the return to the cave. During the intermezzos there should be no movement on stage, and during the last two, no light either. This suggests that during the last two the audience has to imagine the prisoner's ascent to the outside world and his descent to the cave.

Despite my contention that Music Theatre should be relatively easy to produce, *Shadowplay* has proved to be a difficult work to bring off in the theatre, and well-nigh impossible in a concert hall without theatrical lighting. Goehr tells me that he has seen it done in over twenty different ways, and only a few have been satisfactory. The difficulty lies in taking Plato's description of the events too literally. In Goehr's opinion the best production took place at the Opéra-Comique in Paris when the role of the prisoner was played by Jean Babilée, an actor who also had skills as a gymnast. The cave was represented by a large box, its sides covered by white translucent paper. Lights shining on the side nearest to the audience created the impression that everything within the box was seen as a shadow. Thus, with the assistance of a couple of mimes, all the objects and figures in the first two scenes looked like those in a shadow play. When the prisoner was released he too was a shadow. He only became clearly visible when he climbed up a rope suspended from the ceiling, and from near the top he reported on what he could see in the outside world. Goehr always intended that the first two scenes would function as a shadow play, hence the title of the work, but before the production at the Opéra-Comique he had never seen it done so convincingly.

As in *Naboth's Vineyard* the ensemble is an unusual one. Goehr selected alto flute, alto saxophone, horn, cello and piano because they cover the middle register of the tonal spectrum, yet their tone colours are extremely distinctive. They can easily be distinguished even when they play in the narrow tonal bands he uses.

He divided the work into four scenes separated by instrumental interludes, the second interlude marking the division between the two halves of the binary structure. In the first scene the narrator tells us that he imagines a cave with an entrance opening to the light. In the cave are prisoners who have been there since they were children. They are fettered so that they cannot move either their bodies or their heads. Above and behind them is a fire, and in front of this lies a road screened from the prisoners by a wall. Behind the wall people walk carrying objects such as statues and sculptures of animals in wood or stone. These objects are seen by the prisoners only as shadows on the wall they face. Some of the people talk, others are silent.

Apart from the lights needed for the narrator and the instrumentalists to read their parts, the scene starts in darkness with the lighting needed for the cave appearing only gradually. The music is played by all the instruments except the piano. Although it all derives from a twelve-note row, none of the fragmentary shapes produced are the same. To create the illusion of shadows beginning to appear on the wall the prisoners face, the instruments – flute, horn and cello – in particular, create a sense of the ephemeral by both the nature of their fragments and the special effects they employ. However, the harmonics, stopped notes, fluttertonguing and timed tremolos have a totally different effect from when they were used in *Naboth's Vineyard*. Some of these fragments in the last five bars of the scene are taken up by the piano for the first intermezzo, which it performs alone.

The second scene begins with the narrator asking four questions: would the prisoners be able to see only the shadows on the wall; would they be able to see anything of the objects passing behind the wall; if they could communicate would they consider the shadows to be reality; and if they could hear people talking behind the wall would they believe the sound came from the objects being carried? After all these questions Goehr asks the instrumentalists to participate in a mobile, a mobile being a texture in which each instrument has its own short group of notes to play over and over again in its own time until stopped by the conductor. These mobiles vary in length, some being little more than fragments. They are included to relate to mobile sculptures with delicately balanced parts set in motion by air currents. In other words they are objects without stability.

When the narrator says the prisoners believe in the absolute reality of the shadows, they stop moving and we see that one of the prisoners has released himself from his bonds so that he can move his head and see the source of the light and the objects behind the wall. He considers them to be 'toys, playthings, trash, rubbish', so he turns back to his former position where he finds comfort in what he is used to. The intermezzo that follows this scene is given mainly to the cello. Its material is also drawn from the previous fragments, but it plays them in a manner that now has increasing purpose. In it we are to imagine that the scene is changing from the cave to the outside world. Goehr does not show the prisoner's painful ascent, but implies it when the third scene opens and we see the prisoner's state as being 'almost naked, fearful and protesting'.

Until now Goehr has been true to Plato, but now he required Cavander to expand Plato's text to include more incidents and to delay the climactic moment when the sun rises. This creates more opportunity for stage action since there was none in the first scene and, during the second, comparatively little. Goehr also needs time to build the music up to a climax. Throughout the scene the tenor no longer sings the role of the narrator telling the story, but sits in the ensemble to comment and, more significantly, to supply the prisoner's inner feelings.

The scene begins in twilight, and the first of the additional incidents occurs after the prisoner has been dazzled by the light. He now shields his eyes with his hand, which he finds he can name. At the word 'hand' the tenor, as commentator, says: 'Hand – small tree of flesh with branching fingers'. He develops this idea after the second incident when, after wondering whether he ought to return to the cave, the prisoner looks into a pool of water and sees in the reflection that behind him are 'trees … clouds … the light'. At this the commentator says: 'Tree, a hand with branches holds the cloud in its palm'. There is a further development when the prisoner bends down, scoops water from the pool with his hand, and sees the water as being a jewel that gleams in the darkness. Now the commentator says: 'In the palm, the light'. The word 'light' is sung on a high A, as it had been, when in scene one the tenor, as narrator, mentioned that the cave had an entrance opening to the light. It is after its second occurrence of the note that the build up to the climax begins. It arrives when the sun has become completely visible and the tenor once again sings high A, but now as loudly and as long as possible. The long anacrusis to this climax moves further and further away from the fragmentation that characterised the first and most of the second scene.

Lines, even though highly ornamented at times, get longer; three appearing in rhythmic unison and, when the prisoner looks at the water gleaming in his hand, the cello plays the first sustained note in the piece. It is so long that the player has to change bow several times in the course of it. Ideally bow changes ought to be imperceptible, but on this occasion Goehr asks the player to articulate the change with a short accent so that the overall effect resembles a slow pulsation. This pulsating effect becomes more prominent after the prisoner sees the stars and the moon, and the tenor sings sostenuto and very quietly: 'Moon drinks hot Sun and makes it cold'. The last four syllables of this statement are articulated very deliberately. They usher in a return of the mobiles to illustrate the beginning of dawn.

All the instruments except the saxophone have independent repeating figures in the middle register that gradually get faster and louder until their figures appear to gel. They lead us to believe they are contributing to a sustained sound that shimmers and pulsates. Against it the tenor, matched by the saxophone, sings sustained notes that do not shimmer but are absolutely steady. Their durations vary from note to note, so too do their dynamics. But these variations merely heighten the effect of the words: 'Sun lights all in white, white, white flames' (Ex. 6.2).

Gradually the sun rises until it is completely visible and the tenor can finish the sentence by saying '… burns out the dark in bursts of light'. Now we hear the singing of 'light' on a top A as being truly climatic. The mobile continues to get louder, but within a few seconds there is a complete cut off. The musical transformation from a fragmentary texture to its opposite, matching the visual transformation from darkness to light, comes to an abrupt end. The prisoner tells us that he can now see things as they really are, and the cessation of the mobile indicates that with this knowledge he will return to the cave to tell the others about his experience.

The following Intermezzo takes the scene back to the cave, and is scored for all the instruments. Initially they play in a fashion that recalls the exuberance the prisoner experienced in the light. Gradually, however, music associated with

Ex. 6.2 Goehr, *Shadowplay*, 'Sun lights all in white, white flames', bb. 127–39

shadows takes over. The text is Plato's and the tenor becomes the narrator again. He tells us that at first the prisoner, after having been in the light, finds it difficult to distinguish things in the dark. If the others knew this they would think him ignorant. Word would go round that in the world outside he had ruined his sight. Finally he realises that if he tried to unshackle the others and lead them up to the light they might kill him.

If *Naboth's Vineyard* is the equivalent of a sonata allegro, and *Shadowplay* a binary slow movement, it might be expected that Goehr would conclude his Triptych with a rondo finale. I mentioned earlier that the refrain which appears five times in the course of *Sonata about Jerusalem* could be related to the refrain that dominates Monteverdi's *Sonata sopra Sancta Maria*, as well as the recurrence of the music setting the eight verses of the *Lyke-Wake Dirge* in Stravinsky's *Cantata*. But it could also be considered the principal theme of a rondo with four long episodes: (1) the conditions of the Jews of Baghdad, (2) the news a crazed boy brings to the Jews, and their rejoicing, (3) their ascent on to their roofs where they await a miracle, (4) their disappointment, and the mocking of them when they descend.

The refrain is sung in Latin by a small female chorus consisting of two sopranos and a contralto (Ex. 6.3). The words are by the twelfth-century itinerant Italian monk Obadiah the Proselyte: *Sol convertetur in tenebris, et luna in sanguinem antequam veniat dies Domini magnus et horribilis.* (The sun shall be turned into darkness, and the moon into blood before the day of the Lord comes, magnificent and terrible.) Its significance is that, whereas Monteverdi alters the rhythm and articulation of his refrain on each successive occurrence, and Stravinsky alters the words in his, Goehr's is always the same – always the same yet always different, for on each occasion we hear it in a different way, the difference being determined by what it follows.

Goehr's setting of the refrain is surprisingly matter-of-fact for such highly charged words. It creates the impression that, although there will be darkness and blood before the day of the Lord comes, this has to be accepted. The event does not call for lamentation. Nevertheless, when the chorus comes to the word '*horribilis*', Goehr asks for a subito piano on the second syllable, as if the singers needed to stifle the word. All we hear is 'hor' because the rest of the word is masked by the accompanying instruments making in the same bar a crescendo from forte to fortissimo, the implication being that if there is no need for lamentation then there is certainly an element of fear in Obadiah's pronouncement.

Later we discover that the chains of small bells the chorus play before and after they sing identify them as being the Jewish women of Baghdad. The matter-of-fact character of the refrain arises from its moderato tempo, relaxed rhythm, tonal leaning towards B major/B minor, and its immediately recognisable structure.

Ex. 6.3 Goehr, *Sonata about Jerusalem*, opening of Refrain

Ex. 6.3 (*continued*)

This is the old German bar form, AAB, which had its origins in the songs of the twelfth-century Minnesingers, a form in which the length of the two As matches the length of the B. Here the second A is a slight variant of the first. The B also begins in the same way but it reaches its cadence via a longer route. As the work progresses it becomes evident that Goehr makes a feature of bar forms so that the refrain serves as a model for the piece as a whole.

The work employs larger forces than the other two works in the Triptych. As well as a small chorus, a bass is required for narrator, a high soprano for the crazed boy and a boy's speaking voice is also needed for the mocking at the end. The instruments are nine in number: flute doubling piccolo, clarinet doubling bass clarinet, horn, trumpet, bass trombone, piano, violin, cello and double bass. As in *Naboth's Vineyard* there are parts for two mimes. In the score Goehr himself gives instructions on how and when they should act. 'It is not the function of the mimes to reduplicate the telling of a story already told in the text,' he writes. 'The central action of the piece, the desire of unfortunate and persecuted men literally to fly, their trance-like belief that they are flying and their subsequent disappoint-ment and ridiculing seems to form an adequate scenario. It should be done in a manner and utilising visual elements which avoid *all* graphic representations customarily associated with Jewry, and its persecution. In art, persecution, self- or inflicted, and psychological symbols may be misunderstood when made to stick to a particular section of the community or to particular historic events.'

The first episode opens with the entry of the narrator representing the power of the King of Baghdad and the entrance of the mimes representing the Jews. The King is introduced by the bass trombone playing *con forza* music indicating not only his power, but also the effect his words will have on the Jews, for each of its phrases ends with a falling semitone and a stress pattern, which in tonal music is often associated with pathos. Similarly, the music introducing the Jews also con-tains two elements, the first being a quiet, querying variant of what the trombone has been playing, the second suggesting uncertainty. This is achieved by means of a tremolo that gets faster then slower across a wide interval. Development of these elements occurs as soon as the King begins to speak, and later when the mimes act. The King tells the Jews that they must bear a mark on their heads and about their necks, that their women must have a black shoe on their left foot and a red shoe on their right foot, and that little copper bells must be fastened round their necks and on their feet to distinguish them from the other women in Baghdad, and that cruel warders are to be set over all the Jews to humiliate them and to beat them. The mimes, wearing masks, act out these instructions. Their music is in bar form, the As ending with a flourish on the piano (poco liberamente), the B with the tightest and most percussive music so far. It leads straight into the refrain that in this context sounds as if the chorus were indifferent to the plight of the Jews.

The second episode deals with what the crazed boy says and how the Jews respond to his news. Goehr captures the boy's unstable mind with music in which certain words are missed out and the stutter from which the boy suffers grows worse, so that in the end he can hardly say the vital word 'Jerusalem'. He tells the Jews that the time has come when the Lord will gather up his people Israel from all the world and bring them to Jerusalem. However, when the fast tempo expressing their joy suddenly turns to frenzy, their rejoicing is interrupted. In the fast tempo Goehr allowed the singers to reiterate their notes in their own time, but in the slow tempo vocal freedom is replaced by instrumental discipline so that the mood becomes one of unified celebration. The two tempos alternate so that when the refrain follows the slow section it seems to express neither matter-of-factness nor a hint of fear but joyous affirmation.

The third episode is the longest in the work, the structure being bar form writ large. Both the A sections are also in bar form, but the B section has to be much longer than the other two to delay the arrival of the climax. Even so all three sections culminate in a climax, the first being when the Jews put on the green robes of paradise, the second when they climb on to their roofs, the third and main one, when in a state of ecstasy, they wait for the miracle and imagine they are flying.

After the narrator has told us about the putting on of the robes, the mimes take over to act out his words. They have to find gestures to cover the most hesitant part of the work. This occurs at the beginning of the B section. Structurally it marks the nadir before the build up to the last climax, the zenith of the piece. For the first time in the work the music is reduced to fragments. We recognise them as having their origins in the music used for the entrance of the King and the Jews in the first episode. The general pauses Goehr asks for suggest that the Jews are straining their ears to hear some evidence of the miracle that will save them but that all they actually hear are the mysterious noises of the night. During this and the ensuing subsections Goehr does not specify what the mimes should be doing. Musically, however, the music gathers momentum until in the last subsection it becomes a huge upbeat. That the downbeat turns out to be the refrain is a disappointment, a disappointment that mirrors the disappointment of the Jews when they discover that the miracle has not materialised. In conjunction with solemn chords representing their mood we hear something else when they descend from their roofs, the mockery of the bass clarinet and the narrator using an accelerating tremolo to indicate suppressed laughter. Eventually, however, it is the voice of a child which brings the mockery out into the open: 'Ha!', he says, 'the Jews wanted to fly to Jerusalem, but they have no wings.'

As I indicated earlier, Goehr's Triptych is structurally so well balanced and coherent that it is difficult to believe he did not plan it as a whole from the beginning. But evidently he put it together piece by piece. Throughout my account of the work I have drawn attention to the models he called on, yet I have not acknowledged how effectively he was able to absorb them into his own style without making them obvious. This was also true when he used *Il combattimento di Tancredi e Clorinda* for a virtuoso clarinet piece for Alan Hacker paraphrasing the madrigal shortly after completing *Naboth's Vineyard*. It is my opinion that this too can be regarded as Music Theatre. But in the long run it was his use of traditional musical structures and the ideas behind the Epic Theatre of Brecht that proved to be the most valuable influences on the Triptych. It was these that enabled him to construct a type of Music Theatre in the late sixties and early seventies that was entirely his own. I also believe that, although he complained at what Erich Fried had done in his libretto for *Arden Must Die*, he shared Fried's political motives. Although *Naboth's Vineyard* and *Shadowplay* can be looked on as expressing independent moral concerns, looked at in the context of *Arden Must Die* and *Sonata about Jerusalem* Achab's belief that he 'got away with it', and the prisoner's realisation that his companions prefer lies to the truth, can also be seen as a comment on the attitude of the Germans to the Jews during and after the Second World War, awareness of which Goehr has deeply engrained in his mentality.

CHAPTER SEVEN

Maxwell Davies's Monodramas

O F the six music-theatre works Peter Maxwell Davies composed between 1964 and 1974, five are monodramas for a single performer and a small chamber ensemble, while the sixth, *Blind Man's Buff* (1972), is for four perform- ers and a chamber orchestra. As this differs from the other five in both topic and scoring, it will be discussed in a later chapter. The five monodramas fall into two groups. *Revelation and Fall* (1966), *Eight Songs for a Mad King* (1969) and *Miss Donnithorne's Maggot* (1974) have their roots in Schoenberg's *Pierrot lunaire* in that they focus on individuals who have such a distorted vision of reality that they appear to be mad. *Missa super L'homme armé* (1968) and *Vesalii Icones* (1969) have their roots in Stravinsky's *L'histoire du soldat* and the plays of Brecht and they focus on a moral issue, namely the need to distinguish between the true and the false.

Behind all these works, however, lies his opera *Taverner*,[1] the work that affected all his musical thinking from 1956 until he finished it in 1968, a few months before composing *Eight Songs for a Mad King*. The feature they have in common is their use of parody. Maxwell Davies conceived *Taverner* when he was a student at Manchester University. 'I remember thinking that I would have to make a style which would last me through the next fifty years,' he told me:

> a style that would be solid enough ground to construct the edifice of a life-
> time. For me the composers I met at Darmstadt when I was there had not
> faced the issue. By acknowledging only Webern and neglecting everyone
> else they were like flowers that may bloom for a short time in a vase but will
> not put down roots. I came to the conclusion that unlike them I would have
> to have a discourse that was directional if I were to survive. I would have to
> create a sense of progress not only from one musical idea to the next but
> right across the whole length of the work. I had read Schenker's *Der freie
> Satz* and his analysis of Beethoven's Fifth and Ninth Symphonies, and was
> well aware of the need for long-term thinking over a long span of time. I
> was also aware that to sustain a large structure it would have to be done

---

[1] For a detailed discussion of the work, see David Beard, 'Taverner: An Interpretation', in *Peter Maxwell Davies Studies*, ed. Kenneth Gloag and Nicholas Jones (Cambridge, Cambridge University Press, 2009), 79–105.

in ways other than those that Schenker discussed. I realised that it would have to involve a very slow transformation process of say a line of notes or a sequence of note values which would end up being an exact inversion of the original. In fact I had already been turning over in my mind several large-scale canvases involving transformational processes, one of which was an opera about Taverner.

Maxwell Davies began sketching the libretto and some of the music for *Taverner* almost as soon as he conceived the idea in 1956. For his plot he took E.H. Fellowes's account of Taverner's life in the first volume of Tudor Church Music.[2] This had been based on what John Foxe had to say about Taverner in his *Actes and Monuments* (1563), an account that has now been proved erroneous, although Maxwell Davies did not know this at the time.[3] The account interested him not only because it concerned the life of a composer but because it offered a very vivid account of a large-scale transformational process.

John Taverner (1495–1545) wrote some of the finest Catholic Church music of the sixteenth century. Although he became involved in an outbreak of Lutheran heresy at Cardinal College, Oxford, where he was organist and Master of the Choristers, there is no evidence to support Foxe's claims that he was imprisoned for heresy, released on the orders of Cardinal Wolsey for being 'but a musician' or that he abandoned the Catholic faith, became an agent for Thomas Cromwell and took an active part in the destruction of the monasteries, or indeed that under the pressure of his new religious conviction he also abandoned music.[4]

Maxwell Davies had already used a transformational process in the first movement of his Trumpet Sonata (1955). Here a three-note figure is gradually transformed from being a gesture of great clarity and forthrightness when played on the trumpet at the beginning of the movement to become highly dissonant and brutal when played by the piano at the end. When Maxwell Davies began sketching the opera he noticed that these three notes (G-E-D) are those contained in the opening of the Sarum antiphon Taverner used to set the words *in nomine Domini* in the *Benedictus* of his Gloria tibi Trinitas Mass. Shortly after its composition the *Benedictus* became so admired that it was circulated as a detached piece, its plainsong becoming the basis of a long series of instrumental In Nomine pieces (mainly for consorts of viols), which English composers produced up to the time

[2]   E.H. Fellowes, *Tudor Church Music, vols 1–3*: 'John Taverner', ed P.C. Buck *et al.* (Oxford, Oxford University Press, 1922–9).

[3]   Information supplied by Paul Griffiths, *Peter Maxwell Davies* (London, Robson Books, 1985), 47.

[4]   John Foxe's *Actes and Monuments* was published in 1563, 1570, 1576 and 1583 as an ecclesiastical history and martyrology.

of Purcell. The antiphon was therefore the ideal theme with which to represent Taverner's legacy.

Most of the material in the opera derives from the plainsong and the treble theme that accompanies it in the *Benedictus*. Each of its two acts opens with the three-note trumpet gesture, and in the course of the acts this gradually becomes transformed. At the end of the first act, as in the Trumpet Sonata, it becomes dissonant and brutal to reflect the triumph of those forces that have driven Taverner to reject his faith and his art. At the end of the second the transformation results in a performance of the *Benedictus* played by a consort of recorders to express that, although Taverner lies prostrate on the floor because he realises that his actions have resulted in his becoming a victim himself, his musical legacy lives on.

Transformational processes are present in all Maxwell Davies's music-theatre works. Those that are ostensibly concerned with a moral issue start from a state where goodness and truth prevail and proceed to the state where falsehood and the Devil, in the form of the Antichrist, takes over. Maxwell Davies's symbol for the Devil is the traditional one in music: the interval of the augmented fourth, which medieval musicians called the *diabolus in musica*. This association arose from the theory of hexachords used in the Middle Ages and Renaissance, and the use of solmisation to help singers distinguish a perfect fourth (a concordant and therefore a true fourth) from an augmented fourth (a discordant and therefore a false fourth). In *Missa super L'homme armé* and *Antechrist* Maxwell Davies makes the transformational process clear simply by emphasising perfect fourths at the beginning of the work and augmented fourths at the end.

In *Taverner*, he uses the augmented fourth (D-G♯) to form a chord that includes the two whole tones between the interval (D-E-F♯-G♯). It is always scored for low brass. For instance two tubas might be given the notes D and F♯ to play in one octave, and two horns the notes E and G♯ to play in the octave above. Commentators usually call the chord the 'death chord' because it first occurs in the fourth scene of act one when Taverner says 'Death! A thief'. But in his music-theatre works as well as in *Taverner* it symbolises deception and, since it is framed by the augmented fourth, this implies deception by the Devil or the Antichrist. In *Taverner* the chord appears most frequently in the first act's fourth scene where the figures representing deception virtually take Taverner over (Ill. 7.1).

The transformational processes in the other music-theatre works in which apparent madness prevails are less overt. In *Revelation and Fall* Maxwell Davies devises an extremely effective scheme to indicate that the highly disturbed poet who wrote the text moves from a state of extreme agitation to one in which quietude is discovered by means of letting things be, by being prepared to lose control. In *Eight Songs for a Mad King*, on the other hand, peace of mind is only partially achieved. The King is able to stand back from his condition and take

Ill. 7.1 Maxwell Davies, *Taverner*, world première, 1972, Royal Opera House, London

pity on himself even though he leaves the stage howling. Miss Donnithorne (*Miss Donnithorne's Maggot*), however, is another matter. When we first encounter her she is rational enough to invite the people of Sydney to her nuptial feast even though she hopes it will choke them, but when she leaves the stage at the end of the work – after imagining that her lover is about to 'take' her – she dances off to 'a cheap tune summing up the whole masquerade', as Maxwell Davies puts it. During the course of the work she becomes increasingly more involved in her own fantasies.

Musicians acknowledge two forms of parody: firstly the use of borrowed material for serious purposes, the prime example being the Renaissance Parody Mass based on earlier material either by the composer himself or by someone else, and secondly the use of borrowed material for humorous or mocking purposes. Parody in the first sense has formed the backbone of Maxwell Davies's compositional procedures ever since he wrote *Alma Redemptoris Mater* in 1957, but his use of parody in the second sense only came into its own during the period when he produced his music-theatre pieces. It first made its appearance in the first act of *Taverner* and the two *Fantasias on an In Nomine by John Taverner*, which he composed between 1962 and 1964. But in these his use of parody is only sporadic.

On the other hand, the second act of *Taverner*, which he composed between 1966 and 1968, is almost entirely parodic, and so his preoccupation with parody during those years was almost bound to rub off on his music-theatre pieces, especially those composed in 1968 and 1969: *Missa super L'homme armé*, *Eight Songs for a Mad King* and *Vesalii Icones*.

Although *Taverner* played a major role in determining the contents of his music-theatre works, their character arose from the lively public discussion about the future of opera that took place at the first Wardour Castle Summer School in 1964, and the works performed at the second in 1965. It had been decided at the first school that Maxwell Davies would ask the American soprano Bethany Beardslee, whom he had got to know when studying at Princeton, to be the reciter in *Pierrot lunaire*. Everybody I have spoken to who attended her performance says that it was quite extraordinary in its histrionics, and that the event was a never-to-be-forgotten occasion. She performed it in costume, and, according to Robin Holloway, in a style that was 'camp and old lace: creepy Edward Gorey gothic'. There is no doubt in my mind that this performance set the tone for all Maxwell Davies's Music Theatre, and not only the works that, like *Pierrot*, are concerned with abnormal states of mind.

Bethany Beardslee recited *Pierrot* on the Sunday, and Milton Babbitt's equally vivid and demanding *Philomel* on the Monday of the Second Wardour School. On the Friday, in a programme that included the first performance of Birtwistle's *Tragoedia*, Maxwell Davies contributed two new works of his own: the cantata, *Ecce manus tradentis*, and five of his *Seven in Nomine*. The cantata was a choral work that had to be easy enough for the students attending the school to sing after only a few rehearsals. Although it had no influence on the style and tone of his music-theatre pieces about deception and betrayal, it nevertheless exercised considerable influence on the way the wiles of the betrayer or deceiver could be conveyed.

Ecce manus tradentis concerns Judas Iscariot, the arch betrayer and deceiver. The text is taken from St Luke's Gospel for the Wednesday before Easter dealing with the Last Supper, and those passages in St Mark's Gospel dealing with Peter's denial and Judas's kiss. It is a sombre work, and Maxwell Davies feels that ideally it should be performed in a liturgical setting on Maundy Thursday or Good Friday. His model, I believe, was Stravinsky's *Canticum sacrum*, which had made a deep impression on him when its first performance was broadcast in 1956. It too is in Latin, contains choral writing in four-part block harmony, includes instrumental episodes, and gives prominence to low bassoons and trombones in its scoring.

Although the *Canticum sacrum* influenced the sonority and mood of Maxwell Davies's cantata, Maxwell Davies drew specifically on *Taverner* for his material. When, for instance, Christ says, 'This is my body which is given for you … This is the chalice, the new testament in my blood, which shall be shed for you,' the flute plays twice the treble's melody lying above the cantus firmus in Taverner's *Benedictus*. In the first act of *Taverner* the violin had played this melody in the background with 'nauseating vibrato'. In the context of the cantata, however, even though there is octave displacement, there is no obvious parody of it. It floats with clarity above the accompanying choral and instrumental texture.

The most significant reference to *Taverner* is the use of the so-called 'death' chord. The cantata opens with the chorus, accompanied by low bassoons and trombones, singing the incipient to the Gospel to the notes of this chord. Maxwell Davies follows it with an instrumental episode presenting its four notes, with the addition of an extra note, as a line. Although the notes in this line (D-E-F♯-G♯-A) are subject to octave displacement this only partially disguises the fact that it resembles a section of plainsong; except that here it is not an actual plainsong but an invented one, an invented one containing the forbidden interval, the augmented fourth (Ex. 7.1).

Ex. 7.1 Maxwell Davies, *Ecce manus tradentis*, instrumental 'plainsong', fig. A, top p. 6, bb. 1–7

Even when, later on, Maxwell Davies devises another plainsong with an F replacing the F♯ (D-E-F-G♯-A) the augmented fourth is still present. The significance of this is that, whereas Gregorian chant represents the word of God, these quasi-plainsongs have to be construed as representing the word of the Devil. Thus, when the flute enters with the excerpt from Taverner's *Benedictus* mentioned above, the situation is in fact parodic, even though this may not be obvious, for the Taverner quotation contradicts the augmented-fourth-based music lying beneath it: it exposes the travesty. Ultimately, when the soprano sings the line that closes the work, 'And he kissed him', her ecstatic climb to the top of her register and the underlying D-minor harmony cannot detract from the persistent presence of the *diabolus in musica* because until the very last moment D has been sounding with a G♯ above it.

I discuss the works here in chronological order rather than in topic groups. My decision for this order rests on two aspects of Maxwell Davies's Music Theatre that the grouping into topics cannot reveal so clearly: namely changes in the way he organised the structure of the works over the nine-year period they span, and changes in the way he used the visual element in them.

Structuring a piece by means of a gradual transformational process necessitated, when Maxwell Davies conceived the idea, the presence of a line running right through it, a line on which the transformational process could be carried. His model, of course, was the cantus firmus that runs through so many medieval and Renaissance pieces. But whereas the cantus firmus was usually confined to a middle voice, Maxwell Davies's line could also thread its way above or below the textures contained in a piece. *Revelation and Fall*, even though divided into nineteen sections grouped into two parts, conforms to this principle. Apart from one or two short 'breathing spaces' indicated by commas, the structure is continuous, the line remains intact. However, in *Missa super L'homme armé*, his next piece, he abandoned this principle, for although it too is continuous, the work is a montage: it moves from section to section without the presence of a thread running through it. Maxwell Davies told me he considers this procedure to be very useful when writing Music Theatre, and he made some use of it in his following works. Although not montages, these are nevertheless much looser in their construction than *Revelation and Fall*. Essentially *Eight Songs for a Mad King* and *Miss Donnithorne's Maggot* are song cycles. Although the transition from one song to the next may be smooth, the transformational processes they contain are not carried by a continuous line but jump from one event to the next in the process. This also applies to *Vesalii Icones*, the only work that has its topic conveyed by dance rather than text, but here I believe a line can be discovered, and that it lies in the solo role assigned to the cello. It may not be continuous but the gaps it contains are bridged, like the gaps in a medieval or Renaissance cantus firmus, by the sense of continuity created by giving the line to a single instrument or voice.

Revelation and Fall was commissioned by the Serge Koussevitsky Music Foundation and composed in 1965–6. It is scored for a virtuoso soprano and a sixteen-piece ensemble consisting of wind quintet, string quintet, trumpet, trombone, harp and three percussion. Even before a note is played the percussion instruments arrayed on the platform (with three specially invented for the work: a metal cylinder [resonating chamber] with protruding steel rods of various lengths, a clock mechanism to operate a metal tongue vibrating against a resonant sheet of metal, and a knife-grinder) indicate that rhythm and timbre are going to play major roles in the piece. And when it is seen that the soprano has a loudhailer, and that the violins, double bass and harp have their own independent amplification systems, it can be assumed that the sonorities will be surreal, outside the norm.

The piece is a setting in German of the expressionist prose poem *Offenbarung und Untergang* by Georg Trakl (1887–1914), and Maxwell Davies may have been drawn to it partly because it contains images reminiscent of *Pierrot lunaire* (wine, moonlight, blood, night, a corpse), but also because it gave him the opportunity to take musical expressionism to an extreme. He says that when he composed it he thought of it as being a theatre piece only in a very limited way. It was not until it was scheduled for inclusion in the Pierrot Players' third concert on 26 February 1968 that he decided to have the soprano, Mary Thomas, wear a blood-red nun's habit and to assume the role of the sister mentioned in Trakl's text.

Trakl was a highly disturbed man who saw the world as being essentially evil. In some of his poems he finds peace of mind by conjuring up the spirit of a pastoral past. These are the poems Webern turned to in his Trakl settings.[5] In others his fear of insanity and his fascination with decay and disintegration are offset by a struggle to find spiritual order without recourse to the past. Although an obscure poem, *Offenbarung und Untergang* can be classed as one of these. Its title suggests that it reverses the sequence of books found in the Bible, for *Offenbarung* could be a reference to The Revelation of John at the end of the Bible, and *Untergang* to the fall of man described in the Book of Genesis at the beginning.

The poem contains no conceptually coherent sequence of thoughts. Instead it juxtaposes a series of highly charged images apparently unrelated to each other and consequently difficult to interpret. Like the title, many of them have biblical connotations (the juxtaposition of a radiant corpse and a dead lamb in the first sentence could relate to the death of Christ, for instance), but most seem to be the exaggerations and distortions of a man subject to hallucinations of a personal nature. The only image that recurs in the poem is that of the blood flowing from 'the wounded sister'.

The figure of the sister occurs frequently in Trakl's poetry. Although he calls her 'the sister', she was not a nun as Maxwell Davies would have us believe, but his own sister (Margarethe) Grete. She was the only person he loved, the source of the only positive emotion he seems to have experienced; but the incestuous relationships he had with her in his dreams were also the source of his 'unresolved guilt' and his poetry was a form of atonement for this.[6]

---

[5] *Six Lieder nach Gedichten von Georg Trakl*, Op. 14, 1917–22.

[6] Quoting from Trakl's letters, Eric B. Williams refers to Trakl's poems as a form of atonement for his 'unresolved guilt'. *The Mirror and the Word: Modernism, Literary Theory and Georg Trakl* (Lincoln, Nebr., University of Nebraska Press, 1993), 136.

This dichotomy may explain why her presence in his poems took on so many different meanings. For instance, in his last poem, composed after the battle of Grodek, when he was a pharmacist with the Austrian Medical Corps and had to look after ninety wounded men without a doctor or bandages, he sees his sister as a ministering angel, for he has her shadow greeting 'the ghosts of the heroes, their bleeding heads'.[7] But when Grete's shadow appears in *Revelation and Fall*, it is her own head that bleeds. She has been stabbed in the mouth by a black thorn (from Jesus's crown of thorns perhaps?). Although blood falls from her wound into his wine and makes it 'bitterer than opium', the poem ends with a vision of her blood falling gently on his head 'in a fiery rain', a vision Maxwell Davies interprets as being a transformation, the attainment of quietude after a period of intense emotional upheaval. If Trakl ever achieved quietude in his own life it may have been only when he took opium. Otherwise he was constantly in a state of intense emotional upheaval, a condition that became intensified after the battle of Grodek when he committed suicide by taking an overdose of cocaine.

Revelation and Fall lasts about twenty-five minutes, and is a continuous structure based on the seven-note set derived from the chromatic scale used in *Taverner*, here arranged in the order C-E♭-B♭-D-A-B-C♯. As in the opera, this is subject to his idiosyncratic transformational procedures. Nevertheless, throughout the work it returns in its initial order to function as a reference point. In the preface to the original edition of the score (it was revised in 1980) he says that the piece 'represents a marked extension, in comparison with my earlier works in the use of late medieval/renaissance composition techniques ... in the complexity of rhythmic relationships between simultaneous "voices", in the use of cantus firmus with long melismas branching out, and in the use of mensural canons' (these are canons where the following voice has proportionately shorter rhythmic values so that the two voices eventually coincide).

These medieval and Renaissance techniques, however, occur mainly in just one of the nineteen sections that comprise the work. Of greater importance is the way Maxwell Davies structures the work as a whole. Although he insists that it is about the dynamics of the mind and has a structure 'that goes right through the piece', he nevertheless divides it into two parts. These have to be discovered through the way his music proceeds, for there is no division in the score. The first part represents a struggle for spiritual order, and when this is felt to be unobtainable, Maxwell Davies changes tack to veer towards a solution in which the goal is merely peace of mind. There is nothing in the poem to justify the composer's

---

[7] From 'Grodek', in *The Poems of Georg Trakl*, tr. Margit Lehbert (London, Anvil Press, 2007), 183.

division of the score into two parts. The structure Maxwell Davies superimposes on them is necessary only from a musical point of view.

His symbol for spiritual order is the chorale, not a Lutheran chorale, but a hymn-like tune that he specially composed and harmonised, as was traditionally the practice, in block chords, the original purpose being to produce a sense of communal solidarity. There are four chorales in the first part; all are related to the basic seven-note set, but apart from the first and last they are very different from each other. Although they supply a moment of repose after the music that precedes them, they fail to achieve stability; the order they seek is always undermined.

Maxwell Davies's symbol for peace of mind is the aleatoric mobile. This represents, in one vital respect, a musical procedure that differs fundamentally from the chorale. Instead of being harmonised in block chords, the mobile allows each line to float freely in its own tempo. Although this procedure is prepared for during the course of the work, it does not make its authentic appearance until the end. Here two glockenspiels and a set of handbells or crotales are given independent patterns of notes to repeat softly, evenly and slowly in their own tempo. The effect is like looking at a sculptured mobile set in motion by a gentle breeze. Disorder prevails, but it is a disorder that is relaxed, easy-going and peaceful.

The first part opens with an agitated introduction that establishes in two phases the highly charged nature of the work as a whole. In its wake comes the first sentence: *Schweigend sass ich in verlassener Schenke unter verrauchtem Holzgebälk und einsam beim Wein; ein strahlender Leichnam über ein Dunkles geneigt und es lag ein totes Lamm zu meinen Füssen.* (Silently I sat alone with my wine under the charred beams of an abandoned inn; a radiant corpse leaned over a dark pond, and at my feet lay a dead lamb.)[8]

Each of the sentence's three clauses has its own music; all begin hesitantly before becoming more purposeful. But in the first two clauses the purposefulness soon breaks up. At the words 'und einsam beim Wein' the singer uses vocal techniques to suggest that the poet may be drunk, and at 'Leichnam über ein Dunkles geneigt' she stutters as if the sight of the corpse has terrified her. Her sight of the lamb, on the other hand, produces a lyrical phrase which leads into the first chorale.

Like most chorale settings this is in four parts, but instead of giving each line a vestige of melodic independence, Maxwell Davies has three of them move in parallel motion. The fourth is the tune's retrograde transposed up a minor third and is not in rhythmic unison with the others. But just as Bach provided five different harmonisations of the chorale 'Herzlich tut mich verlangen' in the *St Matthew*

---

[8] Translations are those given in the score by Stephen Pruslin.

Passion, so Maxwell Davies gave himself opportunities to present his chorale in different ways. The next, for example, sounds as if Trakl is desperately trying to assert its integrity, for each chord has to be played as long and as loud as possible, with the instruction 'piercing' attached to the piccolo and oboe parts and flutter-tonguing to the clarinet's.

But this outburst has to be prepared for, and Maxwell Davies does this in the way he sets the second and third sentences: *Aus verwesender Bläue trat die bleiche Gestalt der Schwester und also sprach ihr die blutender Mund: Stich schwarzer Dorn. Ach noch tönen von wilden Gewittern die silbernen Arme mir.* (Out of the dissolving blue sky stepped the pale form of the sister, and thus spoke her bleeding mouth, stabbed by a black thorn. Ah still resound for me the silvery arms of wild tempests.)

Maxwell Davies's music for the first of these sentences is slow and reflective. It becomes fast and increasingly more extrovert in the long, highly disordered instrumental episode that leads to the even faster presentation of the third sentence. Here the singer has to place her notes either just before or just after the beat, a form of rubato much practised by jazz singers. But no jazz singer would dare risk bending the tempo in this manner at the speed Maxwell Davies sets for the passage. His tempo makes a mockery of the practice. It is therefore no wonder that the second chorale should place such emphasis on rhythmic unison. Yet its character is too vehement, too aggressive to constitute spiritual consolation.

The third chorale goes to the opposite extreme. It too is a logical outcome from what precedes it, in this case a setting of the words of sentences four and five: *Fliesse Blut von den mondenen Füssen, blühend auf nächtigen Pfaden, darüber schreiend die Ratte huscht. Aufflackert ihr Sterne in meinen gewölbten Brauen; und es läutet leise das Herz in der Nacht.* (May blood flow from moonlit feet and blossom on nocturnal paths where a screeching rat scampers. Flare out you stars in the vaults of my brow, and my heart will peal gently into the night.)

The music for these sentences and the chorale that follows constitute the work's slow movement, and it is characterised by rhythmic freedom. Maxwell Davies sets the fourth sentence as a very quiet recitative, which only the music for the scampering rat disturbs. On the other hand, the fifth gives the impression of being rhythmically free simply because every few bars the tempo suddenly gets faster or slower. These characteristics are brought together in the chorale. Here the violins and viola are given independent lines to be played in a rhythm determined by how their notes are spaced – in proportional notation in other words.

This, of course, is also a form of disorder, but it is different from the disorder in the instrumental episode earlier, and so I think we have to interpret it as being a forerunner of the concluding mobile. It creates the impression that the poet has thought of another way to release himself from his emotional torments. However, the fourth chorale reveals that as yet this thought remains only a possibility. It bears a close resemblance to the first. Its tune, as well as being doubled at the octave and twelfth, and accompanied by its transposed retrograde, is also accompanied by its inversion doubled at the octave and twelfth, and the inversion's retrograde. Had the tune been a twelve-note set then all its forms – prime, inversion, retrograde and retrograde inversion – would be present at the same time. For a serial composer this would represent an even higher degree of order than existed in the first chorale, for there is reflective symmetry between the prime and its inversion, the prime and its retrograde and the inversion and its retrograde. However, even though the chorale has been traditionally associated with spiritual matters, here this association is totally undermined by the trumpeter who has to play the inversion's retrograde muted, and to apply a 'sentimental vibrato' to each note.

The reason for this vulgarity comes out of the music that precedes it, a setting of the last two sentences of the poem's first paragraph: *Einbrach ein roter Schatten mit flammendem Schwert in das Haus, floh mit schneeiger Stirne. O bitterer Tod.* (A crimson shadow with a flaming sword broke into the house, but fled with a snowy brow. Oh bitter death.) Maxwell Davies treats the first of these sentences as being climactic, for the soprano must shout the words 'ein roter Schatten' over and over again through the loudhailer, and then take the remaining words in the sentence to a point when the whole ensemble echoes her assertiveness with repeated notes played quadruple forte. But this violence has an ironic conclusion because for the words 'Oh bitter death' the music is cast in the form of a 'blues' with a walking bass and off-beat 'wows' on the muted trumpet assisted by the horn. Since the soprano is instructed to sing conversationally, the overall effect is like listening to Bessie Smith sing numbers such as the *St Louis Blues* with Louis Armstrong subtly mocking her pathos. This is undoubtedly why Maxwell Davies chose the trumpet to be the instrument that mocks the erudition of the fourth chorale (Ex. 7.2).

The second part contains only two moments of repose, the second being the concluding mobile. Unlike those in the first part they are not purely instrumental. Maxwell Davies involves the singer to give the impression that peace of mind turns out to be of greater importance to the poet than spiritual order. Nevertheless the opening of the second part is far from peaceful for it takes the vulgarity of the fourth chorale into the surreal.

Maxwell Davies divides the single sentence's second paragraph into four sections. The first stops in mid-clause: *Und es sprach eine dunkle Stimme aus mir: Meinem Rappen brach ich im nächtigen Wald das Genick, da aus seinen purpurnen Augen der Wahnsinn sprang; die Schatten der Ulmen fielen ...* (And a dark voice spoke from within me: my horse's neck broke in the nocturnal forest, from its purple eyes madness leapt; the shadows of elms fell ...).

Ex. 7.2 Maxwell Davies, *Revelation and Fall*, 'O bitterer Tod', p. 60

I call it surreal because the singer shouts these words through the loudhailer; harp, double bass and the two violins have to switch their amplifiers on; the first percussionist is instructed to play his drums and suspended cymbal wildly, and the clarinet his descending arpeggios shrilly. The focus of the musical interest, however, lies with the violins, who play in thirds and with sentimental vibrato and excessive glissandos an A minor/major tune Maxwell Davies clearly believes to be the kind Trakl might have heard in some Viennese restaurant. Nevertheless after the word 'fielen' the tempo changes from Allegro to Lento, the dynamics from fortissimo to pianissimo, and the violins put on mutes to play in a very high register the accompaniment to the soprano's expressive completion of the clause: *… auf mich, das blaue Lachen des Quells und die schwarze Kühle der Nacht* (… on me the blue laughter of the spring and the black coolness of night). This is not a mobile, but the way the two violins entwine their lines of counterpoint round each other produces a gentleness and ethereal quality which I consider to be only one step removed from one.

At this stage the structure nears its closing stages, and this means that to round it off the material should begin to recapitulate what has gone before. Maxwell Davies completes the process in two sections. The first looks back at the walking bass heard in the 'blues' number, except that here it is given to the harp. He asks it to be more sonorous and much louder than the playing of the other instruments. Thus its regularity dominates their syncopated rhythms, and provides an ideal complement to the fullness of tone required from the soprano singing the words: *… da ich ein wilder Jäger aufjagte ein scheeniges Wild; in steinerner Hölle mein Antlitz erstarb* (… I was a wild hunter in a snowy wilderness; in a rocky hell my face dissolved).

The following episode is purely instrumental. It recapitulates in varied form that section in the first part where attention was given to the relationship between the soprano and harp, the passage where the singer had to place her syncopations lying just before or just after the harp's quaver beat. But now Maxwell Davies generates more energy and a greater sense of forward direction than he did previously. He achieves this by adding more and more parts so that the whole ensemble becomes involved, and, most significantly, by including a mensural canon to create a sense of 'running to catch up'.

Appropriately, the music for the poem's third and final paragraph, which Maxwell Davies interprets as being the achievement of quietude, is completely subdued, for only the voice, the bassoon and the three percussionists playing glockenspiels and handbells struck with felt-headed beaters are involved. All the rhetoric of the previous sections is stripped away. Initially only the bassoon, playing as softly as possible and at the top of its register, accompanies the soprano who delivers in *Sprechgesang: Und schimmernd fiel ein Tropfen Blutes in des Einsamen Wein; und da ich davon trank, schmeckte er bitterer als Mohn; und eine schwärzliche Wolke umhüllte mein Haupt, die kristallenen Tränen verdammter Engel …* (And shimmering a drop of blood fell into my lonely wine; and when I drank, it tasted bitterer than opium; and a dark cloud surrounded my head, the crystalline tears of fallen angels …). Finally, against the gentle mobile provided by the glockenspiels and handbells, the soprano can sing the only passage of sustained lyricism in the whole work: *… und leise rann aus silberner Wunde der Schwester das Blut und fiel ein feuriger Regen auf mich*

(... and blood ran gently from the silver wound of the sister and as fiery rain fell on me).

In my opinion, although Maxwell Davies had it performed as Music Theatre, *Revelation and Fall* is really a concert scena, for in neither it nor the first version of *Missa super L'homme armé* did he take sufficient heed of how the visual contributions could be introduced. The problems for the singer are these: what kind of gestures can she make when all her attention has to be given to trying to perform the incredibly difficult vocal part Maxwell Davies gives her, and what does she do during the purely instrumental sections when she has to remain silent? Even the acting skills of Mary Thomas were taxed to the hilt at the first performance of the work especially since Maxwell Davies wanted her to be dressed in a blood-red nun's habit. Was she meant to represent the wounded and blood-soaked Sister, or was this another instance of his preoccupation with the subversion of meaning? Was she perhaps the scarlet woman, the great whore of Babylon John refers to in his Revelation? If so, then perhaps this explains why Mary Thomas felt obliged, when the music gave the opportunity, to go over the top when she performed the work. Maxwell Davies was certainly aware that it would tax her to the limit and this is why, when he knew that it would appear in the same programme as *Missa super L'homme armé*, he avoided giving her anything to do in that work.

Like *Ecce manus tradentis*, *Missa super L'homme armé* concerns the betrayal of Christ by Judas and Peter, although here all the excerpts are taken from St Luke's Gospel. They are in the order: Judas's promise to the chief priests and scribes, Peter's denial, and Christ's words about betrayal at the Last Supper. In the original version Maxwell Davies had the Latin text recorded by a boy's voice and relayed to the audience through loudspeakers. Three years later, on 28 September 1971, when the work was given a second performance in Perugia and the Pierrot Players had become The Fires of London, Maxwell Davies instructed the actor Murray Melvin to sit in the audience dressed as a nun and make a dramatic entrance before intoning the text. He wanted him to point to the audience during Christ's accusations, and, at the end, to 'foxtrot out', pulling off his wimple before slamming a door as he left. Clearly by 1971 Maxwell Davies had realised that physical gestures had to be included in his music-theatre scores.

In the revised version Maxwell Davies says that the actor may be a man or a woman. If a woman she must wear a monk's habit and sing the melody of a sentimental hymn tune Maxwell Davies composed for the passage beginning *Et gavisi sunt* ... (And they were glad, and covenanted to give him money. And he promised, and sought opportunity to betray him unto them in the absence of the multitude).

As well as a tape recorder and loudspeakers, the original performance required a pianola with a specially made pianola roll, and a pre-electric horn gramophone with a 78 rpm record of an out-of-tune honky-tonk piano playing a foxtrot. The work is based on Maxwell Davies's completion in fifteenth-century style of the Agnus Dei from an anonymous but incomplete fifteenth-century *L'homme armé* Mass. On the record and pianola roll there is a passage in which he simulates a sticking needle, as well as a second sentimental hymn tune, intended to be Victorian in origin. In the revised version, however, he replaces the tape recorder, pianola and horn gramophone with a live performer.

The purpose of having a man dressed as a nun or a woman as a monk was not just to emulate Schoenberg's use of transvestism in *Pierrot lunaire* but to highlight the work's concern with the subversion of meaning. This had also been his concern in *Antechrist*, the short work that had opened the Pierrot Players' first concert. Maxwell Davies had used the French spelling because his idea for it came from a collection of fifteenth-century woodcut blocks contained in a book published in Paris in 1492, *Traité de l'avènement de l'antechrist*. One of these woodcuts is reproduced on the cover of his score. It shows a stag (in medieval iconography one of the symbols for Christ) sitting on its haunches and being greeted by a priest with the Devil standing behind it. In other words the animal is not what the priest thinks it is. In medieval mythology the Antichrist may appear to be the real Christ but in reality totally opposes Christian precepts. He subverts the meaning of Christianity. And in *Antechrist*, *Missa super L'homme armé* and *Vesalii Icones* Maxwell Davies set out to expose this fact.

He told me that the *Missa super L'homme armé* was his response to one of the outcomes of the Second Vatican Council (1962–5), i.e. permission to substitute the vernacular for Latin in the celebration of the Mass. He felt this would under-mine the mystery of the Mass by taking an expression of the transcendent into the language of the everyday. 'I am not a Christian,' he said, 'but for me the situation symbolised the subversion of meaning and the betrayal of an essential experience.' *Missa super L'homme armé* was therefore a demonstration of how the music of a Mass can be similarly betrayed if it is changed into the music of the everyday.

The Mass he chose had two advantages for this purpose. 'L'homme armé' was a popular song of the fifteenth century, and its melody was the most famous of all cantus firmi used for Mass compositions in the fifteenth and sixteenth centuries. It was the melody composers selected to demonstrate their skill as contrapuntal-ists. The *Historical Anthology of Music* has four examples from *L'homme armé* Masses, all chosen to illustrate either contrapuntal ingenuity or stylistic innova-tions.[9] Dufay's Agnus Dei provides an example of a canonic riddle; Ockeghem's demonstrates the stylistically new way the Flemish school embroidered their

[9] *Historical Anthology of Music*, Archibald T. Davison and Willi Apel, rev edn (Cambridge, MA, Harvard University Press, 1949), nos. 66, 73, 89, 92.

counterpoint; the Agnus Dei of Josquin des Prez is another canonic riddle (this time a double mensural canon notated on a single line), while Pierre de la Rue's two Kyries also contain mensural canons. These are all techniques Maxwell Davies rejoices in using, as we saw in *Revelation and Fall*, but on this occasion he decided to betray the tradition established by these Renaissance masters by denying himself the opportunity to follow in their footsteps, replacing erudition with vulgarity.

The Armed Man[10] may have referred to the English soldier, even Henry V himself, in France during the Hundred Years War, and the melody with its fourths and fifths has the robustness to suggest that opponents should be prepared to withstand him: 'The armed man, the armed man. We must guard ourselves against him. Everywhere it is announced we should arm ourselves with iron coats of mail.' As a cantus firmus it was therefore the opposite to the transcendent music required for the Mass. Maxwell Davies begins his *Missa super L'homme armé* with an instrumental version of 'l'homme armé, l'homme armé' as if it were the introduction to a circus act. He then goes into what he calls 'a more or less straight' quotation of the extant opening of the original Agnus Dei. However, he scores it in a manner suggesting that his aim is ultimately to mock it. The treble's line is given to the cello doubled at the fifth and ninth by the violin and the fifteenth by the piccolo. The countertenor's line is given to the harmonium, which adds occasional ornaments and chords in the Baroque manner; the tenor's to a set of five handbells or crotales, and the bass's to the clarinet playing at the bottom of its register with accelerating flutter-tonguing, additional grace notes, glissandos and exaggerated dynamics. However, when the handbells invert the 'l'homme armé' tune it becomes clear that Maxwell Davies is about to reveal his hand. The scoring changes, alien intrusions, such as glissandos and exaggerated vibrato, increase until the texture breaks up with the harmonium sustaining a bitonal chord, the clarinet playing with 'molto vibrato' the inversion of the first three notes of the cantus firmus, and the cello playing in a different tempo a wildly distorted version of the Agnus Dei's first four bars with octave displacements as well as exaggerated vibrato, dynamics and glissandos.

'In *Missa super L'homme armé*', Maxwell Davies told me, 'I not only broke cover vis-à-vis parody and the subversion of meaning, I also dispensed with having a line which goes from beginning to end, as in *Revelation and Fall* and *Antechrist*, replacing it with the kind of technique one finds in the cinema, a montage of images. Running through the work is my "in style" completion of the Agnus Dei, although this is often obscured by the disparate material that splinters off it.' In his Preface

---

[10] For a theory of how the song was used, see David Fallows, *New Grove Dictionary*, vol. 14, 628: 'the song itself may have been for the mustering of soldiers, conceivably the French initiative of 1440'.

to the published score he described the process in another way. After saying that the work is in three sections each divided into three subsections corresponding to the three subsections of the original Agnus Dei, he continues: 'The eventual treatment stems from the chapter in the *Ulysses* of Joyce corresponding to the Cyclops chapter in Homer. In the Joyce, a conversation in a tavern is interrupted by insertions which seize upon a small, passing idea in the main narrative, and amplify this, often out of all proportion, in a style which bears no relationship to the germinal idea which sparked off the insertion. The insertion is itself a parody of a newspaper account of a fashionable wedding or the Anglican Creed, for instance.'

Maxwell Davies believes that this cinematographic type of procedure enhances the impression of spontaneity required for Music Theatre. In *Missa super L'homme armé* his insertions are parodies of fifteenth- and sixteenth-century religious music, seventeenth- and eighteenth-century Baroque sonatas, nineteenth-century hymns, and twentieth-century popular music in the form of foxtrots and quicksteps. Some of the most interesting are his use of Baroque sonatas. In one instance the handbells play the cantus firmus, the harmonium realises a figured bass and the violin plays the Agnus Dei in imitation of the cross-the-strings leaps found in Bach's unaccompanied violin sonatas and partitas; in another the piccolo plays the cantus firmus, a harpsichord the continuo (this time in a seventeenth-century style), and the cello its solo 'like a bad gamba, sharp on higher notes, scratchy and swoopy' (Ex. 7.3).

As in *Antechrist* the work should end with an assertion of the *diabolus in musica* to emphasise these distortions, but because the the *Missa* is a montage Maxwell Davies cannot generate the logic to make its appearance inevitable or clear. As in *Antechrist*, the work culminates in a state of confusion, but in the *Missa* the confusion begins earlier and lasts longer. It starts just before the voice intones on a C♯ the text relating to events at the Last Supper. But his voice is only one element in a simultaneous montage of different tunes or fragments of tunes on handbells, harmonium, flute, violin, clarinet, cello and honky-tonk piano playing in pitches which cut across the C♯. When all but the tenor and the honky-tonk piano playing the foxtrot in G major fall out, the *diabolus in musica* should reign supreme. But Maxwell Davies wants the foxtrot to be cut off in midstream by the speaker slamming a door upon his exit, and that this should not coincide with the end of the foxtrot. We are therefore unlikely to hear the tenor's C♯ and the piano's low G simultaneously. Even so the persistent C♯ and the equally persistent G major tonality before the music abruptly comes to a halt will continue to live on in the memory even after the door has been closed. The Devil still has the last word.

Although Maxwell Davies is now regarded as being a leading figure in British Music Theatre, he was actually rather slow in realising the principles that lie behind it. As originally conceived, neither *Revelation and Fall* nor *Missa super L'homme*

Ex. 7.3 Maxwell Davies, *Missa super L'homme armé*, cantus firmus as Baroque sonata

armé require any stage action nor do they attempt to find a rapprochement between speech and song. It took the entrepreneurial spirit of the late James Murdoch to prod him into producing something that would involve these features, and to aim at having a commercial success. Furthermore, Maxwell Davies did not realise the importance of the visual until he composed *Eight Songs for a Mad King*.

Eight Songs for a Mad King is still his most frequently performed work, and in music dictionaries it is always singled out as being one of the most significant specimens of Music Theatre. And yet, on his own admission, although dramatically and visually effective, it is nevertheless 'musically thin'. This may well be because, having completed *Taverner*, he felt liberated from the compositional methods that work had imposed on him. One reason for the thinness is that he was too willing to be fashionable. He composed the work in February and March 1969, a period when the use of quotations, indeterminacy and new instrumental and vocal techniques such as multiphonics had become the flavour of the day. Until then Maxwell Davies's use of quotations had been limited to works from the medieval and Renaissance periods, works that music buffs may know but not necessarily ordinary music lovers. Quotations of familiar material had been pioneered by Zimmermann in his opera *Die Soldaten*[11] (1957–60), and by the late sixties the practice had become almost commonplace. In the three years preceding the composition of *Eight Songs for a Mad King*, three works had appeared consisting almost entirely of quotations: Zimmermann's *Musique pour les soupers du roi Ubu* (1966), Stockhausen's *Hymnen* (1967) and the third movement of Berio's *Sinfonia* (1968).

Maxwell Davies's borrowings were a little more modest, but even so they play a significant role in the structure of *Eight Songs for a Mad King*. The one that stands out comes from Handel's *Messiah*. In occurs in the seventh song, when the king sings very simply 'Comfort me' immediately after his mutilation of Handel's version. But in his Preface to the score Maxwell Davies says: 'I have, however, quoted far more than the *Messiah* – if not the notes at least aspects of the styles of many composers are referred to, from Handel to Birtwistle. In some ways, I regard the work as a collection of musical objects borrowed from many sources, functioning as "stage props" around which the reciter's part weaves, lighting them from extraordinary angles, and throwing grotesque and distorted shadows from them, giving the musical "objects" an unexpected and sometimes sinister significance.'

The other innovation – indeterminacy – had its origins in John Cage's music, and in Britain it reached its zenith in the work of Cornelius Cardew, in particular in his graphic score *Treatise* (1967), in which players could interpret his graphs in any way they pleased. But a much less radical form of indeterminacy in Britain sprang from what Lutoslawski had been doing since the early sixties. Evidence of his influence can be found in Maxwell Davies's use of 'mobiles' in *Revelation and Fall*, and the freedom he gives players in certain sections of *Missa super L'homme armé*. But neither of these works can rival the extent of his use of indeterminacy

---

[11] *Die Soldaten* is a four-act opera by German composer, Bernd Zimmermann (1918–70), based on a 1776 play by J.M.R. Lenz and written between 1957 and 1964; it had its first performance in 1965.

in *Eight Songs for a Mad King*. Every page in the score includes several examples. Maxwell Davies's purpose is quite clearly to give the players freedom to support or imitate the lack of determinacy in the King's rantings.

Multiphonics came into vogue after Bruno Bartolozzi published his book *New Sounds for Woodwind* in 1967.[12] Within a short time both Judith Pearce and Alan Hacker, the flautist and clarinettist in the Pierrot Players, became experts in producing two or more notes on their instruments simultaneously, as well as a range of other new techniques. As it turned out the ability to produce multiphonics was not confined to woodwind players, for the South African baritone Roy Hart could also produce chords containing two or more notes. As well as training his voice to produce these he had also managed to extend his vocal range to four octaves. The upper and lower extremes were of poor quality, but in the event they were ideal for the role of a mad king.

Hart had been introduced to Maxwell Davies by James Murdoch, and it was probably this encounter that led him to look for a topic which would allow him to take Schoenberg's *Sprechgesang* one step further. He found it when his friend the Australian novelist and poet Randolph Stow settled in Britain in 1968. Stow's work is characterised by his deep interest in abnormal psychology. Two years earlier, when he had previously been in England, the historian Sir Steven Runciman showed him a small mechanical hand organ once owned by King George III (1738–1820). On a scrap of paper sold with it was written 'This Organ was George the third for birds to sing' [sic].[13] It contained tunes the King wanted to teach his bullfinches. They included 'King Prussia's Minuet, La Promenade, Miss Musgrave's Fancy, The Waterman, He's Ay A-Kissing Me, Le Conterfaite, Scotch Bonnett, and A Spanish March'. When Stow took Maxwell Davies to see and hear the organ the composer immediately knew that he had found the ideal topic for Music Theatre. Not only was it suitable for Hart's voice, it also gave him the opportunity to make use of props, and to be much more specific about how the piece could be staged. Stow duly provided him with words for the tunes. These included sentences actually spoken by the King, but most of the information came from reports of the King's behaviour written by Frances (Fanny) Burney in her *Journals and Letters*[14] who, between 1786 and 1791, was Second Keeper of the Robes to Queen Charlotte.

The props are four large bamboo cages in which sit the flute, clarinet, violin and cello representing, when the King addresses them, his bullfinches. The King's

---

[12]   B. Bartolozzi, *New Sounds for Woodwind*, tr. R.S. Brindle (Oxford, Oxford University Press, 1967).

[13]   See website, Maxopus: http://www.maxopus.com/work_detail.aspx?key=2 (accessed 10 February 2014).

[14]   *Journals and Letters* (London, Penguin, 2001).

Ill. 7.2. Maxwell Davies, *Eight Songs for a Mad King*, 1969

keeper is represented by the percussionist who plays a large bass drum on the King's entry, and the same drum when he follows the King off stage at the end. Although, like *Pierrot lunaire*, the work is essentially a song cycle, Maxwell Davies wants it to be played without a break. On two occasions, between numbers three and four, and five and six, he interpolates instrumental transitions which, in contrast to the songs, are wholly devoted to one of the pieces found on the mechanical organ. The songs themselves only hint at these (Ill. 7.2).

In the first two, 'The Sentry' and 'The Country Walk', Maxwell Davies establishes the context through his use of characteristic figures. 'The Sentry' tells of the time when the King promised to give a cabbage to the sentry guarding the gate to his apartment, and here the figure represents the steps of a slow march. At first all the instruments play a repeated note in the same tempo, but gradually, as if mimicking the derangement of the King's mind, they get out of phase with each other. Later the figure appears in various guises, the most bizarre being when the piccolo plays the repeated note alternatively a quarter tone higher and a quarter tone lower before being told by Maxwell Davies to 'vary it a little by putting it up an octave'. The second song is also based on a regular motion, this time a swishing sound produced by a set of Roto Toms representing the 'green snakes of ivy, pythons' the King sees on his walk.

In 'The Lady-in-Waiting', the third song, the King has the first of his four dialogues with the caged instruments representing his bullfinches. This one, for flute, has the score laid out in the form of a cage. The music for the King is printed on its vertical bars, while the flute's appears between and inside the bars. Maxwell Davies asks the flute to respond to the King's phrases 'with mimicking parodying versions of them, freely' (Ex. 7.4). To accompany the dialogue, the percussionist plays toy bird-calls, and the other players operate mechanical bird noises.

The ensuing instrumental transition takes the music into the structure's slow movement, the dialogue with the cello, 'To be sung on the Water'. Here the King addresses 'Sweet Thames', the clue to the character of the song coming from his last line, 'I am weary of this feint. I am alone'. Hardly has he completed his last sigh when the next song, 'The Phantom Queen', intervenes. This is a set of eighteenth-century dances in which the King asks his phantom Queen, 'Have they chained you too, my darling, in a stable? Do they starve you, strike you, scorn you, ape your howls?' At the words 'starve you, strike you' the flute part, says the composer, 'hurries ahead in a 7:6 rhythmic proportion, the clarinet's rhythms become dotted, and its part is displaced by octaves, the effect being schizophrenic'.

In the next song, 'The Counterfeit', the King talks to the clarinet about his doctors. The piece is cast in the form of a recitative and air, and for the air Maxwell Davies has the clarinet, in imitative counterpoint with the cello, play a jaunty version of the tune of the same name: 'I love Doctor Heberden the best, for he has not told me a lie. Sir George has told me a lie: a white lie, he says. But I hate a white lie! If you are going to tell me a lie let it be a black lie!'

The climax of the structure comes in the seventh song, 'Country Dance (Scotch Bonnett)', when the King seizes the instrument the violinist is playing and smashes it. The music is a 'smoochy' foxtrot and includes the quotation from *Messiah*, 'Comfort ye'. The smashing of the violin is incited by the King's sudden switch of mood when he tries to grab the violin as if he wanted to play it for dancing, and then seizes it when he becomes aware of 'intolerable vileness'. The work ends when his sanity is restored, and against a network of aleatoric gestures on the flute, clarinet and harpsichord, he describes what he has been through. 'Poor fellow, I weep for him. He will die howling'.

Maxwell Davies composed the work when it had already been mooted that King George III may not have been suffering from schizophrenia but from a chronic form of porphyria, a toxic condition, traced to a metabolic disturbance that in acute cases can cause personality changes or mental disorders. Usually attacks of porphyria can last for days or weeks, but if the condition is treated inappropriately they can last for months. Yet whatever caused the King's distress, many of us who were at the first performance of Maxwell Davies's work felt deeply

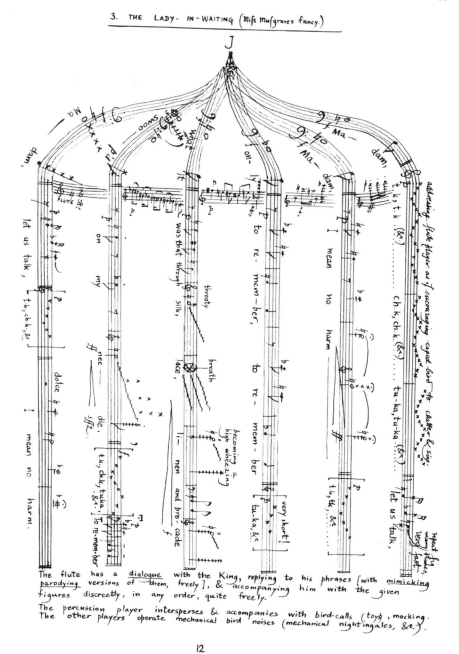

Ex. 7.4 Maxwell Davies, *Eight Songs for a Mad King*, 'The Lady-in-Waiting'

troubled by it. The monarch's condition needed to be pitied rather than mocked. Nevertheless, I now see that although the composer had been tempted to be sensational, he nevertheless took pains to make his audience aware of what it felt like to suffer from such a humiliating illness. All the songs contain a moment when the King stands back from his condition and reflectively sees what he has become. Yet in the barrage of shrieks and howls that assail the listener, such moments tend to get overlooked, certainly when the work is being heard for the first time. Looked at now with a deeper knowledge of Maxwell Davies's other works behind me I can see that madness, the condition when the sufferer is not truly himself, is another aspect of a moral issue that has preoccupied him all his life.

In many ways *Vesalii Icones* is a key work in Maxwell Davies's music-theatre oeuvres, for as well as combining vestiges of montage technique with the presence of a line, it also creates a very satisfactory balance of music and the visual. In 1967 Maxwell Davies acquired a facsimile edition of *De humani corporis fabrica libri septem* (Seven Books on the Structure of the Human Body) by the Flemish anatomist Andreas Vesalius (1514-64). At the time he thought its illustrations would make the starting point for a series of dances, but the idea did not materialise until 1969, after he had written *Eight Songs for a Mad King* and *St Thomas Wake, Foxtrot for Orchestra on a Pavan by John Bull*, a twenty-minute orchestral work for the Dortmund Philharmonic. The trigger was a meeting with William Louther, a black American dancer performing as a soloist with the London Contemporary Dance Theatre. It then occurred to him that Vesalius's illustrations could be used in conjunction with the fourteen Stations of the Cross. With this combination he could create another theatre piece for the Pierrot Players in which betrayal and the moral problem of distinguishing the false from the real would once again be the central issues (Ill. 7.3).

Traditionally, the fourteen Stations of the Cross cover the events that took place on Good Friday: the journey of Christ from the judgement hall to Calvary. But to make his moral point clear Maxwell Davies needed to include events that took place before and after Good Friday: notably Judas's betrayal and the Resurrection. He therefore included only seven of the traditional Stations of the Cross in his scheme: Christ condemned to death, Christ receives the Cross, St Veronica wipes His face, Christ nailed to the Cross, the death of Christ, the descent from the Cross, and the entombment of Christ. To these he added three events included in the Eleven Stations of the Cross ordered in 1799 for use in the diocese of Vienne: the agony in the garden, the betrayal of Judas and the flagellation. The other four stations had no precedent, they were those Maxwell Davies conceived to meet his own requirements. These were Christ before Pilate, the mocking of Christ, Christ prepared for death, and the Resurrection. In *Vesalii Icones* this last is the station when the figure who emerges from the tomb is not Christ but the Antichrist.

Ill. 7.3. William Louther in Maxwell Davies, *Vesalii Icones*, Queen Elizabeth Hall,
London, 1969

Maxwell Davies's sequence is: (1) agony in the garden, (2) the betrayal of Judas, (3) Christ before Pilate, (4) the flagellation, (5) Christ condemned to death, (6) the mocking of Christ, (7) Christ receives the Cross, (8) St Veronica wipes His face, (9) Christ prepared for death, (10) Christ nailed to the Cross, (11) the death of Christ, (12) the descent from the Cross, (13) the entombment of Christ, (14) Resurrection (the Antichrist).

To provide the work with ritual significance each dance terminates with the ringing of Sanctus bells (although on two occasions, after No. 7 and No. 9, these are replaced by jingles which have no associations with the Roman Catholic Church even though some small Sanctus bells do produce a ji-jing, ji-jing, ji-jing sound!). When they ring the dancer takes up his position for the next dance, his posture being determined by those in Vesalius's book. William Louther devised his own choreography, but Maxwell Davies asked him to make it a combination of those features of the human body Vesalius draws attention to, Louther's awareness of his own body, and his response to 'the ritual and emotional experience suggested by the Station'.

The dancer is not the only soloist in the work. Maxwell Davies assigns an equally important role to the cellist, who must sit near the dancer, apart from the other instrumentalists. At the first performance of the work, Jennifer Ward Clarke, the cellist in the Pierrot Players, was required to dress in white. She therefore represented, at least visually, the antithesis of the black dancer who was wearing only the briefest of loincloths. Maxwell Davies says that her presence 'should at many moments be closely integrated with the dance movements', and that she could be become 'in one sense (vis-à-vis the dancer), Pilate, St Veronica, or even a Flagellator, or in another sense the Anatomy Demonstrator'. But Maxwell Davies does not represent these encounters literally. He takes features or characteristics in them and develops them in purely musical or abstract terms. The characteristic feature of Pilate was his hesitancy, his uncertainty, and so when Christ appears before him in the third dance, the cello's music is built almost entirely from short gestures that constantly change course, and consequently lack a sense of purpose. By contrast, in the next dance, when the flagellator performs his task, the music becomes unrelenting. Against a *moto perpetuo* on the upper register of the piano, and an inexorable texture on an anvil and woodblock to represent the cracking of whips, a long uncompromising solo for the cello creates the impression that it is the pitiless flagellator overseeing the beating.

St Veronica was the woman who wiped Christ's face as he laboured towards Calvary and whose handkerchief was believed to have retained the outline of His features afterwards. This was the excuse for Maxwell Davies to demonstrate the comic side of his nature. He begins with the cello playing a slightly altered version of that section in *Ecce manus tradentis* which set the words spoken by Christ at the Last Supper: *Hoc est corpus meum, quod pro vobis datur* (This is my body which is given for you). Accompanying it, the piano supplies a flourish of arpeggios that inflates a fragment of plainsong related to the cello's theme (F♯-G♯-F♯-E-D♯). In fact all the material in the dance is related to the cello's theme. Immediately afterwards, for instance, a slightly distorted version appears on the flute, and then a wildly distorted version on the viola, a version which Maxwell Davies likens to 'a hand-operated cylinder phonograph' because it has to be played on the bridge of the instrument to create a scraping effect. He then immediately embarks on a Schenker analysis in reverse. Whereas the Austrian analyst Heinrich Schenker sought to reduce the structure of a movement in tonal music to its simplest form (harmonically a simple I-V-I procedure, melodically a three-note linear descent from the mediant to the tonic), Maxwell Davies starts with the simplest form and gradually fills it out. In this case a minor third on the flute and clarinet is followed by the viola playing pianissimo and without vibrato the simplest possible version of the cello's theme.

After this has petered out in a downward glissando *a niente*, more 'voices' enter, but instead of reproducing the theme as the cello played it at the beginning of the movement, Maxwell Davies turns some of its details into fragments of the scherzo of Beethoven's Fifth Symphony and then the scherzo of his Ninth Symphony (two works closely associated with Schenker). He continues the process of getting things wrong with an excerpt from the Kyrie of Pierre de la Rue's *Missa L'homme armé* which, as mentioned above, the *Historical Anthology of Music* includes as an example of a mensuration canon, in this case a canon between the tenor and bass. At first the quotation seems to be more or less correct, except that the voices are divided between the instruments, with some placed in the wrong octave or doubled an octave higher. But whereas the flute and viola continue to reproduce the treble and alto of the original, the instruments playing the tenor and bass go astray, and produce chords and scales that render the music absurd. Equally absurd is the rhythm tapped out by the percussionist on a typewriter. It is meant to be a rhythmic canon of the treble part but it goes haywire. To end the dance, Maxwell Davies asks the pianist to start the playback of a tape recording of the flourish at the opening of the movement which the player was told to make on a cheap commercial machine in order to produce hiss and distortion, and then to start a music-box 'chosen for the unsuitability of its tune'. In conclusion the flute and clarinet are each asked to produce a two-note chord that cannot be played multiphonically on their instruments so that one of the notes has to be hummed.

Although Maxwell Davies specifies that the dancer should only reveal he is the Antichrist in the last movement, the presence of the spirit of negation can be witnessed throughout the work. St Veronica wipes His Face is only one example of the way Maxwell Davies makes this obvious. The Mocking of Christ is another. Here the dancer is asked to play on an out-of-tune honky-tonk piano the Victorian hymn in *Missa super L'homme armé* ('a musical style I consider to be almost the ultimate blasphemy') and then a foxtrot ('the epitome of all that is cheap and tawdry'). Also out of tune is the autoharp, a zither on which chords are produced by means of dampers mounted on bars above the strings. Maxwell Davies uses it in the first and third dance where its being out of tune produces harmonic tension with those instruments playing in tune. The first depicts the agony experienced by Jesus on the Mount of Olives, the third when He confronts Pilate. But tension and the impression that things are out of agreement are present throughout the score. This is because at every stage we sense the presence of the Antichrist through the musical symbol Maxwell Davies introduced in *Taverner* and exploited in *Ecce manus tradentis*, the whole tone chord which gives prominence to the augmented fourth, the *diabolus in musica*.

In his programme note for *Vesalii Icones* Maxwell Davies likens its structure to the one he devised for *St Thomas Wake* in that both contain three levels of contrasting material. In the orchestral work the basic level is John Bull's Pavan. Although it appears in its original form only when played by the harp at the end, transformations of it are present throughout the work. Commenting on it is a series of foxtrots played by a dance band sitting apart from the orchestra.

And commenting on both the Pavan and the foxtrots are complex isorhythmic structures played by the orchestra in Maxwell Davies's own style.

The situation in *Vesalii Icones* is more ambiguous. Maxwell Davies says that the basic level consists of fragments of a Good Friday plainsong. But this is impossible to identify because the fragments appear only in accompanying lines, and are the standard formulae found in a great many examples of liturgical chant. Nor do they appear to have any bearing on the pieces of popular music Maxwell Davies includes in the score. Unlike the foxtrots in *St Thomas Wake*, these are not integral to the work nor do they have any influence on the music representing Maxwell Davies's own style, which is fundamental to *Vesalii Icones*. This he bases almost entirely on the two whole tone scales, or alternatively on sets obtained when one scale is filtered into the other.

A clear example of this process can be found in the first dance, *Agony in the Garden*. Here the solo cello playing in a recitative-like manner contrasts with the flute, clarinet, viola and piano playing mensuration canons. The cello could be interpreted as representing Jesus, the other instruments, the disciples. The dance begins with a long declamatory solo for the cello based on the notes of the first whole tone scale (C-D-E-F♯-G♯-B♭). The central notes, D-E-F♯-G♯, it will be remembered, are the notes of the so-called 'death' chord in *Taverner* (Ex. 7.5). Accompanying the cello are the autoharp and the flute and clarinet doubling some of the notes in the solo and sustaining them. (Here can be found figures that could come from plainsong, for example the flute's four-note groups C-D-F-E♭ and E♭-D♭-B-D♭). The lines in the following canons each contain three segments, and in the course of unfolding them Maxwell Davies introduces the other whole tone scale, its presence being confirmed when the cello enters with a quotation from *Ecce manus tradentis* using the notes B-C♯-D♯-E♯. After the second set of canons and during the course of the third the two whole tone scales are interwoven by the cello so that a sense of integration is achieved.

In the penultimate dance, *The Entombment of Christ*, the relationship between recitative and canons is reversed. The canons come first, the cello follows. Here the interwoven whole-tone scales unravel so that the cello's last notes consist of those of the second with only vestiges of the first. The whole of the first scale does not reappear until the end of the final dance, which Maxwell Davies describes as 'going all Hollywood and ridiculous'. It is based on the foxtrot version of the Victorian hymn from the sixth dance (i.e. a combination of the 'ultimate blasphemy' and 'all that is cheap and tawdry') to which a melody associated with 1930s 'swing' is added. Here the cello has a subsidiary role. Any illusion that it may have been occasionally referring to Christ in the previous dances is destroyed. Maxwell Davies goes through the foxtrot twice and on its repetition the mood becomes even more frenetic. But, after the whole ensemble repeats fortissimo a dominant seventh,

VESALII ICONES

PETER MAXWELL DAVIES

1. Agony in the Garden

Ex. 7.5 Maxwell Davies, *Vesalii Icones*, opening, bb. 1–6

the piano silences the noise with the symbol of the Antichrist, the 'death' chord. So if the dancer has not done so already, the music confirms the Devil's presence. The piano plays the chord pianissimo, and the sudden change from fortissimo to pianissimo means that the cello can assume its solo role again and supply pizzicato the notes C-D-E against the piano's held chord. Consequently it relates the end to the beginning of the work. But although a transformation has taken place, as far as the music is concerned it merely transforms a line into a chord.

Vesalii Icones was the work Birtwistle and Maxwell Davies chose as their model for the music-theatre class they ran at the 1970 Dartington Summer School. At it they stressed the need for students to have in mind suitable gestures for the works they were asked to compose, and to this end they employed a mime artist to assist their teaching. But mime artists need only the minimum of instruction; they require only a framework in which to practise their skills. The success of Vesalii Icones as Music Theatre lay in the fact that Maxwell Davies not only gave Lowther the freedom to improvise, he also provided him with Vesalius's illustrations and a suitable framework in which to realise them. It was a solution he carried over into his next monodrama for, unlike Revelation and Fall, the other music-theatre piece he had asked Mary Thomas to sing, Miss Donnithorne's Maggot, also has a vivid framework in which to act.

Maxwell Davies says that Miss Donnithorne's Maggot was conceived at a reception after the first performance of Eight Songs for a Mad King in 1969, and was the result of Randolph Stow saying to him, 'Let's write a funny one, as a sequel.' In his note on the work he does not mention whether Stow had already in mind a work based on the life of Eliza Emily Donnithorne, but as the piece took five years to materialise it may have taken Stow some time to find a suitable subject for the sequel. In the event, Maxwell Davies believes that Miss Donnithorne's music is more introvert, more contemplative and, in his opinion, ultimately more disturbing than the music he composed for George III. It is funny only 'in a most qualified manner'.

Miss Donnithorne may have been one of the models for Miss Havisham in Dickens's Great Expectations. She was born in India, and taken to Australia on the retirement of her father. Four years after his death in 1852 she became engaged to a naval officer. Her marriage and the wedding breakfast were to have been held at her home in Newtown, New South Wales, but her fiancé did not turn up and nothing was heard of him again. Like Miss Havisham she left everything untouched. Stow confesses in the programme note that his portrait of her:

> is a base and cowardly slur on the reputation of an unfortunate lady. It suggests that she had a habit of going berserk, though in fact no one knows what she did in the extraordinary privacy of her own home. It hints that

she drank, though this seems unlikely for commissariat reasons. However, neighbours will talk; and Miss Donnithorne, by her way of life, positively threw down the gauntlet to hers.

Although Maxwell Davies thinks his music to be less than funny, a reading of the seven poems Stow sent him shows that these have as much humour in them as pathos. The problem for Maxwell Davies was that the humour is largely verbal, and verbal humour tends to get lost when set to the virtuoso and sometimes extravagant music he needed to convey Miss Donnithorne's disturbed state of mind. In style the vocal line is similar to the one in *Revelation and Fall* and ideally suited to the vocal technique and histrionic gifts of Mary Thomas.

This is the first piece Maxwell Davies actually calls 'a music-theatre work' on his title page. Like *Pierrot lunaire* and *Eight Songs for a Mad King* it is essentially a song cycle. Maxwell Davies inserts a purely instrumental *Nocturne* after the fourth poem so that like the previous 'mad' work there are eight numbers in all. As in *Eight Songs for a Mad King*, he pays attention not only to the set and props but also to how the singer should act as well as sing the part. In his staging notes he writes with reference to the set and props: 'There should ideally be a set containing a huge wedding cake in an advanced state of decay, the instrumentalists being integrated into the set. The mezzo-soprano soloist playing Miss Donnithorne must be dressed in a period wedding gown with veil, also in a state of decay. Additionally she tears little cakes (made of cardboard paper, to make a lot of noise) or bits from the cake forming the set, in No. 2. In No. 8 she takes confetti from pockets in her dress and throws it about.'

'The music,' says Maxwell Davies, 'refers constantly to the Victorian salon music with which one must assume Miss Donnithorne was familiar.' No. 2, for example, is set as a Victorian ballad. The tearing of paper into little cakes takes place in the second of the four verses, and it is an occasion when Maxwell Davies can be as comic as Stow: 'She wept like a xylophone, she laughed like a tree. / "Alack and alas", she said, "who would not change with me! / To have to herself such a fine tower of cake / here the seaweed does intertwine with the precious coral snake."' The tearing of the paper occurs on the word 'cake'. Maxwell Davies gives the soprano a thirty-two-note roulade for the word. But since each note must be associated with her hands tearing the paper, she has to articulate each note separately (kay-ay-ay). In the course of the roulade she must also get faster and faster in stages so that it can end with her throwing the paper high in the air.

In the following song, which Maxwell Davies calls simply 'Recitative', four of the instrumentalists have to set in motion metronomes clicking at a different pulse. 'This is in order to evoke an empty house full of clocks, at first ticking, and eventually chiming and jangling through the protagonist's disturbed, distorted memories of her tragic wedding day.' The song begins and ends with a line spoken by Ophelia after Hamlet has rejected her and her mind has become unhinged: 'They say the owl was a baker's daughter.' That Miss Donnithorne can equate herself with Ophelia underlines the pathos of her situation, a condition that, despite moments of humour, will increase in intensity as the songs unfold. Stow does this by introducing more and more references to the navy.

They emerge into the open in the sixth number, called *Her Rant*, a rant being a spirited dance movement similar to a jig. This gives the poet and composer the opportunity to introduce sexual innuendo, because at one stage Miss Donnithorne imagines that someone knocks on the door: 'Somebody hacks back the bolts with his hands and advances on me, all womanly, on me alone.' Eventually she imagines seeing her fiancé in dress uniform complete with ceremonial sword. As well as having the viola play pizzicato chords 'like a ukelele' and the cello play similar chords 'like a banjo', Maxwell Davies also takes the word rant in its other meaning, 'to recite theatrically'. To do this he has the soprano sing the number in the dazzling coloratura style of Jenny Lind, the nineteenth-century Swedish soprano.

The sexual innuendo becomes more overt in the next song when Miss Donnithorne listens to the ribald remarks of two boys shouting outside her shutters about (to put it politely) her lack of sexual experience. At first she wants to shoot them, but on second thoughts she ends up by saying, 'Dear boys. Such dear boys. I think I shall adopt a little boy. A little Post-captain / Of the Royal Navy / With a gold moustache.' Maxwell Davies's music for this is mainly for piano and violin, the piano playing in a 'devout' style with decorations *à la Chopin*, the violin in a manner that Maxwell Davies believes to be in the tradition of the Victorian music-hall (even though he claims he doubts whether a well-bred Victorian lady could ever have visited such a common establishment).

The final number is a reel, appropriately a dance for couples, since this is when she imagines she is about to meet her lover. Here we encounter her 'reeling' drunk on dandelion wine, and fantasising that her fiancé is calling to her from an adjoining room. The number concludes with the most overtly sexual *double entendre* of them all. She confesses that she is a virgin and then says three times, 'O chevalier, I come.' On each 'come' she throws confetti into the air before dancing off stage in a state of enrapture. Throughout the song Maxwell Davies makes reference to the wedding marches of both Mendelssohn and Wagner, but at the end he transforms the basic material which in various forms has pervaded the work into what, as mentioned above, he describes as a 'cheap tune summing up the whole masquerade'. And with it we realise why Maxwell Davies thinks the work is funny 'only in a qualified manner', for unlike George III, Miss Donnithorne does not stand back and see herself for what she is. She cannot distinguish between the true and the false. She deceives herself, and consequently, in Maxwell Davies's opinion, she

Ill. 7.4 Mary Thomas in Maxwell Davies, *Miss Donnithorne's Maggot*, world première, Adelaide Festival, 1974

has to be seen as a tragic figure 'imprisoned absolutely in her imagination, forever estranged and alone' (Ill. 7.4).

Although Music Theatre was by no means dead after 1974, I believe that the first performance of *Miss Donnithorne's Maggot* at the Adelaide Festival in March of that year marked the end of the period when Music Theatre flourished in Britain. By then the adverse economic effects of the 1973 oil crisis were beginning to bite,[15] and as a result composers, as with all other creative artists, began to pull in their horns. Those, like Maxwell Davies, who had been among the avant-garde, turned away from experiment and the desire to shock, and made efforts to pursue a more sober attitude in their work. In 1974 Maxwell Davies had already embarked on his First Symphony, and among the models he had turned to were symphonies by Schumann and Sibelius. In fact his change of style is also noticeable in *Miss Donnithorne's Maggot*, for although he takes the vocal part to an extreme as he had done in previous music-theatre works, the instrumental writing and the construction of the piece with its recitatives and strophic forms is much less extravagant and much more formal than hitherto. Perhaps this is why it gets so many performances.

[15] Marwick, *The Sixties*, 7.

CHAPTER EIGHT

Experiment and Protest

WHEN discussing Focus Opera in Chapter Four, I mentioned that it was not until March 1968 that it began to mount Music Theatre instead of small-scale operas. Thereafter, until its demise in 1975, its policy was to produce Music Theatre mainly by young composers, foreign as well as British. Nevertheless, during those seven years only two of the works were specially composed for it. These were Cornelius Cardew's *Schooltime Compositions* (which they presented in the International Students' House on 11 and 12 March 1968 with Ligeti's *Aventures et Nouvelles aventures* and Kagel's *Sur scène*), and Nicola LeFanu's *Anti-World* (presented with Birtwistle's *Down by the Greenwood Side* and another performance of *Sur scène*) performed in the Cockpit Theatre on 29 and 20 June and 1 July 1972.[1]

By initiating its new policy with such controversial works, Focus Opera made a bold statement about its intentions, for as we have seen, both the Ligeti and Kagel pieces were avant-garde in the extreme, and the specially commissioned work by Cardew was by a composer who seven years earlier had embraced the experimental ideas of John Cage and in so doing had rejected a European tradition that had continued since the Renaissance.

Cornelius Cardew (1936–81), the son of artistic parents (his father was a potter and his mother a painter), studied piano, cello and composition at the Royal Academy of Music in London between 1953 and 1957. He worked in Cologne as an assistant to Stockhausen from 1958 to 1960. His interest in Cage stemmed from concerts he heard in Cologne in 1958 and he played a key role in bringing the works of American avant-garde composers to the attention of British audiences.

Cardew's most experimental compositions included *Treatise* (1963–7), a graphic score with scope for considerable freedom of interpretation, and *The Great Learning*, based on translations of Confucius by Ezra Pound. This work led to his forming the experimental Scratch Orchestra with Howard Skempton and Michael Parsons. In 1966, Cardew joined the recently formed jazz improvisation group AMM as cellist and pianist. The Scratch Orchestra came to an end in 1972 and Cardew became more involved in left-wing politics and finding means of using music in support of political causes.[1]

---

[1] Since the first draft of this book was completed a study of Cardew's music and ideas has been published: Tony Harris, *The Legacy of Cornelius Cardew* (London, Ashgate, 2013).

Cardew's early death in 1981 was the result of a hit-and-run car accident.[2]

The controversy sparked by the choice for Focus Opera's triple bill was compounded by the title the Group chose for the programme. As mentioned in Chapter Four, the term Music Theatre was not yet in general use in Britain and they chose to call it '*Three? Avant-Garde? Operas?*', the question marks indicating their uncertainty as to what the genre actually was. But although the commission they gave Cardew was specifically for an opera, when *Schooltime Compositions* was submitted, it did not surprise them that it did not comply with the standard definition of opera as a staged dramatic work based on singing but that, instead, he had taken the word to mean 'working together'.[3]

This definition did not mean that Cardew intended his *Compositions* solely for musicians working together. Like Cage, he wanted music to be an activity everyone could pursue. Instead of producing purely musical scores, he wanted forms of notation that could be interpreted not just by musicians and not solely musically, but by anyone interested in seeing their potential for some form of artistic expression. During the previous few years he had been composing works that set out to achieve this. The most important of them was *Treatise* (1963–7) inspired by Wittgenstein's *Tractatus Logico-Philosophicus* (1921).[4] For this he drew on his training as a graphic designer. *Treatise* consists of 193 pages on which is a continuous design woven from a wide variety of graphic elements that can be interpreted by anyone who has had a visual education. Michael Nyman explains:

> With a score like Cardew's *Treatise* … aural recognizability is both impossible and irrelevant since the (non-musical) graphic symbols it contains have no meanings attached to them but 'are to be interpreted in the context of their role in the whole'. The performer may choose to realise, for example, a circle, as some sort of circular sound, movement or gesture; but it is more likely that he will interpret it in a 'non-representational' way by a melody, or silence, or whatever.[5]

He then went on to compose *The Tiger's Mind*, a verbally notated score that requires neither a musical nor a visual education, simply the ability to read English.

[2] For a comprehensive biography of Cardew, see John Tilbury, *Cornelius Cardew: A Life Unfinished* (Harlow, Copula, 2008).
[3] Desmond Shawe-Taylor, 'How Many Ping-Pong Balls Make an Opera?', *Sunday Times*, 17 March 1968.
[4] Later Cardew described the development of the work in *The Treatise Handbook* (London: Peters Edition, 1971).
[5] Nyman, Experimental Music, 9–10.

Although Cardew had specific performers in mind when he composed *Schooltime Compositions*, he still provided enough material to stimulate just about everyone who wanted to take part. Those who participated included Lou Gare and Keith Rowe, who were colleagues from AMM; John Tilbury, who had been his friend and piano-duet partner for many years and later his biographer; Christian Wolff an American experimental composer; and others who were either friends or his students at the Royal Academy of Music, where he taught composition.

Schooltime Compositions are contained in what pertains to be a school textbook measuring 110 x 155 mm with a label on which can be written the student's name, year and grade. Cardew calls the compositions 'matrices'. He said in the score that they grew around 'such things as words, melody, vocal sounds, triangles, pleasure, noise, working-to-rule, will and desire, keyboards'. He heads the eight pages he needed for triangles 'Triads'. This is because one possible interpretation of their shapes is to think of them as being three-note chords. On the page opposite each triangle or group of triangles he supplies guidelines couched in the language of a mathematical textbook. For example:

As a triangle approaches the equilateral its duration tends to infinity, i.e., the *regularity* of the triangle determines its duration: equilateral triangle = infinite duration; isosceles triangle = medium duration; scalene triangle = short duration; obtuse triangle = very short duration. *Size* of triangle may determine loudness: very small triangle is very loud; large triangle is soft.

Two of the matrices devoted to keyboards have drawings of sections of keyboards on which are printed words. On the white notes of one are the words 'loyal, honest, lovely, good, nice, pretty, friendly, graceful'. Below this, is a skeletal keyboard behind which are two staves on which musical ideas suggested by the words can be written. On the other matrix the keyboard is drawn from another angle and has the words 'arid, spectral, fertile, unknown, soft, remote' printed on the black notes, while on the page opposite is a widely spread ten-note chord with two sets of numbers written by the side of it. Whether the keyboard and the chord have a bearing on each other is difficult to tell, but then ambiguity pervades most of the matrices (Ex. 8.1).

Some are purely verbal. The one headed 'Song of Pleasure' reads, 'I am rowing a boat on a lake / The sounds – the regular / breathing, the small creaking / and thudding sounds of the / oars in the rowlocks, the / water lapping and sucking at / the belly of the boat, the / occasional passing bird – / all combine to make a song / of pleasure.' The one headed 'Desire' reads, 'Want to do something; Do it / Do something without wanting to / Do something wanting not to / Be done to / Be done!' Beneath this, at the bottom of the page, are two footnotes. One says

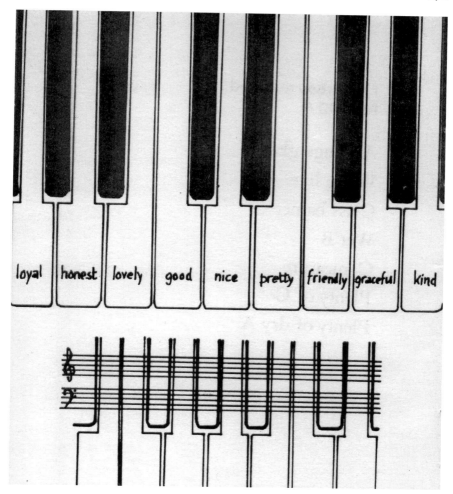

Ex. 8.1 Cardew, *Schooltime Compositions*, keyboard matrices

'Perform all or none of the instructions,' the other, 'Instructions are only to be followed by a qualified person.'

'Melody' consists of two pages containing two scales or modes. Both stretch from a very high to a very low note, and both centre on C♯, but one has forty-two notes the other twenty-four different ones. Above the second scale Cardew writes, 'Play each phrase to make the preceding phrase seem as though it had been played by a child.'

'Working-to-rule' must be 'Making A'. On one page Cardew lists the properties required to make A. They are: 'an A-gauge glass, a White line, a Glass bamer, a Wet B, a C measure, Plenty of C, Plenty of dry A'. On another page he provides the instructions for making it. Unfortunately they did not comply with the fire regulations at the International Students House so 'Making A' was never per-formed. Nevertheless, they offer an insight into his thoroughness in attempting to meet everyone's capabilities:

> When A in the A-gauge glass becomes level with the white line, make more A as follows: 1. Place WET B in glass bamer. 2. Empty one pack of A into the wet B. 3. Draw off two full measures of hot boiling C and pour them over the dry A in the B (using circular motion). 4. Draw off one FULL measure of A and repour it into B. 5. Close B between pours. 6. Never make more A if the A in A-gauge is above white line.

To discover what was in store for those who attended the productions mounted by Focus Opera, the editor of *The Musical Times* asked Cardew to write a short article about *Schooltime Compositions* for the March edition of his magazine. The com-poser entitled it 'Sitting in the Dark,' a reference to what one does when attending a 'real' opera: 'You sit in the dark absorbed in action proceeding in a pool of light. Just like in a classroom: children in the dark of ignorance focusing attention (erratically) on manipulations performed in the light of knowledge by the teacher. Hence *Schooltime*. Children go to Dayschool, grown-ups to Nightschool. We love children in their sagacity; what we love in grown-ups is a childlike quality.'[6]

He follows this with a diatribe pitted against 'the theatrical situation', then goes on to say that each of the *Schooltime Compositions* in the opera book 'is a matrix to draw out an interpreter's feelings about certain topics or materials. These pieces and their interpreters are the characters in the opera. They undergo no dramatic development in the book; [although] in performance they may. The pieces and the performers will be the same in both Dayschool and Nightschool.'

On the grounds that these remarks needed to be amplified, the editor of *The Musical Times* asked Cardew to supply him with more paragraphs. They begin 'Let me explain.' But since his example of a matrix is the sentence 'My heart drink only desert words' in one of Edgar Rice Burroughs's Tarzan stories, his explanation would be helpful only for those who are linguistically sophisticated. More fruitful perhaps is the third paragraph: 'Some matrices serve as a measure of probity (cf. La Monte Young's 'Draw a straight line and follow it'); others as a measure of virtuosity, courage, tenacity, alertness and so on. They point to the heart of some real matter, mental or material. The interpreter knows the general idea of his potential action; he wishes he has talent to play, or sing, or construct, or illumine or take exercise of one sort or another. He can draw out his interpretation in that

---

[6] *The Musical Times*, May 1968, 233–4.

direction. The interpreting route from matrix to action is what determines the condition he arrives in, the spirit in which he undertakes his action.'

London's music critics turned out in force for the first night of the Focus Opera's show. With one exception, all were hostile. Stanley Sadie headed his piece in *The Times* 'Avant-garde, but is it progress?' 'Cardew's *Schooltime Compositions*', he said,

> came over as a 40 minute non-event. The performers did a variety of things: two sat at keyboards, and occasionally played; one had an electric guitar tied to a xylophone, producing noises through an amplifying system with a bow and pieces of chord; one wandered around with electronic equipment; one shone linear patterns on to a wall; two in clownish guise played a game with ping-pong balls; one entertained himself with paper streamers, a balloon, a toy plane and other such things. There was also some singing, and electronic gurgles, buzzes and the like. Nobody seemed to be reacting to anyone else; I had expected interaction to be the motive force of the piece, but perhaps it is naïve to expect a motive force.[7]

The headline for Desmond Shawe-Taylor's review in *The Sunday Times* (17 March 1968) was 'How many ping-pong balls make an opera?', while Peter Heyworth's in *The Observer* was 'Brave new neo-dadaism';[8] and John Warrack's in *The Sunday Telegraph* 'Da-da goes Ga-ga' (17 March 1968). The only sympathetic review was Michael Parsons's in the May edition of *The Musical Times*, but then he was also an 'experimental' composer, and the following year was to join Cardew in founding the Scratch Orchestra:

> In Cardew's *Schooltime Compositions* sound and action instead of underlining each other simply coexisted; interaction arose from the coincidence, overlapping, and juxtaposition in space and time of simultaneous activities, something Cardew would consider more interesting than relationships contrived according to a set plan. Quiet, long-held vocal and instrumental sounds, sometimes electronically amplified and distorted, merged or drew apart in ways which drew one's attention to every slight alteration. John Pitchford gave a performance with newspaper, balloons and other assorted objects that was most inventive when purely and unselfconsciously meaningless, while Robin Page and Eric Brown played a clownish ball game which leant more to entertainment, demonstrating that any activity can

---

[7] *The Times*, 12 March 1968.
[8] *The Observer*, 17 March 1968.

be interesting to watch for its own sake, particularly when taken out of its usual context.[9]

The founding of the Scratch Orchestra emerged out of the improvisation class Cardew held on a Monday evening at Morley College, a class that was almost entirely devoted to ideas about experimental music. It represented the epitome of Cardew's left-wing musical and political idealism, for anyone could join whether they were musicians or not, and those that did could do what they wanted, provided it was an expression on an idea that had been jointly agreed upon by the members of the orchestra.

Cardew's class at Morley College had been initiated by Michael Graubart, who had become its Director of Music in 1968. It was Graubart who had been behind the decision to mount 'Three? Avant-Garde? Operas?' It was therefore unsurprising that, as well as asking Cardew to teach composition at Morley, he should also ask Michael Sargent, the Director of the Focus Opera Group, to take a class on Music Theatre there. It began in autumn 1970, and among the first to join the class was Nicola LeFanu, who following three years at Oxford University and a year at the Royal College of Music had been on the course on Music Theatre run by Birtwistle and Maxwell Davies at Dartington in August 1970. She became its tutor when Michael Sargent obtained a theatre position in Birmingham.

Nicola LeFanu (b. 1947) is the daughter of Irish parents: her father William LeFanu was from an Irish literary family, and her mother was the composer Dame Elizabeth Maconchy. She studied at Oxford, RCM and, as a Harkness Fellow, at Harvard. She has composed more than one hundred works. She has a particular interest in vocal music and has composed to date eight operas. From 1994 to 2008 she was Professor of Music at the University of York, where she gave composition classes to many composers.[10]

For the 1970 Dartington course, the prime concern was the relationship between musical and physical gestures. A performance of Maxwell Davies's *Vesalii Icones* given by William Louther, Jennifer Ward Clarke and the Pierrot Players at the Summer School provided a model, and, in addition, two mimes were employed to help the students. At the end of the fortnight's course the students gave a concert of the works they had composed. LeFanu considers her piece was a 'dry run' for the work she was to compose two years later for Focus Opera. It was the result, she says, of seeing what materialised when she asked a mime and an instrumentalist to improvise on a given idea (the model was Birtwistle's drawing of three straight

---

[9]   *The Musical Times*, March 1968, 233.
[10] Further information about the composer is available from her website: www.nicolale-fanu.com (accessed 11 February 2014).

lines on a blackboard). Improvisation was at the top of her agenda when she began to take a more active role in the Morley College class. She made it the basis of her preparations for the music-theatre piece she was asked to devise, and also for the show Focus Opera wanted her to direct and conduct in June 1972.

The catalyst for the work was a scene in Jacques Tati's film *Trafic* (1971), which, she told me, takes place:

> in an enormous showroom where there's going to be a huge exhibition of cars. It's not yet set out, and the various dealers are walking around it to decide what will be put where. The whole of the floor, a vast space like an aircraft hangar, has been marked out, but not with white lines. The compartments have been made of wire stretched about a foot above the ground so the wires were entirely invisible. However, the people walking about saying, 'I'll go here', 'you go there', have to step over the wires. What you see are therefore lots of people continually coming up against barriers that they can see but we cannot. They have to step over or walk around them. It's a wonderful metaphor because one can see people doing it all the time, at parties for example. My piece is therefore about invisible barriers, in particular about invisible political barriers such as those erected to prevent the Russian *samizdat* poets from publishing their work.

One of these dissident poets was Natalya Gorbanevskaya, a selection of whose poetry had been smuggled out of Russia, translated into English by Daniel Weissbort and published by Carcanet Press in early 1972,[11] Gorbanevskaya was one of seven protesters to demonstrate in Red Square on 25 August 1968 against the invasion of Czechoslovakia by Russia and other Warsaw Pact countries, who objected to Alexander Dubček's liberalisation campaign known as the Prague Spring. Although she was not put on trial with the other demonstrators because she had her three-month-old child with her at the time, Gorbanevskaya was nevertheless arrested the following year, tried and incarcerated in a Soviet psychiatric prison until February 1972.

LeFanu had a particular interest in the plight of Czechoslovakia because her mother, the composer Elizabeth Maconchy, had studied in Prague in the early thirties, and had fond memories of the country. Although Gorbanevskaya's poems published by Carcanet Press date from before 1968, they all betray the deep introspection of a woman encased by invisible barriers. The three that particularly appealed to LeFanu were 'Turn the sky over', 'In my own twentieth century' and 'Only music, nothing else, is left'. In the second of these poems were lines she

---

[11] *Selected Poems* (Oxford, Carcanet Press, 1972).

thought might be the basis of a structure for her projected work: 'my miserable / forever unshared love / among those Goya images / is nervous, faint, absurd'.

The Goya images Gorbanevskaya refers to were probably those depicting the disasters of war painted by Goya after French troops invaded Spain in 1808. In LeFanu's mind this tied in with the invasion of Czechoslovakia and also the invasion of Russia by the Nazis during the Second World War. The latter was the subject of a poem called 'I am Goya' by the Russian dissident poet Andrei Voznesensky, published in 1964 during the Khruschev thaw. The poem is from a collection entitled *Antimiry* (Anti-Worlds), hence the title of LeFanu's work. Seven lines from the poem bring her work to a close. She has them sung by a baritone in Russian, but her programme note contains her translation of them: 'I am Goya / Over the bare fields the enemy swooped, gouging out my eye-craters / I am grief / I am the groaning of war, of glowing ruins in the snow of 1942 / I am hunger / I am the gorge of the puppet-woman, whose body swings like a bell over the empty square / I am Goya.'

To begin her work, LeFanu chose to set Gorbanevskaya's 'Turn the sky over', confining the other two poems to her programme note on the grounds that they offer the best indication of what the work is about. If the invasions of Czechoslovakia, Spain and Russia focus on barriers erected in the public domain, then 'Turn the sky over' focuses on barriers erected in the private domain, barriers needed for personal protection. The poem speaks about moving between opposites, the need to find a balance, and ultimately the temptation to sink deep into one's inner self, a meaning made clear in the last few lines of the poem: 'Balance yourself and the world, / the world and the ladybird, / the wavelet and the wave / that drags you down to the bottom. / And go down to the bottom, softly / banging the moist doors behind you.'

LeFanu scored *Anti-World* for a female mime who must also be a dancer, a soprano, a baritone and three instrumentalists: alto flute, clarinet doubling amplified bass clarinet, and percussion. The alto flute functions as the soprano's alter ego, while the clarinet, particularly the bass clarinet, functions as the baritone's. With this small ensemble, recruited mainly from her class at Morley College, she was able to construct a network of relationships built on the intertwining of a musical progression involving the two singers and their alter egos, and a visual progression involving mainly, but not exclusively, the mime. The musical progression moves from introspective lyricism to rhetorical declamation, the visual progression from farce to tragedy.

The venue for the work's first performance was the Cockpit Theatre, a small theatre in Marylebone, London, with an open stage and seats that could be arranged in different ways. At the side of the stage was a staircase leading to a gallery that the performers could use but not the audience. This is where LeFanu placed the baritone and the bass clarinet when 'I am Goya' was being sung. Among her props was a large version of a wheel found in a pet hamster's cage, a wheel from which it is impossible to escape, but which in this case functions as the wheel of fortune. The only other props were mobiles such as wind chimes that could be placed in various places across the stage, that can be heard as well as seen, and when set in motion might help to break down barriers between singers and instrumentalists.

Although *Anti-World* is continuous and seamless, LeFanu divides it into four sections. The first begins with the soprano entering from the auditorium singing the first setting of 'Turn the Sky', her introspection made clear by her intermittent humming and whispering. When she confuses the poem's two stanzas and sings 'turn the world' instead of 'turn the sky', the alto flute takes over. It too begins off stage and eventually peters out. Counterpointed against this musical progression is the farce performed by the mime, percussion and clarinet. Initially the function of the percussionist is to be the clarinet's dogsbody. He enters wearing sandwich boards containing only the letter S preceded by an apostrophe; he then has to fetch a chair for the clarinettist when ordered to do so. Meanwhile the mime, who throughout the piece attempts to break down barriers and establish rapports between herself and the others, enters as if on a tightrope, wobbles violently and repeatedly crashes into an invisible door. Even though she thinks the soprano and flute may be responding to her when they start singing and playing again, all her attempts to establish rapport are thwarted.

Her failure results in the second section being entirely devoted to how the others, including the soprano and flute, exert complete control over her. Their improvisations and sudden silences make her dance so jerky then so wild that eventually she is forced back against the wheel. As soon as it begins to turn, the barriers that have been enclosing her are broken. Her fortune changes and she can take charge of the action.

The third section is concerned with her efforts to make the instrumental-ists play in a manner that allows her to dance gracefully rather than jerkily. Imperiously she flicks her wrist at each of them to order them to begin playing. But once again she cannot control the soprano whose singing of another version of 'Turn the Sky' becomes so introspective that eventually the mime has to force a confrontation with her. Initially she seizes the soprano's music and tears it in two. When this has no effect, she threatens her with an apparently heavy object that she has in her hands. Now farce takes over again, for when she releases the heavy object it turns out to be a feather, which the mime blows away. Nevertheless, it reduces the soprano to whispering again. After murmuring 'the world and the ladybird / the wavelet and the wave / that drags you under to the bottom', she lies on the ground remaining in a crouching position with her eyes open until the end of the work.

LeFanu tells me that she intended this outcome to represent Gorbanevskaya's imprisonment, but having witnessed how she had the soprano retreat into herself in the first section, she believes that the audience are more likely to think that the soprano has deliberately erected a complete barrier between herself and the world, an opinion that appears to be confirmed when the alto flute in its role as the soprano's alter ego sustains unobtrusively a long melodic line, which until the end of the work it must perform as if 'totally oblivious of its surroundings'.

That these surroundings are tragic begins to emerge as soon as the soprano adopts a crouching position, for immediately afterwards the clarinettist steps over her and goes up the stairs into the gallery, takes up the bass clarinet and switches on the amplification. The indifference of the clarinet to the soprano's inert body horrifies the mime, her feelings being intensified when the amplified bass clarinet delivers violently four high notes that sound like shots from a rifle (Ex. 8.2). The mime tries to escape, but cannot. Instead she is obliged to adopt what LeFanu calls 'the Goya position', a reference to Goya's painting *The Third of May, 1808: The Executions at Principe Pio Hill*, in which a white-shirted Spanish partisan has been forced on to his knees, and who, with arms outstretched and terror in his eyes, faces a French firing squad. When from the gallery the baritone accompanied by the bass clarinet sings an impassioned aria which verbally presents facts about the invasion of Russia during the Second World War, all we see on stage are the twitches of the mime in her death throes. Yet the flute plays on even after the baritone has sung his last 'Ya Goya gove'.

LeFanu continued her association with the Focus Opera Group until autumn 1973, when she went to America as a Harkness Fellow and Mendelssohn Scholar. Although she composed no more Music Theatre for Focus Opera after *Anti-World*, she conducted Jeremy Dale Roberts's *Reconciliation* when it was given as part of a triple bill in December 1972. By then Focus Opera had become absorbed into the Morley Music-Theatre Group and the triple bill was given at the Emma Cons Hall at Morley College under the auspices of the Morley Group. As well as including *Reconciliation* and a new production of Stravinsky's *Renard*, the programme also contained Melanie Daiken's *Mayakovsky and the Sun*, a work in seven scenes for speaker, singers, chorus, mime and ensemble, which that summer had been given at a fringe event at the Edinburgh Festival. Although well received both in Edinburgh and in London, further performances are unlikely because the score and parts have been mislaid. I did not attend the performances and apart from reports received from those that did, which I paraphrased in Chapter Four, I am therefore unable to discuss in depth what appears to have been a particularly bold and imaginative work based on the principles of Russian Futurism.

Jeremy Dale Roberts (b. 1934) studied composition at the Royal Academy of Music with William Alwyn and Priaulx Rainier before taking a degree in music at

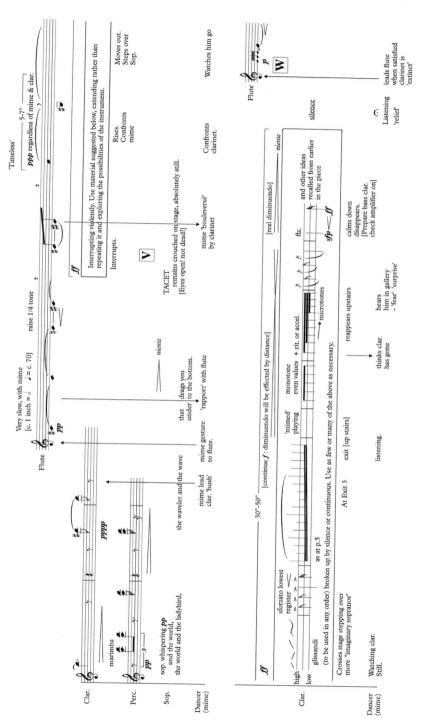

Ex. 8.2 LeFanu, *Anti-World*, clarinettist steps over soprano and departs stage

the University of Durham. His compositions range through a variety of unusual combinations of instruments but he has also written many pieces for the piano, most notably the *Oggetti – omaggio à Morandi*, inspired by the still-life paintings of the great twentieth-century Italian artist Giorgio Morandi. He also taught for many years, at Morley College, the Royal College of Music (1966–98, where he became Head of Composition) and as Visiting Professor of Composition at the University of Iowa (1999–2000 and 2004).

Dale Roberts's *Reconciliation* had received performances before being taken up by the Focus Opera Group. It had been composed in 1969–70 to a commission from Radio Suisse Romande and was first performed in Neuchâtel before being broadcast. Because it was originally intended for radio it can be performed without any visual component. It only becomes Music Theatre when visual elements are added, as they were when it was given in London. In this respect it resembles Schoenberg's *Pierrot lunaire*, which also holds up well when broadcast. The resemblance is strengthened by its scoring for, like *Pierrot lunaire*, it was written for a speaker and an ensemble consisting of flute, clarinet doubling bass clarinet, violin, viola and piano. However, here, the speaker has to be a man using normal speech rather than *Sprechstimme* and the violin and viola must be played by two players rather than one. Furthermore, during the course of the work the speaker must play two suspended cymbals and a tam-tam, the flute a pair of bongos, and the clarinet maracas and tambourine.

The texts are two 'Uneasy Love Songs' by the American poet Philip Oxman, called respectively 'The Fear of Confinement' and 'The Fear of the Open'. 'The reconciliation of the title', Dale Roberts told me, 'is effected between the verbal texts of the speaker, which are themselves antithetical in expression and phonetic in character, and the non-verbal sounds of the instruments.'

On stage, the speaker should be positioned on the left-hand side of the platform, the instrumentalists on the right. The two poems are to be shown on two large, brightly lit panels situated behind them so that the audience can follow visually the attempts of instrumentalists to draw the speaker into their fold of pure sound, and the efforts of the speaker to resist them. In the final 'dissolve', when reconciliation is achieved, there should be a gradual extinguishing of light.

The work begins with the speaker reciting the two poems unaccompanied. Although entitled 'The Fear of Confinement', the first poem presents images that seem to express freedom rather than confinement. They are also clearly sexual in intent, the last lines, for example, being, 'From his back time, / Lively with bison, man will ride on megaliths ... / Kind on his love-mount and gay of her. Lo! / Her mane fills his mouth and heart. Lo! / A human brain grows out of earth'.

'The Fear of the Open' explores a different imagery. It contrasts the apparent freedom that insects enjoy with the confinement to which men subject themselves.

Here the last lines are, 'But some men are never ended praying: God / Is a rise and fall in them. All: / Mistral and tramontane have stunned the Levantine / Maintaining the dead past. We are our dreams again'. As this last sentence is being recited the speaker strikes the tam-tam and the flautist the bongos. And with the entrance of non-verbal sound into the proceedings, the subsequent repetitions of the two poems are subject to comments from the instruments who play with them, break them down, and examine their significance both as sound and as symbol.

As soon as the instruments enter and the speaker embarks on a second reading of the poems, the pacing of his recitation begins to be taken out of his hands, for he has to take heed of the ways his diction is being commented on. This clearly irritates him. On one occasion he claps his hands at the ensemble only to have the flautist clap back at him; on another he flicks his fingers at them, the response from the violist and cellist also being like for like.

This conflict increases when the speaker embarks on yet another reading of the poems. During this the ensemble mocks him. Under the influence of the instruments, particularly the bongos, he turns the phrases 'quick in us' and 'dead in us' into rhythms associated with music rather than speech. Ultimately the ensemble's mockery forces the speaker to stop when only halfway through his repetition of the first poem, and, as a result, all attention has to be focused on the lyrical melody the strings begin playing, a melody which anticipates, at least in character, the melody that will bring the work to a close. The speaker's response to this is to intone the second poem 'in the manner of a liturgical incantation: i.e. rapidly and monotonously, without emphasis'. But by ignoring the rhythms and inflections that make the poem a poem, the speaker destroys its identity. To make amends he is obliged to focus on what he has just eliminated, to devote his attention to the phonetic content of the poems. But in so doing he jumbles the words up and deprives them of any meaning they may have had. Words become sounds, and to emphasise this Dale Roberts asks the instrumentalists to extract a word from a list compiled from words in the poems, words containing either 'n' or 'ng', then to repeat them in their own time so that they overlap and produce a verbal drone (Ex. 8.3).

To accompany them, and indeed to enchant them by his non-verbal action, the speaker rolls one of his suspended cymbals to create an equally sustained sound. Then after opening wide his arms in a gesture of acceptance, he closes them over his chest and bows his head in a gesture of confinement. But as if realising that his function in the work was to be a speaker and an actor, he engages in a 'flyting' with the pianist. This marks the climax of the conflict between the speaker and the ensemble for after each of the piano's ad lib phrases the speaker indulges in expletives. Once the two combatants are silenced by the bongos, the speaker makes his

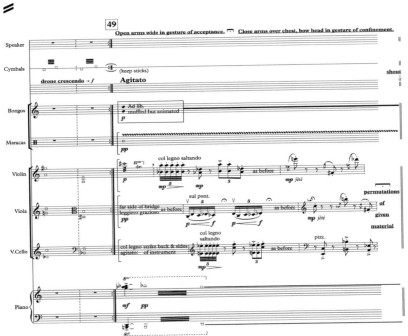

Ex. 8.3 Dale Roberts, *Reconciliation*

last attempt to recite words from the text, but eventually all he can produce are four syllables separated by deep breaths: 'air ... are ... our ... fear'. The conflict is over, and the fact that music has won the day is celebrated by the flute playing a melody that perhaps everybody has been waiting for, not least the unseen woman who can be heard singing the single note that brings the work to an end.

Whenever Nicola LeFanu talks about *Anti-World* she insists it is essentially political. This only becomes evident in the final scene, where the mime represents the execution of a patriot by the French in Spain, the baritone sings of atrocities committed by the Nazis in Russia, and the soprano represents the immediate outcome of the Russian invasion of Czechoslovakia. But *Anti-World* was composed in 1972, and those who attended the first performance may have wondered why LeFanu had not found a way of including the American invasion of Vietnam as this would have been in most people's minds at the time.

Ostensibly the Americans had bombed North Vietnam and sent combat troops to South Vietnam in 1965 to bolster the South Vietnam régime against the threats posed by the Communists in the north and by the Communist Vietcong in the south. Yet this rationale did not mask the fact that the American action was an invasion in most people's view. Evidence of their brutal campaign, their killing of innocent civilians, the use of napalm to defoliate the countryside became common knowledge through the press, television, and the publicity given to the court martial of Lieutenant William Calley between November 1969 and March 1971 for the massacre of at least twenty civilians at My Lai. It was during this period that the protests against the Vietnam War, especially in Britain and America, reached their height. Although protests and demonstrations had been sweeping across Europe and America since the early sixties, when black civil rights in America had been the prime issue, and although they eventually embraced almost everything that troubled and angered students and other citizens of the two continents during the late sixties and early seventies, it was the Vietnam War that was the biggest cause of dissent.

It troubled LeFanu as much as anyone, but she had seen Peter Brook's *US* when it had been performed by the Royal Shakespeare Company at the Aldwych Theatre in 1966, so that when she came to write *Anti-World* she realised that, whatever protest she might make against the war, it would pale into insignificance compared to what Brook had done. All she could do in twenty minutes, with a small theatre and a limited cast, was to provide some historical precedents for what was happening. However, most of the London music critics were unable to make the connection, yet the only difference between her protest and those that had taken place in the streets of Paris and London and were continuing to take place in the campuses of American universities in particular, was that hers was veiled rather than overt. In a later review in *The Musical Times*, Richard Cooke almost, but not quite, grasped the point: 'It is possible that the Soviet invasion of Czechoslovakia was present in the composer's mind at the time. However, to pursue the political analogy further would probably be misleading.'[12]

Although neither of the next two works I discuss exploited the music-theatre genre to make a direct attack on the American action, they were nevertheless open about their opposition. They are George Newson's *Arena*, which the BBC commissioned for a Prom in the Roundhouse on 6 September 1971, and Anthony Gilbert's *The Scene-Machine*, which the Kassel State Theatre commissioned, and which was first performed in German at the Kassel State Theatre in April 1971, and then in English at Sadler's Wells, by the New Opera Company in March 1972.

George Newson (b. 1932) was born in London's docklands and as a child he taught himself to read music and to play the piano. When he was fourteen he won a scholarship to the Blackheath Conservatoire of Music in London. In 1955 a second scholarship allowed him to study composition at the Royal Academy of Music with Alan Bush and Howard Ferguson. During the late 1950s and early 1960s he came into contact with Elliott Carter and John Cage and also studied with Luciano Berio, Bruno Maderna and Luigi Nono.

In 1967 he was awarded a Winston Churchill Fellowship to research electronic music in the US. This led to invitations from Berio and Gottfried Michael Koenig to work in the studios of the RAI in Milan during 1968 and the University of Utrecht in 1969. He has held a research fellowship at Glasgow University, and was lecturer in electronic music at Goldsmiths College, London, and composer-in-residence at Queen's University Belfast.

Alan Bush, his teacher at the Royal Academy of Music, was a committed communist who was still writing his agitprop opera, *The Men of Blackmoor*, when Newson became his pupil. He felt that, as Newson came from a working-class background, he ought to be a 'working-class composer'. But, when at the end of his studies, Newson went to Darmstadt and fell under the spell of Berio, and later, when he worked in the electronic studios at Utrecht and then with Robert Moog in New York, Bush accused him of being a traitor to his roots. He had deserted what should have been his true path.

Nevertheless, when Newson came to compose *Arena*, he based it on a form of theatre that had close associations with the working class especially during the Victorian and Edwardian eras. This was music hall: a term used for both a building and a genre. Although music hall rapidly declined after the First World War, it was kept alive by a popular television programme called *The Good Old Days*, and, in a spectacular way, by variety shows at the London Palladium.

---

[12] *The Musical Times*, vol. 116, 1975, 961–3.

Newson chose this form of theatre because the Prom was scheduled to be given at the Royal Albert Hall, which although not a music hall was nevertheless an arena where all kinds of different events took place (boxing matches as well as concerts and military celebrations, for example). His plan was, therefore, to compose a work that would reflect the diversity of its use. But when the BBC decided to change the venue for the Prom from the Royal Albert Hall to the much smaller Roundhouse to prepare the ground for the concerts of experimental contemporary music they intended to mount there, Newson had to amend his plan. He now arranged the six movements he intended to write into two types. The second, third and fourth movements would be solo items reflecting the relative intimacy of the traditional music hall, while the first, fifth and sixth would involve all the performers. Apart from the short first and sixth movements, all would relate to events at home and abroad that had been recently in the news, the most important being those mirrored in the fifth movement: the 1970 general election, Black Power, the civil rights protests, and above all the shooting of four students at Kent University in Ohio by the National Guard on 4 May 1970. This would mark the climax of the work, and ultimately would be seen as its *raison d'être*.

Arena was never intended to be repeated. It was an occasional work specifically scored for Cleo Laine, Jane Manning, the King's Singers, Alan Hacker, the Goldsmiths College Music Society Choir, and the woodwind, brass and percussion sections of the BBC Symphony Orchestra conducted by Pierre Boulez. Newson selected the actor Joe Melia to be the master of ceremonies, and Leonard Smith to write his script. The work opened with various members of the orchestra drawing attention to themselves by making their warming-up exercises prominent. This was followed by everyone behaving like showmen calling out for customers, their cacophony being followed by the orchestra, now fully under the control of its conductor, playing rhythmically varied block chords to demonstrate their unity. The master of ceremonies then had the opportunity to introduce Boulez and the orchestra to the audience. 'This then is the Roundhouse, the arena. Hail gladiators all! Monsieur Boulez is at the stand, *maestro furioso* of orchestral karate, ready to defy with only one hand this lurking crew of stringers, bowmen, harpies, ear blasters, heavy breathers, pipers, snare snatchers and tuners of skins.' At this, certain members of the orchestra, particularly a clarinettist, interrupt him to continue drawing attention to themselves. 'Listen to it. An ego vibrates. I was a natural until Benny Goodman stole my G. There he goes again. That's how he stopped Dizzy Gillespie! He-man tells all. Everyone, you see, must have their say. Performers must be heard. Some though are better than others.'

These last remarks are an introduction to the first of the music hall turns, a piece called 'Black Magnificat' sung by the King's Singers with trumpet, trombone and percussion accompaniment. The King's Singers, two countertenors, tenor, two baritones and bass, were so named because in 1968, when they were founded, five of them had been choral scholars at King's College, Cambridge. Since then they had become successful not only for their professionalism and rather camp humour, but because they had a repertory that embraced styles including popular music as well as Renaissance polyphony. Newson had chosen his topic because he had been deeply distressed when he heard about the death of Judy Garland in 1969. She had died in London seemingly from an overdose of sleeping tablets. The event was given widespread press coverage because it seemed to be tied up with her rather pathetic efforts to regain the success she had previously had, particularly as a child. Newson selected the Virgin Mary's canticle, 'My soul doth magnify the Lord', because it can be turned into a black magnificat, when the words are used in an attempt to magnify the speaker rather than the Lord. He cast the King's Singers contribution almost entirely in the language of show biz or the theatre, using the broadest backstage slang to set the stage, their first words being 'Spielers, sharpers, hoggers of the mike'. He follows this by having them sing a series of pathetic pleas such as, 'Light me … Let me be seen … I'll thrill you.' In the end when they seem satisfied with the attention they have evoked, they can say, 'Give me your hearts, your loves … My soul is crowned.' Interpolated between these passages, and enhancing the theatrical hyperbole, are comments from the master of ceremonies: 'Dr. Johnson said – how beautifully he said it – "That the mind is its own peace is the boast of a fallen angel that has learnt to lie." Who could deny that now, when we all contend the arena.'

The King's Singers also feature in the next item, a homage to Stravinsky, who had died on 6 April 1971. Its title, 'My dancing days are over', is a response to the words that open the second Ricercar in Stravinsky's Cantata of 1952, 'Tomorrow shall be my dancing day.' Newson's piece is a lamentation that intersperses references to Tallis's *Lamentations of Jeremiah*, sung by the King's Singers, with settings of the words 'My dancing days are over' sung by Jane Manning. Like the King's Singers, Jane Manning had also become a star performer, in her case mainly for her extraordinary skills as an interpreter of difficult contemporary music. But on this occasion Newson chose her for the purity of her voice, partly because he wanted to reserve vocal virtuosity for when Cleo Laine was to be the soloist, but mainly because Jane Manning could elaborate the repetitions of 'My dancing days are over' with the ease of someone who was also skilled in baroque ornamentation. The King's Singers, as well as singing in Latin the opening lines of the *Lamentations* ('Quomodo sedet civitas plena populo …'), enter into dialogue with the soprano when they ask her to dance for them. Her response is a line from the *Lamentations*, 'the young men have ceased from their musick'. She then joins the King's Singers and the quintet of low instruments accompanying the singers to bring the piece to the end with 'For these things I weep'.

Neither 'Black Magnificat' nor 'My Dancing Days are Over' had been triggered by events of national importance, but those that triggered 'Garden Fête', the item that Cleo Laine sings, were of particular national significance, for they related to the Women's Liberation Movement: first the invasion of the Royal Albert Hall in November 1970 by women angered by the Miss World competition taking place there, then the Women's Day marches the following March and the spectacular show *Sugar and Spice* that the Women's Street Theatre Group mounted in Trafalgar Square at the same time.

Newson's contribution to the movement was a piece in which Cleo Laine could tell the story of the events in the Garden of Eden from a woman's point of view, or rather from several women's points of view. Cleo Laine had become a world-class jazz vocalist with a range of over four octaves, and an actor's ability to move from one type of delivery to another in a flash. At one moment she could tell the story in a cockney accent, in the next she could appear to come from down-town New York. Her script had little respect for Genesis. Its account of the expulsion from Eden bears witness to the tone of the piece in general: 'In fact the old misery guts turned up himself, pink and white in his deep celestial bath. "Not in my garden", he said, "Not on your nelly". I couldn't help thinking the dodgy old ponce had rather laid it on, the whole thing, me with my lot, dreamy Daniel's, his blue-eyed boy and your friend and mine, dead on, the fabled Mr. Charm. Anyway we were long gone in the sin bin – out baby – permanently.'

These words, which Cleo Laine speaks rather than sings, bring to an end the series of three movements I have likened to music hall turns. In the context of the work as a whole they could be considered a means through which the impact of what follows is intensified. From now on there will be no more amusing introductions from Joe Melia. Instead he plays the role of a newscaster and a speaker who has to use a megaphone to be heard over the welter of information being hurled at the audience. Newson calls this composite final section 'I'm in the Game', a quotation from a speech delivered at the 1970 general election by Enoch Powell: 'I'm in the game. I shall continue to play, and I do not use the game at all lightly.' Powell was referring to his dismissal from the Shadow Cabinet for his 1968 'rivers of blood' speech, and his determination to continue speaking out against what he believed was the threat from black immigration. But the general election was only one of the events Newson deals with in the movement, for his intention was to create a montage of quotations that would cover most of the main political events in Britain and America during 1970 and 1971. To do this he had to make use not only of the soloists, the orchestra, a speaking chorus and a singing chorus, but also a film made specially by the television director William Fitzwater. This was shown on screens erected behind the performers, and included riots and acts of violence from all over the world. As a consequence

Ill. 8.1 Newson, *Arena* with singers Cleo Laine and Jane Manning, and conductor
Pierre Boulez

Arena obtained the necessary visual dimension that could classify it as Music
Theatre (Ill. 8.1).

Structurally 'I'm in the Game' goes through several phases, each one adding
to the intensity that culminates in the shooting of the four students at Kent
University. The first phase focuses on the general election. It begins with the
newscaster telling us that there are sixty Labour marginal seats. We are then
bombarded with information about the swings needed in each constituency for a
Conservative victory. In addition, piled one on another, we hear what politicians
had to say. This is cast as a game, one side trying to get the better of the other as in
a football match. Then on top of the electioneering we hear the slogans and peti-
tions of those agitating for students' rights, racial equality, women's liberation,
and all other groups who wanted their claims to be heard in Britain. Gradually
the focus shifts to America. Within the hullabaloo still pervading we hear what
appears to be a report of proceedings in what could have been Congress or the
Senate: 'What do you think the students are trying to say?' 'They are trying to
say that they want to stop the killing; they are trying to say that they want to
end the draft; they are trying to say that we ought to get out of Vietnam.' Then

more and more American issues come to the fore, prominent among them being Black Power. By then Joe Melia has to speak through a megaphone to be heard. Suddenly we hear him say 'Clear the area – leave the area – you must leave the area!' After this come the fatal shots (Ex. 8.4).

Newson then has a soprano sing the last words of the girl who was shot, words which she uttered on the telephone to her father immediately before the incident: 'I will do what I can do to protest peacefully, but I shall not do anything dangerous. I shall take care.' The speaker then brings the movement to an end by quoting what her father said to the press after the shootings: 'Is this dissent a crime? Is this a reason for killing her? Have we come to such a state in this country that a young girl has to be shot because she disagrees deeply with the action of her government?' (In this case the action of her government was the bombing and invasion of Cambodia by the American military.)

As I said above, this incident not only constitutes *Arena*'s climax, it is also its *raison d'être*. This became absolutely clear when I interviewed Newson, because he returned to it over and over again. By referring to it so dramatically he was himself protesting against the Vietnam War and its extension into Cambodia. What disturbed him was the reaction of the critics to the show. To a man they condemned him for bringing politics into what purports to be Music Theatre. Stanley Sadie, in *The Times*, concluded: 'There is an element of pretension, perhaps even impertinence, about dealing with such momentous socio-political issues in a work whose appeal is so deliberately popular.'[13] But, of course, there were precedents for this. They had forgotten that Brecht and his associated composers had used Music Theatre for political purposes.

Anthony Gilbert was born in London in 1934. After early work as a translator, he studied piano at Trinity College of Music under Denis Holloway and took up serious composition in his early twenties, studying first with Mátyás Seiber, then with Anthony Milner and Alexander Goehr at Morley College, London, and later with Gunther Schuller at Tanglewood. During the 1960s he composed virtuoso works for small ensembles. He joined Schotts publishers, eventually becoming Chief Editor of contemporary music and Head of Production. In 1970 he became Granada Arts Fellow at Lancaster University and went on to teach composition at the Royal Northern College of Music. He has written for most of the major ensembles and soloists, including the Arditti Quartet, London Sinfonietta, Manchester Camerata, Hallé Orchestra and Lindsay Quartet, and received major commissions from the BBC and from the Cheltenham Festival and Kassel State Theatre. Throughout his professional life, Gilbert has been closely involved in the promotion of performances of new music. Until his retirement at the end of

---

[13] 'Prom with knobs on', *The Times*, 8 September 1971.

Ex. 8.4 Newson, *Arena*, 'I'm in the Game', Kent State shootings

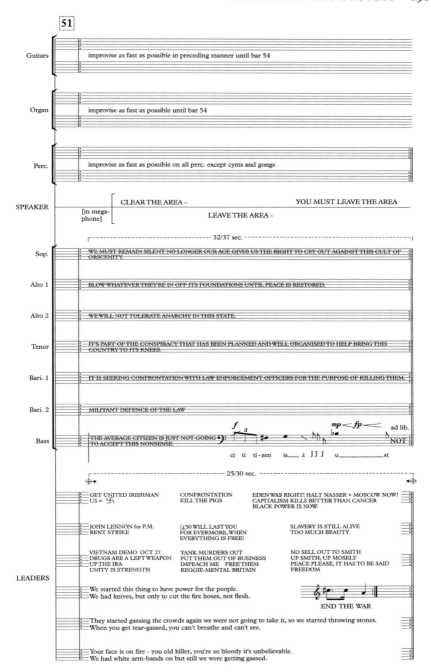

Ex. 8.4 (*continued*)

1999, Anthony Gilbert was Head of Composition and Contemporary Music at the Royal Northern College of Music in Manchester.[14]

That Gilbert's *Scene-Machine* was commissioned by an opera house, and its two versions were first performed in opera houses, would seem to preclude it from a study of Music Theatre. But as I mentioned in Chapter One, when I was reporting on what had been said in the discussion on 'opera today' at the Wardour Castle Summer School in August 1964, Gilbert had then insisted, to Tippett's annoyance, that opera ought to be concerned with contemporary issues and be more concentrated in its form. As an example he cited Hindemith's *Das Badener Lehrstück vom Einverständnis*, now judged to be a predecessor of Music Theatre. As the work Kassel had commissioned him to write had specifically to be a *Lehrstück* intended for young people, and as *The Scene-Machine* has many of the attributes of Music Theatre, I feel justified in classifying it as such.

The Scene-Machine, which Gilbert himself called an 'entertainment in one act with a message for the times', looks at the protests against the Vietnam War from a different perspective. Briefly, it tells the story of a young protest singer called Frank, who sells his soul to commercialism, becomes a pop star and is eventually killed by his former fans for deserting the ideals he once held.

Gilbert's story had its origins in a bedside story he told the three daughters of Alexander Goehr when he was their babysitter one evening in the late sixties. It was transformed into a stage piece the next morning when he was visiting Schotts, his publisher. Gerd Albrecht, the Intendant of Kassel's State Theatre, telephoned Schotts to ask if the publisher knew of a composer with experience in writing music for young people, who might be interested in composing a theatre piece 'with an ethical message for young people'. Gilbert was the obvious choice because he had recently composed *Shepherd Masque* for young voices and *Peal II* for jazz or school orchestra. When the telephone was given to him, he told Albrecht the story he had improvised for the children the previous evening confirming that essentially it was an allegory with an ethical message that girls as young as four, seven and nine could understand. As a result he immediately received a commission for a work based on an ethical message.

He scored *The Scene-Machine* for three solo singers (baritone, mezzo-soprano and tenor), a chorus of adolescents, a thirty-eight-piece orchestra, a three-piece pop group and an electronic tape. He also required an amplification system, a white grand piano, and an amplified guitar to be on stage in the last two scenes.

[14] Further information about the composer can be found on his website: www.anthony gilbert.net (accessed 11 February 2014).

His main prop was a monstrous puppet figure that could be assembled and taken apart on stage, and in which the mezzo-soprano could stand.

Gilbert had already mapped out the work before he asked the poet George MacBeth to supply the libretto. Slightly amended for clarification with the use of square brackets the titles of the scenes are:

Scene 1: The Song, Report I, Chorus in Praise of Frank.

Scene 2: Report II, First Interview.

Scene 3: Appearance of Monstrous Puppet, Pavan, Scene of Bizarre Seduction, Transformation I [the puppet becomes a woman], Transformation II [Frank becomes the woman's puppet].

Scene 4: Litany of Disapproval, Report III

Scene 5: Scene of Bizarre Transformation, Report IV, Pavan, Second Interview, Report V.

Scene 6: Debased Version of the Song [including the death of Frank, the reappearance of the monstrous puppet, and at the end an echo of Frank's original song sung by some of the adolescents] (Ill. 8.2).

Ill. 8.2 Gilbert, *The Scene-Machine*, Kassel State Theatre, 1971

Like Birtwistle's *Punch and Judy*, the structure is both circular and progressive. It returns to its starting point yet goes through a series of transformations. Where Gilbert differs from Birtwistle is in the range of musical styles he employs. They include plainsong and folk as well as a broad spectrum of contemporary music idioms such as serial and aleatory techniques, jazz and pop. He also exploits a wide range of vocal techniques, folk singing, pop singing, operatic singing, falsetto, warbling, chanting, parlando, *Sprechgesang*, speech, shouting, whispering and murmuring.

Frank's song in the first scene is a quasi-folk song in the hypodorian mode which he accompanies on his guitar with the notes of the Dies Irae plainsong. Fragments of this also occur in other places throughout the work, giving warning that eventually the 'Day of Wrath' will arrive. The words of the song are cast in six verses with a refrain placed after the second, fourth and sixth. The verses provide a summary of the situation in Vietnam:

> I hear the leaves burnin' somewhere in Vietnam – I hear the trees turnin' ... the birds flyin' ... the small children dyin' ... the hate risin' ... I see it rim the black horizon somewhere in Vietnam.

The first two lines of the refrain, on the other hand, give us the voices of the American military, the 'dark angels' being their term for the Vietcong: '"Kill the dark angels, kill, kill the dark angels" – That's what I hear them say, all night, all day.'

The following spoken report by the narrator (played by the tenor), accompanied by a jazz 'walking bass', tells us that this is a message for the times:

> It hints at what needs changing, it's not ranging very wide perhaps: it overlaps with what the papers say each day, but still it's filled with what he feels, he's honest and concerned ... Salute him, it's his golden hour.

At this, Frank's fans emerge from scattered positions in the auditorium, their calls so written that they seem to echo round the building: 'You are the light we admire; you are the source of true fire.' Then after they converge and mount the stage they all individually shout 'Make the scene man, make the scene.' This they follow by briefly providing the work's message: 'Be true to what you believe, sing out the truth you conceive.'

In the narrator's second report he tells us that he's going to assume the role of a correspondent for *The Golden Echo*, a magazine for pop fans, and that he's going to interview Frank. On this occasion he speaks in a 'brisk parlando': 'Frank ... will you tell all our teen fans why you come quite so strong against the Americans, pro Viet Cong?' To which Frank replies, 'Look, war's a drag, man.' Then after several similar exchanges Frank is asked, 'So, finally, if I may be bold as to lay my main quiz on the line: why do you so hate the whole show-biz machine?' This time Frank says, 'Make love, not war.' Throughout the interview certain woodwind instruments are tuned slightly sharp and flat, 'so as to play not quite in unison'. The point of this is not only to point out that Frank and the interviewer are out of kilter, but that Frank's answers miss the interviewer's point. 'Make love, not war' tells us nothing about why he hates show biz, it only suggests that in his heart of hearts, like so many young people in the summers of 1967, 1969 and 1970, he is ready to devote himself entirely to love.

Scene three opens with the appearance of his seducer, a woman in the guise of a monstrous puppet figure, who is assembled during the course of an orchestral interlude. While this goes on, a collage of transistor radios beaming out 'Mozart, Tchaikovsky, T.V commercials, slogans, and other sounds characteristic of the world of big-business music' rotates around the auditorium and increases in intensity. At first, the voice of a woman coming from inside the puppet is distorted by frequency modulation: 'I … I … I … I am the spirit of the world and offer you its kingdom furled in banks of green.' At this Frank responds with 'Niet', and indeed after all her efforts to win him over, his replies are gruff and dismissive. She begins to succeed only when the puppet is transformed into a woman. She then alters the words of her initial statement so that they become more personal, 'I am the spirit of your dream, and offer you the golden stream of a poet's fire.' Gradually Frank succumbs to her, his replies being in song rather than the *Sprechgesang* he had been adopting previously. When she assures him that her sole intent is to offer him 'the leisure of possession', he is transformed into her metaphorical puppet. Their exchanges develop into a love duet that ends when she sings, 'all my life long', and he, 'like honey I belong'. The fact that their last syllables are identical, and that they end on a perfect fifth indicates that they are virtually at one. Frank's fans, however, are appalled by this. At first the words they pass from one to another are whispered: 'Is that a fair theme for a song? Are you not bound by her thong?' But as scene four progresses, and Frank's replies become more and more evasive, the fans' anger becomes more and more intense until they eventually shout, 'Take more care, man, take more care.' Frank ignores their advice, for in the next narrator's report we hear that he is about to become a cog in the show-biz machine. 'I hear his mistress on the wing, she's singing. Bring the golden boy on, let's enjoy seduction as destruction. Now she takes him in her arms and charms' (Ex. 8.5).

On stage in scene five should be a white grand piano 'in prime condition', 'strummed by the woman if possible or else by a splendidly dressed accompanist, as well as a steel-strung acoustic guitar, later amplified, for Frank to pluck'. To destroy him, the woman takes the words of Frank's original song apart line by

Ex. 8.5 Gilbert, *The Scene-Machine*, 'Take more care man'

line, substituting words suitable for show biz. When the verse 'I see the small children dyin' somewhere in Vietnam' is replaced by 'I feel my baby flyin' into the sweet heart of me' the pop group becomes increasingly predominant to match the growth of the song's new version. Shortly afterwards Frank and the woman become so amorous that words no longer seem to matter. Even the altered refrain is reduced to repetitions of 'Kiss me again.'

'So as you see', says the narrator in his next report, 'he's lost in passion, following the fashion of the times.' He then interviews Frank (whom he now calls Lord Faust) for a second time, but in this it is Frank who dominates the encounter. He only needs the shortest of questions to tell the interviewer that he has made a fortune and that he has become a new Super-Show at Tele-City. The narrator then becomes the compère at the Super-Show. Accompanied by parodies of 'There's no business like show business', and adopting a 'sleazy patter', he urges Frank's new pop fans to give 'a gorgeous welcome to our Wild Lord Faust'. These new fans, however, can only shout, 'Ooh, ah, ugh, aye, ee, ah, aye'.

They continue to shout in this fashion after the debased version of Frank's song gets under way, debased not only in terms of its words but also in terms of its music, references to the Dies Irae being reserved for later. When Frank comes to the refrain following the fourth verse, which is now 'Kiss, kiss me, my angel. Kiss, kiss me, my angel, that's what I want to say, all night, all day,' Frank's first fans surge on to the stage saying, 'How can you swallow such lies? The show bird shines in your eyes.' Frank, however, appears to be unaware of the rising opposition, for he sings on, as though in a trance. He even manages to sit on the puppet's knee. But when his first fans become more and more violent in their attempts to destroy the puppet figure, he topples to the ground, apparently killed. This hardly gets noticed in the general mêlée and the repeated shouts of 'Break her down, man, break her down.' Eventually the puppet figure is indeed broken down, Frank's body is discovered and carried away, but even as his first fans echo fragments of his original song to indicate that they will continue to protest, the monster machine appears again whole, winking and shining as before.

I was unable to attend the performances of *The Scene-Machine* in Kassel or London, but I gather from what Gilbert has told me and from Peter Heyworth's highly perceptive review of the Kassel production in *The Observer*[15] that both performances had production problems. These arose, I suspect, because both the Kassel State Theatre and the New Opera Company failed to realise that, although commissioned as an opera, it is actually closer to Music Theatre. They failed to recognise that its models were the music-theatre pieces composed by Weill and

[15] *The Observer*, 11 April 1971.

Hindemith in the late twenties and early thirties, particularly Hindemith's *Das Badener Lehrstück*, which also contains a scene in which a huge puppet is dismembered. According to Gilbert, in the Kassel production 'Frank was black and jazzy, and the Mezzo was a very large, warm Cherokee American, very compelling if a little too Wagnerian.' But in Heyworth's opinion:

> the Kassel production seemed to create more problems than it solved. To introduce a ballet that the score does not call for … and then, because the dancers cannot distinguish the music's rhythms, to install a jazz drummer on the level of the stage where he naturally obscures the orchestra in the pit, is a prime example of producer's licence. So was a failure to provide the monstrous puppet-figure, who should serve as an embodiment of musical commercialism. As a result, the most crucial encounter in the opera [i.e. the dialogue between Frank and the puppet after its first appearance] opens with an extensively lengthy passage of off-stage singing by a voice amplified to a degree that made it hard to hear the orchestra.

Originally the Kassel producer wanted a huge inflatable doll to be the monstrous puppet-figure. This could then shrink to become the mezzo herself. But this idea was abandoned before the first performance. In London, Frank was an operatic baritone, the electronic tape was jettisoned and the puppet-figure was a large doll on wheels which was supposed to roll down stage on rails, 'a strategy', says Gilbert, 'which failed embarrassingly, at least once'. Gilbert had first conceived the idea of a monstrous puppet when telling Goehr's children the original bedtime story. At that time he too had thought of it in terms of an inflatable doll, but since this had proved impractical in Kassel, he now believes that the best solution would be to have images of the monstrous figure shown on screens at the back of the stage by means of back projections. This easy solution might ensure that *The Scene-Machine* will receive more performances than it has done. It may now be a period piece, but the message it delivers is still and always will be pertinent.

CHAPTER NINE

Instrumental Theatre

As discussed in Chapter One, Instrumental Theatre falls into two types: one expands the concerto principle, the other relates to rituals. The word concerto is related to *concertare*, the Italian for 'join together' or 'unite'; at other times, however, it can be related to the original Latin meaning of *concertare*, 'to fight' or 'to contend'. It is this latter meaning that informs the theatrical concertos of Thea Musgrave and Jeremy Dale Roberts, although for both composers the former meaning also covers the condition the combatants find themselves in at the end of their respective works.

Musgrave was born in Edinburgh in 1928 and is several years older than the other British composers whose works I discuss in this book. She studied with Nadia Boulanger in Paris between 1950 and 1954, after attending Edinburgh University. In 1958 she attended the Tanglewood Festival and studied with Aaron Copland. She subsequently became Guest Professor at the University of California and her involvement with the musical life of the United States led her to settle there in1972. From 1987 to 2002 she was Distinguished Professor at Queen's College, at City University, New York. Performances at the Edinburgh Festival brought her early recognition, but it was her Concerto for Orchestra (1967) that marked her dramatic style of instrumental writing, a style further explored in three solo concertos in the late 1960s and early 1970s. Although she gradually adopted a twelve-note style she was not committed to it, and as a consequence she was never a member of the avant-garde. In fact, most of the British composers I discuss considered her to be a member of the establishment. What they could not deny, however, was her theatrical flair. *The Decision*, the opera she completed in 1965, proved to be the first of six. Her four theatrical concertos are her Concerto for Orchestra (1967), Clarinet Concerto (1968), Horn Concerto (1971) and Viola Concerto (1973). All require a symphony orchestra so that in this respect they fall outside the usual practice of scoring Music and Instrumental Theatre for relatively modest forces.

She had prepared the ground for them in her Second Chamber Concerto, which William Glock commissioned for a concert at the 1966 Dartington Summer School. She scored it for the same instruments Schoenberg had selected for *Pierrot lunaire*: flute doubling alto flute and piccolo, clarinet doubling bass clarinet, violin doubling viola, cello and piano. Although the work lacks a visual dimension, it involves role-playing. The instrument she assigned for this task was the viola.

It plays Rollo, the name Charles Ives invented to describe the character of the second violin in his Second String Quartet (1907-13). Ives called this piece a 'String Quartet for four men who converse, discuss, argue (politics), fight, shake hands, shut up, then walk up the mountain to view the firmament'. From the tunes he quotes, the discussion and argument concerns the Civil War, and from the way he differentiates the instruments, it is clear that the person who tries to bring order to the proceedings is Rollo. Rollo is 'genteel, conservative and timid', and is given only 'nice' tunes to play.

Musgrave's work, unlike Ives's, is not a conversation on a topic, but a concerto designed to give space for the instrumentalists to demonstrate their skills in a quasi-conversational manner, and above all to give them the opportunity to assert their independence. The work consists of a series of short movements played without a break. Within each movement are sections to be played strictly in tempo, and other sections where the instrumentalists can play ad lib without any bar lines to coordinate them.

Rollo first enters the scene when the other players reach an impasse in their efforts to agree with each other. The first of his 'nice' tunes is *The Keel-row*. Later when he gets no response to this he doubles his efforts with *Swanee River*. This time he does get a response, but only to the rising minor third contained in the tune. He has to wait until he plays the hymn *All things bright and beautiful* before the other instruments become really interested. Before long they play their own versions of it, but when they also drag in *The Keel-row* and *Swanee River*, their playing defies what Rollo has been trying to do. Rhythmical anarchy prevails (Ex. 9.1). Nevertheless in the last ten bars when the tempo becomes a calm Adagio, *concertare* in the Italian sense replaces *concertare* in the Latin sense. Rollo wins the day.

Musgrave's four concertos involving full orchestra are split into two groups. In the Concerto for Orchestra and Clarinet Concerto, the role of Rollo, the person who tries to keep everyone in line, is given to the conductor, while in the Horn and Viola Concertos the conflict lies in the relationship between the soloist and those sections of the orchestra playing the same instrument, i.e. the horn and viola sections.

The Concerto for Orchestra contains four long movements played without a break, each movement being faster than the one before. During the first (misterioso, adagio) there are ad lib, asynchronous passages as there had been in her Second Chamber Concerto. In these the conductor abandons beating time and brings his stick down only when a vertical arrow in the score indicates when the ensemble should be exact. He loses more control over the players in the second movement (andante velato), when at the end of one or two ad lib passages Musgrave asks two or three of the woodwind players to increase their tempo on

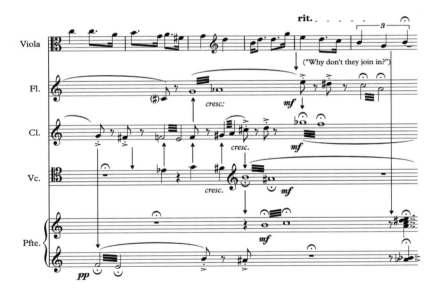

Ex. 9.1 Musgrave, Second Chamber Concerto

their own initiative to 'rapido'. This is the tempo the conductor must take before returning to the strict andante tempo.

Before long the first clarinet takes advantage of his vulnerability by standing up and playing a short cadenza. Later, after the third movement (liricamente) has got under way, the clarinet plays a longer cadenza. Musgrave marks it 'fantastico', and it leads to a section in which the clarinet becomes the leader of a concertante group of seven instruments representing all the principal sections of the orchestra. If they can stand when playing, they do. However, despite the conductor's attempts to interrupt their 'fantastic' ad lib proceedings by having the horns and remaining brass play strictly controlled music, they pursue their rebellion until, in an act of supreme defiance, the brass stand up and virtually everyone plays ad lib scales and arpeggios in a 'rapido' free-for-all. After this everyone sits. It becomes clear that if the concerto is to be completed order must be restored. The conductor must have control. Nevertheless, near the end of the concluding presto the clarinettist plays by himself three short phrases softly and expressively in a slower tempo, the first two ad lib, the last, as if capitulating totally to the will of the conductor, 'in tempo'.

In the Clarinet Concerto, where the clarinet is now the accredited soloist, Musgrave reverses the situation. The conductor must ultimately bow to the will of the clarinettist. There is still the contrast between strict and ad lib observance of the beat, but now all the ad lib sections are led by the soloist, who has three concertante groups at his disposal: trumpets, trombones, tuba, contrabassoon and double bass make up the first; alto flute, bass clarinet and accordion the second; and vibraphone and harp the third. The first group must be positioned on the right side of the orchestra, the second group left of centre, the third on the extreme left. There must also be enough space for the soloist to walk from his normal position next to the conductor to stand in front of the three groups in turn before returning to his starting position again.

This circular motion implies that the structure of the concerto ought to be a rondo, and basically it is, Musgrave's pattern being: A-B-A-C-D-B/C-A. A is a dynamic, strictly measured tutti with or without the soloist; B and C slow, relatively static ad lib episodes led by the soloist; and D a fast central development section based on A but in which strict and ad lib sections alternate. The soloist's journey round the orchestra begins during the second A and finishes during the recapitulation of C. The groups he leads in the B section (violins and violas, and then a woodwind sextet plus harp) are not given concertante status, but nevertheless function as one.

Although the Concerto is continuous, the alternations between strict and ad lib in the D section create the impression that it is not unlike the end of the first act in a two-act *opera buffa*, i.e. the moment when everything is in utter confusion.

Essentially the section is a tutti. At first the interruptions from the soloist and his concertante group (alto flute, bass clarinet and accordion) do little to disturb its strictness, but when the soloist walks to his next concertante group (vibraphone and harp) to be in readiness for the B/C section, at least half the orchestra, including each individual string player, takes to playing ad lib. Order is restored only when the soloist from his new position indicates that the recapitulation of B and C is imminent.

Throughout the work one of the most prominent motifs has been the repetition of a single note. In the opening A section, where the tempo is crotchet = 138, it was represented by a series of repeated semiquavers. Later in the work it is also represented by repeated crotchets or minims in slower tempos. The motif becomes particularly prominent at the end of the B/C section, when the woodwind sextet and harp accompanied by the strings under the direction of the conductor play simultaneously repeated notes in various speeds within a slow andante tempo (crotchet = 72). Set against them, the soloist assisted by the bass clarinet plays repeated semiquavers in the original tempo (crotchet = 138). This is the moment when the conflict between the conductor and the soloist reaches its climax, because while the conductor continues to beat crotchet = 72, the soloist, turning to the percussion, horns and most of the other woodwind and the bass clarinet, places his instrument in his left hand and, with his arm, beats crotchet = 138. What the soloist is doing is telling the conductor that to end the concerto the opening A section ought to be recapitulated, only this time it has to include himself. Being his accompanist, the conductor has to give way, and in so doing order and conformity are restored (Ex. 9.2).

As mentioned above, Musgrave's Horn and Viola Concertos are built around the rivalry between a soloist and, respectively, the horn and viola sections of the orchestra. The Horn Concerto had its roots in her *Night Music* for chamber orchestra, a piece she wrote before composing her Clarinet Concerto. It explores the spatial relationship between the orchestra's two horn players, who change their positions during the course of the work. When they sit close together they produce lyrical music, when they stand on opposite sides of the conductor and are therefore some distance from each other, their music becomes dramatic. Ultimately, when one remains on the platform and the other gradually disappears into the distance, the relationship ends and so does the piece. For Musgrave this was her first example of 'space music'.

The horn's capacity to create a sense of space arose mainly through its association with hunting. The sound of hunting horn signals echoing and re-echoing across the countryside in a hunt may now be a thing of the past, but Berlioz recalled it in his Royal Hunt and Storm music, so too did Wagner when Siegfried hunted in *The Ring*. In fact *The Ring Cycle* opens with eight horns echoing each

Ex. 9.2 Musgrave, Clarinet Concerto

other, except that there the purpose was not to evoke a hunt but to symbolise the awakening of consciousness. Musgrave's orchestra consists of double woodwind, four horns, three optional extra horns, two trumpets, trombone, harp, celeste, prepared piano, three percussion and strings, so that, although it is much more modest than Wagner's orchestra for *The Ring*, nevertheless she also has eight horns at her disposal (the eighth being the soloist). Ideally the work ought to be performed in a concert hall with a balcony above the back and sides of the auditorium. At the beginning of the performance the trumpets and trombone sit behind horns two, three and four, who in turn sit behind the woodwind at the centre of the platform.

Throughout the work the soloist remains in his position next to the conductor. The instruments that move are the first horn, who begins by playing off stage behind the orchestra before proceeding to the back of the auditorium; horns two and three, who move to the front of the auditorium to sit at opposite sides of it; and the two trumpets, who move in opposite directions to sit behind the first violins on the left and the double basses on the right. At the end of the work, with the trombone remaining in situ, the soloist will be encircled by brass instruments. In addition, if the hall does have a balcony, the three extra horns will be positioned to sit above horns one, two and three.

The work's structure, like those of the Concerto for Orchestra and Clarinet Concerto, is continuous. It opens with a slow movement in which the soloist can expose his range and expressive powers. Musgrave directs it to be played *misterioso: come un sogno* (like a dream). Against a hazy, shimmering background, the solo horn gives the impression that, like the horns at the beginning of *The Ring*, he too is emerging into consciousness. But on this occasion, when he exposes his range, some of his high notes have to be played *cuivré*, the technique that requires the player to tense his lips to produce a harsh, brassy sound. Throughout this first movement the orchestra's brass section are silent, but after several repetitions of the *cuivré* sound they spring into life as a concertante group, their first response being an equally harsh sound, a flutter-tongued chord sounding like a raspberry being blown at the soloist. It makes an appropriate introduction to *parodia con violenza*, where whatever the soloist does is echoed either derisively or ironically by the concertante instruments (Ex. 9.3). After a while the first horn, from its offstage position behind the orchestra, begins to parody not only what the soloist has just been playing, but what he also played in the first movement. In the process he completely 'up-stages' the soloist.

Echoes are also prevalent in the following *capriccioso*, indeed many of them are also parodies. During the course of it the two trumpets move to their new positions on either side of the orchestra, and standing deliver a series of fanfares, the trumpet on the right being just behind the trumpet on the left. Meanwhile,

Ex. 9.3 Musgrave, Horn Concerto, 'Parodia con violenza'

Ex. 9.3 (*continued*)

the first horn goes to the back of the auditorium (ideally without being seen), and the second and third horns to the left and right sides. After the trumpets are joined by the trombone to improvise 'wild fanfares', the movement ends with a cadenza for the soloist, its main feature being a two-note motif in which on most occasions the second note is hand-stopped. This lowers the first note's pitch by a semitone and produces a muted effect that sounds as if it were more distant than the first. It also becomes prominent in the tapestry of recapitulations that bring the following *andante espressivo* and the work as a whole to an end. During the course of this *andante* all the horns in the auditorium, including the extra horns on the balcony, stand up, and from this moment on the space is filled by the sound of horns echoing and re-echoing throughout the concert hall. We also become aware that the horns are now reconciled to the soloist. Their echoes are no longer parodies, and when the soloist plays the last two-note motif, he and all the brass and woodwind instruments make a crescendo through the second note so that it no longer sounds more distant then the first, but appears to be coming nearer.

In a symphony orchestra horns occupy a privileged position. Berlioz and Wagner were not the only composers to give them decisive material in their operas and orchestral works. Violas, on the other hand, are the butt of a great many orchestral jokes. They are considered to be failed violinists and, because they rarely have anything conspicuous to play, they always appear to be depressed. Thea Musgrave, however, not only plays the viola herself, she is also married to Peter Mark, the virtuoso American violist. It was therefore not surprising that when she came to write a concerto for her husband she would also want to redress the ridicule and neglect violas suffer. This is why she has the nine orchestral violists sit in the positions usually occupied by the first violins, and the first violins positioned where the violas normally sit. Yet when the concerto gets under way it soon becomes clear that she too cannot resist poking fun at the violas. They become the target of her jokes.

The work consists of a sequence of recurring tempos held together by a lively *allegro molto*. There are no designated concertante groups, but the soloist has to give cues to various groups that sit near to each other in the orchestra without moving from his place next to the conductor. There are even more ad lib sections and opportunities for limited improvisation than there were in the Horn Concerto. It is after one of the latter that the dramatic relationship between the solo viola and the orchestral violas begins. Once the soloist has established his virtuosity in the opening *allegro molto*, the tempo changes to *andante: espressivo molto* to give him the opportunity to explore his more reflective skills. To accompany him Musgrave asks the three horns to improvise slow expressive melodic lines from five given pitches. As if incensed by the privilege given to the horns, the violas are told to 'ad lib, dramatically, as if trying to attract attention'. But their aggression provokes the soloist to respond 'angrily, as if to hush them up'. They, however, are not prepared to be hushed up, for they repeat their demand to be noticed, even going to the extent of cajoling the soloist by imitating him. Eventually the conductor has to silence them.

Musgrave then moves into a section she marks *dolcissimo*, where the solo viola is accompanied by a quasi-concertante group consisting of flute, bass clarinet and harp, who sit behind the violas and therefore need to have eye contact with the soloist. Out of respect for this, the violas remain silent. They are also silent when later, in a section marked *giocoso*, the soloist has to direct a quasi-concertante group consisting of the principal cello, bassoon and the six double basses situated on the other side of the platform where there is no need for any eye contact. Here the violas are silent only when the soloist plays with the bassoon, cello and principal double bass. Once the other double basses begin playing a descending canon pizzicato, the violas make even greater demands to be noticed. They therefore interrupt the *giocoso* by entering one by one in an ascending canon that they cap by abandoning imitation to pursue their own courses. When this fails they try again, this time making the canonic entries closer together and even more vigorous. But before they cap their efforts, they stand up. This time their free-for-all is silenced by the trombone, when he too stands up to play ad lib and *molto drammatico* a declamatory passage the violas are forced to listen to. No sooner are they silenced than the soloist turns to them and invites them to join him in playing the type of expressive melody they had wanted to play earlier in the work. Later he also gives them the opportunity to join him in playing a particularly demanding virtuoso passage that takes them from their lowest register to their highest. From then on, they no longer oppose the soloist, they assist him. Their constant reference to the note that terminated the virtuoso passage enables to soloist to weave his valedictory lyricism around something firm and stable.

Traditionally, concertos have contained a cadenza. In the classical concerto it was an improvised elaboration by the soloist on the cadence leading into the closing tutti of the work's first movement. However, starting with Beethoven, composers have often preferred to write their own, and have them accompanied at times. Musgrave includes only one cadenza in the four concertos just discussed. It is the notated and accompanied cadenza that occurs after the clarinettist has stood up to assert his independence in the Concerto for Orchestra. By contrast, in Jeremy Dale Robert's Cello Concerto there are three cadenzas. They are placed at the beginning, in the middle and at the end of the work, and all are very unconventional.

Equally unconventional is the way the sixteen strings that accompany the soloist are positioned. Dale Roberts divides them into two clearly separated orchestras. The one sitting on the left consists of six violins, two violas, two cellos and a double bass, while the smaller one on the right contains four violins, two violas and one cello. The double bass stands on a rostrum placed some distance behind the players of the first orchestra; the second orchestra's cellist sits on the opposite side of the platform hidden behind screens. Dale Roberts designates this cello the Doppelgänger, the soloist's 'familiar' or ghostly double. He too is a soloist, and because he is totally divorced from the rest of the orchestra, he has to follow the conductor's beat on a closed-circuit television set. Like the principal soloist and the double bass, the second soloist is amplified, in his case all the time, not intermittently. In this work nobody stands up or walks around, but nevertheless a strong sense of movement is created by having the second soloist's loudspeakers placed in positions creating the illusion that his sound appears to be wandering, sometimes distant, sometimes close at hand, sometimes as if it were coming from just behind the first soloist, at other times as if it were omnipresent, saturating and pervading the whole acoustic.

The idea lying behind these unusual circumstances was to create a concerto in which the soloist represented someone who was ill, struggling with pain, and terrified by the prospect of death. The three cadenzas provide a frame for two laments and a central movement entitled Capriccios, a reference to the set of eighty etchings by Goya depicting people being menaced by grotesque creatures for their 'error and vice'.[1] The Doppelgänger is not the only image suggesting menace. Others are the casting of the violins and violas of the second orchestra as Furies, and the casting of the amplified double bass, which intermittently knocks as if it were a deathwatch beetle. Dale Roberts tells me that the Capriccios are meant to represent a hall of mirrors, a succession of encounters, through which the protagonist endures, turns a corner and is at last reconciled.

With the work's first movement consisting of Cadenza I, Lament I, Cadenza II and its third of Lament II, Coda, Cadenza III, the eleven episodes compromising the central movement function as the axis of symmetry for the distorted mirror imagery of the outer movements. But distorted mirror images penetrate the whole fabric of the work, 'structure, layout, material, characterisation, texture, every-thing'. This idea, he says, probably came from Jean Cocteau's film Orphée where the modern-day Orpheus goes into Hades through a mirror. In keeping with Cocteau's film and Goya's etchings, he wanted his work to be the equivalent of a study in black and white, hence the absence of wind and percussion instruments in the two orchestras.

In the first cadenza, the soloist has merely to react spontaneously to the events around him, not only to the variety of short, agitated, seemingly unrelated figures the strings play, the ominous pizzicatos of the amplified double bass, but also to

---

[1] See Robert Hughes, Goya (New York, Alfred A. Knopf, 2006), 181.

the gestures improvised by the Doppelgänger. 'The purpose of these', says the composer, 'is to confuse the various groups of instruments, inviting them to assail the principal soloist in their different ways.' Eventually, he says, the Doppelgänger should 'gain ascendancy over the whole ensemble', using non-musical sounds 'with the despotic energy of a poltergeist'. But although he encourages the soloist to enter into a struggle with these events, it is not until the first lament begins that his struggle becomes evident. In this, and also in the second lament and second cadenza, the Doppelgänger and the amplified double bass are absent, so that what we witness in the first lament is the soloist's struggle with the strings and with himself. However, he proves unable to sustain the kind of line we associate with a lament, for everything he does dissolves, falls into disarray. The frustration this produces spills over into the second cadenza, which Dale Roberts marks 'frenzied'. Unlike the first, this cadenza is notated and unaccompanied. But it soon evaporates, and in its place the strings provide an example of how to create a line that includes a mock lament from the two viola sections, a derision that triggers the return of the Doppelgänger and the amplified double bass.

During the course of these short episodes we witness the transition from *concertare* 'to contend' to *concertare* 'to join together'. Music inspired by Goya's grotesque, nightmarish images therefore fade into the distance as the movement proceeds. No better way to illustrate this transition than to look at the duets between the soloist and the amplified double bass in the second and eleventh. On both occasions the soloist must pluck his strings with a plectrum and be amplified to create 'a brilliant enhancement' of its tone. This means that, in the second, the soloist can match the musical grotesqueries the double bass has been producing. In the eleventh episode, however, he outstrips his opponent, for here the double bass is reduced to thrumming over its strings with a soft-headed stick before knocking on the belly of his instrument with the palm of his hand to acknowledge the receding of the deathwatch beetle image.

The soloist's newly found confidence means that when he plays the second lament he can sustain a line, making it sound even ecstatic at times. When the Doppelgänger joins him for the last cadenza, he no longer encounters animosity, for the expressive up-beats his ghostly double plays are clearly invitations for the soloist to respond to them. This the soloist does, and when reconciliation has been achieved, and the Doppelgänger fades away, the soloist glissandos up to a sustained E natural, a pitch that heralds the end of the work. Throughout the work the soloist has had to have his lowest string, his C string, tuned down a minor third to A, its timbre being so unusual that every time it sounds (and this is quite often) it strikes the ear as being potentially significant. Although the work is serial, there are hints that A is its tonal pole of attraction. In which case the sustained E natural, being its dominant, is the traditional place where the embellishments that constitute a cadenza should occur. And so they do, but in this case virtuosity is inappropriate for the soloist's newly found peace of mind. All he can do is descend quietly and slowly across two octaves as if dying away. It is left to the double bass to supply the resolution. This he does by lowering his C string down to A with his peg so that the glissando sounds like a sigh.

Although rituals, with their repeated, often ceremonial, actions are associated primarily with religious observance, they can also have social and personal functions. Of the three composers who chose rituals to be the basis of their instrumental theatre, Gilbert was drawn to their religious significance, Birtwistle to their social use, and Erika Fox to their personal function. Gilbert's *Brighton Piece* (1967) uses the Catholic Mass not to celebrate it but to use it as a protest; Birtwistle's *Verses for Ensembles* (1969) creates a ritual out of the spatial relationships between choruses of instrumentalists; while Fox's *Lamentations for Four*, *Round for Fourteen Strings* and *Exercise for Two Pianos* (1973–4) employ the ritualistic movements of instrumentalists to keep intense emotions at bay.

Anthony Gilbert composed *Brighton Piece* at the request of Alexander Goehr, who wanted a work with theatrical elements for a solo percussionist and players from his Brighton Festival Ensemble for the first Brighton Festival in 1967. As mentioned in Chapter Four, the percussionist was to have been Michael Colgrass, the virtuoso American player and composer who was also having a work (*Virgil's Dream*) performed at the Festival. Gilbert had intended that the theatrical elements would be the sight of Colgrass virtually dancing round the vast array of instruments he had to play. Unfortunately, before Gilbert had completed his piece he learned that, because Colgrass was an American and not officially recognised as a soloist, the Musicians' Union had forbidden his participation. As there were no English players to rival Colgrass's dexterity, his part had to be modified for two players. In fact, a third had to be roped in for the first performance. On that occasion the first and third percussionists played all the percussion instruments on the left-hand side of the platform, while the second played the equally large array on the right-hand side.

The five-piece ensemble accompanying them (clarinet, trumpet, horn, trombone and cello) sat behind the percussion, the three brass instruments being positioned on a higher level than the other two. In addition the clarinet has to double on Ab (piccolo) clarinet and bass clarinets, while the horn has also to play a small natural horn capable of playing very high notes. All five players have to double on two types of percussion instruments: walnut shells and coins with which to strike the set of bells suspended from their stands. Gilbert admits that by increasing the number of percussionists from one to two or three he had reduced the theatricality of the piece visually, but his intention was always to make theatricality involve the presentation of exaggerated effects: hence the extremely high clarinet and horn notes, the occasional use in the brass of wide rather than tempered major thirds, the huge dynamic contrasts and the exaggerated use of glissandos. The purpose of having these exaggerations, he tells me, was to produce a sort of concerto grosso, 'more gross than grosso', the percussionists being the concertino, the other instruments the ripieno.

Brighton Piece was originally called *Introit, Gradual and Two Chorals*. 'When dreaming up the piece', Gilbert says, 'my mind was still semi-focused on my seven-minute Missa Brevis for a-cappella choir of two years before, which I was then preparing for publication. This had been conceived during the early stages of my rebellion against the edicts of Catholicism, not least the Pope's recent agreement to the use of the vernacular in the mass, rather than Latin. But because my assertively Latin Missa places great emphasis on the pleas for mercy in the text at the expense of praise, it did not meet the approval of the choirmaster of the Edinburgh Cathedral Choir for which it was written. After toying with the idea of turning it into a concert piece with a brass backing, I realised the piece I was writing for Brighton could be a frame for the Missa Brevis. It would make a work consisting of Introit, Kyrie and Gloria, Gradual, Sanctus and Benedictus, Choral 1, Agnus Dei, Choral 2.'

The combined version of the two works has yet to receive a performance, but the idea of writing a work with two pieces that interlock with each other was something Gilbert followed up on several occasions. His First String Quartet (1972), for example, can either be played by itself or interlock with his four *Little Piano Pieces*. In this case the two pieces comment on each other. Likewise, as ritual theatre, *Brighton Piece* can stand on its own.

Gilbert says that as with a lot of his music 'there's a personal sub-text in both the Missa and *Brighton Piece*. In this case a certain anger and frustration at what seemed and seems a tinge of hypocrisy underlying all religious movements claiming to do good in the name of the biblical God. This is embodied in the Mass, which, while claiming to be an act of worship, is also very clearly a plea for forgiveness. So the theatre in *Brighton Piece* is ritual theatre, protest theatre even, for those with ears so attuned.'

And those who do have ears to hear will soon recognise the protest in *Brighton Piece*. It does not require knowledge of the Roman Catholic liturgy, even though the traditional structures of the Introit, Gradual and Hymn stand behind the movements. (Gilbert uses the terms 'choral' or 'chorale' rather than 'hymn' because the word chorale was common usage for any passage presented in block harmonies during the sixties. In the Roman Catholic Masses he attended, he says, 'there were often hymns for the congregation, after the Consecration/communion or sermon and at the very end'.)

It begins with a summons, the call of a horn repeating the note A, marked 'campana in aria', to create the brassiest sound the instrument can produce. It finds a response, a resolution, on the note G played by the other instruments in the ensemble, who reiterate it in their own ways. Traditionally the Introit alternates an intoned verse and a plainsong antiphon with the intoned Gloria Patri replacing the third of the four verses. The Gradual has soloists alternating with a choir, often in highly melismatic plainsong, while the Choral harmonises its simple melody equally simply. Having established the essential characteristics of these structures in his first three movements (intoned long notes, melismatic elaboration, simple harmonies) Gilbert takes the music to a point where the characteristics are so exaggerated that they do indeed sound like a protest.

However, in Choral 2 he takes a different course since this is where resolution must appear. Here the simple harmonies are replaced by rising glissandos that start slowly but accelerate so that they appear to be floating away into the stratosphere. At this point the ripieno players join the concertino players by tapping out rhythms freely and sweetly (*libero e dolce*) on their suspended bells. Gilbert tells me that it was always the practice in the church he attended for a bell to ring out at the end of the second hymn. The work ends not only in compliance with his particular church's custom, but also with the ripieno players becoming percussionists so that a sense of reconciliation is attained.

Verses for Ensembles was the second work Birtwistle entitled 'verses'. The first was his *Verses* for clarinet and piano dating from autumn 1965, when he was still absorbed in theatrical problems following the 1965 Wardour Castle Summer School. It is a short, six-minute piece consisting of eight movements that go through the same material from different perspectives. Although the two instrumentalists remain in the same position throughout the piece, Birtwistle was at pains to show that through his music he could appear to alter the spatial relationships between them. In the first verse, for instance, the piano with its flamboyant gestures sounds as if it is near at hand, while the clarinet with its repetition of a single note, pianissimo, sounds as if it were in the distance. Eventually, in the last verse, this relationship is reversed, for he makes the clarinet sound near at hand, while the piano appears to be in the distance.

At the same time Birtwistle achieves a transformation of the status of the two instruments. In the first verse it sounds as if the piano is the soloist and the clarinet the accompanist. It is only in the last verse that the usual relationship of the two instruments in a clarinet recital is achieved, i.e. that the clarinet is the soloist and piano the accompanist.

Verses for Ensembles is bigger in every way. It lasts almost half an hour, and is scored for thirteen players: three percussionists, a woodwind quintet and a brass quintet. As in the *Verses* for Clarinet and Piano, one of its main aims is to exploit spatial relationships, except that now the movements from back to front and front to back are real. Where *Verses for Ensembles* differs from the smaller piece is that, like *Tragoedia*, it exploits relationships between soloist and ensemble as well as those between ensemble and ensemble. In my first book about the composer, I explained the tensions between the individual and the group in such works as follows: 'In effect, they are projections of an internalized conflict which probably besets all children from a cohesive working-class community who consider them-selves outsiders, the conflict between the necessity for individual self-assertion and the equally strong pull of the group.'[2]

The three percussionists, the woodwind quintet and the brass quintet can all produce two ensembles. The percussionists have ensembles of pitched instruments and unpitched instruments. The woodwind quintet produces two by exchanging higher-pitched instruments (piccolo, E♭ clarinet, oboe, B♭ clarinet and bassoon) for lower-pitched instruments (alto flute, B♭ clarinet, cor anglais, bass clarinet and contra-bassoon) and vice versa. And the brass quintet, sitting from left to right (trumpet 1, trombone 1, horn, trombone 2, trumpet 2), form an ensemble when they play as a quintet and when they play as a quartet of two trumpets and two trombones to perform the brass ritornellos.

Birtwistle has these ensembles placed on four levels of a tiered platform. At the back on level four are the tuned percussion instruments (three glockenspiels and three xylophones), below them on level three are the twenty-six untuned percus-sion instruments; one tier lower on level two are the brass, while below them on level one are the high woodwind and low woodwind, their stands being placed in diagonal rows on either side of the platform so that they make the shape of a forward slash on one side and a backward slash on the other. In addition there are two stands placed as far apart as possible at the front of level one for those asked to play solos, and two stands as high up and as far apart as possible at the very back of the platform for the trumpets, when they have to play six peremptory fanfare-like passages (Ex. 9.4).

Altogether there are twenty-six verses and eighteen occasions when the players change positions. These are when the percussionists move between levels three and four, the trumpets between levels two and four, the woodwind players move from one side of the platform to the other according to whether they play their high-pitched or low-pitched instruments, and when the high-pitched woodwind as well as the horn and trumpets move to the stands at the front of the platform to play their solos.

Birtwistle arranges the twenty-six sections into three large groups to produce an ABA structure: A consisting of verses 1–10, B of verses 11–21, and the second A of verses 22–6. B is the simplest, most consistent of the three groups. It consists of solos for the high-pitched woodwind (in the order bassoon, B♭ clarinet, oboe, E♭

[2] Hall, *Harrison Birtwistle*, 52.

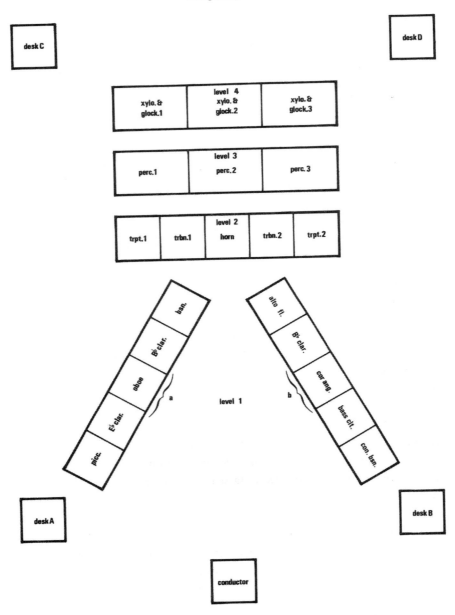

Ex. 9.4 Birtwistle, *Verses for Ensembles*, seating arrangement

clarinet, piccolo) accompanied by the untuned percussion and the horn with the soloists standing at the left-hand desk and the horn seated at the right-hand desk.

Interpolated between the solos are ritornellos for the trumpets and trombones. Just as the five solo verses use the same basic formula presented from different perspectives, so too do the six ritornellos. Whereas the different perspectives in the solos derive mainly from the options Birtwistle provides, in the ritornellos they derive entirely from his options. As a unit the players can choose between being very soft or very loud, whether mutes are used and what type they should be, while individually they are given a choice as to how their four pitches can be articulated, phrased or elaborated.

There are also sections in the A groups that contain options: one is for the low-pitched woodwind chorus slowly playing music that rarely rises above a whisper, another for when the horn has a solo. As in *Refrains and Choruses* and *Tragoedia*, the horn has a privileged position. It accompanies all the solos in the B group and is the only instrument to have two solos for itself. Throughout the piece it gives the impression that it ought to be the work's protagonist. This is because from the very first bar, whenever it is not accompanying, its manner is aggressive and self-assertive. When, for example, its first solo is interrupted by the first brass ritornello, its fast, 'wild', triple forte gestures suggest a fit of temper.

That the horn never achieves its ambition is largely owing to the trumpets. They always perform as a pair. In Verse 3, when they stand at the two solo desks, they deliver not a solo but an extremely tightly knit duet, their notes and rhythms always in close proximity. Their next prominent appearance is in the longest verse of all, Verse 9. For this they have to walk from level 2 up to the two desks in the two corners behind level 4 to deliver the six peremptory fanfare-like passages mentioned above, the last three being canons, the last two of which can be in a tempo of the players' choice. They become so dominant that the horn cannot compete with them. It is obliged to take a subsidiary role in the solos it accompanies in the central B section of the work. Nevertheless, the horn has another opportunity to assert itself, for it is given another solo to play in the recapitulation. But this is shorter than its previous solo, and it is played with the hornist sitting in his position on level 2 rather than standing at the left-hand solo stand. Now there is no interruption from the brass ritornello, no need for the horn to lose its temper, and on this occasion it is immediately followed by the exact recapitulation of Verse 9.

During the first part of the coda that follows, the trumpets vacate their positions at the back of the platform, but instead of going back to level 2, as they did on the previous occasion, they go to the two solo desks at the front of the platform. From there they sustain a series of long notes: the last two being E for the second, and A for the first. But the decisive move to bring the work to an end is the horn's ascending chromatic scale to join the A played by the first trumpet. With this we assume that some kind of reconciliation has been achieved.

Like Gilbert's *Brighton Piece*, Erika Fox's Instrumental Theatre also has its roots in religious ritual, in her case from her very orthodox Hasidic background. She was born in Vienna, and when she was three, in 1939, her parents escaped the Nazis and brought her to England where they turned one of the rooms of their London house into a synagogue. She studied composition at the Royal College of Music with Bernard Stevens, and later with Jeremy Dale Roberts and Harrison Birtwistle.

If she could not always witness the male-dominated Hasidic ceremonies, she nevertheless had them always within earshot. Hasidim is a mystic Jewish sect founded in Poland in about 1750. It places great emphasis on emotion and religious exultation in its prayers, and this finds expression in music and dancing. The basis of its music are wordless melodies called 'Nigunim' that can be traced back to Eastern European village songs. In prayers a Nigun has to be sustained for some considerable time, and to do this it has to be repeated, but never in the same way, for the intensity of the emotion demands that each repetition should express a different aspect of the exultation. In Hasidic ceremonies everyone takes part in singing whatever Nigun has been chosen for the occasion, but each person sings it in his own way; they never sing in unison. What Fox heard during her childhood was an extremely intense, highly emotional heterophony taking place within a ritual context. And because she had discovered when she was allowed into the 'shtiebel' as a child that there is constant movement in these ceremonies, she regards the ritual as being essentially theatrical.

Virtually all her music is theatrical. But the three instrumental-theatre works she composed in 1973 and 1974, *Lamentations for Four*, *Round for Fourteen Strings* and *Exercise for Two Pianos*, bear witness to another influence on her music and instrumental theatre, as, in 1970 and 1971, she attended the courses run at the Dartington Summer School by Birtwistle and Maxwell Davies in 1970 and Birtwistle alone 1971. On both occasions most of the discussion was devoted to how physical gestures could be related to musical gestures, and to assist the students in composing a piece for the concert at the end of the course an experienced mime was engaged.

As was his wont when teaching Music Theatre, Birtwistle began by telling the students that the best way to proceed was to think of an idea or a gesture that could be realised both musically and visually. He then drew two parallel lines on the blackboard, told them this was the idea, and instructed them to get on with it. Fox interpreted the lines as implying direction, and her contribution to the concert was a piece in five self-contained sections for clarinet and mime that would frame the four pieces the other students were going to produce. She borrowed the idea from Birtwistle's *Four Interludes for a Tragedy* for basset clarinet

(1968), which were intended to be a ritual frame for a concert in two halves. And just as Birtwistle's interludes were variants of the same thing, so too were her five sections. For Fox, the thing to be varied was a series of slow, concentrated movements initially made by the mime alone. Then followed three sections in which the clarinet and mime presented contrasting versions of this type of movement. Finally, in the last, they revealed the common identity of what they had been doing. To make the work as formal as possible, and to create a ritual framework for it, she asked the mime to light a candle before each of the five sections, and to extinguish it when each was completed.

Many of these features can also be found in her work, *Lamentations for Four*, the four being two cellists and two percussionists. To lament is an act that can be realised both musically and visually. Musically it finds expression in the intense, highly charged heterophony of the two cellos, visually in the two percussionists acting as if they were at a funeral. The two cellists must sit side by side at the centre of the platform, while the two percussionists must move between three percussion 'positions' placed in an oblique semicircle behind and to one side of the cellists. Sometimes the percussionists have to carry instruments from one position to another, and when they do they must take 'slow, measured steps'. She also says they must be 'sombrely dressed, and play their instruments with as few jerky movements as possible, in a calm, deliberate and formal manner, thus providing a ritualistic "frame" for the cellos'.

The purpose of having a ritualistic 'frame' is to distance the intensity of the cellos' lament from the audience, for although Fox thought of the piece as being a funeral march, it is not a meditative expression of grief, but, as characterised by the singing of a Nigun, an outpouring of emotion, in this instance the emotion she felt at her mother's funeral in Israel. Rather than a lyrical outpouring, the cellos play a series of instrumental gestures that explore just about all the sounds a cello can produce, their intensity being enhanced by having them frequently play in such a high tessitura that a sense of tremendous strain is induced. At the same time, although the percussionists may walk and be dressed sombrely, they too contribute to the heterophony, even when playing instruments that cannot produce a definite pitch (Ex. 9.5).

Musically a round is a perpetual canon at the unison or octave for three or more voices; visually it applies to a dance in which the dancers are grouped in a circle. In *Round for Fourteen Strings* Fox has it also mean turning round and changing round: changing round in the sense that the four types of instruments she has at her disposal – eight violins, three violas, two cellos and double bass – reverse their normal function in a string orchestra. Instead of having the violins and occasionally the cellos supply the melodies, she has them provide the accompaniment and support. She gives the melodies to the violas and the double bass. The violins are

Ex. 9.5 Fox, *Lamentations for Four*, opening, bb. 1–20

asked to stand in a large circle facing inwards with their stands placed equidistant from each other. The violas and cellos sit within the circle, the violas behind the cellos, while in front of the circle, i.e. outside it, there must be two stands, the one on the left for the principal viola, when he steps forward to lead his section in an expressive canon, the one on the right for the double bass. On a given signal the violins must move from stand to stand in a clockwise direction usually when still playing. The work ends when they have completed seven moves and they have returned to their starting point.

Structurally the work divides into two parts, each culminating in unisons played by the whole ensemble apart from the double bass: a rhythmic unison after the third move in the first part, a melodic unison before the seventh move in the second. The double bass is excluded because in the passage leading up to the rhythmic unison he is given a virtuoso part to play 'quasi cadenza', and in the passage that brings the work to an end, after the seventh move, he plays his own version of the unison melody unaccompanied. While he plays it the other players must stand or sit still with their bows across their strings as if playing.

The work begins with everybody playing as loudly and ferociously as possible a heterophony built from eight notes played on the lowest string of each instrument in fast down-bows. Thereafter, apart from when they play the passages in either rhythmic or melodic unison, the four types of instruments go their own ways. The violins provide brilliant textures to give the work rhythmical impetus. These textures change whenever they move to the next stand in their journey round the circle, so that the ritual frame of the work is defined both musically and visually. The violas supply the canons at the unison. But they follow each other so closely and so freely at times that they can slip into either heterophony or unison. They play each of the canons in a different way, the differences ranging from playing with exaggerated vibrato to plucking the strings, from bowing or tapping the strings with the wood of the bow to, more conventionally, the use of mutes. These are put on for the most expressive canon when all the violas stand up and the principal goes to the solo stand. The cellos have two types of music, and in both they play in rhythmic unison. They either supply the harmonic support, or move into a high register to create an intensity unique to their instrument. This occurs on two prominent occasions. The first coincides with the violas playing their canon with the wood of their bows, the second when they double the violas in the passages leading up to the melody which everybody apart from the double bass plays in unison. This melody and the distillation of it in the double bass's solo that brings the work to an end exposes the mode on which the whole work has been based. It is a symmetric mode that begins and ends on F and contains within itself three smaller symmetries (F-F♯-G / B♭-B-C / E♭-E-F). As this pursues a regular course returning upon itself, it too can be considered round.

Fox dedicated her *Exercise for Two Pianos* to Dale Roberts, who had been her teacher for several years. It could, therefore, be considered an exercise she might have submitted to him for his approval. But, as in her other instrumental music-theatre works, the title means other things: the exercise involved from walking from piano to piano, and the way the pianists exercise their virtuosity. The two pianos must be placed equidistant from the audience and about five yards apart, the tail-end of the piano on the left facing the left-hand rear corner, that of the piano on the right the right-hand rear corner. This means that the pianists always have their backs to the audience, so that, apart from when they walk from one piano to the other, the audience can never see their facial expressions. They epitomise visually the marking 'non espressivo' that litters the work. And in that their walking must be quiet and slow they represent, like the percussionists in *Lamentations for Four*, the ritualistic dimension Fox demands. Their movements involve (1) the pianist at the left-hand piano walking to the piano on the right to play primo to the other pianist's secondo in a piano duet, (2) the pianist playing secondo walking to the piano on the left so that the two have changed places from the ones they originally occupied, and (3) the pianist now at the right-hand piano walking across to the left to play secondo to the other's primo. They only play by themselves in the transitions when one of them is walking. When the piece draws to a close the pianists have been involved in all the possibilities of solo, duet and two piano playing.

Ideally both pianos should have sostenuto pedals. This allows the work to open with a dense five-strand texture occupying the upper registers of both pianos in which a slow 'chorale' in block chords played an octave apart by both pianists can coexist with four independent lines, the two for the pianist on the left (hereafter called the first pianist) being in one metre, the two for the second pianist in another. All five strands represent heterophony, simultaneous variations of a single melody. At first they are strictly notated, but after a while the second pianist begins to play ad lib to demonstrate his virtuosity, so that the strict and free run side by side. Later, after the players have gone through movements one and two, and have exchanged pianos, their virtuosity becomes competitive. They indulge in a conflict that results in what can only be described as a head-on collision, both pianists playing simultaneously, and as loudly as possible, a cluster covering just about all the notes in their upper registers. What was once ordered has now become totally disordered.

However, it becomes clear in the following slow-moving section that this is not the end of the work. As in *Round for Fourteen Strings*, the first climax initiates a second part that will end amicably. On this occasion the denouement is not a melody played in unison but a series of repeated demi-semiquavers instructed to be played mechanically. Set against them is the return of the chorale, now in its inverted form but still with the ubiquitous expression mark 'non espressivo' attached to it. Fox has left us in no doubt that, despite its romantic associations, the piano is fundamentally a percussion instrument producing noise by having hammers strike its strings.

CHAPTER TEN

Game Playing and Clowning

INTEREST in basing Music Theatre on children's games arose in 1957, when David Holbrook published an anthology of sixty-five games 'to give some indication of the fine qualities of these songs, dances and rituals which made up the unwritten culture of the English child.'[1] Among the composers who read Holbrook's book was David Lumsdaine. Although he never made use of the games it describes in his own music, he recommended the book to John Tavener, his former composition student, when he was looking for a children's funeral game to be enacted alongside the adult contributions in the *Celtic Requiem* he was planning to write for the London Sinfonietta. To meet his requirements, Tavener selected not only *Jenny Jones*, which Holbrook had drawn particular attention to for its theatricality, but also other singing games dealing with death and resurrection.

Holbrook's was not the only book to discuss children's games in the late sixties. In 1969 Clarendon Press published Iona and Peter Opie's *Children's Games in Street and Playground*, which included 170 games collected from all over the British Isles, although their book did not discuss *Jenny Jones* or others mentioned by Holbrook. Then, in 1970, Cambridge University Press published *Sound and Silence: Classroom Projects in Creative Music* by John Paynter and Peter Aston. This was a highly influential book based on the work done by two composers at York University, who wanted music teachers to encourage children and young people to compose music for themselves. Their book ends with suggestions for dramatic works children could invent. Their belief was that 'the child-like sense of wonder can perhaps best be expressed in terms of magic and ritual. It demands action, and the music of its rituals is part of the action. It is theatre.'[2]

Eventually, despite the interest these books created, only Tavener, Maxwell Davies and John Buller produced works based on children's games. These were *Celtic Requiem* (Tavener), *Blind Man's Buff* (Maxwell Davies), *The Mime of Mick, Nick and the Maggies* and *Finnegan's Floras* (Buller). However, all four require larger forces than is normal for Music Theatre. They last respectively twenty-five, twenty, seventy and twelve minutes, and all need a stage director. *Celtic*

---

[1] David Holbrook, *Children's Games* (Bedford, Gordon Fraser, 1957), 12.
[2] John Paynter and Peter Aston, *Sound and Silence: Classroom Projects in Creative Music* (Cambridge, Cambridge University Press, 1970), 335.

Requiem is scored for high soprano, chorus, children's chorus, organ, and an orchestra that includes strings and an unusual assortment of wind and percussion; *Blind Man's Buff* needs a boy soprano (or high soprano), mezzo-soprano, dancer, mime, a seven-piece stage ensemble and, in the pit, a string orchestra of at least fifteen players; while *The Mime of Mick, Nick and the Maggies* requires soprano, tenor, baritone, speaker, a chorus of thirteen and an ensemble of fourteen, and *Finnegan's Floras* needs seven women, seven men with hand percussion and a piano. Tavener's work had its first performance on 16 July 1969 at the Royal Festival Hall with soprano June Barton, the London Sinfonietta with the London Sinfonietta Chorus and children from Little Missenden Village School, conducted by David Atherton; while the Maxwell Davies and Buller pieces were performed at the Roundhouse by the BBC. *Blind Man's Buff* (commissioned by the BBC) was performed by Josephine Barstow, Mary Thomas, Mark Furneaux, and members of the BBC Symphony Orchestra and Chorus, and conducted by Boulez on 29 May 1972; *The Mime of Mick, Nick and the Maggies*, with Jane Manning, Philip Langridge, Michael Rippon, Denys Hawthorne, members of the BBC Symphony Orchestra and a section of the BBC Singers, was conducted by Elgar Howarth on 6 February 1978. *Finnegan's Floras* had its première five months earlier on Radio 3.

Tavener's starting point was James Carney's translation of poems by the Irish poet Blathmac, son of Cu Brettan, in the collection *Early Irish Poetry*,[3] which Tavener had come across on a visit to Ireland. Of the four poems Tavener selected for the work, one was the keening, 'O father you have left us, Ochon!' (which was clearly intended for men to recite); two were for a female mourner and more personal in character, while the fourth was a prayer addressed to 'loving Mary'. This gave him the idea that different types of mourning could be superimposed upon each other so that, as he had done in his Prom piece *In Alium* (1968), he could create a work exploiting acoustic space. His model was Britten's *War Requiem* (1962), which is cast on three spatial planes. In the foreground, behind a symphony orchestra, are the tenor and baritone soloists with a chamber ensemble expressing, through poems by Wilfred Owen, the grief and 'the pity of war' experienced at a personal level. Positioned behind them are a soprano and a large choir singing the *Missa pro Defunctis* to express formal mourning, while in the background a boy's chorus and an organ give promise of deliverance on an impersonal level.

Tavener differs from this arrangement by having in the background a continuously held chord of E♭ major to represent the presence of God in all things. Nearer at hand he has sung seven sections of the *Missa pro Defunctis* to represent formal mourning. Still closer he has settings of the Blathmac poems, verses 1, 3 and 5 of

---

[3] Ed. James Carney (Cork, Mercier Press, 1965 and 1969).

'Ascension Hymn', a poem by Henry Vaughan, and 'Lead Kindly Light', a hymn by Cardinal Newman, to represent personal mourning, while in the foreground he has a group of children playing *Jenny Jones* and other funeral games to 'alleviate' the gloom of the adults.

The Royal Festival Hall was chosen for the first performance both to give the children space to play their games and because Tavener needed width as well as depth for his work. For the *Requiem* and Cardinal Newman's hymn, he required three SATB choirs each with its own group of instruments placed on tiers across the platform; to sing the Celtic contributions he required that three male soloists from the three choirs should be amplified, and that the high soprano should sound as if she were on yet another level. If I remember correctly, at the first performance she stood fairly well back and more or less at the centre of the spatial distribution. At the very back and absolutely central to the distribution is the organist who helps to sustain the chord of E♭, and who at the climax of the work, during the singing of the hymn, creates a deafening noise, after which the hall is plunged into darkness so that, when this touch of melodrama is over, we are conscious of the sound of the choirs completing pianissimo 'Lead Kindly Light', as if nothing had happened.

Jenny Jones has twenty verses arranged in pairs. In the first five, the children ask to see 'poor Jenny Jones', and are told by Jenny's mother that they can't see her because 'she's scrubbing … she's washing … she's ill … she's dying … she's dead'. In the concluding group the children want to know how they should dress for Jenny's funeral. Should they come 'in yellow … in green … in white … or in black? Since black is for mourning, black will do.'

Holbrook notes that any number of children can play the game. After one girl is chosen to be Jenny she crouches behind her mother, who holds her skirts out to hide her. The other children stand in a line facing them, moving backwards and forwards as they sing: 'We've come to see poor Jenny Jones.' When the mother tells them Jenny is dead, Jenny lies on the ground and crosses her arms. At the end of the song two of the children pick Jenny up and, after placing her in her grave, the others mourn her, weeping into their handkerchiefs. One child sprinkles earth on Jenny saying: 'Ashes to ashes and dust to dust, / If God won't have you the devil must.' At this Jenny jumps up, and the other children run away shouting 'The Ghost'. Whomever the ghost catches becomes the next Jenny Jones.

Although Jenny must be a girl, Tavener does not exclude boys from the game. They can also take part in the other games, as well as the nursery rhymes and nonsense songs he inserts into those sections of the Requiem Mass he selects for the work. He arranges these into three main parts: Requiem aeternam, Dies irae and Requiescat in pace. The Requiem aeternam contains the Irish material and the Kyrie; the Dies irae includes the Tuba mirum, Recordare, Lacrimosa, the Tuba mirum again, the Confutatis maledictis and an echo of the Lacrimosa; and the Requiescat in pace the Vaughan song, the Newman hymn and the Amen.

The Requiem aeternam opens with the children chanting 'Ene, mena, bora mi' to select which girl will play Jenny. Tavener then has the three male soloists and the high soprano presenting simultaneously the Irish material, the men intoning their keen independently of each other, and the woman singing her song, 'The ebbing that has come to me', freely and without any sense of key other than when she terminates each paragraph with a high E♭. Against them the three choirs and various instruments reiterate the E♭ chord so that it sounds like a tolling bell. When the children sing they too are in E♭. But in this section they give us only verse one of Jenny Jones ('Is Jenny Jones at home?') and verse five ('Jenny Jones is dying'). The Kyrie is scored for two solo tenors, the Christe for two solo contraltos, and the repetition of the Kyrie for two solo basses. Now the E♭ chord is supplied by three double basses. Against these the children sing verse one again followed by verse six ('Jenny Jones is dead').

To lead into the Dies irae, Tavener asks for some children to repeat 'Jenny Jones is dead' sadly and others to weep into their handkerchiefs. Here instead of the E♭ chord being confined to one group of instrumentalists, it is passed slowly from one instrument or instrumental group to another, the changes anticipating the greater activity the Dies irae will offer.

As in all Requiems, the Dies irae is musically the most dramatic part of the work. For his Tuba mirum, Tavener has the three choirs present antiphonally the E♭ chord loudly and in repeated demi-semiquavers so that they sound as if they were trumpets echoing across space. Against them the children play a slow game of hopscotch, which Tavener believed represented the soul's path through purgatory.

The Recordare Jesu pie, in contrast, needs to be introspective and reflective. For this the three words are presented in four speeds simultaneously. A solo alto has the fastest version, a solo tenor a slower version, and a solo bass an even slower version. The remaining sopranos, altos and tenors pass the four syllables of Recordare from one to another at the slowest pace of all. The children's activities during this section are focused on the swing they have in their 'playground'. When one child swings the others sing 'One to earth and one to Heaven, / And THIS to carry the soul to Heaven'. On 'THIS' the child on the swing has to be given a large push. When one child gets off the swing and another takes over, the children repeat nonsense rhymes: 'Wingy wongy', 'Half a pound of twopennny rice', and when the swing is slowing down for the last time, 'Die pussy, die'.

Before the Recordare gets under way, the children begin to ask how they should dress for Jenny's funeral. In counterpoint to their song and while they are starting the swinging game, the soprano sings the first phrase of a line from another Irish text, 'Heart of my heart'. She will sing the next phrase 'whom I shall see' at the end of the Lacrimosa, but she will not complete the line until she sings at the end of the Confutatis maledictis, 'no more'.

In the Lacrimosa the sopranos, altos and basses join forces for the words 'Lacrimosa dies illa'. But although in unison, the syllables are still sung separately and still passed from section to section. However, the handovers are more rapid. During this section the children begin playing the game *Green Gravel* (Ex. 10.1). 'For this', writes Holbrook, 'they hold hands in a ring facing inwards and walk round singing the first stanza ('Green gravel, green gravel, the grass is so green, / The flowers are all faded and none to be seen, / O (Susan), O (Susan), your sweetheart is dead, / He's sent you a letter to turn back your head'). As they sing the last line the girl named in the third line turns round about and holds hands again, facing outwards. Then the circle dances the other way and sings the second stanza ('Wallflowers! Wallflowers! Growing up high, / We are but little, and we shall have to die! / Excepting (Susan Winters), who's the youngest girl. / O for shame, and fie for shame, and turn you back home again'). Each girl is mentioned in turn again, whereupon she turns about and faces inwards, and the game goes on until everyone is facing inwards again.'[4] Holbrook notes that this game comes partly from an adult funeral ceremony,[5] the green gravel being the subsoil turned when the grave is being dug. Tavener restricts the turning to one child, and he concludes the section with some children pulling on an imaginary rope and singing 'Ding, dong bell', and others chanting 'Mother, mother, I feel sick … Doctor, doctor shall I die … Yes my dear and so shall I … How many carriages shall I have, One two three four …'.

The children play a version of the game *Green Grass* during the other version of the Tuba mirum, when the words are sung by the basses in each choir. In this version ('Tripping up the green grass …') 'all the children hold hands in a line, and one stands in front. They sing the first three verses dancing backwards and forwards, clapping their hands at the end of the third verse, the gist of these verses being that the boys want the girls to come out and play; if they do they she'll have a nice young man, and if they don't he may die and leave his wife a widow. The boy in the front asks one girl: 'Will you come out?' and she answers 'No!', and then the company dances singing the fourth verse: 'Naughty man, he won't come out …' (Of course the words 'man', 'he' and 'lad' must be changed to 'girl' and 'she' if the player who is asked 'Will you come?' is a girl). When the boy asks again, the girl must answer 'Yes' and she joins him to dance round for the last verse while

---

[4] Holbrook, *Children's Games*, 63–4.
[5] Ibid., 63.

Ex. 10.1 Tavener, *Celtic Requiem*, 'Lacrymosa', beginning

the others clap their hands ('Now we've got our bonny lad'). This game is sung through until everybody has joined the first boy in the dancing line.

The Confutatis maledictis ('When the wicked are confounded') is the fastest, most energetic section of the work. While the choirs are engaged with repeating the text in fast rising arpeggios, the children dance round the 'corpse' of Jenny Jones clapping, whirling 'thunderspells' (bull-roarers) and singing the last verse of *Jenny Jones*: 'Black is for mourning, mourning, mourning, / Black is for mourning, so black will do.' When the Confutatis maledictis is concluded, the children throw earth on the grave, one of them chanting, 'Ashes to ashes and dust to dust, / If God won't have you the Devil must.' Jenny then jumps up, and to the cries of 'The Ghost', she even chases some children through the auditorium. To echoes of the Lacrimosa, others join hands in a ring with one girl kneeling in the middle covering her face with her hands to the accompaniment of 'Poor Mary sits a-weeping, / On a bright summer's day ... Poor Mary, what're you weeping for ...?

Tavener does not set the words 'Requiescat in pace' in the *Celtic Requiem*. He begins the last part of the work with the sopranos, altos and tenors sounding 'like swaying bells' as they sing in unison on the note E♭ the Irish text: 'Come to me loving Mary, that I may keen with you, your very dear one.' This leads straight into 'Lead kindly light'. Here, as in the Introit and Recordare, the music is performed in three tempos simultaneously. The first choir sings the hymn as it should sound, the second sings it slower, and the third slower still. Above them the high soprano sings a setting of Henry Vaughan's 'Ascension Hymn'. The melody is written unbarred and in semibreves with long rests between the phrases, and Tavener says it has to be sung 'without expression', the notes sounding 'slow, equal, unrelated'.

Although the *Celtic Requiem* as a whole is rooted in E♭ major, here most of the notes are outside this key. The only E♭s are those at the end of certain phrases, when they are placed in the soprano's highest register. Meanwhile, the children, who are very much down-to-earth, are preoccupied with the Mary who will ultimately be the next Jenny Jones. Not only do they sing 'I'm waiting for a sweetheart on a bright summer's day' they also give us the courting song, 'Poor Mary Sits A-Weeping', and chant 'Mary had a little lamb, / They shot it in the head', / And everywhere that Mary went / it bled and bled and bled ... Mary had a little lamb / Her father shot it dead, / And now it goes to school with her / Between two chunks of bread.' The courting song results in Mary finding Peter, whom she kisses and marries. During this episode the children slowly dismember a toy lamb. Later, in the Amen, when they set in motion toy tops in the pitch of E♭ representing the risen Christ, they put it together again. The work ends with the amplified voice of Jenny's ghost singing: 'Mary I'm on your one step, / Mary I'm on your two step.'

The new girl hides behind her mother's skirts. Her friends form a double line with candles and carry the corpse of the first Jenny off the platform suggesting different colours to precede the black for the new Jenny's funeral: 'red for the soldiers, blue for the sailors, black for the mourners of poor Jenny Jones'.

The *Celtic Requiem* proved to be as successful as Tavener's dramatic cantata *The Whale*, which the London Sinfonietta had prèmiered at its opening concert in January 1968. Indeed they were so successful that, when recordings of the BBC's transmissions of the two works were played to The Beatles, both works were recorded for commercial release by Apple, the recording company they had formed to encourage new creative works of all kinds.

When other composers wanted to make use of children's games, they were precluded from making use of David Holbrook's book and having a group of children on stage in case they were seen as imitators. Maxwell Davies found what he needed in the last scene of *Leonce and Lena*, a comedy by the early nineteenth-century German playwright Georg Büchner, where the characters play what is essentially a game of Blind Man's Buff; while John Buller, who had a penchant for setting particularly challenging texts, turned to the 'Night Games' episode in the second part of James Joyce's *Finnegans Wake* for his two works in the genre: *The Mime of Mick, Nick and the Maggies* and its short offshoot *Finnegan's Floras*.

In the game Blind Man's Buff children blindfold one of their playmates, test whether he can see, make him confused by asking him silly questions, and twirl him round until he becomes dizzy. He then has to identify whoever he touches as he gropes around. The rest of the children amuse themselves by dodging under his arms, making noises behind his back and buffeting him. When he catches someone and guesses who they are, that person is blindfolded in turn. The game had particular interest for Maxwell Davies because, as we have seen, without exception, all his music before *Blind Man's Buff* was concerned with what is real and what is not real, what is meant and what is parody. The opportunity to write the work came from a BBC commission for a music-theatre piece to be given at one of Boulez's 'experimental' concerts at the Roundhouse six weeks before the first performance of Maxwell Davies's opera *Taverner* at the Royal Opera House on 12 July. It is no coincidence that both *Taverner* and *Blind Man's Buff* contain a King and a Jester, who is not always what he seems to be.

Maxwell Davies calls *Blind Man's Buff* a 'masque'. Unlike his previous music-theatre works, which were all monodramas involving a small or relatively small instrumental ensemble, the BBC's commission allowed him the compose a work for two singers, a dancer doubling mime, a brightly dressed stage band consisting of flute (doubling piccolo and alto flute), clarinet, horn, ukelele (doubling mandoline), guitar (doubling banjo), harp and percussion, and a string orchestra in the pit. At the first performance, Boulez conducted sections of the BBC Symphony Orchestra, and Maxwell Davies also had at his disposal the services of the television director William Fitzwater.

Like many comedies, *Leonce and Lena* is based on obstacles to an inevitable marriage, except that here the obstacles are those erected by the couple themselves. The play is in three acts. In the first two acts, King Peter of Po has arranged that his son, Prince Leonce, shall marry Princess Lena of Piddle. But the two have never met and have no desire to marry: he, because he has no desire to rule, even though he is promised the crown when he marries; she, because she does not want to become her husband's shadow. They therefore both quite independently escape into the countryside, where they meet by chance and fall in love without knowing each other's identity.

In the third act Valerio, Leonce's companion, asks them to put on masks and duly presents them to King Peter and his court as automatons constructed from pasteboard and watch-springs. Since they want to get married, and since the King has promised his citizens a royal wedding, he decides that in the absence of Leonce and Lena the automatons shall be the royal couple. But no sooner is the short marriage ceremony over than, to everyone's surprise, not least the King's, the couple remove their masks to reveal who they are. The King hands over the crown to Leonce, who, with Lena's meek acquiescence, makes plans on how the country should be run. Addressing the compliant Lena, he says,

> Look, how my pockets are stuffed with toys and dolls. Should I trick them out in false moustachios for you, and buckle on swords? Or should I swaddle them in suits, ready for politics and diplomacy, and sit looking on through a microscope? Or do you want a barrel-organ, with milk-white aesthetic mice carved in a ring? Or shall I build you a theatre? … But I know what you would really like. Let all clocks stop, and tell only dandelion time, and surround the country with burning mirrors to abolish winter, and distil for us the sun's rays from Ischia and Capri, for ever.

Thus the comedy ends with Leonce and Lena behaving in the manner they had sought to avoid, for he has become the ruler, she his shadow.

Those words were Maxwell Davies's translation of Leonce's speech, and in *Blind Man's Buff* he puts them in the mouth of Valerio so that he avoids making the ending too sad from Lena's point of view. But this is only one of the changes he made to Büchner's play. To transform the piece into children's theatre with masque-like characteristics, he cast King Peter as a Boy King (treble or high soprano), Valerio as the Court Jester (mezzo-soprano), and Leonce and Lena as a dancer and mime.

The masque was an English form of courtly entertainment that reached its peak in the early seventeenth century.[6] It consisted of music, poetry, dances, costumes and scenery performed by a group of revellers wearing masks. As often as not the King took part, indeed it was the only theatrical event in which he was allowed to take part. The subject matter was heroic, mythological or allegorical, and the purpose of the event was to honour the King's greatness. In *Blind Man's Buff*, however, the King is a pantomime figure who sings nursery rhymes, stabs a large pantomime penknife into his large pantomime heart, dies later in a grossly exaggerated manner and reappears as a ghost, who, resurrected, can go on singing. The work is therefore a parody of a masque.

At the head of the score, Maxwell Davies provides notes for the production:

The King, in full regalia, sits in majesty on a throne, surrounded by the Jester and musicians. The Jester should be in male full evening dress, but with jester's cap and bauble, which rattles, and the musicians should be dressed brightly as courtiers. The Mime and Dancer each have hermaphrodite, black and white costumes, with jester's caps identical to that of the mezzo-soprano, whose singing role they act out visually; they have alchemical sun and moon symbols on their chests. On dying, the King dons a deathmask. The Resurrection of the King should be realised by a large banner on poles, depicting the Spirit, raised behind as he sings (still enthroned). The Mime and Dancer will need a large supply of masks (animals, devils, popes, ladies, etc.), and each will require a pair of large mirrors, which tie over the palm and wrists, for the Mirror Dance ... The stage should be a simple platform, with simple lighting, which lights should be able to be turned against the audience during the 'blinding' at the end. There is no 'set' as such.

Structurally the work consists of a number of set pieces divided by episodes to advance the action. During the Overture the King and Jester enter slowly and take up their positions with the Jester sitting at one side with a conventional old-fashioned music lectern for her score. The first set piece is a nursery rhyme for the King: 'There was a man of double deed / Sowed his garden full of seed. When the seed began to grow, / 'Twas like a garden full of snow,' etc. During this the Dancer and Mime enter dancing and miming his song as they go. The King and Jester then have their first encounter. The King asks the Jester, 'Who are you?', and the Jester replies on behalf of the Dancer and Mime, who peel off a succession of masks, 'Am I this, or this, or this or that?' The episode ends with the King telling

---

[6] For examples and further information see David Lindley, ed., *Court Masques: Jacobean and Caroline Entertainments, 1605–1640* (Oxford, Oxford University Press, 1995).

the Jester that he must be something, whereupon the Jester has a set piece about not being able to know who he is when surrounded by mirrors. To confirm this, the Dancer and Mime put on paper crowns and perform a mirror dance. The Jester then informs the King that the Dancer and Mime are automatons, and in response to this the King sings another nursery rhyme: 'There was a mad Prince and he had a mad Wife, / And they lived in a mad, mad town; / And they had children three at birth, / And mad they were every one.'

The King then pronounces the two automatons man and wife, and after they have danced a wedding dance they remove their masks to disclose their real faces. The King feels tricked, but nevertheless he gladly relinquishes his throne. The Jester then sings about what Leonce will do when he becomes ruler, words which, as indicated above, Büchner had given to Leonce. At the end of it the lights become painfully bright and are turned towards the audience. The Dancer and Mime, blinded by the light, grope their way out through the auditorium, and the ghost of the King along with his Jester bring the show to an end with the third nursery rhyme, the second verse being the one that relates the work most closely to *Blind Man's Buff*: 'Stick, stock, stone dead, / Blind man can't see. / Every knave will have a slave, / You or I must be he.'[7]

Maxwell Davies's music is governed by a three-note motif (F-G-A), which he varies and elaborates in every possible way. It first becomes prominent when the King asks the Jester 'Who are you?' On this occasion the intervals are a falling major seventh (F-G) and a rising major second (G-A). It is these intervals that begin the overture, which is a set piece for the strings, sounding as if it were a parody of a consort piece for viols that composers such as Alfonso Ferrabosco, William Lawes and John Coprario might have written for a seventeenth-century masque. In context it makes a perfect foil for the scoring of the King's first nursery rhyme that follows. Here the instruments are ukulele, banjo and dulcimer, the first two being strumming instruments a busker might play when improvising his accompaniment, making this too parody. The Jester, on the other hand, becomes associated with the three wind instruments in the stage band. But when he assumes the role of ruler after the King's death, and sings 'Look how my pockets are stuffed with toys,' he too is accompanied by strumming instruments. This reversal must also apply to how the King is accompanied when, as a ghost, he sings his last nursery rhyme. On this occasion the instruments are the strings playing in the contrapuntal manner they established in the overture. By this means Maxwell Davies establishes that at last the King's greatness has been honoured. As the lights fade after they have been blinding the audience, the King

---

[7] The nursery rhymes are numbers 322, 327 and 221 in *The Oxford Dictionary of Nursery Rhymes*, ed. Iona and Peter Opie (Oxford, Clarendon Press, 1951).

is joined by the Jester to sing the nursery rhyme's last line, 'You or I must be he.' They begin by singing the words one by one antiphonally. But now the notes are A-F-G not F-G-A, and as their voices fade away the basic motif becomes even more ambiguous. In this version of Blind Man's Buff, identities are never really confirmed.

John Buller (1927–2004) showed early promise as a chorister at St Matthew's, Westminster. However, although he had a composition accepted by the BBC in 1946, he turned away from music, having been discouraged by his family, and became an architectural surveyor. In his thirties he turned to music again, studying first at Morley College and then for a BMus at the University of London. In the 1970s he became a full-time, professional composer. He attended the 1965 Wardour Castle Summer School and became a friend of Birtwistle and Maxwell Davies. In 1975–6 he was Composer-in-Residence at the University of Edinburgh and in 1978 he was awarded an Arts Council bursary. In 1985–6 he was Composer-in-Residence at Queen's University, Belfast. *Proença*, a commission for the Proms Jubilee season in 1977, was chosen by the 1978 International Rostrum of Composers in Paris. In 1978 *The Mime of Mick, Nick and the Maggies* was staged by the BBC at the Roundhouse. *The Theatre of Memory*, commissioned for the 1981 Proms, was also selected by the International Rostrum of Composers (1982). His opera *Bakxai* had its first performances by the English National Opera in May 1992, and this was followed by *Bacchae Metres*, an orchestral work, in 1993. *Illusions*, commissioned by the Cheltenham International Festival, was premièred there in 1997 by the BBC Philharmonic Orchestra.

John Buller's early fascination with James Joyce's *Finnegans Wake* (1939) resulted in five works: *Two Night Pieces from Finnegans Wake* for soprano, flute, clarinet, cello and piano (1969) take their texts from pages 427, 143 and 556, while the other four relate to the episode on pages 219–59,[8] when Chuff, Glugg and Issy, the children of H.C. Earwicker, play the game *Angels, Devils and Colours* outside their father's pub in Dublin. *Poor Jenny*, a portrait of Issy for flute and percussion (1971), is based on the singing game *Poor Jenny sits a-weeping*, while *Scribenery* for solo cello (1971) is a portrait of Glugg after he has been sexually humiliated by Issy. The two other pieces, *Finnegan's Floras* (1972) and *The Mime of Mick, Nick and the Maggies* (1971–5) are both music-theatre works.

One reason for Buller's preoccupation with *Finnegans Wake* is because Joyce's highly convoluted prose is infused with references to music. Behind the texts of *Two Night Pieces*, for instance, lie Cavaradossi's 'E lucevan le stelle' from act three of Puccini's *Tosca*, Philip Rosseter's lute song 'What then is love but mourning' and William Byrd's 'Shall I go walk the woods so wild'. Joyce does not quote the

---

[8]   London, Penguin Books, 1992, reprinted 2000.

words of these pieces verbatim. His purpose is to give the impression that his novel represents H.C. Earwicker's dreams during the course of a single night. They are the product of the subconscious rather than the conscious mind. As well as occasionally making direct references to the music of the three composers, Buller also alludes to them through his use of motifs, which he constructs by either contracting or expanding the intervallic content of the originals, his purpose being to make his music as evocative and as dense in its allusions as Joyce's prose.

In his preface to the score of *The Mime of Mick, Nick and the Maggies*, Buller tells us that in Joyce's many-layered and multi-allusive texts, 'children's games merge as in a dream, with life/sexual games to form an episode of "Universal History", depicting humiliation and extreme loneliness, and recovery from such rejection, fused with the mythologies of the fall, of parenthood and the family, with jealousy and with incest'.

Throughout most of *Finnegans Wake*, Earwicker's twin sons are called Shaun and Shem, his daughter, Isobel. They take on the names Chuff, Glugg and Issy in the first section of the second part when they enact *The Mime of Mick, Nick and the Maggies*. In this Chuff is St Michael; Glugg is Lucifer (Old Nick); and Issy is the leader of a group of seven girls who are Floras when they are nice to the boys and harpies (maggies) when they are not. Neither Holbrook, nor Iona and Peter Opie, make mention of *Angels, Devils and Colours*. The nearest to the game Joyce describes is a guessing game the Opies call *Fool, Fool come to School*, a game in which the guesser, 'who is styled the "fool" or the "little dog", moves out of earshot while each of the others assumes a fancy name. The guesser has then to decide which person has acquired a given name, and, as is most likely, his guess is incorrect, they laugh at him for his trouble.' In an extended footnote two pages later the Opies mention a game from Kent called *Angel and Devil* in which an angel comes to the door seeking ribbons, and takes away the child with the colour she wants; and a game from America called *Colors* in which 'the angel and devil each seek to acquire children (under the guise of colours)'. However, they fail to provide details of how these games are played.[9]

Briefly, in *Angels, Devils and Colours*, Glugg is the fool who must guess the colour Issy and the girls have selected. Had he not been such a fool, he might have guessed that the answer lay in the colour of their knickers, the colours of the rainbow, which when combined produce heliotrope, the colour of the sun. But on the three occasions he is given to provide the answer he fails. After the first two, Issy and the girls tease him mercilessly by flirting with Chuff, and after the third,

---

[9] Iona Opie and Peter Opie, *Children's Games in Street and Playground* (Oxford, Clarendon Press, 1969), 285 and 287.

his brother beats him up. Eventually Father summons them to come home, and Mother takes them in for tea, homework and bed.

Buller sets most of Joyce's text, the biggest cut being between page 236, line 18 and page 239, line 28 where the imagery adds nothing to the plot. As is usual in Music Theatre, all the participants are visible. On the right-hand corner of the stage is a raised platform with a plank or ramp leading up to it. On this platform are Issy and the seven Maggies. The instruments, apart from the keyboards, sit in a diagonal line in the centre of the stage with Glugg standing in front of them on the left and Chuff on the right. At the back of the stage, sitting behind a table with a collection of hand percussion, are the girl's six boyfriends, and on their right are the three keyboard instruments, celeste, electric organ and piano. In his production note Buller says, 'Stage production should be discreet – not too much: it would interfere with the night-language blurring of everything becoming something else if it were made too dramatic and theatre-like.' Nevertheless, he says, 'There will be some movement to and fro. Glugg must approach the girls three times and attempt each set of questions from the ramp; Chuff and Glugg should at times confront each other.' When they all go home to tea, Chuff and Glugg should join the girls on the raised platform, and when Joyce indicates thunder and the fall of the curtain before prayers are said with a 100-letter word 'the platform lights should flash on and off as in a storm'. Ordinary (non-evening) clothes should be worn, 'but the rainbow girls should have sashes [not knickers!] of their seven colours with letter cards (backed in the same colour) which when turned round reveal the letters of the word RAYNBOW'. Chuff and Glugg could wear Victorian-style bowler hats, Glugg throwing his away on his first rejection. 'But the intention', says Buller, 'is merely to form a frame and space for the players to express their parts through the text and the music.'

The work progresses through thirty continuous sections each with a distinctive character. The first begins with the instruments tuning to A, and when the speaker, either live or on tape, reads the shortened and slightly altered playbill, they play different three-note, six-note or nine-note ostinatos, mostly in regular semiquavers but with each instrument being allowed to slightly vary their beats so that the required blurring is created. Finally the seven girls and then Issy, Chuff and Glugg enter independently, each with their own ostinato, and the section comes to an end with an abrupt stop.

The second section, which Buller in his score calls 'Chuff, Glugg, the girls and Issy hinting at colours', establishes the character of the participants and the instrument or instruments they will be associated with. Most of Joyce's text is in the third-person singular but Buller treats it as being in the first-person singular. Chuff, a forthright, confident character, is invariably accompanied by two muted trombones to enhance the bold, regular rhythms that will identify him. Glugg

has uncertain rhythms that tend to stumble from one to another, a characteristic shared by the cello accompanying him. The girls either pass each word in
a sentence from one to another or say the same thing in sequence, their nature
being characterised by the hand percussion played by their boyfriends, as well as
by piano, glockenspiel and, occasionally, triangle and jingles. Issy has a flute to
accompany her and both have music that can become highly ornate.

In an article published in *Tempo* before the first performance, Buller tells us
that all the material is derived from children's songs or singing games, and gives
examples of how and why their intervals are expanded or contracted for expressive purposes.[10] Issy's material comes from *Poor Jenny is a-washing*, Glugg's from
Rosin the beau, Chuff's from *St Patrick was a gentleman*, and the seven girls and
their six boyfriends have sets derived from *Twinkle, twinkle little star*, *Ring-a-ring
of roses*, *Sur le pont d'Avignon* and *When I was a young girl*.

Buller's first example indicates how carefully he tries to match his music to the
complexity of Joyce's language. It comes from the fifth section, when Issy, sitting
by the river, is thinking sadly about Glugg, the brother she has just jilted, her old
love, and then erotically about Chuff, the brother she now fancies, her new love.
To convey the transition from old to new in this part of her monologue she traces
the cycle of a woman's life backwards. Buller's music for the passage has two
strands, one for the soprano, the other for the alto flute. For Issy's strand he takes
a seven-note phrase from *Jenny is a-washing*, which divides into two segments,
one of four notes the other of three. He then begins to expand the intervals to
represent, in contradiction to the text, a progression that gets bigger rather than
smaller (i.e. from baby to dame).

The Mime of Mick, Nick and the Maggies took Buller four years to complete.
After struggling with it for a year, he took time off to write *Finnegan's Floras*,
a much shorter piece (twelve minutes compared to one hour) scored only for
the seven girls, their seven (not six) boyfriends playing hand percussion, and a
piano. It is a reworking of four episodes in the longer work: (1) the character and
appearance of the girls (page 226, lines 21–9 of Joyce's text); (2) the naming of their
colours (page 226. lines 30–3); (3) their praise of Chuff (page 234, line 34 to page
235, line 10; and (4) moonrise (page 244, lines 3–12). The music is similar, but the
passages for Issy, Chuff and Glugg in counterpoint with the chorus in the second
episode are replaced by the girls singing in counterpoint words that come from
page 226 of Joyce's text. As they sing, they make slow circlings round each other,
pointing toes.

Buller called the work *Finnegan's Floras* rather than *Finnegan's Maggies*
because the sections chosen reflect the 'sweet side' of the girls' natures. In this

---

[10]   John Buller, '*The Mime of Mick, Nick and the Maggies*', *Tempo*, 123 (1977), 24–9.

work they stand in a line at the front of the platform, while, as in the other work, their boyfriends and the piano are positioned at the back. Also, as in *The Mime*, each girls wears a sash of her own particular colour of the rainbow, and carries a card indicating the same colour as the sash. Each card carries a letter to identify the colour. When the cards are turned to face the audience at the beginning of their chorus they read WRYNABO. They become RAYNBOW only momentarily during the course of their gyrations. They then move to positions that make the letters read WOBNYAR. In *The Mime* these gyrations were meant to tease and confuse Glugg, but in this piece, the girls are described affectionately by their boyfriends.

During the other episodes visual movement is achieved by having the girls either circle round each other or perform small dance steps. In Moonrise, however, visual movement is only suggested.[11]

The first performance of *Finnegan's Floras* was given on Radio 3 in September 1977. It was preceded by an explanatory talk by the composer followed by a reading of the text by Patrick Magee. When the première of *The Mime of Mick, Nick and the Maggies* took place in the Roundhouse four months later, the BBC decided that, as described in Chaper Four, since the text was too long to be read beforehand, the audience should be given the printed text. But the house lights were lowered and they couldn't read it. On the evidence of their reviews of the concert, this angered the critics. 'At the best of times', wrote Edward Greenfield in the *Guardian*, 'words are indistinct in the Roundhouse, and even in Joyce some sort of rhyme and reason has to be conveyed.'[12] As a result *The Mime* did not receive a good press. Writing in *The Financial Times*, Dominic Gill said, 'for those in the hall, there was more of Joyce in the ten minutes of Berio's deft, delicate, humorous tape-piece *Thema* which began the evening than in the whole of Buller's hour'.[13]

Even so, for most of us, *Finnegans Wake* cannot be read without a crib, so even if the audience had been allowed to follow the text during the performance, they may not have been able to unravel its complexities. Buller must have been aware of this when he was composing *The Mime*, because the passage after the one for Issy and the alto flute cited above, although perfectly clear musically, totally obfuscates Joyce's words. The passage is the chorus which the girls and their boyfriends sing just before the girls name their respective colours. While they sing,

---

[11]   Closer analysis of Buller's methods of relating words and music had been intended but permission to quote from James Joyce's text was refused. Although Finnegans Wake is out of copyright in Europe, it is still protected in the USA.

[12]   *The Guardian*, 31 August 1976.

[13]   *Financial Times*, 3 September 1975.

the girls also dance. The music is on three levels. On the lowest, the tenors sing one two-part canon, and the basses another two-part canon simultaneously; above them the two mezzo-sopranos and three contraltos sing in close harmony, sliding from one note to another to create a whooping effect; while the two high sopranos with careless brilliance complete the line. Each level is in a different tempo. The men are instructed to sing 'Giocoso, very lightly and clearly' (crotchet = 84), the mezzo-sopranos and contraltos must be 'a little faster than the men' (crotchet = 92), while the top sopranos must be 'quick' (crotchet = 132). To add to the verbal confusion, the sentence the men sing comes from a different part of the text to the one the girls sing. This provides ample proof that although Buller attempted to find a correlation between text and music by means of children's songs (in this case, 'Sur le pont' and 'When I was a young girl'), he focused first and foremost on the music. He was not 'setting' Joyce's text, he was using it to create his own type of Music Theatre.

When Mark Furneaux contributed his expertise as a mime and clown to the course on music and gesture that Birtwistle and Maxwell Davies ran at the 1970 Dartington Summer School of Music, some of the students were inspired to include parts for a clowning mime in the Music Theatre they composed later. Nicola LeFanu, for example, introduces her mime in *Anti-World* by having her walk on stage as if on a tightrope and then bumping into an invisible door. But the student Mark Furneaux influenced most on that course was Bruce Cole, who, between 1971 and 1973, produced four music-theatre works, three of which had roles for clowns and clowning that were central to the action.

Bruce Cole (b. 1947) studied composition at the Royal Academy of Music with Birtwistle. His works have been commissioned and performed by The Fires of London, London Sinfonietta, Scottish National Orchestra, Gemini and the Royal Choral Society. In 1981 he established The Lewisham Academy of Music for young people in South East London. He has composed for both television and the theatre and was musical director to two circus companies. In 1986 he was appointed Fellow in Community Music at the University of York, responsible for under-graduate and postgraduate programmes and outreach work including disability arts, placements with the education departments of orchestras and rehabilitation work with young offenders.

Having been one of Birtwistle's students at the Royal Academy of Music between 1968 and 1972, he also attended Birtwistle's music-theatre course at Falmouth Art College in autumn 1970, when Mark Furneaux and four members of the Pierrot Players were in attendance. He remembers devising an instrumental piece for flute, clarinet, violin and cello in which the interruptions of Mark Furneaux, dressed as a clown, affected both how they played and what they played. Two years later, when Cole had completed his studies at the Academy, he taught music part-time at the Grey Coat Hospital School in London and became the music director of Furneaux's *Raree Show*, an itinerant street circus, where he learnt how to do just about everything connected with the circus. He was responsible for the music but also he had to be the electrician, stage manager and occasionally one of the clowns as well.

At Dartington, and entirely separate from the course, Birtwistle had conducted the Pierrot Players in a performance of Cole's *Caesura*, which had been composed at the Royal Academy the previous year. However, when it was performed in early 1971, the Pierrot Players had become The Fires of London, therefore Maxwell Davies conducted it. Its success persuaded Maxwell Davies to commission a music-theatre piece from Cole. The work was called *Pantomimes* and it had its first performance in the Queen Elizabeth Hall on 12 February 1972. In Cole's opinion it was a disaster. It had been under-rehearsed, and it needed a designer and a puppeteer to manipulate its puppets. The *Times* critic William Mann gave it a lukewarm review: 'Cole's music is only quite pleasant but not really captivating, partly because the dramatic happenings just occur; they don't convey meaning, nor do they astound.'[14] Even so, Maxwell Davies thought it worthy of a second performance, and this gave Cole the opportunity to revise it, the main alteration being the inclusion of Mark Furneaux and a circus act. But by the time Cole had revised the work in November 1973, his other music- theatre works, *Harlequinade*, *Epic for a Charlady* and *The House on Secker Street*, had all been performed. The revised version of *Pantomimes* turned out to be his last, for in 1973 he became composer-in-residence for the Inner London Education Authority (ILEA) and had to devote himself to writing more educative music for children. Later his interest in out-of-school musical activities led him to become a community composer, an occupation that led to the appointment as Fellow in Community Music at York University.

His four music-theatre works fall into two pairs. *Pantomimes* and *Epic for a Charlady* are what he calls 'Theatrical Lieder Recitals' because both draw on German song cycles to provide a background to the strange transformations they contain; while *Harlequinade* and *The House on Secker Street*, which were written for children to perform, are examples of expanded Music Theatre.

Cole scored *Pantomimes* for the members of The Fires of London (mezzo-soprano, flute, clarinet, violin, cello, piano and percussion) plus a mime and a guitar. It had started life as a guitar piece for Mick Taylor, then of The Rolling Stones, whom Cole had been teaching to play the piano. This is not included in *Pantomimes*, but nevertheless proportions arising from the open strings of the guitar provide the harmonic framework of the piece, and halfway through,

---

[14] *The Times*, 14 February 1972.

when the guitarist feels he is being neglected, he substitutes his acoustic guitar for an electric instrument so that its dynamic power can replace the soprano as soloist. But then the whole piece is about how one thing can replace or become another.

In an article Cole wrote before the first performance of the original version of *Pantomimes* in the January 1972 edition of *The Musical Times*, he mentions that its title derives from the ancient Roman pantomime in which a solo singer, accompanied by a small group of musicians, acts both as the narrator and as the characters of a drama. 'It also relates to the Victorian pantomime,' he adds, 'an entertainment form composed of songs and musical "numbers", conjuring tricks, and transformation scenes, which often involve the character of Harlequin'.[15]

Cole based the work on an exercise he devised at Falmouth Art College: a sequence of events interrupted by the appearance of a clown who influences both what is played and how it is played. Here the events are those taking place in a puppet show that draws its characters from the commedia dell'arte. For his texts Cole turned to Joseph Addison's translation of his Latin poem *Machinae gesticulantes* (Gesticulating Contraptions, i.e. puppets), from which he selected -verses about the deaths of Columbine and Harlequin. He also included lines from *La vie de Scaramouche*,[16] a biography by Angelo Constantini about the seventeenth-century clown Tiberio Fiorelli, and the last eight lines of 'Pause' from Wilhelm Müller's *Die schöne Müllerin*.

His stage plan consists of a grand piano situated on the extreme left of the platform. At the back of the right-hand side are the other instruments, the most prominent being the guitar. In front of them stands the conductor, while centre stage are three mobile proscenium arches of different sizes, with fairground lights around their edges. Among the props there must be two large rod puppets and three smaller puppets, one with removable arms, legs and head, another with a neck capable of extending to two feet, and a third with a head made from a blown-up balloon. Also needed are a very large alarm clock and a double-bass case marked fragile, containing props for the circus act, among them a broken-down guitar (Ill. 10.1).

The work opens with the soprano dressed in 'a severe dark gown' standing in the well of the grand piano from where she sings the line 'And I shall sing' as if she were about to list the items in a Lieder recital she was about to give. But before she can begin, a crazy cadenza for the clarinettist intercedes. As a result she inexplicably changes her mind and embarks on a song about the death of a puppet. During this she is interrupted by an assertive cadenza for the pianist, who, like

---

[15] *The Musical Times*, vol. 113 (January 1972), 38.
[16] First published in Paris in 1695.

Ill. 10.1 Cole, *Pantomimes*, performed by The Fires of London at Queen Elizabeth Hall, London, 1975 with Mark Furneaux and Mary Thomas

the clarinettist, clearly wants to challenge her role as a soloist. Neither of these, however, is as disruptive as the interruption of a clown, who, on the ringing of the alarm, enters with his double-bass case.

The first thing he has to do is mend his guitar. To do this he takes a huge screwdriver, fiddles with the back of the instrument, pulls out a clock mechanism, a string of sausages and a dead chicken. He then sets up his stand, trips over it, takes off his coat, brings on a proscenium arch, steps through it and with a theatrical gesture pretends to play on his guitar the accompaniment to the soprano's singing of 'Scaramouche's Song' with its catchy refrain 'Ut, re, mi, fa, sol, la'. After the second of the song's three verses he slowly opens the curtain of the proscenium arch to reveal the soprano as Harlequin clutching a small puppet like a doll. To prepare for the next song (Harlequin's song about the death of Columbine), the soprano must speak the words of the third verse without any expression, and deliver the refrain in a loud stage whisper.

In a footnote, Cole says that Harlequin's lament 'should be mock-tragic as in the traditional Harlequin role. The singing should be very bad, like an ageing alto with a too-difficult part.' As she sings, the clown has to stand in a smaller proscenium arch behind her mimicking and parodying her movements. The lament ends with the soprano screeching out the words, 'The riddle of an asses bray' like a comically bad coloratura soprano, then singing 'I shall die of love' innocently, like a choirboy, finally delivering 'a noble suicide' in the manner of a very grand operatic prima donna.

She then assumes the role of the messenger announcing the death of Harlequin. As she sings, she tears apart the first small puppet, treating its head like a yo-yo, watches the clown hang the second puppet, and bursts the balloon that serves as the third puppet's head. On reaching the lines 'Farewell dear lute for I shall sing no more. I leave you pitifully' the electric guitar with its fuzz box on plays a cadenza aided by the pianist. Eventually after the soprano, pianist and guitarist have themselves become puppets on the point of death, the soprano gets round to giving us what she had hoped would be the start of her Lieder recital. But instead of presenting us with Schubert's setting of 'Pause', she speaks its last eight lines in German in a dull expressionless voice. These are the words the young miller addresses to his lute asking why its ribbon hangs down so far. When translated into English they end 'Often it flutters across the strings with a sighing sound. / Is this the echo of my love's sorrow, / Or could it be the prelude to new songs?' Appropriately, elaborating the word FINE in his manuscript score, Cole has drawn the figure of a clown looking doleful but with mischief in his eyes.

Epic for a Charlady has only a pianist to accompany the soprano. Before composing it Cole had attended the first UK performance of Berio's *Recital I for Cathy* at the Roundhouse in March 1973, and he tells me that in several respects Berio's piece was a model for him, particularly when the pianist becomes involved in the action. His piece was commissioned for International Women's Year (1973) by Dorothy Irvine, an English soprano living in Sweden. He composed it in English and it was performed untranslated in a Swedish theatre before being filmed for Swedish television. Cole says that it grew out of his interest in pop culture, 'with its goddesses of stage, screen and discotheque'. Those he selected were the great French tragedienne Sarah Bernhardt (1844–1923), Marilyn Monroe (1926–62), who had already become a screen legend, and Janis Joplin (1943–70) whom most aficionados considered the finest white blues and soul singer of her generation.

Like *Pantomimes*, *Epic for a Charlady* is about transforming identities. In this case, Bernhardt, Monroe and Joplin are characters a charlady working on the *Titanic* assumes when she is cleaning a stateroom that has its furniture under dust sheets. The purpose of having a charlady was because Cole wanted his central character to be someone who would have liked to be a star but would never be one. Charladies were stock characters in the Victorian music hall, so the charlady's show can be preceded by a typical Victorian monologue that can set the scene aboard the *Titanic* before and when it hits the iceberg. Cole can therefore include accounts by actual survivors of the disaster as well as the hymn, 'Nearer my God to Thee', which passengers were reputed to have sung as the vessel sank. But since *Epic for a Charlady* is a fantasy that takes place in the charlady's mind possibly

Ill. 10.2 Cole, *Epic for a Charlady* performed in Stockholm, 1976

long after the event, Cole can treat the demise of this 'maritime star' as if it were 'a sort of film show, with everyone singing and dancing as the ship goes down'.

The work opens with the charlady coming on stage to clean the stateroom. As she goes about her business she notices she is being watched by the audience. Anxious to make a good impression, she provides it with anecdotes about herself, the ship's captain, the wealthy passengers and a crew preparing to make a film. In the process she takes off the dust sheets one by one only to discover that, beneath the one covering the piano is a pianist, who, on being revealed, immediately starts to play the instrument. Using his improvisations as a background, she delivers an off-the-cuff monologue about a sea captain who had murderous intentions, a delivery she interrupts with frequent asides to both the audience and the pianist. This leads her to talk about icebergs, and as she does she pulls out of her bag a faded gown that she gets into with the help of the pianist. With this she is ready to start singing (Ill. 10.2).

During her first song, a Vocalise and Aria, she takes off her headscarf, brushes her hair and puts on jewellery. In the process she provides another premonition of what will happen on the *Titanic*, for she sings about the cicada, an insect whose song is so energetic, she believes, that it dies of exhaustion after two days. She, however, is far from being exhausted, for on the number's completion she rushes off stage to return in a new gown. Graciously acknowledging her ovation, she takes her place by the piano as if to give a Lieder recital. In this number she has two songs, whose music is based on Schumann's *Frauenlieder und Leben*. One relates to Sarah Bernhardt, the other to Marilyn Monroe. Cole draws most of his textural material for the Bernhardt song from her *Mémoires*[17] and the final scene in Racine's *Phèdre*, and most of the material for the Monroe song from Norman Mailer's biography of her[18] and Edgar Allan Poe's 'To Helen', a poem about a beautiful woman who, having made a great impression on those she met, finally commits suicide.

Cole calls the next number a Nocturne. This is not about any particular star but about stars who get thrown aside when they lose their glamour or fashions change. The text is an adaptation of the English folk poem, 'John Barleycorn', which uses the annual harvest as a symbol of the fate that happens to us all, except that Cole transfers the scene from England to Hollywood, where the harvesters are photographers, agents and publicists. During the course of it, the pianist takes a camera and the singer strikes poses like a model. It is here that clownish elements enter the proceedings, because to get some decent shots the pianist acts out a pantomime around her. Meanwhile, as she is coming to the end of her account of a human harvest, she see a corpse lying on the ground, pushes the pianist out of the way and plonks herself down at his instrument. At this point there is a total blackout.

When the lights go up again, the pianist is back at the piano and the singer reappears this time as a pop star. 'The effect', says Cole, 'should be tawdry and decadent.' He sustains the sense of fantasy by composing the song so that it sounds like a jumble of half-remembered pop songs the charlady might have heard on the radio (Ex. 10.2). But before she can finish this number the *Titanic* begins to sink, and we hear 'Nearer my God to Thee' on the piano. The soprano does a quick change back to a charlady. She puts back the dust sheets, and tells the audience in a chatty, matter-of-fact voice that six months after the ship went down they made a film of it. 'They even had the original soundtrack playing over the speakers in the saloon – sold a million, everyone was talking about it.'

Cole's 'Cantata for a Fairground', *Harlequinade* was first performed in the Queen Elizabeth Hall on 16 January 1972, a month before *Pantomimes* received its first performance in the same hall. The two had also been commissioned at more or less the same time, and this is why they share similarities, the most obvious

[17] Sarah Bernhardt, *My Double Life: The Memoirs of Sarah Bernhardt* (New York, SUNY Press, 1999).
[18] Norman Mailer, *Marilyn: A Biography* (London, Hodder and Stoughton, 1973).

VII
Discotheque

Soloist reappears as a 'pop-star'. The effect should be tawdry and decadent - in the words of the song; 'an ageing queen of rock'. She is perhaps wearing hippie-type beads, sequins on her face, or a shaggy 'Afro-style' wig. She carries a (dummy) hand microphone and, where appropriate, uses it to adopt the attitudes of a pop singer. Lighting should be multi-coloured and vulgar, with flashing lights and perhaps neons or strobe-lights. Singer is lit by a follow-spot.

NOTE Singer's costume should be geared so that she can make a fairly quick return to the charlady, following the song - though this change need not be too literal, and certainly not a Cinderella-like transformation. Rather, she should appear to have regressed somewhat.

Ex. 10.2 Cole, *Epic for a Charlady*, 'Discotheque', opening

being the presence of Harlequin in both. Each was intended to appeal to children, but *Harlequinade* requires children to be participants too. The commission for it came from the Finchley Children's Music Group and its conductor, John Andrews, who had given the first performance in May 1971 of another work they had commissioned from Cole: *Autumn Cicada*, 'Ko-uts on Japanese texts for children's voices, harp and four handbells'. But whereas Cole had selected the texts for *Pantomimes* himself, as he was also to do later for *Epic for a Charlady*, the text for *Harlequinade* was written by Anne Millar, a librettist whom John Andrews had recommended. This explains why its plot is free from the ambiguities and inconsistencies of the other two.

For *Harlequinade* Anne Millar was able to forge a plot in which the individual items flow more easily from one to another than in *Pantomimes*. A *Harlequinade* is a form of English pantomime based on the *commedia dell'arte*, which centres on the efforts of Harlequin and Columbine to pursue their love affair despite the opposition of Pantaloon, Columbine's father, and the evil machinations of Pierrot, Harlequin's rival. To these easily recognisable identities Millar added a Jack-in-the-box to function as a narrator and protector of the two lovers, and a Policeman, who, like Columbine, also becomes one of Pierrot's victims. At the climax of the story Millar draws on early film. Pierrot ties Columbine and the Policeman to a railway line, then, urged on by Jack-in-the-box and the bystanders at the fairground, Harlequin races to rescue them from the oncoming train, releasing them just in time. After that Pierrot gets his just deserts. He indicates that his next victim is going to be Jack-in-the-box, but when he knocks on Jack's box, Jack jumps up and throws a custard pie in his face.

The setting is a fairground with various sideshows, each occupied by one of the principals. The one placed in the centre of the stage, however, is reserved for cards displaying pictures of the train as it gets closer. All the parts, apart from Pantaloon (a tenor), can be performed by children. Those who are not principals function as bystanders and are divided into two choruses of SSA, each having percussion instruments to play. In the pit are seven adult instrumentalists: a string quartet that usually accompanies the Jack-in-the-box, and a wind trio of oboe, clarinet and trumpet that underscores the action. (This division of the ensemble into two more or less independent streams bears witness to the influence of Elliott Carter's music Cole so much admired, as does the superimposition of different pulses and rhythmic articulations within the textures. It is a feature, incidentally, that also characterises *Pantomimes*.)

Since *Harlequinade* was written for the Finchley Children's Music Group, Cole made sure that all the children taking part had something to do for at least most of the time. Their activity is not to sing songs, but to provide a background to the action. They do so either by playing their percussion instruments or by producing a background murmur with their humming, whispering and their singing of long notes often no more than a semitone apart. It is they who introduce Jack-in-the-box and the event that sets the action in motion, for between them they provide the sentence, 'Jump Jack jump when master knocks.' After Jack has appeared and introduced the pantomime routine of Harlequin and Columbine, the children echo what he has said by slowly repeating some of the words he had used, i.e. 'Clinging', 'Pairing', 'Unwinding', 'Playing'.

They start playing their percussion instruments when Pierrot enters brandishing a chopper. Since his presence is ominous so too is the sound that the children produce: tam-tams and bass drums played with soft beaters to create a menacing rumble. After Pantaloon has been killed and Pierrot threatens Jack, the children blow whistles to summon the policeman. To accompany the policeman the children play a combination of tam-tams, suspended cymbals, milk bottles and wood blocks. But they take a more decisive role in the proceedings after Pierrot ties Columbine and the Policeman to the railway line positioned in front of the central booth: they are responsible for producing the sound of the approaching train with snare drums to imitate the sound of its wheels and recorder mouth pieces to reproduce its whistle. Gradually more and more instruments are added to create the illusion that the train is getting nearer. When it actually passes, the noise becomes deafening, but by then Harlequin has rescued Columbine and the Policeman, and has been hailed as a hero.

The children revert to being bystanders after Pierrot gets his come-uppance. Now it is Columbine who sings 'Jump Jack jump when master knocks,' and while the ensemble, including Pantaloon and Pierrot, assemble to bring the show to an end before dispersing to their booths, the children return to repeating the words 'Clinging, pairing, unwinding, playing'.

Such works involving children are expanded Music Theatre because they usually have more participants and are longer than those intended for professionals. *Harlequinade* is a fairly modest example because it lasts only half an hour, and at that time, the Finchley Children's Music Group contained no more than forty children. *The House on Secker Street*, on the other hand, lasts for well over an hour, and was intended for the combined forces of two schools: The Grey Coat Hospital School, a Church of England Comprehensive School for Girls in Pimlico, London SW1, and St Matthew's Primary School in nearby Victoria.

It was the custom for the Grey Coat School to put on a concert every Easter, but when Cole was one of its music teachers in 1972–3 he was given the libretto for a music-theatre work the poet and teacher Michael Johnson had written. As it related to the events during the three days following Christ's crucifixion transferred to Secker Street in nearby Lambeth, and contained a circus ring and significant parts for clowns, it was exactly what Cole needed for a music-theatre work that would be suitable for Easter while satisfying his taste for clowning. The result was a composition that related the events of Easter to the everyday world the children were familiar with and that told the story in a manner the children would enjoy. Originally he thought it would be given in the Grey Coat School's assembly hall or a concert hall, but when the vicar of St Peter's, Eaton Square heard about it, he suggested that, as many of the children involved would be his parishioners, it ought to be given at St Peter's, even though it meant turning the church into a theatre.

Because their parts are scored for tenors, two of the characters, the Observer and the Ringmaster, have to be played by adults. The rest of the cast can be made up of children of all age groups. Their parts include the Street Speaker (Punch), and five circus clowns (one of whom is a Pierrot). There are also walk-on parts for clowns, acrobats, performing animals, dancers, the people of Secker Street and their children, postmen, milkmen, and characters from the life of Christ. Cole also includes three choruses (Senior, Junior and Primary) and four instrumental groups: the School Orchestra (the violins also playing wine glasses, the wind instruments, spinning tops and melodicas), the Recorder Consort, the primary school's 'Orff' Percussion group, and a group of percussion instruments including suspended cymbals, thunder sheet and gongs, which substitute for an electronic tape if unavailable. Cole was at pains to make sure that none of these groups would be neglected, and that in the case of the instrumental groups, even beginners could take part.

The action takes place in three locations: Secker Street itself, the playground adjacent to it, and a Circus Ring. The story covers the period after Christ was placed in the Holy Sepulchre on Good Friday until the celebrations on Easter Sunday. Structurally the work is framed by an Introduction and an Epilogue, and Interludes between the events that take place during the Three Days. The score contains details pertaining to production and lighting as well as to how the instruments have to be played. To represent the placing of Christ in the tomb, the slow and mysterious Introduction, scored for the Primary Percussion Group, culminates with large drums playing the rhythm of a slow march. This leads to a Prologue in which a large body of people converse with each other. Among their snippets of conversation might be heard, 'There's nothing special about Secker Street, nothing special at all,' or 'It's dead in Secker Street. Everything is pretty well dead.' An Observer steps forward to tell us that after Christ died they wrapped his body in a shroud and laid it in the wash-house of a house in Secker Street. To dispel the gloom, a procession of circus clowns appears blowing party squeakers, waving balloons and chanting nursery rhymes. Since they are like the clowns in Furneaux's *Raree Show*, they have a different slant on death: 'Baby, baby if he hears you / As he snuffles round the house, / Limb from limb he'll tear you, / Just as pussy tears a mouse.' They are silenced by the arrival of the Ringmaster who tells them, 'No-one must know it's here, you understand? It infringes the public health acts, keeping a dead body.'

Then as the Senior Chorus ask 'What shall we do?' comes a pantomime consisting of various incidents from Christ's life. It concludes with the Recorder Consort playing a version of the chorale 'Christ lag in Todesbanden', one of several Easter hymns pervading the melodic material of the score. When it fades away, a procession of sad, performing animals do their tricks. But they do so reluctantly, preferring to dance to a round sung by the Junior Chorus repeating the words the people of Secker Street spoke earlier: 'It's dead in Secker Street. Everything is pretty well dead in Secker Street.' Gradually the action focuses on three performing animals standing on high pedestals, as a symbol of the three crosses of Calvary. Later when shepherds and three kings appear, the people disperse. Then, once again, clowns take over. Five of them perform their knockabout business to the music of a waltz, which gets faster and faster, and results in chaos. When the Ringmaster drives them off, the Observer tells us it is now midnight in Secker Street, 'the tiny houses bend under night's weight'.

On the Second Day, the scene is set exclusively in Secker Street, and depicts the normal life of its inhabitants. As dawn breaks, postmen, milkmen and newspaper boys deliver their goods, then gradually people go on their way to work, saying when they pass it, 'This is the house, number nine – quiet as the grave,' then later, 'This is the house of God, cold as a coffin, cold as Christ.' A Street Speaker dressed as Punch assails them, 'Here's one afloat on the Styx, seeking three nails and a fortune.' But when he stops speaking and pelts them with rotten fruit, they flee in all directions.

The scene then changes to the playground in the afternoon. Some of the games the children are playing, such as Hopscotch, are simple. Others are complex. Two are games of chance for percussion instruments. One involves a pack of cards. For example, if a jack is drawn the player must 'repeat a single sound and get faster', if a queen, 'repeat a single sound and get slower', if a king, 'repeat a single sound and get louder', if an ace, 'repeat a single sound and get softer'. Cole calls the second game 'a musical snakes and ladders'. Each box is numbered and contains music. The players land on the boxes according to the throw of a dice. They must then repeat the music over each number until their turn to throw the dice comes round again. While the games are being played other children dance and sing nursery rhymes such as 'The cock he is a crowing, a crowing, a crowing; the cock he is a crowing for it is Easter-tide'.

When the people of Secker Street come home from work it is time for an Easter Carnival. They process up and down the street, but as their procession gets faster and faster the five circus clowns appear again. The Carnival immediately stops.

Quietly and solemnly the clowns intone a chant containing instructions: 'Lift the shroud. The knots are very loose. Feel the heart beat.' This astonishes the crowd, 'What shall we do?', they ask.

The action then focuses on a solitary Pierrot bearing a cross. He prays, and his prayer reveals what worries the people of Secker Street: 'This is a house of shadows,' he says, 'the shadow of owls, and the shadow of God.' With this, the Second Day ends. In the words of the Observer, 'The coffee-cold moon stares in at the wash-house cobwebs and the roped decay. Secker Street's Priests sleep.' But although its priests sleep, the ordinary folk are having nightmares: 'Who shall distinguish between us? Who shall distinguish between Barabbas and Messiah?'

On the Third Day the setting is the Circus Ring again. It opens with the Ringmaster cracking his whip. At first his clowns dance slowly and grotesquely, but eventually, when the recorder consort begins to play the folk song 'John Barleycorn', they dance to it more purposefully. And while they dance they recite the poem that tells why John Barleycorn must die. They are then joined by the group of five clowns, one carrying a cross. When these five reach the Ringmaster, they begin a slow ring-a-roses dance around him. Gradually it gets faster and faster, and as it does the clowns festoon the Ringmaster with streamers so that he becomes entangled in them. When the dance reaches a climax, they plaster him with custard pies before carrying him off clutching the cross. Left behind is the Pierrot praying for the Resurrection: 'I have seen God. He has looked at me with the pits of his eyes. I breathe his breath clutching this calm shroud. O God, if there is body, bone, matter in this shroud, let it rise, walk, greet us.' Eventually the wash-house shadows stir, and as they do the sound of an off-stage choir of clowns can be heard. Pierrot and the people continue to stare at the shroud, when suddenly the clowns burst in blowing hooters and squeakers, the work ending with the throng passing through the audience and into the distance.

CHAPTER ELEVEN

Musica Poetica

M USICA Poetica was the title of the course Wilfrid Mellers taught when he became a Reader in the Department of English at York University in 1964. When the university was founded, there were no plans to establish a Music Department. Instead it included music as a linked study with English, and it appointed Mellers, who, in the thirties, had read English and Music at Cambridge University. He was both a composer and a distinguished musicologist, whose writings had covered an unparalleled range of musical topics, including, in 1964, the first major study of American music: *Music in a New Found Land*.[1] When Mellers accepted his appointment he decided the emphasis of the course would be on theatre. This reflected the fact that earlier that year he had composed a piece for a concert to celebrate Shakespeare's quatercentenary at the 1964 Cheltenham Festival: *Rose of May: A Threnody for Ophelia* for speaker, soprano, flute, clarinet and string quartet. The commission had been for a work that would include actors from the Shakespeare Memorial Theatre and musicians. Mellers chose to set the three songs Ophelia sings in *Hamlet*, framed by an actress reciting the lines given to the Queen when she reports on Ophelia's death: 'There is a willow grows aslant a brook …' Those taking part were the actress Diana Rigg, April Cantelo (soprano) and the Wigmore Ensemble.

To give emphasis to the theatrical context of the Queen's speech, Mellers asks the actress to 'begin very lazily and slowly' before adopting a normal narrative style, and to reverse this procedure for the lines which end the speech: 'Pull'd the poor wretch from her melodious lay / To muddy death'. And to emphasise the purely musical aspect of the score, he concludes the three ballads in which Ophelia sings her songs with cadenzas for respectively clarinet, flute and voice. Thus poetry is both spoken and sung, and music also has the opportunity to come into its own.

Six year later Mellers composed *The Ancient Wound*, another work that deals with the death of an innocent victim, and which also has its poetry both spoken and sung. But before then he had to compose two large-scale works, *Life Cycle* for the opening of the Sir Jack Lyons Concert Hall at York University in 1969, and in the same year *Yeibichai* for the BBC Proms. Shortly after he had been installed in the English Department, York University decided that, with the prospect of

---

[1] London, Barrie & Rockliff, 1964.

the Sir Jack Lyons Concert Hall being completed, a Music Department ought to be established, and that Mellers should be its Professor. His two co-founding members of the department were composers David Blake and Peter Aston.[2] *Life Cycle*, a cantata for two student choirs and student orchestra containing exotic percussion, sets words from Khoisan and Inuit dance songs, while *Yeibichai* is a 'night chant' for coloratura soprano, soprano and baritone, scat singer, chorus, two speakers, jazz ensemble and orchestra, which in Mellers's words in the preface to the score: 'overtly concerns "regression" to the savage state, to nature, the birds and beasts, in order to be born again'.

The Ancient Wound was written in conjunction with the Canadian poet Peter Garvie for a performance at the Victoria Fair at Victoria University, where Mellers was a visiting lecturer during the summer of 1970. The title was taken from Alessandro Striggio's libretto for Monteverdi's *Orfeo*: 'Your words are gentle, / But in my heart revive / The ancient wound of love'. The gist of the piece, however, has its roots in Rilke's poem 'Orpheus, Eurydice, Hermes'. In this, Eurydice is seen as being independent of her husband, a woman who in death 'is deep inside herself, who is filled beyond fulfilment'. Mellers's piece takes place in modern times on the banks of a lake in northern British Columbia, in a nearby hospital as well as in the underworld. Orpheus and Eurydice have lost their ancient identities. They are now a fisherman and his wife, and she is fatally injured by a herd of cattle instead of a snake.

Mellers scored the piece for singing actress with two actors, a non-singing chorus of nine voices, a string trio, a wind trio, three keyboard instruments, three percussion players and electronic tapes. As in *Rose of May*, the work revolves around three lyrical songs the woman sings during the course of her recollections: a Summer-song, sung when her husband is out on the lake fishing; a Fall-song, when she realises that the hospital is not her home; and a Winter-song, when she recalls that her husband 'can't believe in the world below'. The spoken words are provided by speeches in verse for an Ambulance Man and a Doctor, who between them describe the events that led to her fatal injury, her death in hospital, and the moment when she follows her husband out of the underworld, and 'her hand slips out of his, like a boat drifted free, [and] very slowly his head swivels'. 'The only real "character" is the woman', said Mellers, 'and only she is required to make any pretence of acting. The Ambulance Man and the Doctor are choric figures who

---

[2] Both Blake and Aston composed works for the stage during the sixties and seventies but they were not performed as part of the university's music-theatre repertoire. Blake composed *It's a Small War*, a musical for schoolchildren in 1962, and an opera, *Toussaint*, in 1977 for the English National Opera. Aston wrote a children's opera, *Scarapant the Sorcerer*, in 1969.

should be presented in static stylization ... The chorus represents animate Nature and the hidden world of the unconscious.'

Both *Rose of May* and *The Ancient Wound* were written for professionals to perform, but for a younger generation, who wanted to compose Music Theatre at York, professionals were not available. This meant that Roger Marsh, Richard Orton, Steve Stanton and Trevor Wishart had to compose works for undergraduates, postgraduates and members of the faculty to perform. Some of them may have had acting ability, but none were trained singers. This was why the appointment of Bernard Rands to the music faculty in 1969 was so important for them. Rands had studied and worked with Luciano Berio in Italy, and was therefore able to introduce them to what Berio had done with Cathy Berberian's voice in works such as *Thema (Omaggio a Joyce)* (1958), *Visage* (1961) and *Sequenza III* (1966).

Thema (Omaggio a Joyce) was an electronic piece based on Berberian's reading of the 'overture' to the Sirens episode in James Joyce's Ulysses. This is already becoming music, but when the passage is treated as a 'sound system' its constituent elements are transformed by electronic manipulation into a form of music in which sound per se is predominant.

Visage is also a piece for electronic tape but is based on recordings of monologues improvised by Berberian, each monologue containing vocal gestures and phonetic material suggested by a particular language. Apart from the word 'parole' which Berberian struggles to articulate on two occasions, there are no other words in the piece and we have to find meaning through her laughs, sobs and moans.

Sequenza III for solo soprano, on the other hand, has to be performed 'live'. In this, Berio took a minimalist text consisting of nine phrases ('give me / a few words / for a woman / to sing', etc.). These he interchanged. He also broke them down into their phonemes, which he further combined with other phonetic material: vowels and consonants drawn from the International Phonetic Association's alphabet and exploited for their ability to offer a stuctured notation of speech sounds. He then shaped the sounds so that they become increasingly songlike until eventually the piece ends with 'pure' wordless singing.

But Berio was not the only figure to influence York composers in the early seventies; equally important were the late prose works and plays of Samuel Beckett. This can be clearly illustrated in Roger Marsh's *Cass*, the first music-theatre piece that the younger generation at York produced in the early seventies. 'Cass', said Marsh, 'combined the non-linguistic expressionism of Berio's *Visage* with the minimalism and hopeless landscape of Beckett's *Lessness*.'

Roger Marsh (b. 1949) studied composition in London with Ian Kellam, and later at the University of York with Bernard Rands. Between 1976 and 1978 he attended the University of California, San Diego on a Harkness Fellowship before lecturing in Music at Keele University until 1988. He then returned to York.

In 1993 he was visiting composer at Harvard University. He co-founded (with his wife, the singer Anna Myatt) the contemporary music ensemble Black Hair, known for its performances of new music and Music Theatre. He is currently Professor of Music at the University of York. Although he has written music for a wide range of genres, his work has often had a theatrical quality.

Cass (1970) is an abbreviation of Cassandra, the prophetess who, in Aeschylus's *Agamemnon*, tries to warn the Elders of Argos about Agamemnon's imminent death. But because she is doomed never to be believed, when she does manage to tell them that Agamemnon will lie dead before their eyes, the Elders abruptly silence her. In Aeschylus's play Cassandra is highly articulate when she tells them why Apollo gave her the gift of prophecy, but in *Cass* she is virtually speechless; she can only struggle to say the name Agamemnon syllable by syllable. Marsh scores his twenty-five-minute piece for female voice, flute, six men and a 'jug' blown by a player across the mouth of a large empty glass acid jar to produce a low moan. He describes the work as a modern-day dithyramb in which a wild-haired Cassandra appears as a vision above a chorus of wizened elders, who are 'rooted to the spot' and capable only of contemptuous spits and weary sighs.

The action takes place on an open stage with a six-feet-high platform at the back. On the top of the platform sits Cass dressed in a long white dress with long sleeves. She is young 'but her face is that of a tired gaudy whore'. In front of her on her left sits the flautist, and on her right the jug-player, both of whom wear pale blue gowns. Evenly distributed at ground level, and looking in different directions, are six elders in simple white smocks. According to the score's stage directions, 'Their hair is grey and bunched wildly, their faces pale and wizened with dark eyes and wrinkles. They stand with legs apart and bowed, arms awkwardly at side, heads pushed forward slightly, rooted to the spot.' Marsh insists that the players should appear to have been in place for several hundred years before the piece begins and indefinitely in place after the work ends. 'Where it is difficult to give this impression,' he says, 'the chorus should take about five minutes (perhaps more) to shuffle from six different entrance points until they are in position.'

We may assume that the flute is Cass's alter ego, and that the jug has a similar relationship to the chorus. I say this because the flute has a three-note refrain that it repeats throughout the piece: two fast grace notes (C-G) leading to a semibreve (A), i.e. a fourth followed by a whole tone. This, I believe, relates to the names of the musical notes found in Agamemnon's name: A-G-A-E, a whole tone followed by a fourth.

Unlike Cass, the flute can articulate freely, and in doing so it can help Cass in her struggle to articulate the four syllables of Agamemnon's name: A-GA-MEM-NON. Its three-note refrain is not only a constant reminder that in musical terms

Ill. 11.1 Marsh, *Cass*, with Melody Lovelace and Randall Giles

the first four vowels in his name contain a whole note and a fourth, it also enables her to get started on her efforts. Following the flute's first two notes, G and A, Cass begins with an attempt to say A-ME, the first and most of the third syllable of his name. She omits the second syllable because the flute has just supplied their phonemes. The whole passage, beginning with the flute's entry and ending with Cass's 'A-ME', takes less than a minute to perform, but in this time Cass gives a hint that she fears for her own life as well as Agamemnon's. She indicates this through her bodily and facial gestures. Marsh's performance instructions begin just after the flute has sounded its initial G:

> Cass begins to stir imperceptibly, straightening up, removing hands from face. Her features should not be clearly discernible until a moment or two [before she begins to speak] ... She peers into the distance straight ahead, looking confused, puzzled ... Nervous, timid, unsure, she looks surprised at the sound she has just made and tries to summon more confidence ... As she hits the E she turns her gaze nervously to the left with a jerk of the head and remains in that position; eyes wide open – like a hunted deer listening for the hounds. (Ill. 11.1)

She does not attempt to utter the first two phonemes of the fourth syllable (NO) until one of the Elders delivers it, and she imitates him irritably. A more extended flute passage that results in a minor version of its refrain (C-G-Ab) stimulates her into repeating aggressively her first efforts, this time with the addition of NO. But when she starts yet again she cannot get beyond E, which she turns into a prolonged wail. At this point the Elders begin their mockery of her. But although Cass appears to be defeated, their mockery leads to the work's turning point.

This begins when the flute plays the six semitones between G and C in a detached and irregular manner, 'trance-like, without tone or energy, often sharp or flat by a ¼ tone'. When Cass hears this she becomes unusually peaceful, as if hypnotised. She then copies the flute, playing with the syllables she has used already, taking special delight in GA the new one. But she has still not completed the name, and in her efforts to reach ON she becomes increasingly more frustrated, annoyed and frightened. Just as the Elders supplied NO for her earlier, they now supply ON, the last syllable of 'ailion', one of the two Greek words that have been their entire repertoire: 'ailinon ailinon eipe', a line by Aeschylus meaning 'sing the song of woe, the song of woe'. Whereas Cass's utterances have been confined to syllables, the chorus cannot only pronounce their words cleanly, they can also make use of phonemes ('e' as in pet, and 'o' as in pot) as well as other syllables ('ei' with a falling inflection to indicate a low sigh, 'ei' with an upward inflection to indicate a question, and the elision of 'ei' and 'e' to anticipate 'eipe').

Structurally the work alternates between four episodes for the chorus and four for Cass and the flute. As in a concerto, the entrance of the soloists is preceded by an introduction. In this case the Elders anticipate Cass's difficulties with a rhythmic texture that makes use of the phonemes and syllables as well as the low moan of the jug before mumbling in a jumbled fashion Aeschylus's text. In their second episode, they introduce an unvoiced, wheezy chuckle into their mumbling of the text. But when Cass fails to get beyond E. they devote their third episode to vehemently mocking her in a spirit of disgust.

Finally, after Cass has managed to articulate ON, their voices gradually fade away, leaving the flute to bring the work to a conclusion with a line that is both a recapitulation and a development of what it has played before. At first it seems to be joyous, but eventually it gives way to the moan of the jug and Cass's answering sigh. Although Marsh makes no mention of Clytemnestra and Aegisthus, he assumes, I think, that his audience will be familiar with Aeschylus's play, and that throughout his version of the events leading up to Cassandra's prophecy, it will be aware that she has known that she too will be murdered.

Richard Orton's *Mug Grunt* (1972) has at least one clear parallel with *Cass* in that it involves the articulation of a single word. But whereas *Cass* draws its model from classical Greek tragedy, *Mug Grunt* is based on something much closer to home: the sight of three men drinking beer in a pub, and trying to converse. *Mug Grunt*, says Orton in his programme note:

> presents many paradoxical faces. It is a work of music-theatre, for three actor-musicians, which is both complex and minimal. It may appear to make a social statement about, for example, communication or non-communication, appropriate to the skills of actors, but it is at the same time a precisely scored counterpoint of actions that require the command of the musician. It is a difficult work to perform. since both sounds and actions must be memorised totally, and yet to an audience can appear improvised and informal. Its presentation may be comic or sinister, or perhaps even both.

Whereas Marsh, Stanton and Wishart were postgraduates in the early seventies, Orton (1940–2013) was a member of the music faculty, appointed by Mellers. He was born in Derby, and left school at sixteen to work in a bank. He later took piano teaching and class teaching diplomas at the Birmingham School of Music and subsequently won a Choral Scholarship to St John's College, Cambridge, where he took the BA and BMus degrees in Music. As a Lecturer in Music at the University of York he pioneered and established the University's Electronic Music Studio (EMS) in 1968. In 1986 he founded courses in Music Technology with his colleague Ross Kirk. He took early retirement from the University of York in 1998 and was honoured by the university with a lifetime Emeritus Readership.

It was Orton who had suggested that the teaching at York should be based on projects rather than lectures. But although he had the facilities to make *Mug Grunt* an electronic piece, he realised that its basic gestures would be more effective if presented live. Like Marsh, he was influenced by both Berio and Beckett. He raided *Thema* as well as *Visage*, and also Beckett's plays, *Play* and *Come and Go*.

Beckett's *Play* is a conversation piece for a man and two women who are encased in three identical grey urns with only their faces visible. At the beginning and end they all speak at the same time, and these sections constitute a chorus lit by a single light. At other times their speech is provoked by a spotlight swivelling at maximum speed and highlighting one face after another.

Come and Go, on the other hand, is a 'dramaticule' lasting only a few minutes. In it three women, Flo, Vi and Ru, sit side by side, very erect, facing front, hands clasped in laps. Starting with Vi, who sits in the middle, each goes off stage, then comes back after the other two are sitting next to each other. When Vi returns the pattern becomes Vi, Flo, Ru; after Flo goes away and comes back it becomes Vi, Ru, Flo; and after Ru goes away and comes back it becomes Ru, Vi, Flo. At the end they join hands: Vi's right hand with Ru's right hand, Vi's left hand with Flo's left hand, Flo's right hand with Ru's left hand, Vi's arms being above Ru's left arm and Flo's right arm.

In his performance notes for *Mug Grunt*, Orton says that the three performers should walk on to the platform each carrying a large mug in his right hand:

> The mugs contain liquid refreshment and the three enter in a relaxed manner, talking with each other, and sit down on three chairs that have been placed facing the audience. As they finish drinking, they gradually become stiffer in appearance, more erect in the chair, facing straight ahead, like automata. If light is used, it should change from natural lighting to coloured spotlighting on the performers: I blue, II purple, III red. They remain in this position for perhaps 20 seconds after the last drop has been drained, then the notated work begins.

It consists of signs for the relative pitches of the grunts (low, medium or high) combined with signs for the position of the head and arms (Ex. 11.1). At first the grunts are just short gruff noises in the throat with the mouth closed, but in the third of the work's three parts the men have to deliver a text with their mouths closed until one of them brings the work to an end by tonelessly uttering the word 'yes'.

The three are requested to observe four head positions: straight ahead, to the left, to the right and above. These are combined with six positions of the right arm holding the mug: stretching to the right, across the body to the left, to the front and above the head, doubled to the side and doubled horizontally to the floor. In the last two positions, the mug is held upright near the mouth. Any of the head positions may be found with any of the arm positions, making a total of twenty-four combined positions.

In the first of *Mug Grunt*'s three parts are four sections, each terminating with a group of either vocal or physical gestures performed as fast as possible. The first is confined to grunts, the second introduces gestures, while the third and fourth treat the man in the middle as a soloist who has to alternate between grunt and action so quickly that the others are mainly confined to cadences.

The second part places the three on an equal par. Here Orton creates the impression that the piece is like playing a game. He bases it on the Krak-Krek-Krik episode in Beckett's novel *Watt*. In this the eponymous hero remembers lying in a ditch and hearing the sound of frogs croaking. Krak croaked on a count of eight, Krek on a count of five and Krik on a count of three. This meant that they created a counterpoint of croaks before reaching simultaneity. Orton extends the procedure by alternating the grunts with the twenty-four combined positions of

Mug Grunt

for 3 voices/actors

Richard Orton

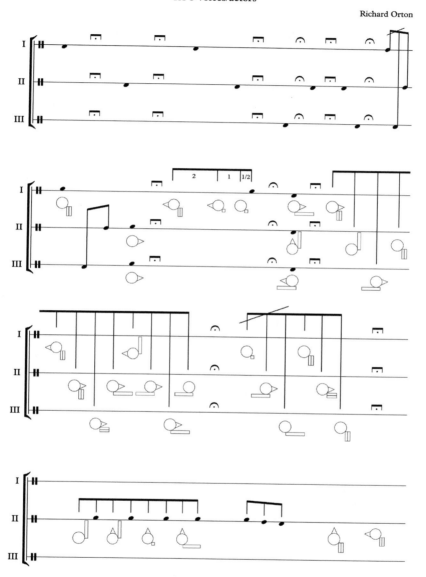

Ex. 11.1 Orton, *Mug Grunt*

Mug Grunt

Notation

Throughout the score proportional notation has been used. Exceptions are groups (marked 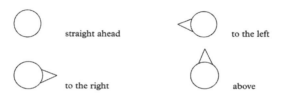), "as fast as possible", and the pause signs: ⌢ which indicates a pause of 2 seconds, and ⊓ which indicates a pause of 5 seconds.

••• are grunts made with the closed mouth - low, medium or high in pitch indicated by the position of the dots with respect to the line.

There are four notated head positions:

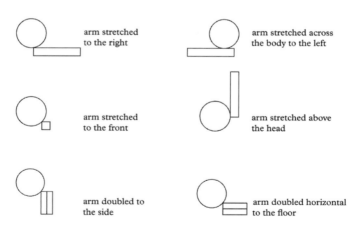

These are combined with the following six notated positions of the right arm, holding the mug:

In the last two positions, the mug is held upright near to the mouth. Any of the head positions may be found with any of the arm positions, making a total of 24 combined positions.

Ex. 11.1 (*continued*)

head and arms, and by having the first man count five, the second eight and the third eleven between what they do.

When they reach simultaneity Orton brings the structure to a close with a series of choruses. The first has the men doing their utmost to articulate a nonsensical text with their mouths closed: 'I will why until love yesterday edge nothing less.' The second chorus asks them to follow with their eyes the simultaneous movement of the mugs. They then must 'turn mug upside down', 'slowly tilt mug to face mouth', 'slowly clamp mug on mouth', then to speak into mug, randomly allowing each syllable of the nonsensical text to be heard accented by momentarily removing the mug. This process should get faster and faster until everything stops. Finally, after the first man says 'to', and the third 'ter-day', it is left to the second to drop his mug and hand into his lap and murmur tonelessly (like Molly Bloom at the end of Joyce's *Ulysses*) 'yes'. *Mug Grunt* was first performed in 1972 by Tom (Archer) Endrich, Roger Marsh and Steve Stanton. Shortly afterwards Roger Marsh and Steve Stanton made a pact to compose a solo piece for each other. The outcome was Marsh's *Dum* and Stanton's *Andante cantabile*.

Dum is a psychological drama: the drama of a man who also struggles to free himself from his preoccupation with sin, guilt and death by making use of six poems that have expressed attitudes which he hopes can release him from his mental prison. To represent the man's predicament, Marsh built a six-feet-high, four-feet-square wooden cage, hung with hundreds of metallic items, 'to be played from within the cage, by the trapped soloist, as though attempting to escape'. However, in 1977, when he himself performed the work in America, and the cage was still in York, Marsh reduced the number of percussion instruments, and this is the version printed in the score.

On a platform approximately eight feet by four feet, he placed, looking from left to right, a metal bucket containing one or two metal objects to anchor it, as well as a small 'tinkly bell attached to the inside by a string', a chair, a stool on which is another metal bucket half full of metal objects as well as a tam-tam beater, a lectern with a hammer, a saucepan lid and a solid block of wood, and, on the extreme right, a medium-sized tam-tam.

The six poems Marsh draws on are: (1) Emerson's 'Grace' ('How much, preventing God! how much I owe / To the defenses thou hast round me set'); (2) John Donne's 'Batter my heart, three person'd God'; (3) Christina Rossetti's 'Despised and Rejected' ('My sun has set, I dwell / In darkness as a dead man out of sight'); (4) an anonymous medieval 'Hymn to the Virgin' ('Of on that is so fayr and bright'); (5) lines from Canto XII of Dante's *Purgatorio*; and (6) Rupert Brooke's 'The Hill' ('Breathless, we flung us on the windy hill, / Laughed in the sun, and kissed the lovely grass').

In a programme note Marsh calls the work:

> Dum's dream. It is the dream of a human fly caught up in a complex web, and determined to improve the situation. He adopts a number of attitudes, one of which must surely secure release, the pomposity of Emerson, the escapism of Brook, the defeatism and aggression of Christina Rossetti's recluse, and so on. If none of this is quite clear, neither is the constant presence of the Lord's prayer, filtering through the haze, first in Greek, then in Italian, and finally in English as the nightmare/comedy reaches its horrifying point: 'and forgive us our trespasses as we forgive them …'.

In Danish and Norwegian, 'dum' is an adjective meaning foolish or stupid, and in English it could be an abbreviation of 'dumb'. However, in Latin it means 'whilst' and may refer to the Christian belief that man is trapped on Earth whilst preparing for eternal life. Marsh never gives us the poems in full, he supplies only snippets of them. The bulk of the six sections into which the work is divided is taken up with vocal gestures and mixed-up syllables and phonemes of the poems.

To illustrate what Marsh does, here is Emerson's poem 'Grace' as it appears in print:

> How much, preventing God! how much I owe
> To the defenses thou hast round me set:
> Example, custom, fear, occasional slow,
> These scorned bondmen were my parapet.
> I dare not peep over this parapet
> To gauge with glance the roaring gulf below,
> The depths of sin to which I had descended,
> Had not these me against myself defended.

The snippets Marsh supplies are underlined in the score, and include the names of friends Dum calls out to: 'how much? how much? Set! Example!, fear, Ned! I dare not peep over this parapet, Sue!, to which, hey Basil!, ended? Hey Basil!, Sue!, ended? dead' (Ex. 11.2).

Other words and phrases are given in their phonetic spelling, but in every case, including the references to the Greek version of the Lord's Prayer, they distort the original. Perhaps the most significant is the alteration of 'descended' and 'defended' into 'ended? dead'. This and the hysterical gestures that pervade the section expose the fear that lies behind Emerson's pomposity. Apart from when Dum has to strike the saucepan lid with the hammer on the phoneme 'ow' (in

for Steve
DUM

ROGER MARSH
(1973/77)

Ex. 11.2 Marsh, *Dum*, part 1

'slow'), and then, at the specified time, to slam it down on the lectern when the name Ned appears, only the hammering of the lectern is employed in this section.

In contrast to Emerson's self-satisfaction, Donne calls on God as if he were speaking to his mistress: 'Yet dearely I love you, and would be lov'd faine, / But am betroth'd unto your enemie: / Divorce mee … / Take mee to you, imprison mee, for

I / Except you enthrall mee, never shall be free, / ... ravish mee.' For Marsh, Donne's attitude is histrionic. He has Dum adopt what he calls a 'Shakespearean' tone when he says, for example, 'Yet dearly I love you and would be loved'. He also has him assume the role of an Italian tenor, and shout the name Mimi at the top of his voice while simultaneously striking the gong. However, as the performing instructions accompanying his final remarks indicate, Dum cannot sustain his play-acting: 'imploring–pained–sobbing–sinking–sinking–elbow on lectern, head in hand, defeated'. After this all he can do is utter the phonemes of 'amen' one by one.

'Despised and Rejected' is a dialogue between Christ and a sinner who has become a recluse, and Marsh draws on it for both his third and sixth sections. In the third he confines himself to Christ asking to be admitted to the sinner's house. 'Open, see / Who stands to plead with thee. / Open, lest I should pass thee by, and thou / One day entreat My Face / And howl for grace, / And I be deaf as thou art now.' The tone is generally pathetic, but on one occasion Dum inserts the word, 'Santificato', which he pronounces in comic Italian. Then after a garbled version of 'My Feet bleed, see My Face, / See My Hands bleed that bring thee grace, / My Heart doth bleed for thee, / Open to Me', Dum, still defeated, fades into silence.

The words between the vocal gestures in the fourth section veer between medieval English, Latin and Italian. Dum now turns to the Virgin Mary for assistance : 'Ic crie to the, thou see to me, / Levedy [Lady], preye thi Sone for me, / *Tam pia*, / That ic mote come to thee / *Maria*'. To emphasise the name *Maria* he simultaneously hammers out a series of semiquavers on the lectern with a small solid block of wood. He employs an even more dramatic gesture at the end of the section. This draws on a garbled version of the poem's second and third stanzas, which Marsh rearranges so that the cry *ave* in the line 'With *ave* it went away ...' occurs at the very end. He re-enforces it with three loud thumps on the lectern followed by an even louder blow on the tam-tam, which coincides with Dum turning 'Ave' into a wail. Dum then carelessly throws the tam-tam beater over his shoulder and proceeds to centre stage, facing front, expressionless, so that after a pause he can recite the opening interchange between Rupert Brooke and his friend in 'The Hill': 'Breathless, we flung us on the windy hill, / Laughed in the sun, and kissed the lovely grass. / You said, "Through glory and ecstasy we pass; / Wind, sun, and earth remain, the birds sing still, / When we are old, are old ...'.

This is the longest unaltered quotation in the work, and 'The Hill' is the only secular poem that Marsh chooses. Although he summarises its content when his notation indicates the approximate pitch and rhythm he requires ('And when we die all's over ... And life burns on ... said I heart ... Heaven is now, is won'), he nevertheless inserts the opening of the Lord's Prayer before leaving incomplete the word 'faith': 'We have kept the f ... [faith]'. Nor is he able to compete Brooke's last line, when the friend suddenly exposes his fear of death: '[And then] you suddenly cried, and ... [turned away]'. Marsh then prepares us for the last section of the work by asking Dum to take the first bucket and move to the chair. 'With eyes constantly fixed on audience, sit, clutching the bucket on lap, arms wrapped around it possessively, peering suspiciously over the top of it.'

In this sixth section we return to Christina Rossetti's 'Despised and Rejected', where, because only the words of the guilt-ridden sinner are used, the attitude is at first gruff and embittered then very ill-tempered. Marsh combines snippets of these with an incomplete passage from the Lord's Prayer: 'Give us this day out daily bread, and forgive us our trespasses, as we ... for ...'. Throughout the section he treats the missing syllable 'give' as if it were a leitmotif, as he does the phrases 'Trouble me no more' and 'Leave me in peace'. But Dum never finds peace. Every time he says 'give', he throws as hard as possible an object from the first bucket into the second. Later more objects are thrown into the second bucket. Finally, when the words 'for ever and ever amen' are reached, Dum throws everything remaining in the first bucket into the second and screams 'Amen, amen, amen, amen, And! And!' After this comes a blackout.

Steve Stanton (b. 1950) obtained his BA in Music from the University of York and went on to complete a doctorate in composition. In 1977 he joined City University, where he pursued his interests in in Oriental music, African American music, European folk musics, oral tradition and popular music idioms, and inter-disciplinary studies in twentieth-century Music Theatre and the performing arts.

Although the agreement between Marsh and Stanton was that they should compose solo works for each other, the literary material Stanton drew upon necessitated also a chorus of nine voices in the background. In a programme note about the work he composed, *Andante cantabile*, he says the piece:

> is essentially a contemplative monologue into which are woven various and fleeting references to Dante's *Purgatorio*, Samuel Beckett's *The Lost Ones* and E.M. Forster's *The Machine Stops*, whose common theme is that of some imaginary place where human souls are confined to an eternity of waiting, longing for release, dreaming of a way out. Here, ecstasy and agony, hope and suffering, poetry and music, encountered initially as distinct and separate, and finally driven into one frenzied whole, are regulated by an awesome and omnipotent life force: the machine, now on the threshold of grinding to a terrifying halt.

E.M. Forster's short story 'The Machine Stops' (1909) describes a world in which most of the human population has lost the ability to live on the surface of the Earth. Individuals live below ground in isolated cells, their bodily and spiritual needs met by an omnipotent Machine humming constantly in the background.

The story concerns Vashti and her son Kuno, who, when he hears the humming falter, believes that the Machine is breaking down. But the Machine has become a kind of god, and although humans created it, they have forgotten how to repair it. Eventually the Machine collapses and, with it, 'civilisation' too.

Stanton chose this story because most of the University of York's Music Department had been involved in the making of *Machine, An Electronically Preserved Dream* (1971), an electro-acoustic composition by Trevor Wishart, who was then a postgraduate student specialising in electronic music. In *Machine*, Wishart had combined spoken texts, pre-recorded factory sounds, and the carefully directed improvisations of the York Chamber Choir. This meant that although *Andante cantabile* is self-sufficient, those who had heard *Machine*, or had contributed to it, would realise that it too could be described as a dream.

The publication of Beckett's *The Lost Ones* in English also dates from 1971. Stanton chose this because, although it describes the atmosphere of another kind of Purgatory, it suggests a means of escape. Beckett begins his piece elliptically:

Abode where lost bodies roam each searching for its lost one. Vast enough for search to be in vain. Narrow enough for flight to be in vain. Inside a flattened cylinder fifty metres round and eighteen high for the sake of harmony. The light. Its dimness. Its yellowness. Its omnipresence as though every separate square centimetre were agleam of the same eighty thousand of total surface. Its restlessness at long intervals suddenly stilled like panting at last. Then all go dead still. It is perhaps the end of their abode. A few seconds and all begins again.

Beckett's text then goes on to say that the only objects in the cylinder are ladders positioned so that the lost bodies can ascend to niches halfway up the wall. These lead to tunnels which could be the means of escape. But to the frustration of those who attempt to escape, the tunnels go nowhere (Ill. 11.2).

Dante's *Purgatorio*, on the other hand, does go somewhere; it leads to *Paradise*, and it is towards this goal that the soloist in *Andante cantabile* purports to be heading. Stanton casts him as a sham Dante, someone who acts the part of the poet traversing through Purgatory to reach Paradise. He focuses particularly on the period when Virgil, who has been Dante's guide, leaves him to find his own way to Beatrice, for it is she who will take him through the Garden of Eden to Paradise. I call him a sham because he is dressed as a Mafioso wearing 'a white suit, white trilby, white tie, black shirt, white shoes with white spats, sunglasses, with a black handkerchief hanging from his breast pocket'. In addition he has a 'rich, healthy suntan', and maintains an 'obvious broad Italian accent which by its inflective and stress characteristics occasionally affects his English narrative'.

Ill. 11.2 Stanton, *Andante cantabile*, La Jolla, California, 1977

The nine 'lost ones' sit in a line on armless chairs wearing a variety of dirty, shabby, ill-fitting greatcoats, footwear and flat caps. They look pale, ill, bruised and bloody. Behind number five is the central portion of an aluminium ladder, and behind the first two and the last two are the loudspeakers relaying the hum of the Machine. At the beginning, the nine are completely covered by a black drape. The soloist enters by climbing up the ladder from below. He then goes along the line removing the drape. Once exposed, the lost ones create vocal mobiles, and 'a collage of gentle muzak' becomes the Machine's hum. The mobiles consist of unvoiced phonemes connected by glissandos, with the words 'grazie' and 'fratello' uttered intermittently in stage whispers. As these are addressed to the soloist, the soloist replies by first quoting the opening of Dante's *Purgatorio*, 'Per correr miglior acqua' (To run over better waters) then by imitating their glissandos and muttering. To frustrate them even further he then quotes an English translation of a passage from near the end of the first canto of the *Purgatorio*: 'For to the second realm I tune my tale, where human spirits they purge themselves, and await to leap up into JOY CELESTIAL.' (The capital letters in the score emphasise the importance the soloist must give to them.)

The first part of the work's title, *Andante cantabile, omaggio a Rossetti*, refers to *Andante cantabile, molto espress, bel canto con molto vib*, the performing instructions for the improvised aria the soloist must sing with phonemes drawn from the name Beatrice. *Omaggio a Rossetti*, on the other hand, refers to Dante Gabriel

Rossetti's *Dante's Salutation of Beatrice* (1849), a painting showing in its left panel Dante's Salutation of Beatrice in Florence (as depicted in *La vita nuova*); in the right panel, his Salutation of her in the Garden of Eden (as depicted in *Purgatorio* XXX); and in the centre her death.

It is during the improvised aria that the hum from the Machine begins to falter. Mention of the Machine first occurs shortly after the soloist has delivered 'Joy celestial'. On hearing the word 'machina', some of the lost ones superimpose on their first mobile a second mobile employing unvoiced speech: 'forse che di sedere in avrai distretta, a machina, forgive us, please forgive us, we must keep going, we cannot stop, we must, we cannot, a salire alle stelle'. Eventually, as if to allay their fears, the soloist provides them with the opening of 'The Machine Stops': 'Imagine, if you can, a small room, hexagonal in shape, like the cell of a bee. It is lighted neither by window nor by lamp, yet it is filled with a soft radiance. There are no apertures for ventilation, yet the air is fresh. There are no musical instruments, and yet, at the moment that my meditation begins, this room is throbbing with melodious sounds.'

Nevertheless when the hum gets louder, like Kuno, the soloist predicts that the Machine might indeed stop. He therefore includes prayers to the Machine as well as to Beatrice: 'Machina! Our fathers trusted in thee; they trusted and thou didst deliver them. They cried unto thee and were delivered.'

Eventually, after the hum of the Machine gets louder and louder, it does stop. Everybody freezes: the lost ones in fear, the soloist in amazement. 'Now, the stars', he says, and he himself begins to hum, 'come la macchina'. At this the lost ones go rapidly through their mobiles. But since, in the best musical tradition, a recapitulation has been initiated, the soloist abandons his hum and embarks on a 'Coda – Cadenza' in which he recalls previous material 'to help pass the time'.

While this proceeds, the lost ones perform five visual mobiles. In the first, each of them touches his or her neighbour's right then left knee, their hands passing very slowly through a vertical semicircle. Upon contact they rapidly recoil and scream. In the next they touch in a similar manner both their neighbour's right knee and left knee simultaneously, as well as their own breasts and hair. Again each gesture is accompanied by a scream. In the third they add to these the covering of their eyes or face. Next they combine these gestures with the word 'fratello' uttered as they point to the top of the ladder. Finally they add begging hand gestures to their pleas of 'o fratello'. But their brother, the soloist, shouts 'stop, a way out' at them. Then, with his eyes also fixed on the ladder, 'he covers the chorus one by one with the drape, proceeds to the ladder, puts on his sunglasses, examines the audience, looks up the ladder, beings to climb up it, stops, looks at audience, looks up the ladder, then at the audience again, hesitates, says in an Irish accent, "what use to go up yet?", climbs down the ladder and disappears'.

Trevor Wishart (b. 1946) was educated at the Universities of Oxford and Nottingham and obtained his doctorate from the University of York. He originally studied chemistry but soon switched to music. His experience of Darmstadt led him to compose complex instrumental music and he also experimented with recordings of the sounds of industrial machinery. Committed to new approaches to music making, he has developed many new instruments (as signal processing software) for musical composition, is a founder member of the 'Composer's Desktop Project', a composers' cooperative, and author of *On Sonic Art and Audible Design*. He was Edgard Varese Visiting Professor of Music at the Technical University in Berlin 2004, and Composer Fellow at the University of Durham between 2006 and 2009, before becoming Artist in Residence at the University of Oxford, supported by a Leverhulme Fellowship.

Fidelio (1977) is the second of two music-theatre works Trevor Wishart composed in the mid-seventies. But only *Fidelio* received its first performance at York. The other, *Scylla and Charibdis* (1976), had its première at La Trobe University in Melbourne. Both were orientated to the absurd, except that unlike those specimens by Kagel, Ligeti and Stockhausen, they were aimed at specifically political targets.

As well as *Machine* and *Journey into Space*, the electro-acoustic works he produced in the early seventies, Wishart also composed, in association with Mick Banks and his alternative theatre group, *John Bull Puncture Repair Kit*, three soundscapes, site-specific events that were absurd without being overtly political: *Landscape* (Calder Valley, Yorkshire, 1970) featuring airborne musical instruments, hilltop vocalising, military fireworks and black ice cream; *Seaside* (Filey, 1971) with beach art and white gongs in the sea, and the school-based event *Wicked Wizard of Whitworth* (1972).

The term 'soundscape' – the relationships between people and their acoustic environment – was coined by the Canadian composer R. Murray Schafer, who in 1969–70 enjoyed a period of residency at York. Although he was at the university mainly to contribute to John Paynter's seminars on creativity in music education, he had also composed an electro-acoustic work called *Kaleidoscope* (1967), and was in the process of composing two music-theatre works: *Patria 1: Wolfman* (1966–74) and *Patria 2: Requiem for the Party Girl* (1966–72). These were eventually to become part of a cycle of twelve in which theatre as ritual takes place in a specific outdoor environment in order to convey a sense of homeland. But although Wishart was influenced by Schafer in his electro-acoustic works and soundscapes, by the mid-seventies, when Schafer's influence had waned, he chose to write Music Theatre that involved only modest forces, and had to be performed indoors rather then outdoors.

Scylla and Charibdis represents two countries or multinational corporations competing with each other in terms of the noise they can make. Their champions are Hell's Angel bikers, who produce the full range of vocal sounds through their separate microphones. But as well as trying to be aurally supreme, their champions also hurl luxury objects at each other. When one of these objects hits the metal screen behind each of them, the screen loudly emits a quotation from either the Communist Manifesto or the US Bill of Rights. In addition each biker has an *agent provocateur* in the audience. His job is to try and get those in the auditorium to increase the noise by delivering abusive political slogans through a microphone.

Eventually there is relative peace when noise and abuse are replaced by bird calls and 'mood music for young lovers'. But the hypocrisy of this soon persuades the combatants to renew their battle. It ends when the sound and light systems suddenly fail, and the audience is plunged into darkness and silence.

Scylla and Charibdis was never performed at York, perhaps it was too absurd, too provocative and too impracticable. However, Wishart's *Fidelio*, scored for flute (or clarinet), mime, six suitcases and six cassette tape recorders was performed in 1977. It concerns monopoly capitalism as opposed to competitive capitalism. A solitary flautist walks on stage and plays, two octaves higher, Don Fernando's aria 'Es sucht der Bruder seine Brüder' ('A brother has come to seek his brothers') from Beethoven's *Fidelio*. As it draws to a close, a stranger enters carrying a suitcase containing a cassette tape recorder playing the same music. He places it in front of the flautist before turning back and leaving the stage. The flautist responds by playing simultaneously a more complex version of the aria, treating the music coming from the suitcase as his accompaniment. The stranger then brings in another suitcase, this one with a tape recorder playing the more complex version of the aria the flautist has just played.

The process is repeated until there are five suitcases containing tape recorders piled up in front of the flautist. On each occasion the flautist has to devise ever more complex versions of the aria, either by expanding its pitch range or by finding new ways to ornament it. Eventually, he runs out of ideas and the suitcases are completely obscuring the audience's view of him so that he has to leap into the air in order to be seen. He then rushes to the front of the platform, but when he shouts for attention, the tape recorders, being imitators, shout too. Realising that he is defeated, the flautist falls to the ground. This time the stranger enters with a suitcase large enough to contain the body of the flautist, which he wheels off with the flautist inside it. After a few moments he returns with the large suitcase and places it on top of the others. Immediately the tape recorders play their versions of the aria again. The one in the large suitcase, however, has a tape loop that emits only the flautist's shout.

Fidelio, it is true, bears little or no relationship to the *musica poetica* envisaged by Meller. However, even though different avenues were pursued, the combination of poetry as sung and poetry as spoken in a theatrical context continued to thrive in York. To illustrate this, I fast forward to 2002, to Roger Marsh's *Albert Giraud's Pierrot Lunaire* (2002), a setting for speaker and various vocal ensembles of all fifty of the rondels in Giraud's *Pierrot* cycle. This work had its origins in 2000, when Marsh was Composer in Residence at the Hilliard Ensemble's annual Summer School for vocal ensembles at Schloss Engers on the Rhine. His self-imposed task was to compose for each ensemble a number of part songs that would make a composite work that they could perform at the end of the week. He had been studying Giraud's work for two years, following his earlier composition on a performing translation of the twenty-one numbers in Schoenberg's *Pierrot*.

For the Summer School he selected the first twenty-two rondels on the grounds that the first, 'Je rêve d'un théâtre de chambre' (I dream of a chamber theatre), sets the scene, and the twenty-second, which ends with the lines 'Je disparais sans une plainte, / Dans une immense mer d'absinthe' (I disappear, without a cry, / In an immense sea of absinthe), makes a suitable conclusion. If the ensembles on the 2007 recording of the work (NMC D127) are anything to go by, the four-man Hilliard Ensemble were given numbers 1, 9 and 13 to sing, while the largest ensemble, which was virtually a chamber choir, had to learn numbers 2, 4, 7, 12, 19, 21 and 22. Other ensembles were a mixed-voice trio (STB) and a female trio, which for some settings were combined. In addition Marsh also supplied a solo setting for the mezzo-soprano, Linda Hurst (No. 18 Suicide), who was there as a tutor.

Marsh finds much to admire in Giraud's poems. This is why, although he also wanted to present them in his native tongue, he was at pains to preserve the originals. He had therefore commissioned Kay Bourdier to supply him with literal English translations that a speaker could weave into his French settings. By so doing he could present their meaning directly to an English-speaking audience. But to ensure that the French originals and the English translations could be heard clearly, he had to compose the songs so that music and speech did not impinge on each other.

Usually the translations are placed at cadence points in the interstices of the music's flow. But there are several exceptions to this. One is Marsh's setting of No. 5, 'Lune au lavoir' (Like a pale washer-girl / She washes her white silks), which he scores as a duet for soprano and tenor, the soprano singing her slow-moving line in French, the tenor his equally slow-moving line in English. Another is No. 20, 'Coucher de soleil', in which the speaker is also absent. Here to capture the image of the sun splitting its veins on a bed of red clouds, the song is cast as a scherzo with French and English intertwined. It leads into 'Lune malade', the first of two slow songs that, together, take nearly eleven minutes to perform.

Later Marsh set the remaining poems in Giraud's cycle, which he also distributed between the various types of vocal ensembles, making the first twenty-two Part One, and the remaining twenty-eight Part Two, into a composite work lasting 108 minutes. In the second part he added violin, cello, piano and organ to accompany the singers when appropriate. As he had done at the end of Part One, he ends Part Two with the speaker reciting the poems in French rather than English. In it Giraud confesses that Pierrot has been himself in disguise, and that he is presenting these poems to his beloved.

At York University it had become the custom to begin the academic year with a theatre project that involves all new students and as many of the existing students as want to join in. In 2002 *Albert Giraud's Pierrot lunaire* was given in its entirety 'by an enormous cast of student singers, actors and instrumentalists', says Marsh, 'with five or six Pierrots in costume and all manner of theatrical paraphernalia to help bring the poems to life on the stage'.[3] This, I believe, was what he had in mind for the work from the beginning, and is the fullest expression of *musica poetica* too.

---

[3] Sleeve note with the 2008 CD of the work on NMC D127.

CHAPTER TWELVE

Continuations

Iᴺ my conversation with Maxwell Davies before I wrote this book, he described the optimism composers felt during the sixties:

> There was a feeling among all composers of hope for the future; that we were moving into areas of experience and technique that had never been done before. At the time I didn't think the sixties were anything special at all. I thought that this is how things were in every generation, striving to make things work. What united all composers was a sense of optimism. But this optimism gradually evaporated after about 1973. The music we had created in the fifties and sixties was not being played. Glock had retired, and the spirit of adventure which had characterised the Proms, for example, quickly evaporated. Perhaps we had been over optimistic.

As mentioned in Chapter One, 1973 was the year of the international oil crisis, when, in Arthur Marwick's words, 'the doubling of oil prices led to widespread recession and a general crisis of confidence'.[1] It ushered in a period when composers of Music Theatre felt the need to be simpler, more direct, less experimental than they had been. This explains why *Miss Donnithorne's Maggot* (1974) is based on Victorian salon music, Wishart's *Fidelio* (1976) on a phrase from Beethoven's opera, Birtwistle's *Bow Down* (1977) on one basic pulse and three basic intervals, and Buller's *The Mime of Mick, Nick and the Maggies* (1977) on children's songs.

The same ethos applies to the music-theatre works composed thirty years later and beyond, which I want to discuss briefly in this chapter: Goehr's *Kantan and Damask Drum* (1999), Maxwell Davies's *Mr Emmet Takes a Walk* (2000) and Birtwistle's *The Io Passion* (2004), and as an addendum to these Birtwistle's double bill *Semper Dowland, semper dolens* and *The Corridor* (2009), and Eve Harrison's *The Rose Collector* and *Hera's List* (2011).

In the years between 1974 and 2000, Maxwell Davies composed two operas: *Resurrection* (1987) and *The Doctor of Myddfai* (1995); two chamber operas: *The Martydom of St Magnus* (1976) and *The Lighthouse* (1979); and two children's operas: *The Two Fiddlers* (1978) and *Cinderella* (1980). His music-theatre works were *Le Jongleur de Notre Dame* (1978), *The Medium* (1981) and *The No. 11 Bus*

---

[1] Marwick, *The Sixties*, 7.

(1984). In addition, he composed seven music-theatre works for children: *The Rainbow* (1981), *The Great Bank Robbery* (1989), *Jupiter Landing* (1989), *Dinosaur at Large* (1989), *Dangerous Errand* (1990), *The Spider's Revenge* (1991) and *A Selkie Tale* (1992).

In the same period Goehr produced two operas: *Behold the Sun* (1985) and a reconstruction of Monteverdi's lost opera, *Arianna* (1995), while Birtwistle composed four operas: *The Mask of Orpheus* (1986), *Gawain* (1991), *The Second Mrs Kong* (1994) and *The Last Supper* (2000); one television opera, *Yan Tan Tethera* (1986); one music-theatre work, *Bow Down* (1977); and one specimen of Instrumental Theatre, *Secret Theatre* (1984). Altogether, Maxwell Davies, Birtwistle and Goehr composed thirteen operas in the period, but only eleven music-theatre works, and of these seven were for children. This mirrored the decline of interest in Music Theatre after the seventies and indicated too that there were fewer ensembles willing or able to stimulate it. The Pierrot Players ceased to exist after 1971, the following year the Music Theatre Ensemble folded, and in 1987 The Fires of London gave their last concerts. *The No. 11 Bus*, which Maxwell Davies composed in 1984, was the last music-theatre work he wrote for them. By 2000 Goehr, Maxwell Davies and Birtwistle were highly respected members of the musical establishment. Goehr had become Professor of Music at Cambridge University in 1976, Maxwell Davies had been knighted in 1987 and Birtwistle received the same honour in 1988. Usually they were prepared to write Music Theatre only if they were commissioned to do so. And when they were, it was expected that they would produce substantial works to justify the fees their agents demanded.

Kantan and Damask Drum, commissioned by Theater Dortmund, lasts just over ninety minutes, and was first performed in Dortmund in a German translation on 19 September 1999, before being produced in English at the 2001 Aldeburgh and Almeida Festivals. *Mr Emmet Takes a Walk*, commissioned jointly by the St Magnus Festival, Psappha and Muziektheater Transparant, lasts just under an hour, and was first given at the Pickaquay Centre in Kirkwell as part of the St Magnus Festival on 16 June 2000. *The Io Passion*, commissioned by Almeida Aldeburgh Opera and the Bregenzer Festspiel, lasts at least seventy-five minutes, and was first performed at The Maltings on 11 June 2004 to open the 2004 Aldeburgh Festival. As well as being expansive, these works epitomised their composers' debt to the past far more than in their earlier pieces, and focused even greater attention on what had been their prime concerns.

Although Goehr embraced extreme avant-garde ideas when he was a student, it soon became evident that he could not break entirely with tradition. As we have seen, the three music-theatre works that make up his first triptych were all indebted to Monteverdi's *Il combattimento di Tancredi e Clorinda*. When he decided to write another triptych of music-theatre pieces thirty years later, he once again chose to base them on another older tradition: two Noh plays and a short farcical Kyogen, types of theatre which flourished in Japan five hundred years ago.

Kantan and *Damask Drum* were both plays by Zeami (c. 1363–c.1443), who, with his father Kwanami (1333–84), pioneered the Noh tradition. The texts, in Goehr's version of them, were based on translations from the Japanese and the modern adaptation by Yukio Mishima. Goehr said in a programme note that he made no attempt to recreate the style of the original Noh theatre: 'this is a modern music-theatre composition for singers, a dancer and an instrumental ensemble, done in the belief that the dramas, originating from far away and long ago, may be understood by modern audiences'.

Kantan takes up the topic Goehr explored in *Sonata about Jerusalem* and his opera *Behold the Sun*: namely, the way dreams can be shattered by reason or by the light of day. It concerns a young traveller called Rosie who is making his way to 'the Hill of the Flying Sheep' where he hopes to find enlightenment. Feeling tired, he knocks on the door of a cottage and asks the woman who opens it for a night's lodging. She points to a bed in the corner, but warns the young man not to sleep on the pillow. The man who left it there had said, 'Whoever sleeps on it will wake to see his whole life, past and future, as if in a dream.' The young man does not heed her advice. He puts his head on the pillow and immediately falls asleep. During his dream the woman leads in an exotically dressed envoy 'from another world', who tells the young man that the Emperor is dead, and that Rosie must rule in his stead. He is given an embroidered robe and transported in an elegant palanquin to the palaces of the ancient Kings. When he gets there, a fantastically dressed courtier tells him he has occupied the throne for fifty years, and that if he drinks the wine the courtier offers him he will enjoy a thousand more years of kingly life. The illusion ends when the woman wakes him up with a bowl of porridge. Rosie realises that the glorious years lasted only as long as the porridge took to soften in the pan. 'Pondering on my condition,' he says, 'I see, that when life's done, a hundred years of happiness, ambition, pomp, and length of days fade. O, immeasurable wisdom! Is this not what I set out to learn.'

Damask Drum is about an old gardener who is deceived by two mischievous boys. He has fallen in love with the lady who sits at the window overlooking the garden, and he has been writing to her every day. But the boy he has been asking to deliver the letters confesses to the other boy that he has not delivered the letters, he has kept them. After reading one of them, they decide to tease the old man by writing a letter to him as if it had come from the lady. In it they say that if the old gardener were to beat the damask drum hanging on a tree next to the pond the lady would come to him. But when he beats the drum, it makes no noise so the lady does not come. In despair the old gardener drowns himself in the pond. The boys confess what they have done to the lady, but already the curse of the old gardener's ghost is beginning to have its effect. As she walks in the garden the ghost dances in a circle round her, stamping his feet as he does. But the lady fails to hear the stamping, just as it was impossible for her to hear the silent damask drum, because now she is deaf.

(Un)fair Exchange switches from deafness to blindness. A blind old man with a young wife asks her to take him to where the cherry blossom is in bloom. If he cannot see it then at least he can sniff it. When they reach the cherry blossom, she gives him a little cup of saké, and the old man dances.

They are observed by a man with a monkey, who asks the young wife why she has an old man for a husband. He could fix her up with someone young, he says. His suggestion is greeted with derision, and she offers her husband another cup of saké. They then both dance. Afterwards, the monkey man calls her away from her husband again, and repeats his suggestion. This time she says that if she could see the young man he talks about she will think about it. By now the old man has become irritated by her disappearances, and decides to fasten her sash to his belt to keep her by his side. At that the monkey man quietly releases the woman, and in her place he ties his monkey to the old husband's belt. The woman now capitulates to him, and the two run off together. When the husband asks for another drink and a kiss, it is the monkey who replies. 'My God!', says the old man. 'My wife's hairy.'

Taken together, the common theme uniting *Kantan, Damask Drum* and *(Un)fair Exchange*, is deception, just as it had been in the first triptych where Naboth was deceived by the Elders acting under the instructions of Jezebel, the prisoners in the cave were deceived by the shadows on the wall, and the Jews of Baghdad were deceived by the belief that they could fly to Jerusalem. As indicated in his score, Goehr originally placed the Kyogen after *Damask Drum*, and this, I believe, was how it was done in Dortmund. But when the work was performed in England, he placed it as an interlude between the two Noh plays. This made the structure better balanced in the length and contents of the items. It also conforms to the Japanese principle of having the play containing demons or vengeful ghosts placed last in the sequence.

Goehr requested that the staging should also be similar to the Noh model. A small male-voice chorus should be placed at the back, and the instruments placed at one side and be visible throughout the triptych. Ideally the wooden floor should have resonant properties, which, in the case of *Damask Drum*, would make the old gardener's stamping sound extremely loud. The set should be confined to a single tree placed at the back of the stage. This means that all actions involving props have to be mimed. Miming had also been exploited in *Naboth's Vineyard* and

Sonata about Jerusalem, and it draws the staging of this new triptych close to that in the original one. So too does the use of the chorus, except that now it no longer functions as a narrator but as an extension of a solo voice, as it does in the Noh theatre. To Western audiences this may be disorientating. It gives the impression that the feelings and actions of the individual are not his own. However, this impression cannot be sustained, because, for example, when the young traveller in *Kantan* has been woken by the woman, he speaks as if he were still dreaming, while the tone of the chorus which alternates with him is strictly matter-of-fact.

In Noh theatre the instrumentalists are three drummers and a flautist. Goehr expands this ensemble by having three percussionists, a harp, an electronic sample programmed to produce sound representing, for example, the Japanese *sho*, a nasal organ, a metal organ and an electric piano, six violins, one viola and one cello. In addition, *Damask Drum* calls for an alto flute and an alto trombone. The overall tessitura of the ensemble is therefore light in bass sonorities. But this helps to give a Japanese quality to the sound. 'From Japanese practice', he says in a programme note, 'I culled a free modality which characterises action and protagonist, but straightaway composed vocal melody with an independent bass from which I could derive harmony. In the Noh, flute and drum parts stand in an heterophonic relation to the voice and I retain this practice to create polyrhythmic structures, where vocal and instrumental lines are metrically though necessarily complementary.'

In contrast, Maxwell Davies's music for *Mr Emmet* is nearer to home. It is based on melodic phrases from four works: the F minor Prelude in the Second Book of Bach's 48, the introduction to the first movement of Schumann's Second Symphony, Donna Anna's *come furia disperata* ('like a fury I'll pursue you, haunt you to your dying day') from the opening scene of Mozart's *Don Giovanni*, and the closing segment from the last of four choruses Andrea Gabrieli composed for a production of Sophocles's *Oedipus Rex (Epido Tiranno)* which took place in Venice in 1585, the words of this being 'And now I close my eyes in eternal darkness'. However, as the Mozart and Gabrieli passages are given to instruments, only very sophisticated music lovers will be acquainted with the words. What the rest of us may be able to grasp, however, is that the phrases represent a potted history of music. If placed in their correct historical order, the Gabrieli represents both the Renaissance period and choral music, the Bach the Baroque period and keyboard music, the Mozart the Classical period and opera, and the Schumann the Romantic period and orchestral music. All are heard in the introduction to the work, and Davies says in his programme note that 'everything thereafter is derived by variation, transformation and development'.

There are several reasons why Maxwell Davies selected these pieces for his source material. One is that Mr Emmet, as well as being a businessman dealing in industrial cleaning equipment, is also an amateur musician. He plays the piano and the cello, and he refers to Bach and listens to Schumann on the radio when by himself in the final scene. Another is that, by selecting phrases that have certain melodic or rhythmic features in common, Maxwell Davies can transform one type of material into another with ease. He can produce a texture that is in a constant state of flux, so creating a situation where nothing is as it seems, where nothing is certain, a philosophy, as we have seen, that has permeated all his Music Theatre, except that in *Mr Emmet* it is overt. (Perhaps it is worth noting that in Hebrew 'emet' means 'truth'.)

He scores the work for soprano, baritone and bass, and ten instrumentalists. The baritone plays the role of Mr Emmet, while the soprano and bass cover all the other roles. The instrumentalists are those he would have had in The Fires of London (flute doubling piccolo and alto flute, clarinet doubling bass clarinet and saxophone, violin, cello, keyboard instruments and percussion) plus horn, trumpet, double bass and a separate viola player. Five of the instrumentalists are required to be on stage to accompany the action from time to time so that the ensemble, although it need not necessarily be in view, must nevertheless be in easy reach of the stage. Only a baby grand piano has to be on stage all the time. It must be adapted so that it can play pre-recorded CDs (like a hotel pianola) as well as being played 'live'.

Maxwell Davies's librettist for *Mr Emmet* was David Pountney, who also produced the work's first run. He had also supplied the libretto for *The Doctor of Myddfai*, a strange tale that hinges, I believe, on the premise that, as with Davies's music for *Mr Emmet*, nothing is as it seems. Pountney describes *Mr Emmet* in the programme note as being:

> part thriller, part mystery, part black comedy ... As an ordinary man with a brisk practical sense [Mr Emmet] is a well known entrepreneurial stereotype. He has come to some unidentified town to sign a contract involving industrial cleaning with an Hungarian client called Gabor. The action covers the few hours between Mr Emmet's arrival in the town and his inexplicable suicide after the contract has been signed.

Pountney casts the work as 'a dramatic sonata' and divides it into exposition, development, recapitulation and coda: the standard sections in classical sonata form. But it is sonata form at its most unorthodox, for the exposition is subdivided into sections associated with nineteenth-century Italian opera (Introduction, Duet, Arioso, Cabaletta and Trio), the development is cast as a series of five episodes (The Piano, The Park, Hotel Room, The Mountain and The Teacher), the interludes separating them being recordings of Mr Emmet running, breathing and reciting lists of various sorts, while the recapitulation, far from casting the exposition in a new light or summarising it, is a monologue dealing exclusively with Mr Emmet telling us that he is driving his car to where he can walk to a railway track on which he can place his head.

In his programme note, Maxwell Davies says that when writing the music for the work it helped the composition process to imagine that the music's time span was the split second before the train arrived:

> The whole action was to occur in that out-of-time moment before self-inflicted sudden death, with the brain in overdrive, and memories, events, justifications and fantasies teeming through the mind in that split second. However, this is but one possible interpretation – the text revealed, in the course of composition, a criss-crossing of reality, dream and waking fantasy, opening up a kaleidoscope of possible interpretations.

The work opens with a funeral march that leads to the sound of a train passing, horn blazing with Doppler effect.

This not only prepares us for the opening of the exposition, and hints at the outcome of the work, it also indicates that the action, dialogue and music will be based on incongruities and non-sequiturs. For example, even though the bass line from the first four bars of Bach's Prelude, which opens the march, may contain the seeds of the Schumann, Gabrieli and Mozart quotations, there is no reason why it should be immediately followed by the Gabrieli. Nor is there any reason why the Gabrieli should be followed by the music given to the right hand in Bach's Prelude, or why this should be immediately followed by a variation of what the horn and trumpet play in the Schumann, or why the Gabrieli should be returned to.

Similarly, there is there no reason why a funeral march should be followed by scenes from a musical comedy. Nevertheless, when the passing train has gone on its way, the lights go up on an industrial room where two cleaners, Ka and Mr Todd, are scrubbing blood and viscera from the walls and floor. They place these in plastic bags, which they label and fasten with security tags. Todd is wearing a check tweed suit with yellow rubber gloves, Ka 'something short and snappy'. Their song and dance routine, which Maxwell Davies directs to be sung 'brightly, with gallows humour', comes to an embarrassed stop when Mr Emmet enters. 'Am I lost?', he asks, and presents them with his card. Ka points out that the back of the card is blank but if a special solution were applied to it she could learn the truth as opposed to the lies on the other side. At this, Emmet loses his temper saying that there are no lies. But when he opens his briefcase, and appears to be preoccupied with various calculations, Ka and Mr Todd provide us with samples of the truth Ka has learned by applying her cleaning fluid: 'Behind the wall of this chest / An empty echo chamber'; 'On the pink tip of his tongue / A cautious laugh'. After a series of similar observations, Mr Emmet tells them that he's closing down the plant where they're working, 'Buying it up, Shutting it down, Selling it off.'

The set consists of mobile transparent walls that can change colour. In the first of the five central Encounters, the baby grand piano is at the back of the stage against a blue background suggesting the sea. After Mr Emmet goes over to it to play a line of a tune, he confesses that he felt strangely disturbed when he first arrived, but music soothes the nerves: 'useful at a time like this' he adds. A Security Man approaches with a note informing him that Mr Gabor will meet him at a café in the park. But the Security Man is more than he seems, and warns Mr Emmet to take care.

In the first of the interludes that separate the Encounters, we hear the sound of running and breathing, and Mr Emmet listing the things he must remember: 'Tissues, My wife, Irises, Headphones, The map, Choose the music, The lake in spring, My first day at school, My mother's jewellery'. The scene then changes to the café in the park. A woman is seated at the piano playing a medley. She joins Mr Emmet at his table saying that she's never answered an ad before. When he tells her he's never placed an ad before, she asks whether he's a spy, to which he replies 'Since that I was a little boy', adding, 'Why is my mother at the piano?', a question which receives the answer, 'Refreshing her memories'. The woman then recites verses that could have come from his nursery. Suddenly Mr Emmet becomes cheerful and relaxed. 'Shall we go to bed, Or for a walk in the Himalayas, Or on Safari, Or work in the garden?' 'Yes, oh yes', says the woman and leaves excitedly. She returns after Mr Emmet encounters a waiter with whom he has more comic banter. On her return the woman is pushing a bed on to the stage into which Mr Emmet falls, and on which, as indicated in an extremely graphic musical interlude, they make love. The Encounter concludes with Mr Emmet referring to his childhood, particularly his toy trains.

After the second interlude listing what he has to do, Mr Emmet is in his hotel bedroom waiting for a telephone call from Mr Gabor, who had failed to turn up at the café. He says he has been six days in the bedroom, and is complaining about the heating system. After ringing the hotel's receptionist for assistance, a maid, the housekeeper and finally the heating engineer appear. The Encounter ends with the engineer telling him there is nothing wrong with the heating system. The heat comes from inside Mr Emmet. As he goes out he tells Mr Emmet that Mr Gabor will meet him at 16.00 in the local railway station.

This means that Mr Emmet has spare time, so he takes to the mountains complete with a knapsack. On the way up he meets an old crone who is so frail that he offers to carry her to the top. He calls her mother, and when he tells her they will never make it to the top she replies, 'I know, son. That is why I left you, and leave you now. When I conceived you I lay on my back with my arms in the cool water of that forbidden sea. I bathed you there, illegally, and bore you, my poor guilt-ridden boy.' Throughout this encounter the voices have been accompanied mainly by the flautist sitting cross-legged on the stage.

The next interlude lists things to avoid: 'Bindweed, Latin Grammar, Untidy cupboards, Arrogance, Skiing badly, Airports, Ducking the issue, My mother's voice, Frankfurt, Being abandoned'. He might have added the name of his piano teacher, for the next Encounter begins with Mr Emmet happily playing the piano before his teacher arrives. When he does it seems they will play a duet together, but then the teacher begins to give him terse instruction, and the music becomes increasingly demanding. At last Mr Emmet slams the piano shut and cries, 'Damn perfection!' At this point Varoomschka enters and, accompanied by Mr Emmet and a saxophonist, sings a torch song 'à la Piaf'. After a while Mr Emmet becomes so carried away by the song that he joins in the reprise: 'For Love is the heart, But death is the core. Yes, love is a circle, But death a straight line, For love is a miracle, But death is divine. For love is just the purest chance But death, she is for sure. Love loves to join in every dance, But death is chaste and pure. Yes love is a folly, But death is the cure.'

During this reprise, Todd sets a table with three chairs, and the flautist, viola player and contrabassist enter to play Tafelmusik. The occasion is the dinner party during which Mr Emmet and Mr Gabor sign the contract, with Varoomschka acting as the witness. After this, in the monologue that Pountney calls a reca-pitulation, Mr Emmet's memories, dreams and waking fantasies come to an end. Accompanied on stage by the cellist, he approaches the realm of certainty. What he does cannot be acted on stage. He merely tells us that he is calm, that he is driving his car to the spot he has selected, that he parks the car, locks it out of habit, puts on his headphones, listens to Schumann, walks, runs forward, kneels, and then 'For an eternity, I feel the cold steel on my forehead, the scythe and the flail.' We then hear the sound of the train siren, the two walls bang shut and Mr Emmet disappears.

In the coda we see Ka and Todd scrubbing again, but this time rather listlessly. Ka says she's upset, and when asked why, she replies, 'It's not everyday someone takes the trouble to make friends with death.' After Todd repeats, 'It's not every-day,' we hear the distant sound of a train siren, and bird song, with rooks. The two walls then open out to reveal the piano, now closed. On top of it is a black cello case.

The story of Birtwistle's *Io* attempts to explain why cattle, particularly cows, are plagued by gadflies. It can be found in Volume 1, Section 56 of Robert Graves's

The Greek Myths.[2] Although Graves does not include Ovid's Roman account of the myth, he draws on all the available Greek sources. These vary considerably, but Graves puts first the one that represents the core of the story. It claims that when Io was tending her father's sheep on Mount Nenea (now Lerna) she was seduced by Zeus, who turned her into a heifer when he saw his wife Hera coming to rebuke him. To punish Io, Hera had a gadfly sting her and chase her all over the world. Birtwistle's interest in the myth, however, was not the fate of cattle, but its psychological relevance for a man and a woman of our own time who became estranged when visiting Lerna on holiday.

The work is scored for two actors, two sopranos, two baritones and an ensemble consisting of basset clarinet and string quartet. The actors and singers represent three aspects of a single man and a single woman. A baritone plays Man 1, an actor Man 2, and the other baritone Man 3. Woman 1 is given to an actress, Woman 2 and Woman 3 to the sopranos. All have also to double the characters involved in the myth: Zeus, Hera, Hermes, Io and her father Inachus, and the Gadfly.

Many of the details of the piece were decided in a series of workshops held in the National Theatre Studio by those participating in the original production. They included Stephen Plaice, the librettist, Stephen Langridge, the director, and Alison Chitty, the designer. Before presenting them with his ideas, Birtwistle drew a sketch of the set he wanted. It divided the stage into four boxes.[3] The two downstage (i.e. at the front of the stage from the audience's point of view) would consist on the right-hand side of a room in a suburban terraced house, and on the left-hand side a street outside. The two upstage boxes would be the same but the other way round, i.e. the room would be on the left, the exterior of the house on the right. At the back of the downstage room, and at the front of the upstage room, there would be a window with a blind and a door. This meant that the audience would be seeing the inside and outside of the house from four different perspectives, two on the horizontal plane, two on the vertical. To make the situation even more like a mirror, Birtwistle wanted the action taking place upstage to be exactly the same as that taking place downstage. In the course of the workshops it was decided that the room would contain an occasional table, armchair (with

---

[2]   Harmondsworth, Penguin, 1955.

[3]   The stage layout suggests the four regions of a Johari window (a technique created by Joseph Luft and Harry Ingham in 1955 in the United States, used to help people better understand their mental instability). They represent: (1) what one knows about oneself and is seen by others; (2) what one does not know about oneself but what is visible to others; (3) what one knows about oneself but what is hidden from others; (4) what is completely hidden, i.e. what is unknown about oneself and unknown to others. (See Joseph Luft, *Group Processes: An Introduction to Group Dynamics* [Palo Alto, National Press Books, 1970], 57.)

book), mirror, writing table and upright chair, while the road outside would have a streetlamp.

Birtwistle divides the work into seven Fits preceded by an Antefit, using fit (or fitt) from Old English meaning a struggle, a term also used in medieval romances for a section of the narrative (Birtwistle had previously used it in his opera *Gawain*). Because the shape of a heifer's horns resembles the shape of the new moon, Io became the moon goddess, and to convey this each Fit should have a phase of the moon visible above the stage. There is, however, no moon in the Antefit. It consists of a silent summary of the recurring actions in the Fits presented upstage, with the streetlamp on and the blind pulled down so that we see the movements only as shadows.

In Fit I (The House) the basic external events are presented silently, mostly in mime, as they always will be throughout the work. There are sixteen in number: (1) The streetlamp goes off. (2) Man 1 enters and waits under the lamp, his eyes fixed on the window. (3) Woman 1 enters from inside the house. She lifts the blind and looks out of the window. Since she stands fully revealed in the window, the man steps back at the same time to avoid being seen. (4) She goes over to the mirror, checks herself in the glass, flicks her hair and goes out again. (5) The man moves from the streetlamp up to the window of the house, and looks in for a few minutes. When she comes back, afraid she might see him, he returns to the streetlamp and continues to watch. (6) The woman enters with a tea-tray. She sets the tray down on the table, and sits down in the armchair. She pours herself a cup of tea and drinks. (7) She finishes the tea and clears the tray from the table then goes out. (8) The man also exits. (9) The streetlamp goes on, indicating that for the rest of the Fit the action takes place after sundown.

The instrumentalists then play the first of seven Nocturnes, after which the action resumes. (10) The woman re-enters. She switches on the standard lamp and draws down the blind on the window. She picks up her book. She takes it to her chair, sits down and begins to read. Gradually she falls asleep. (11) During her sleep she sits bolt upright. Then a few moments later she slumps back down in the chair. She sits bolt upright again and flicks away a fly in her sleep. (12) The man re-enters, crosses diagonally straight to the door and delivers a letter, leaving immediately. (13) The letter landing on the mat wakes the woman from her sleep. She re-reads a passage in her book, then puts the book down. Only now does she pick up the letter from the mat. She opens it and scans the contents. (14) She angrily stuffs the letter back in its envelope. She goes over to the writing desk and sits down in the upright chair, opens a drawer in the desk and takes out a pen and some paper.

The last two events overlap. (15) She begins to write ... (16) The man re-enters and stands under the streetlamp, watching the window. He approaches the door

... (15) The woman finishes writing her letter. She puts it in an envelope and scribbles an address ... (16) The man is about to knock, but he hesitates, turns and goes back to the lamp ... (15) The woman gets up, checks herself in the mirror, applies her lipstick. She brushes away a careless hair, or maybe it's a fly. She puts on a scarf. Then she switches off the standard lamp and goes out ... (16) The man waits by the streetlamp.

These events are repeated in each of the following Fits, except that on some occasions the length between them becomes expanded, on others contracted. In Fits IV and V events 1 to 9 are omitted. Nevertheless in each Fit the basic external events remain the same. They imply that time is cyclic, as do the phases of the moon, except that the lunar cycle takes longer to complete. What changes and represents linear time cutting across these cyclic oscillations are the events in the woman's dream as she sleeps. This is because in each Fit her dream is different. Apart from the dream in Fit V, they focus on different aspects of the myth. Gradually these not only culminate in a climax, they become transformed. At this point dream and reality fuse so that the audience may well believe that maybe everything has been a dream.

Fit II (Letters) contains three insertions providing oblique references to the Io myth, as well as clues as to why the relationship between the man and the woman has broken down. The first insertion occurs between events 3 and 4 after Woman 1 has moved to the window, lifted the blind and looked out of the window. In the window on the other side of the stage, Woman 2 (soprano) appears and sings an Arietta comparing England in a cold summer to summer in the Mediterranean. In the course of it she makes references to another story about Io included in Graves's account. They are 'The fear of the knock', and '... With Antioch's queen'. Antioch, the place formerly known as Iopolis, is where Io was buried after she had been re-transformed into human form. According to Graves, in honour of Io, 'The Iopolitans knock at one another's doors in the same way every year, calling out. "Here I am, Io" on each occasion.'[4]

The two other insertions are the reading of the letter the woman receives from the man, and the letter she writes to him. Both are spoken by Woman 1, but during the reading of the man's letter, Man 3 (baritone), singing off stage in *Sprechgesang*, takes over from her from time to time, and during the writing of the woman's letter, Woman 3 (soprano), also singing offstage, provides some of the woman's inner thoughts. The first letter is strange because it inverts what happened between Zeus and Io. The man writes, 'I don't understand how it's come to this. Neither of us could have foreseen what happened between us that afternoon in Lerna. I had read about the mysteries, but nothing had prepared me for how

[4] Graves, *The Greek Myths*, vol. 1, 191.

strong their revelation would be. Yet, despite your promise, you have now chosen to withdraw altogether, as if, having initiated me, you don't wish to come near the source of that pleasure again.' He then goes on to say that every time something reminds him of her, 'it sends a sting through me like a scorpion'. In the basic myth, however, it is Io who is initiated into the pleasures of sex, and it is Io who is stung.

In her reply, Woman 1 says, 'Your impatience is forcing my hand. I warned you that after what happened with Z ... I could not commit myself to anybody ... What manifested itself in that room didn't belong to us. We disturbed something we shouldn't have.' Off stage, Woman 3 mentions the dress she wore for him, the ways he touched her, her fear, the window melting as if it wasn't there. Then, more graphically, she recalls 'the beating of wings ... hot and cold like ice ... I split ... sun burst in the room scorching me, the white light in my head ...'. Finally when Woman 1 says, 'At the height of our ... in the heat of the moment', Woman 3 adds, 'I want to hurt you, leave on you an indelible stain.'

At this stage the audience will want to know what prompted these ambiguous comments. What are the mysteries? What happened with Z ...? Why does the woman want to hurt the man? They soon discover that the answers come in stages. In each successive Fit they are taken deeper and deeper into the reasons why the woman responds to the man as she does. The first indication occurs near the beginning of Fit III (Mysteries), when in event 5, Man 1 looks in through the window and says, 'Bull at gate ... don't give her the satisfaction'. Then when the woman pours herself a cup of tea and drinks, he reacts by saying, 'Another man's poison', and finally when she finishes her tea and goes out he becomes as crude as Zeus will be after he has turned Io into a heifer, 'Meant nothing ... vain cow'.

In this Fit the Arietta comes after the Nocturne, when Woman 1 draws down the blind. As in Fit I, Woman 2 sings it standing in the window on the opposite side of the stage. Her first lines refer to the man standing outside in the dark, 'My lover in darkness, how does your night fall?' She concludes by seemingly taking the man's part, 'The poppies are folding, the fields are poor. Let me come back tomorrow. Reveal the door.' However, the main insertion in this Fit occurs after Woman 3, still off stage, supplies the passage Woman 1 is reading in her book:

The myth of Io offers a primitive pre-dramatic representation of the moon-goddess. In ancient ritual, the moon was often worshipped as a celestial cow, because the new moon resembled cow-horns. In dramatic ritual, this cow would have sported three colours: white for the new moon, red for the harvest moon, black for the moon when it had waned. These represent the three phases of the moon-goddess – the virgin, the woman and the crone.

At this point the Woman 1 falls asleep, and in her dream we witness not what has just been read out but a fairly full version of the basic myth. Hermes, Io, Inachus and Zeus appear and enact the myth in ritualistic images. They do so in the manner of a primitive theatrical masque, their smooth and lyrical movement being in direct contrast to the staccato and jerky nature of the music. Hermes stands by the woman's chair and tells the story in Greek, the translation being given by Woman 3 still off stage and still speaking: 'When Io the maiden comes of age,' she translates, 'her father Inachus, fearing a thunderbolt, sends her to the slopes of Lerna to tend his cudding flocks.' We then see Inachus anointing and laying Io out for the gods on the writing desk which has become an altar. Following this we hear and see how Zeus is the first to take advantage of her vulnerability for 'soon she's bouncing on his fingertips'. Hermes tells us how Hera suspects what's happening, how Zeus turns Io into a heifer and offers her to Hera, who summons a gadfly to sting and to go on stinging her so that she is perpetually reminded of her crime. When Woman 1 flicks away a fly in her sleep, the mythic characters do likewise before disappearing.

Fit IV eliminates events 1 to 9 so that the whole episode takes place at night. There's a full moon and according to the Fit's subtitle it's a 'Rough Night'. It opens with a Nocturne, but on this occasion Man 1 uses it to accompany himself in a song expressing his feelings as a rejected lover and his hope that things might change. After Woman 1 has entered, switched on the standard lamp, started reading her book and fallen asleep, Hermes enters again; with him are Io and Inachus. This time we get a cruder, more graphic description of the myth. Inachus tells Io to hide herself, and she drops on the floor 'in a supine ball'. When Zeus enters, he leaps on to the desk and grunts at her like a bull. Enticing her with his low bellowing, he raises her up and is just about to couple with her when Hera arrives. She immediately summons the gadfly. We hear Io's bloodcurdling screams followed by a long instrumental passage vividly describing the extent of her suffering. Woman 1, still sleeping, sits bolt upright in the chair, brushes away a fly, and slumps back into her chair; before departing, the myth characters do likewise. We are then taken through events 12 to 16 except that during her silent reading of his letter and her silent writing of her reply, Woman 3 recapitulates, off stage, what the woman had said and thought in Fit II, ending with 'I want to hurt you.'

Fit V (Quartet) takes up this threat and expands it into a huge row between the couple. The fit also begins with a Nocturne, but in this Man 1 now becomes the jealous lover as he waits outside under the streetlamp. 'Where are you tonight?' he asks, 'Will you come home kissed and flattered by everyone's lips but mine?' Woman 1 re-enters, switches on the standard lamp, sits down, starts reading then falls asleep. No actors take part in her dream, only the four singers: Man 3 and Woman 2 on the left side of the stage argue with Man 1 and Woman 3 on the right side. Two arguments run in parallel with each other: Man 3 battles it out with Woman 3, and Man 1 battles it out with Woman 2. However, Woman 3 becomes increasingly involved with the accusations Woman 2 is levelling at Man 1, egging her on at the expense of her own argument. The gist of the male arguments is that the woman has completely wrecked the man's life, that she is an unfeeling bitch. She says she never promised him anything, it was too early, he knew she wasn't ready. They then start a slanging match, adding insult upon insult to each other. Eventually Man 3 works himself up into a fury, and when Woman 3 tells him to control himself, he replies, 'Control myself? But this is your dream ... I'm just the man inside your head, the me you imagine wants to blame you.' And when Woman 3 asks, 'Then who am I,' Man 3 says, 'You're just the woman inside her head, the one she thinks she wants to blame.'

This initiates a period of relative calm, except that in events 13, 14 and 15, when Woman 1 silently reads the man's letter and writes her reply, the off-stage pre-recorded spoken voices of Man 3 and Woman 3 repeat odd phrases from Fit II and the dream in Fit III. In this context they anticipate what is to happen in the next Fit, when the hurt Io suffers at the hands of Zeus and Hera goes even deeper than before. They are spoken by Woman 3: 'At the height of our ... In the heat of the moment ... The tail's frantic switch ... That mysterious bond'.

Birtwistle subtitles Fit VI 'Opera', because as well as having a dramatic scena for Io and Zeus, it contains three set pieces: an aria for Io and two ariettas for Hera. He now restores events 1 to 9. As in Fit II, when the woman opens the blind, another facet of herself appears in the window on the opposite side of the stage. However, now it is Hera not Woman 2 who stands in the window, and the arietta we would have expected her to sing at this juncture comes after the Nocturne. The gist of the arietta is that Hera wants to please her husband by cooking him what he likes, by putting on flattering make-up and asking for a kiss. When we come to the woman's dream, however, Zeus is taking advantage of seeing Io counting Inachus's sheep. After every number she calls out, he responds with a 'baa', revealing himself to be Zeus when number eleven is reached. Grabbing her he says 'Bolt from the blue. Two billion volts down the jagged yellow wire, straight into you.' Freezing in fear, she lets him control her limbs. She 'splits', he 'elevates', and with his thrusting grunts and her ecstatic cries their intercourse eventually reaches a climax.

When Zeus lets her go and turns her into a heifer, Hera approaches. 'He didn't like me,' says Io. 'He's turned me into something safe, chucked me like a dirty rag.' Hera then sings her second arietta, but this time it's like a dance. 'Pretty little pouting mops, How I despise your golden locks ... I want to hurt you and I must, a punishment that never stops.' A gadfly appears, and to it Io sings 'an aria of complaint'. When she and the gadfly disappear to let the domestic events resume, we see Woman 1 writing her letter. Once more there are interpolations from Man 3 and Woman 3 off stage: 'Like a scorpion … the javelin's hiss … the tail's frantic swish … that mysterious bond'.

The last Fit (Sacrifice) is also framed by the sixteen events established in Fit I, but the contents of the later insertion events are inverted. In the arietta Woman 2 sings when Woman 1 lifts the blind, we are told that she has become the rejected lover. But the most significant inversion occurs in event 10, when the woman dreams, only this time it's not Woman 1, the actress, but Woman 2, the singer, who sits in the chair. Almost immediately after falling asleep, she gets up and goes over to the mirror, where she applies her lipstick. Meanwhile Man 1 has gone over to the other side of the mirror and insults her: 'Unfeeling bitch! Rancid whore! Man-beater! She-devil.' Totally ignoring his abuse, she reaches through the mirror and smears lipstick over his lips without encountering any resistance. Taking her scarf, she loops it round his neck and drags him to the chair by the desk so that he is lying right across it. She then begins to write on the man's chest so that it feels as if gadfly were stinging him. When she has put down her pen she leaves, and Woman 3, who has entered unnoticed during the ritual, takes her place in the armchair where Woman 2 had fallen asleep. But this time the letter Man 1 posts does not fall on the mat, it hangs in the letterbox, and so the woman ignores it. Instead she wakes up of her own accord and becomes Io, saying, 'Here am I, Io, buried in Antioch … May the spirit of Io come back … Here am I, Io, wait for my knock.' She switches out the standard lamp and goes out, leaving Man 1 on stage brushing away a fly.

In this account of *The Io Passion* I have been focusing on the stage action and plot, and have paid little or no attention to the music. Suffice to say that, not only does it accompany the action, it also supplies dimensions that seem to lie deeper than even those in the woman's dream. Of particular interest are the seven Nocturnes. Those in Fits IV and V are placed first and accompany what amounts to an aria for Man 1. The others are purely instrumental and mark the transition from morning to evening or vice versa. Most of them are instrumental arias for the basset clarinet, and demand to be heard as music *per se*. When they occur, stage action is suspended. The most likely explanation for their presence is that, like the four Interstices in Birtwistle's *Monodrama*, they provided moments for reflection.[5]

This interpretation gains credence when we turn to Birtwistle's next two pieces of Music Theatre, *Semper Dowland, semper dolens* and *The Corridor*, the double bill that opened the 2009 Aldeburgh Festival. The brochure advertising them

---

[5] For a detailed analysis of the music see Beard, *Harrison Birtwistle's Operas and Music Theatre*, 307–16.

described them as being 'The Theatre of Melancholy'. (There is a predecessor to the first of these: *An Heavyweight Dirge* for eight musicians and conductor written by Dominic Muldowney, Birtwistle's one-time assistant at the National Theatre, while still a student at Southampton. This is an experimental transformation of Gesualdo's equally melancholic madrigal *Moro lasso* of 1612.)

The Corridor has at its heart the moment when Orpheus, leading Eurydice through the corridor from Hades to the outside world, turns and loses her forever. To prepare the ground for this event, Birtwistle did something he had never done before: he devised a music-theatre piece built on the music of another composer. In his *Second Book of Lute Songs* of 1600, John Dowland included a song based on a piece that had became so popular he decided to compose not only a song but also a set of seven pavans for lute and a consort of five viols. The song was 'Flow my tears, fall from your springs. / Exiled for ever let me mourn', and the pavans, *Seaven Teares Figured in Seaven Passionate Pavanes*, were the first items in a volume of consort pieces called *Lachrimae*. As well as being variations of the original lute piece, each of the pavans represented differ- ent ways on reflecting on the sorrow of the words. With these Birtwistle had a frame into which he could slot six of Dowland's other lute songs that gradually become more and more introspective: 'Lend your ears to my sorrow', 'I saw my lady weep', 'I must complain', 'Sorrow stay', 'Come heavy sleep' and 'In darkness let me dwell'. Birtwistle substituted harp for lute in the songs, and scored his arrangements of the pavans for violin, two violas and two cellos, adding in five of them a flautist playing piccolo, alto flute or bass flute, and a clarinettist playing B♭ clarinet or bass clarinet. As Guy Dammann aptly puts it in *The Times Literary Supplement*,[6] '[Birtwistle] uses his variations to amplify and explode Dowland's rhetoric of "tearful" minor sevenths and appoggiaturas. The flute and clarinet first moderate the viol-like tone of the five string instruments then pull gradually away, lines and textures dissipating. The two composers' idioms seem to rub against each other; while the songs acquire a freshness and sharpness in their new musical settings.'

In *The Corridor*, Birtwistle reduces the number of instruments to five: flute, clarinet, violin, viola and cello. These sit in a line upstage and are called 'The Shades'. Whereas in *Semper Dowland, semper dolens* the pavans are consistently reflective, and songs increasingly more so, in *The Corridor* Birtwistle and his librettist David Harsent provide a clear distinction between what Eurydice thinks, feels and does in the corridor, and the reflections of Orpheus after he loses her and talks only to the trees and rocks. One measure of this distinction is that, when he reflects, he is accompanied by a harp as in Dowland's songs.

[6]   10 July 2009.

The work opens with a duet, Orpheus urging Eurydice on as they go through the corridor, Eurydice hesitating. Eventually, when he realises that she is not by his side, he turns. During this duet the man and the woman move from downstage right to downstage left, where the man remains throughout the piece. She, on the other hand, continues to walk, from downstage left to downstage right, when she expresses her inner feelings in song, and then upstage, when she becomes a narrator and speaks rather than sings. As the narrator, she is out of character, foresees the future and communicates with the shades, who answer her questions with musical gestures, then she exits upstage. She returns downstage left after Orpheus has had his moments of contemplation. These are six in number, and since they slot into the seven solo episodes for Eurydice (four when she sings alternating with three when she speaks), the structure of the work, after the opening duet, resembles that of *Semper Dowland, semper dolens* and, more remotely, *The Io Passion* with its seven Nocturnes.

Maxwell Davies, in his programme note for *Mr Emmett Takes a Walk*, said that it is the last music-theatre work he intended to compose. But even if Birtwistle said the same about *The Corridor*, Music Theatre in Britain has not perished. In 1994, thanks to a grant from the Ralph Vaughan Williams (RVW) Trust, the Royal Northern College of Music was able to mount a year-long music-theatre project, in the course of which two of the Manchester composers who championed the genre in this country were represented: Goehr by *Shadowplay* and Birtwistle by *Down by the Greenwood Side*. Alongside these were works by Judith Weir: *King Harald's Saga*; and by Alison Bauld: *Banquo's Burial* and *Lady MacBeth's Sleepwalking*. In *King Harald's Saga* the single soprano has to sing eight roles, dramatically retelling Harald Hardrada's doomed invasion of England in 1066. Alison Bauld, the Australian-born composer, actor and singer, brilliantly performed her own two short works.

Musical genres are never static and Music Theatre, as we have seen, is particularly flexible and has allowed composers enormous scope for experiment. Just as new ensembles provided exciting outlets for the works composed in the sixties and seventies, so new groups and companies continue to offer opportunities for the current generation of composers. The term Music Theatre is not always used but, although the new groups often refer instead to opera, the scale and experimental nature of the works they encourage and produce suggest that Music Theatre would be a more appropriate expression.

Tête à Tête, founded in 1997 by Bill Bankes-Jones, Orlando Jopling and Katie Price, has an annual festival that actively seeks new works, many of which fall into the category of Music Theatre rather than full-scale opera. Eve Harrison's *Hera's List*, discussed below, was performed at the 2012 Festival at the Riverside Studios, Hammersmith. Tête à Tête encourages experimental Music Theatre, and it exploits new media to stimulate interest, with video clips of its productions available to all online.

The Opera Group,[7] based at King's College, London, tours two new productions each year, in opera houses, theatres and festivals both at home and abroad. In 2009 it staged Birtwistle's *Down by the Greenwood Side*; in the same year premièred George Benjamin's 2006 music-theatre work, *Into the Litte Hill*, and in 2012 it revived Birtwistle's *Bow Down*.

Music Theatre Wales is a touring company based in Cardiff. It commissions new works and produces others that are rarely performed. To date it has commissioned twelve new works and has also revived productions of earlier works by Birtwistle and Maxwell Davies. Some projects, such W11 opera, have survived from the seventies. Since it was founded in 1971, it has commissioned and produced thirty-three new operas for its cast of children and young people. Despite the current straitened economic climate that has made arts funding dwindle, these and numerous other small groups are thriving and keeping Music Theatre alive. Furthermore, just as computer technology was the impetus for innovation by composers in the sixties and seventies, so now digital technology, the Internet and other new media offer exciting new horizons for today's composers.

Music Theatre in its current incarnation is a topic for others to explore, but to show how the tradition is being developed, I will look briefly at the work of Eve Harrison, the composer of *The Rose Collector,* which had its première in a Spotlight concert at the Royal Northern College of Music in Manchester on 1 April 2011, and *Hera's List*, which received its first complete performance by the University of York Opera Society and at the International Anthony Burgess Institute in Manchester on 25 November 2011.

Like those composers who began to compose Music Theatre in the sixties, Eve Harrison had to make her pieces short and easy to produce. *The Rose Collector* lasts eight minutes, *Hera's List* half an hour. Both could be described as modern fairy tales, best suited for an audience of teenagers and young adults, and both break new ground. *The Rose Collector*, for example, breaks the distinction between Music Theatre and Instrumental Theatre not only by having its bassoonist walk around, but by having both its bassoonist and harpist talk.

These two instruments and a soprano, who has three gongs to play (B♭-high, G♭-medium and B♭-low), constitute the *dramatis personae*. As the work was commissioned by the bassoonist Adam Summers, he has the lion's share of the music. The story revolves around the soprano's obsession with roses and her

---

[7] Editor's note: Opera Group joined with Mahogany Opera in 2014: http://www.mahog anyoperagroup.co.uk/ (accessed 19 February 2014).

determination to have them all for herself. As well as standing in front of her gongs, which she turns to imperiously and strikes from time to time, she also walks into the auditorium in pursuit of new varieties for her garden: 'Agatha Incarnation', 'Astrid Späth Striped', 'Yardley Baroque' and so on. Her theft of the roses is discovered by the bassoonist when he circulates around her gongs and walks into the auditorium. 'They are all gone', he reports to the harpist. The two instrumentalists are determined to stop her activities. She accuses them of having 'simple eyes, unrefined minds, not worthy of the proud flowers' grace'. But ultimately it is the roses themselves who win the battle.

The bassoonist tells us that the beauty of the flowers has given them the power to climb out of their plot, 'at first for space, but then for revenge'. Then the harp continues the story by saying, 'Through the decaying window sharp stems unfold. Her soft down pillows provide no protection.' As she suffocates, whispering the names of her flowers, the bassoonist calls her 'The Queen collector', and adds 'Her beloved prizes can breathe alone at last. Victorious.'

The common denominator binding *The Rose Collector* and *Hera's List* is the desire for independence and freedom. Eve Harrison scores the latter for a baritone (playing the part of Ashdon, a young man who has lost his wife and children), three sopranos and three mezzos (who play the parts of the goddesses Hera, Kore, Demeter, Hera, Terpsichore, and Hecate doubling those of Bacchae, Aphrodite, Xenaea, Pasiphaë, Fortuna and Jocasta) and a 'band' consisting of flute (doubling piccolo), clarinet, horn, percussion, violin and cello.

The work could be considered a twist on the story of Cinderella, the twist being that the lonely person who sits by the fire is a man not a girl, and the fairy godmother is a rather incompetent Olympian goddess with a bad memory. As she did for *The Rose Collector*, Harrison wrote her own text. She divides it into two acts separated by an interlude. Act One takes place in Ashdon's living room, where there is a fireplace, table, chair and sofa; while the four scenes in Act Two alternate between a rowdy dance club and Mount Olympus.

It opens with Ashdon sitting by the hearth lamenting his loss. Observing him are Hera, Hestia and Demeter, who are bored, tired of the constraints their myths have imposed on them. Believing that Ashdon is wasting his life and freedom, Hera decides to play a game with him by making a list of those goddesses who might make him a wife and sort him out. First on the list is Kore, the daughter of Demeter, but Hera has forgotten that for half the year Kore has to descend into the underworld to be Persephone, the wife of Hades. Kore, thinking that by becoming Ashdon's wife she might be free of her commitment to Hades, willingly agrees to seduce and marry Ashdon. Eventually she and Ashdon fall in love. Yet she cannot escape the summons of Hades. Therefore she is denied love and freedom, and Ashdon becomes lonely again.

Ill. 12.1 Harrison, tableau from *Hera's List*. Performers: (from left to right) Demeter –
Catrin Woodruff, Hera – Lisa Coates, Kore – Fiona Constantine, Terpsichore – Caroline
Challis, Hestia – Rachel Gilmore

Undeterred, Hera says she will find another goddess for the man. In the interlude she goes through her list with Ashdon. But Aphrodite, followed by Pasiphaë,
then Jocasta, Bacchae, Xenaea and Fortuna, all turn out to be unsuitable for one
reason or another. Finally she selects Terpsichore, the goddess of dance. And it is
with her that we are taken into the first scene of Act Two: the rowdy dance club
(Ill. 12.1).

Here Terpsichore, singing as she dances, is trying to persuade the reluctant
Ashdon to join her. Nudging each other, the members of the band tell him that
with her he's sure to find fun. But the goddesses on Mount Olympus are becoming increasingly distressed by the condition of Kore, who has returned to them.
Her grief at the loss of Ashdon persuades them that Terpsichore might suffer the
same fate, and they resolve that Hera's game must come to an end. They therefore
send for Hecate, the goddess of magic and necromancy, to weave her spells on
Terpsichore and those in the rowdy dance club. There, Terpsichore's dancing is
becoming increasingly frenzied. To stop her, Hecate casts a spell over the music,
but even though its rhythm becomes extremely irregular, Terpsichore asserts her
independence and continues to dance. For the others at the dance club, however,
Hecate's magic has produced terror. Snakes appear, and Ashdon sees the ghosts of
his wife and children. But the sight of them makes him realise that they have been
dead for three years, yet he has still not moved on. 'Terpsichore has got it right,'

he says. 'Her focus and delight have made her indestructible. I must trust myself. Find my own way out … someone else can play this miserable game. I'm free.' Back on Mount Olympus, however, the goddesses are now squabbling among themselves. Hera admits that her game has come to an end: she was only having fun. Now it is she who is lonely.

Although *Hera's List* has many of the attributes of a Christmas pantomime, it also complies with most of the points I made in my definition of Music Theatre in Chapter One. I said there that Music Theatre is a flexible genre totally distinct from opera or ballet. It never relies exclusively on singing, dancing or speaking, but combines these elements, or draws on folk or popular types of theatre to create a unique composite style of its own. I then went on to say that music-theatre works are intended for the concert hall or a theatre with an open stage, and should be short enough to be included as an item in a concert containing other types of music. Sometimes the instrumentalists are asked to take part in the action. Without exception they set out to be surprising, to include moments of humour even when the topic is serious, and to convey a spirit of adventure.

A film was made of the first performance of *Hera's List* and it indicates that it took place on a platform with the goddesses in flowing white robes situated on the left side of the platform from the audience's point of view, Ashdon and his living room situated in the centre, and the band situated on the right. To indicate that the goddesses were 'other worldly' they were bathed in a blue light. However, as the work proceeded these locations proved to be inadequate, simply because there was no location for the dance club other than in Ashdon's living room. At those times I wondered whether the work should have been performed in a theatre where Christmas pantomimes are normally given, a theatre large enough to have a revolve that could rapidly swivel away Ashdon's living room, and leave more space for dancing. But perhaps I'm niggling. What cannot be doubted is that in *The Rose Collector* and *Hera's List*, Eve Harrison has not been afraid to be adventurous, a quality that throughout its history has been the hallmark of Music Theatre.

Bibliography

Reference

Cambridge Companion to Twentieth-Century Opera, ed. Mervyn Cooke (Cambridge, Cambridge University Press, 2005)

Concise Oxford English Dictionary (Oxford, Oxford University Press, Updated Edition, 2009)

The New Grove Dictionary of Music and Musicians, ed. Stanley Sadie (London, Macmillan, 1980 and 2001)

The New Harvard Dictionary of Music, ed. Don Michael Randel (Cambridge, Mass., Belknap Press of Harvard University Press, 1986)

The Oxford Dictionary of Nursery Rhymes, ed. Iona and Peter Opie (Oxford, Clarendon Press, 1951)

The Oxford English Dictionary (Oxford, Clarendon Press, 1989)

The Rough Guide to Classical Music, ed. Joe Staines (London, Rough Guides, 2010)

General

Bartolozzi, B., *New Sounds for Woodwind*, tr. R.S. Brindle (Oxford, Oxford University Press, 1967)

Beard, David, *Harrison Birtwistle's Operas and Music Theatre* (Cambridge, Cambridge University Press, 2012)

_____'Taverner: An Interpretation', in *Peter Maxwell Davies Studies*, ed. Kenneth Gloag and Nicholas Jones (Cambridge, Cambridge University Press, 2009), 79–105

Berio, Luciano, *Luciano Berio: Two Interviews with Rossana Dalmonte and Balint Andras Varga*, tr. and ed. David Osmond-Smith (New York, Boyars, 1985)

Blake, David, 'Hanns Eisler', *The Listener* (15 September 1966), 398

Boulez, Pierre, *Orientations: Collected Writings* (London, Faber, 1986)

Boulez, Pierre and Célestin Deliège, *Conversations with Célestin Deliège* (London, Eulenburg Books, 1976)

Brecht, Bertolt, *Brecht on Theatre: The Development of an Aesthetic*, ed. and tr. John Willett (London, Eyre Methuen, 1978)

Buller, John, 'The Mime of Mick, Nick and the Maggies', *Tempo*, 123 (1977), 24–9

Burney, Frances (Fanny), *Journals and Letters* (London, Penguin, 2001)

Cardew, Cornelius, 'Sitting in the Dark', *The Musical Times*, 109:1501 (March 1968), 233–4

_____*The Treatise Handbook* (London, Peters Edition, 1991)

Carney, James, ed., *Early Irish Poetry* (Cork, Mercier Press, 1965 and 1969)

Cott, Jonathan, ed., *Stockhausen: Conversations with the Composer* (London, Robson Books, 1974)

Dalmonte, Rossana and Bálint András Varga, *Luciano Berio: Two Interviews*, tr. and ed. David Osmond Smith (New York: Marion Boyars Publishers, 1981)

Davison, Archibald T. and Willi Apel, *Historical Anthology of Music*, rev. edn (Cambridge, Mass., Harvard University Press, 1949)

Dunsby, Jonathan, *Schoenberg, Pierrot lunaire* (Cambridge, Cambridge University Press, 1992)

Esslin, Martin, *Brecht: A Choice of Evils* (London, Heinemann Educational Books, 1970)

_____*The Theatre of the Absurd*, rev. and enlarged edn (London, Pelican, 1967)

Fearn, Raymond, *Italian Opera since 1945* (London, Routledge, 1998)

Fellowes, E.H., *Tudor Church Music*, vols 1–3: 'John Taverner', ed. P.C. Buck et al. (Oxford, Oxford University Press, 1922–29)

Foxe, John, *Book of Martyrs*, 9th edn (London, Company of Stationers, 1684)

Fuchs, Peter Paul, ed., *The Music Theatre of Walter Felsenstein* (London, Quartet Books, 1991)

Gann, Kyle, *No Such Thing as Silence: John Cage's 4'33"* (New Haven, Yale University Press, 2010)

Giraud, Albert, *Pierrot lunaire* (Paris, Alphonse Lemerre, 1884)

Glass, Philip, *Opera on the Beach: Philip Glass on his New World of Music Theatre*, ed. Robert T. Jones (London, Faber and Faber, 1988)

Goehr, Walter and Alexander Goehr, 'Arnold Schoengerg's Development towards the Twelve-tone System', in *European Music in the Twentieth Century*, ed. Howard Hartog (London, Routledge and Kegan Paul, 1957), 76–93

Gorbanevskaya, Natalya, *Selected Poems*, tr. David Weissbort (Oxford, Carcanet press, 1972)

Graves, Robert, *The Greek Myths* (Harmondsworth, Penguin, 1955)

Griffiths, Paul, *György Ligeti* (London, Robson Books, 1983)

_____*Modern Music and After*, 3rd edn (Oxford, Oxford University Press, 2011)

_____*Modern Music: The Avant Garde since 1945* (London, J.M. Dent, 1981)

Grock, *Grock: King of Clowns*, tr. Basil Creighton, ed. Ernst Konstantin (London, Methuen, 1957)

Hall, Michael, *Harrison Birtwistle* (London, Robson Books, 1984)

_____*Harrison Birtwistle in Recent Years* (London, Robson Books, 1988)

_____*Leaving Home* (London, Faber and Faber, 1988)

Harris, Tony, *The Legacy of Cornelius Cardew* (London, Ashgate, 2013)

Harvey, Jonathan, *The Music of Stockhausen: An Introduction* (Berkeley and Los Angeles, University of California Press, 1975)

Henze, Hans Werner, *Bohemian Fifths*, tr. Stewart Spencer (London, Faber and Faber, 1998)

Holbrook, David, *Children's Games* (Bedford, Gordon Fraser, 1957)

Huebner, F., 'Entering the Stage: Musicians as Performance in Contemporary Music Theatre', *New Sounds*, 36:2 (2010), 63–74

Joyce, James, *Finnegans Wake* (London, Penguin, 1992)

Karlinsky, Simon, 'Russian Preliterate Theatre', in *Confronting Stravinsky: Man, Musician and Modernist*, ed. Jann Pasler (Berkeley, University of California Press, 1986)

Kurz, Michael, *Stockhausen: A Biography*, tr. Robert Troop (London, Faber and Faber, 1994)

Leach, Robert, *The Punch and Judy Show: History, Tradition and Meaning* (London, Batsford Academic and Educational, 1985)

Ligeti, Györgi, *Ligeti in Conversation* (London, Eulenburg Books, 1983)

Lindley, David, ed., *Court Masques: Jacobean and Caroline Entertainment, 1605–1640* (Oxford, Oxford University Press, 1995)

Luft, Joseph, *Group Processes: An Introduction to Group Dynamics* (Palo Alto, National Press Books, 1970)

Marwick, Arthur, *The Sixties: Cultural Revolution in Britain, France, Italy and the United States, c.1958–c.1974* (Oxford, Oxford University Press, 1998)

Metzer, David, *Quotation and Musical Meaning in Twentieth-Century Music* (Cambridge, Cambridge University Press, 2003)

Millington, Peter, 'The Origins and Development of English Folk Plays' (Unpublished Ph.D. Thesis, University of Sheffield, 2002)

Nyman, Michael, *Experimental Music: Cage and Beyond*, 2nd edn (Cambridge, Cambridge University Press, 1999)

Opie, Iona and Peter Opie, *Children's Games in Street and Playground* (Oxford, Clarendon Press, 1969)

Osmond-Smith, David, *Berio* (Oxford, Oxford University Press, 1991)

Partch, Harry, *Genesis of a Music: An Account of a Creative work, its Roots, and its Fulfillments*, 2nd edn (New York, Da Capo Press, 1979)

Paynter, John and Peter Aston, *Sound and Silence: Classroom Projects in Creative Music* (Cambridge, Cambridge University Press, 1970)

Reich, Willi, *Schoenberg: A Critical Biography* (London, Longman, 1971)

Salzman, Eric, 'Speaking in Tongues or Why Should Eclectic Be a Bad Word?' *Theater* Magazine, 39:3 (2009), 2–9

Sheppard, W. Anthony, *Revealing Masks: Exotic Influences and Ritualized Performance in Modernist Music Theater* (Berkeley and London, University of California Press, 2001)

Seabrook, Mike, *Max: The Life and Music of Peter Maxwell Davies* (London, Victor Gollancz, 1994)

Stravinsky, Igor and Robert Craft, *Dialogues* (London, Faber Music, 1982)

_____*Expositions and Developments* (London, Faber and Faber, 1962)

Tilbury, John, *Cornelius Cardew: A Life Unfinished* (Harlow, Copula, 2008)

Trakl, Georg, *Poems*, tr. Margit Lehbert (London, Anvil Press, 2007)

White, Eric Walter, *Stravinsky: The Composer and His Works*, 2nd edn (London, Faber and Faber, 1979)

Williams, Eric B., *The Mirror and the Word: Modernism, Literary Theory and Georg Trakl* (Lincoln, Nebr., University of Nebraska Press, 1993)

Index